D1174856

ACCOUNTING for RELATIONSHIPS

ACCOUNTING for RELATIONSHIPS

Explanation, representation and knowledge

Edited by Rosalie Burnett,
Patrick McGhee and David Clarke

METHUEN
London and New York

First published in 1987 by
Methuen & Co. Ltd
11 New Fetter Lane, London EC4P 4EE

Published in the USA by
Methuen & Co.
in association with Methuen, Inc.
29 West 35th Street, New York NY 10001

**Printed and bound in Great Britain by
Biddles Ltd, Guildford and King's Lynn**

British Library Cataloguing in Publication Data

Accounting for relationships: explanation,
   representation and knowledge.
   1. Interpersonal relations
   I. Burnett, Rosalie   II. McGhee, Patrick
   III. Clarke, David D.
   302   HM132

   ISBN 0-416-41410-9

Library of Congress Cataloging in Publication Data

Accounting for relationships.
   Bibliography: p.
   Includes index.
   1. Interpersonal relations.   I. Burnett, Rosalie,
1946– .   II. McGhee, Patrick, 1962– .   III. Clarke,
David D.
HM132.A25   1987   302.3'4   87-14211
0-416-41410-9

Contents

Acknowledgements

Before making an issue of accounting for relationships within these pages, we could first detain the reader here by accounting for the book. And – as prefacing pages to books often show – there too hangs a tale. But that would quickly bring us round to relationships again, and the chapters within are a better source for that. Therefore, suffice it for us each to acknowledge people who have helped make it possible.

The first-named editor has most to thank Peter Burnett, for doing all that a best friend and lover is able to do short of the work itself. Others she would like to thank – for moral or practical support, or for the rewards of their warmth – are (alphabetically): Charles Antaki, David Burningham, David Clarke, Steve Duck, Michael Hall, Pauline Harrison, Mary Ann Kernan, Sonia Livingstone, Robert McHenry, Phillipa Merriman, Frank Swartz and Sue Wilkinson.

The second-named editor would like to thank Margaret Godel, Audrey Nicholson, Sue Widdicombe, Maria Yapp, Chris Topham, David Clarke, Rom Harré, Bob Hoyle, Peter Manning and Nina Nowakowska for their emotional and intellectual support. His portions of this work he dedicates, with love, to his father.

The third editor would like to acknowledge with gratitude the 'big three' relationships in his life, with his wife Brigitte, and his parents. Thanks are also due to the Economic and Social Research Council for financial support, and to the Department of Experimental Psychology, and Wolfson College, Oxford, where the third editor was based until recently.

Oxford, April 1987

Notes on contributors

CHARLES ANTAKI is lecturer in Social Psychology at the University of Lancaster. He is editor of *The Psychology of Ordinary Explanations of Behaviour* (London: Academic Press, 1981) and (with Brewin) *Attributions and Psychological Change* (London and New York: Academic Press, 1986) and is co-editor (with Lewis) of *Mental Mirrors* (London and New York: Sage, 1986).

LESLIE A. BAXTER received her Ph.D. in speech communication from the University of Oregon in 1975. She is currently associate professor and chair of the Communications Department at Lewis and Clark College, Portland, Oregon. Her many publications have included work on interpersonal relationship formation and dissolution, interpersonal persuasion and conflict management, and mass media portrayals of social behaviour.

FRANCES BERENSON is a tutor in Philosophy in the Department of Extra-mural Studies, University of London, and has been a lecturer in Philosophy and Education at the University of London. She is author of *Understanding Persons: Personal and Impersonal Relationships* (Brighton: Harvester Press, 1981).

CHARLES R. BERGER is professor of Communication Studies and director of the Communication Research Center at Northwestern University. His general area of research interest is in the relationship between cognition and communication. His current research programme concerns the roles played by plans in the production of human action. He recently co-authored (with Chafee) the *Handbook of Communication Science* and he is the editor of *Human Communication Research* (London: Sage), the journal of the International Communication Association.

ROSALIE BURNETT obtained her D. Phil. at the University of Oxford in the subject of personal relationship conceptualization. She was formerly employed as a probation and after-care officer, and is now a relationship guidance counsellor. She is author of *Intimate Awareness: Thinking, Knowledge and Understanding in Personal Relationships* (London: Methuen, in press).

DAVID D. CLARKE is lecturer in Psychology at Nottingham University. He was previously a research fellow of Wolfson College and senior research officer in the Department of Experimental Psychology in the University of Oxford. He is author of *Language and Action* (Oxford: Pergamon, 1983) and co-author (with Harré and De Carlo) of *Motives and Mechanisms* (London: Methuen, 1985) and (with Crossland) of *Action Systems* (London: Methuen, 1985).

STEVE DUCK is Daniel and Amy Starch research professor in Communication Studies at the University of Iowa. He has played a major role in establishing personal relationships as a recognized research field as the founding editor of the *Journal of Social and Personal Relationships* (Sage), and is joint-convener (with Gilmour) of the International Conference on Personal Relationships, and joint-convener (with Harvey and Cutrona) of the Iowa Conferences on Personal Relationships. His eighteen books on relationships include *Human Relationships: an Introduction to Social Psychology* (London: Sage, 1986) and the *Handbook of Research in Personal Relationships* (Chichester: Wiley, in press).

KENNETH GERGEN is professor of Psychology at Swarthmore College, Pennsylvania. He received his Ph.D. from Duke University, and previously taught at Harvard. He has published numerous influential books and articles. His works include *Toward Transformation in Social Knowledge* (New York: Springer – Verlag, 1982), *Historical Social Psychology*, (edited with M. Gergen) (Hillsdale, NJ: Lawrence Erlbaum, 1984) and (with Davis) *The Social Construction of the Person* (New York: Springer – Verlag, 1985).

MARY GERGEN teaches psychology at Penn State University, Delaware County campus. She received her Ph.D. from Temple University, and previously worked as a researcher at Swarthmore College and Harvard University. She is author (with K. Gergen) of *Social Psychology* (Orlando, Florida: Harcourt Brace Jovanovich, 1981) and editor of *Feminist Thought and the Structure of Knowledge*.

JOHN HARVEY is professor and chair of the Department of Psychology at the University of Iowa. Previously he was at Vanderbilt and Texas Tech Universities. His major focus is on attribution theory, especially as applied to dynamics in close relationships. He has been co-editor (with Ickes and Kidd) of the three-volume *New Directions in Attibution* (Hillsdale, NJ: Lawrence Erlbaum) series and co-author (with Weary) of *Perspectives on Attributional Processes* (Iowa: W.C. Brown) and (with Kelley and others) of *Close Relationships* (San Francisco: Freeman). He was founding editor of the *Journal of Social and Clinical Psychology*.

JOHN J. LA GAIPA is professor of Psychology at the University of Windsor, Ontario, where he has taught for twenty years. He was previously employed as a research psychologist with the Defense Department in Washington, DC. His main research interest is friendship, about which he has written extensively, contributing to numerous books and journals.

SONIA M. LIVINGSTONE is currently lecturer in Social Psychology and Mass Communication at Brunel University, and has completed her D. Phil. at the University of Oxford on the subject of viewers' interpretations of soap opera characters. She has published articles on the structure, viewing reasons and interpretation of television programmes.

PATRICK McGHEE is currently research fellow in Psychiatry at St George's Hospital Medical School, London. He took a degree in Psychology at the University of Glasgow, and completed a programme of doctoral research at the University of Oxford. His current research interests include impression management, personal relationships, community psychiatry, and the relations between social psychology, pragmatics and literary theory.

DOROTHY MIELL is lecturer in Social Psychology at the Open University. She obtained her Ph.D. from the University of Lancaster on the subject of strategies in the development of personal relationships. Her research interests also include occupational stress on personal relationships.

SALLY PLANALP is assistant professor at the Department of Communication, University of Colorado. She received her Ph.D. from the University of Wisconsin, Madison. Her research interests include interpretative processes in relational communication, discourse processing, and theoretical issues in social cognition, and she is the author of articles about these subjects.

JOHN SHOTTER has recently relinquished a readership in Psychology at the University of Nottingham to take up a chair at Rijksuniversiteit, Utrecht. His numerous writings include *Images of Man in Psychological Research* (London: Methuen, 1975) and *Social Accountability and Selfhood* (Oxford: Blackwell, 1984).

MELINDA A. STANLEY is a Clinical Psychology intern at the University of Pittsburgh School of Medicine. Her main research interest is applications of social psychology to clinical problems and health behaviour, and she expects to receive her Ph.D. from Texas Tech University in 1987.

ANN L. WEBER is a social psychologist who is currently associate professor of Psychology at the University of North Carolina at Asheville. She received her Ph.D. at the Johns Hopkins University. The area of close relationships is the focus of her research and teaching interests, and she is the co-author of chapters and books on the subject, and is also active as a consultant.

SUE WILKINSON is lecturer in Psychology at Liverpool Institute of Higher Education, and honorary research fellow in the Department of Psychology at Liverpool University. Her research interests include the areas of self and identity (particularly within the context of social relationships) and the psychology of women. She is the editor of *Feminist Social Psychology: Developing Theory and Practice* (Milton Keynes: Open University, 1986), and series editor for the *Gender in Psychology* series (Milton Keynes: Open University).

Introduction

Rosalie Burnett

To place this volume into a research history context, it is relevant to note that not much more than a decade ago, the concept of 'personal relationships' was scarcely used by academics outside of applied fields like psychoanalysis and social work. Before 1979, Steve Duck's *Personal Relationships and Personal Constructs: A Study in Friendship Formation* (1973) was the only social psychological monograph with the term 'personal relationship' in the title (Duck 1984). Now it labels an expanding and dynamic interdisciplinary field, with the achievement and further promise of wide applicability and influence. Yet some areas of personal relationship phenomena have been slower to capture research time and attention than others. One such area comes under the heading of people's 'accounting' for relationships – their views, theories, understanding, conceptions, knowledge and so forth, and how reports, explanations and discourse construct relationship meanings and are implicated in the way we conduct our personal encounters. Without minimizing either the role of the individual from within person-to-person affairs, or the 'social facts' that precede and survive them, it can be argued that 'accounting', in the broad sense in which we mean it, is constitutive of reality in relationships. At one end of the line, there are individuals, couples and small groups thinking and talking about their relationships and, in so doing, creating their own major life experiences; somewhere else along the line are official accounts of how things are, from family rules to academic generalizations; and then, further along (the scale is large), are stories – some here before us that we tend to believe and accept as 'reality', some we might help to assemble and invent ourselves, and others we cannot predict.

In a recent review of the domain, Duck and Perlman (1985, p. 5) suggested: 'The single most important question for research in the future is to discover how "relationships" are created, both subjectively and objectively, from strings of interactions, and from the changing beliefs that persons form about them.' The major role here implicated for the inner world of the individual in private construal and dyadic negotiations of personal reality accords with one of our central concerns in inviting the following contributions. An emerging consensus is that progress in understanding relational phenomena awaits full investigation of the subjective dimension of relationship experience. The relevant thread here is recognition of the formative role of individual perceptions, perspectives and knowledge about relationships – a product of which is a person's relationship accounts. Another connecting thread concerns the knowledge structures (e.g. schema, prototypes) that underlie relationship accounts, and the integration of these with systems of affect and thinking processes. With regard to the objective dimension, main strands are relationship events in the short term, and the cultural dissemination of relationship meaning over the long term.

Another of our central concerns has been with the role of language. Without in any way assuming that all accounts are directly translatable into words and sentences, in a book about accounting, language must be major currency, and we take what people say seriously for several reasons. It is not just, as Clarke points out in his chapter, that by disregarding common sense, academics lose credibility and respect among lay persons; language is an index to common sense knowledge, 'which constitutes the fabric of meanings without which no society could exist' (Berger and Luckmann 1966, p. 27) (there are many access problems and communication obstacles, of course, some of which are aired within). Including and beyond this, it is the multiple role of language in acquiring, formulating and expressing accounts – and particularly language as a social device used for extra-linguistic purposes – that makes it so crucial here. A theme therefore is 'accounting' as a communicative vehicle for conveying and generating meaning – in other words, the pragmatics of using 'accounts'. In their chapter, Gergen and Gergen refer to there having been 'a shift in sensibility that is both subtle and profound ... sensitizing us to the pragmatic purposes to which person talk is put within social relationships', and, indeed, this change of emphasis is one that guided our choice of contributions. It is no coincidence that a number of the authors are affiliated to Departments of Communication Studies, yet collaborate with or regard themselves as social psychologists.

There have been other shifts of concern, heralding and reflected in this volume. Investigators from different disciplines, though journeying via alternative routes, seem to have been arriving at the same crossroads simultaneously. A stage has been reached whereby social science is confronting matters by-stepped for many years or brushed aside as incommodious. Psychology, for instance, not so long ago still amounted to a form of 'indoctrination' in mechanical empiricism and what Liam Hudson has called 'the atomistic habit of mind', which 'whatever its virtues . . . is ill adapted to the elusive, shifting world of everyday meanings' (1972, p. 39). Time was when investigation was characterized by 'an avoidance in research of personal feelings, or personal experience' (Hudson 1972, p. 41) and when 'any idea that we were there to uncover the mysteries of the human mind . . . would have been greeted by embarrassment; the kind . . . that hardens . . . into contempt' (p. 40). But psychology can no longer be accused of avoiding messy human relationship affairs. Of major importance in this has been the business of 'scientizing' the study of personal relationships, and here the key role of individuals, namely Steve Duck and Robin Gilmour, should be noted: there can be little doubt that a turning point came as a result of their efforts, with the combined influence of the First International Conference on Personal Relationships, 1982, and a multi-volume work on personal relationships, followed by the inception of the *Journal of Social and Personal Relationships*. Nor is investigation continuing to ignore the mysteries of the human mind; another subtle shift has been towards tolerance of, graduating towards insistence on, including emotion as part of human enquiry; or there is, at least, acknowledgement of the seriousness of the omission. Thus, with the entrance of these newcomer subjects, 'personal relationships' and 'emotions', into mainstream psychology, its traditional halls, not long since exclusive to the formality of precision, cognition and empiricism, now admit the ambiguous uncertainty and hot-head informality of private emotions and trivial interpersonal matters. There has been a joining with other fields of investigation that have been affiliated to more practical and professional rather than purely academic walks of life, such as family therapy, marital relations, kinship networks, social support, psychodynamics and interpersonal communications.

Academic movements and social trends mutually inform one another; and outside science, but 'rubbing off' on it, there have been corresponding value and belief shifts; for instance, more explicit discussion of 'relationships', a merging of sex roles, and mutual admission of the viability of each others' gender characteristics. Perhaps most significant among these is the emerging phenomenon of tough and/or rational men (*all* 'men', in other words) seriously admitting to needs and feelings, and so beginning to legitimize traditionally female values. As Gilligan has said: 'the discovery now being celebrated by men in mid-life of the importance of intimacy, relationships, and care is something that women have known from the beginning' (1982, p. 17). As such influences filter back to research levels, and given the increasing importance placed on the voice of common sense, we can expect this voice, significantly, to be sometimes of a higher pitch; i.e. for the academic to hear the woman-indoors as well as the man-in-the-street, and for the neglected discourse of women now to have distinct reverberations through the slopes of masculinely biased scientific traditions. Through a mixture of trends, tolerances, acknowledgements and defeats, a point has arrived whereby all the indeterminacies of personal relationships can be countenanced, and daily domestic and recreational exchanges have attained a weight sufficient for them to be admitted as a scientific subject. These trends have been separate, but in reciprocal influence they bolster each other's permissibility.

Echoes of Berger and Luckmann (1966) in some of the preceding will not have been missed. The different contributions capture the dialectic between a small-scale relationship reality constituted by subjective meaning – private perspectives, perception and accumulation of knowledge – which, in turn, has been formed by internalization (into hierarchies of the mind) of distant, large-scale social construction of objective 'truths' and beliefs about relationships. On one level, there is what each thinks and knows, some of which is communicated (whether as academics choosing and reporting on areas of interest, or as people in relationship making sense, actualizing goals, etc.), and then on another level, what we become and what we experience in our relations with each other. To join these, we go from private construals and inner speech, used in the struggle to understand and integrate new information with old knowledge, to ways of talking, communication acts and decisions, and to plans and achievements based on what is axiomatic – until there is a change of opinion, cultural 'climate' or social construction. These levels are selectively represented in the divisions of this volume: in Section One, the private (between you and me and the sense in which we know), in Section Two, the use of what we know to get a message across, keep memories alive, cope within a social network and strive after goals, and in Section Three, the evolving construction of relational reality balanced 'twixt immediately modified and unquestioningly reified cultural meanings.

'Accounting' is a multi-faceted concept. As well as 'accounts' and 'accounting', within the following pages there is much reference to various synonyms and related terms – like 'stories', 'reports', 'narratives' and 'explaining', 'representing' and 'telling'. The range as well as distinctive uses and different emphases make the domain we are covering complex, and inevitably there is potential for confusion and ambiguity. Like a large rambling house, visitors need to be shown their way around and have rooms they otherwise might miss pointed out to them; and even occupants may dwell only in certain rooms, keeping others locked or treating them as junk stores. Or there may be similar occupants in other houses, who, despite a capacity to be of support and help to each other, never meet. Investigators use the concepts concerned in diverse ways, and may not be aware of colleagues in other corners of the neighbourhood. There is a pluralism involved, such that even those working within the 'house' or area may require clarification. To extend the house/neighbourhood analogy, we feel there is need for some new development and expansion. This book is a start. Some of the houses and occupants are missing: there are gaps in coverage, notably a developmental perspective, and it would have been valuable to include accounts or meta-accounts of a sociologist, an anthropologist and a historian. We could not attempt to be comprehensive, but trust the student of the area to note the empty houses in the district and to consider making visits elsewhere in search of missing parties. We don't consider any under-population to be remissive: this is a new neighbourhood, an over-spill, and the book will have done its job if it acquaints readers with a selection of the relevant work and demonstrates the force of relationship construal, representation, communication and other key issues.

There is at least a dualism involved. To use the distinction drawn by Antaki and Fielding (1981) in respect of 'ordinary explanation', for the researcher, accounts and accounting are of importance either as research tools or as phenomena in their own right. In the former sense, an account is a vehicle for accessing and conveying relevant information and knowledge, and it is ultimately the information yielded that matters. However, it is necessary to understand accounting as a phenomenon in order to assess its limitations and significance as a social tool. As a phenomenon, the range of concern includes implicit accounting as well as accounts as overt or communicable products, and covers social uses and functions, plus content – the emerging theory, knowledge or explanation. It may be helpful to depict the field of interest as including both accounting as a capacity for attaining meaning, and as a device for making sense of each other. The *double entendre* in the concept of 'accounting for relationships' is not just there as a convenient linguistic device to link two disparate areas. We believe there is value in connecting both accounting in the sense of constructing meaning and explaining within relationships *per se* (whether by investigators or ordinary people) and accounts as relational discourse, constitutive of meaning in the pragmatic sense. Though the enterprise is formidably large, it is our view that scientific explanation of understanding and knowledge in personal relationships and also the construction of social meaning can each be enlightened by work in the other. Thus these are the two frontiers (together with where they merge) for work reported in this volume.

SECTION ONE

The coverage of the book ranges wide and away from intimacy between particular individuals, the *sine qua non* of personal relationships, but this, properly, is the level at which the book begins. Section One, Interpersonal Understanding, includes chapters relevant to the individual's role in creating relationships. They deal with the inner (mental) world and the psychological processes that underlie understanding and knowledge of individuals in relationship. 'Accounting' in this section is how one person comes to explain or understand his or her own relationships; and any accounts, whether in the abstract or more concrete sense, are self-directed, motivated towards insights, detailed knowledge of persons and appropriate perceptions of changing relationship matters. To focus on this, the wider issues are suspended or treated as of secondary interest to this personal context of the individual's subjective contribution. Contributors here are concerned with explaining, describing and evaluating the process of acquiring intimate knowledge, developing understanding in new relationships and maintaining ongoing awareness over the long term. Collectively, the concern is with how we each arrive or fail to arrive at interpersonal knowledge unique to particular relationships.

Clarke's chapter makes a fitting start, first, because the psychological theory he presents is 'grand' enough to provide an integrated theoretical basis for much about mental processes that is to follow and, second, because the multiple relevance of the 'accounting' concept, referred to above, is evident within his chapter. There is relevance with respect to methodology; data to support his theory were based on participants' accounts, and he raises the investigative problem of how much accounts are to be trusted and taken at face value when used as research tools. Theoretically, his chapter is about people 'accounting' for each other, through an awareness of known persons' patterns of emotional responding. He introduces a tripartite model of the mind, which includes a dominant affective level, and then reports on studies that support the theory that emotions are 'driving forces' and that interpersonal decisions are reached via a 'dialogue of emotions', and that it is these rather than events, cognitions and specific actions that are the essence of personal understanding.

From the different tradition of a philosophical background, Berenson presents a complementary thesis; namely, that it is only because we are emotional beings, able to identify each other's way of feeling, and are characteristically emotional in our responses, that we come to know and understand others as individual persons. Contrary to philosophy's conventional treatment of emotions as obstacles to sense-making, she argues that if our reasoning was emotionless, we would be without qualities in ourselves essential for noticing intrinsic aspects of others, and therefore would be incapable of knowing each other. In opposition to philosophical tradition, in which emotions have been represented as obstructive and anathema to arriving at knowledge, she argues that emotions are intrinsic to being human and being in relationship, and so to be human is to use them, naturally and constructively. Both Berenson and Clarke, in pushing forward emotions as a vital force in interpersonal accounting (i.e. in the sense of understanding), are going against the more conventional moulds of their respective disciplinary backgrounds; it is appropriate and timely to bring into prominence this other dimension of being human, which insists, and which enables view. The place of emotions they both propose with regard to accounting for relationships is in respect of understanding as opposed to accounting about relationships to others. 'Accounts' as a device are features of their respective contributions, but only incidentally. For Clarke they are tokens for purchasing information from research participants, and, equally, have the same currency for people's interpretation and understanding of each other. That is, they are accepted as research tools, and as one of the means people have for representing their feelings to each other. Berenson uses accounts of a specific kind — literary examples — to illustrate her argument.

The next three chapters deal more with cognitive than emotional underpinnings of people's relationship accounting, though there is, as in later chapters, at least tacit acknowledgement of the part played by affect. Wilkinson makes exemplary use of 'accounts' as a tool, finding partici- pants who were especially good at providing them, using detailed extracts to let them speak for themselves in her discussions, and, being both a participant and investigator herself, making double use of them to explore perceptions and metaperspectives in getting to know another. Her data indicate the importance of perceptions unique to the individuals involved, as distinct from generalizations. She uses accounts to demonstrate the reciprocity of self-knowledge and other-knowledge and suggests that a lack of correspondence between metaperspectives is implicated in rela- tionship failure and breakdown. Miell uses 'accounts' of a non-verbal kind (graphs, in this case) to explore how retrospective construals of a newly developing relationship are modified over time in the light of an evolving cognitive context. The way in which participants reorganize remembered events so that they conform with their present position, anticipates one point made by Livingstone in Section Three, about the possible distortion of cultural representations to fit with the interpretative position of the individual. Burnett takes a sceptical look at the extent and depth of interpersonal awareness, in the context of studies concerning the content and incidence of thoughtfulness about and within relationships.

SECTION TWO

Section Two, Accounting in Use, moves from the private world of interper- sonal discovery and sense-making to the more practical business of using accounts and the underlying cognitions. The widening focus is on the expression, use and functions of accounts, interactive processes and the employment of general relationship cognitions. The last three chapters group together more easily than the first three, but they form a collective in that they move beyond the more intimate setting of in-depth detailed understanding to a wider interactional setting and towards a working knowledge of how to act in relationships. In contrast to the previous section, where the emphasis was on perception and other-orientation, here the concern is more with cognition and self-serving functions and uses of accounts; the focus goes from acquiring knowledge and understanding to making use of it.

   Some of the chapters here reach marginally beyond the concerns of the section, but are not sufficiently micro-scale to belong to the intimate realm of the previous section, or removed enough from intra-relationship issues to be deferred to the wider perspective of Section Three. Certainly, the chapter by Antaki has relevance beyond the themes here of function and interaction–knowledge links, and might well have appeared at the start of the book to provide an introductory typology. Antaki's chapter finds a place here because he deals with investigators' uses of the concept of 'relationship accounting', and because the application of a performance analogy highlights the more expressive aspects of accounting. However, as well as its intrinsic interest in revealing important features of relationship accounts, the value of his guide extends beyond itself to help connect and organize in a domain of potential confusion where, as he suggests, there is a tendency to mark out territories. In other words, his classification has an extrinsic value in linking the different positions the sectioning necessarily separates. The typology suggested by Antaki serves a bridging role by connecting 'hidden' and 'unarticulated' accounts on one side of the divide and metacognition and illocutionary effects on the other.

The change of emphasis in this section implicates some flexibility of definition with regard to the 'accounts/accounting' multiface. 'Accounts', including self-reports, essays, justifications, communications, and other more concrete forms, are sometimes featured, but so too are components of knowledge, such as plans, expectations, schemata, which can be said to underlie people's knowledge of relationships. The concept of 'accounts' is most applicable in the first two chapters; in the next three it is 'accounting' in the sense of knowing and cognitions which is applicable, and Baxter relates her investigation of cognitions to tacit understanding, strategies and the functional value of accounting or not, as the case may be, to each other.

Weber, Harvey and Stanley touch on the Section One theme of sense-making, but widen their survey of accounts to consider, in passing, accounts as a research tool, but particularly the various motivations and functions of accounts following terminated relationships. In stressing utility and the associated maintenance work, the account is reified in their discussion, so that it becomes an object, comparable to, say, a photograph album in which memories of idealized versions of relationships are preserved, or objectified devices by which commitments and promises are honoured and old feelings and memories can be displayed and stored. La Gaipa, drawing from a long-term research programme on friendship, describes studies dealing with predictive and prescriptive expectations, looking at how they serve as interaction guides. La Gaipa's systems approach sets private meanings and ideals in the context of social prescription, group networks and the situational constraints and needs of specific populations (e.g. the elderly; cancer patients). His discussion balances a person's inbuilt guide to relational information, in the form of schemata based on predictive expectations, against reference to external authority in the form of prescriptive and normative information. Thus, his review instances the dialectic between private meaning (the person as his own authority on friendship) and social construction (the influence of norms and situation on conceptions of a personal relationship). In addition to presenting a very detailed empirical review of people's friendship accounts, from kindergarten to old age, this chapter also exemplifies academic accounting for relationships – in this case, based on close to two decades of empirical investigation, using thousands of statements, essays, questionnaires and other kinds of accounts, converted via multi-dimensional scaling to generalizations about the meaning of friendship. Despite his broader concerns, expectations come under the heading of schemas, and La Gaipa's discussion of behavioural links point in the direction of the next three chapters.

The last three chapters in this section are unified by their focus on the use of relationship knowledge in conducting relationships. Planalp describes work to show how the elaboration of tacit relational knowledge on the one hand and the course of a relationship on the other both progress in a complementary way, and examines the cognitive processes with which schemas and events are 'inextricably linked'. Berger, more specifically, deals with how plans are applied, using the example of the various strategies there are for initiating relationships. Baxter looks at how people use their relationship knowledge to achieve their objectives in relationships, often without the necessity of direct communication; she proposes that being able to avoid explicit communication, with the complications and face-loss this could bring, is one way in which such knowledge is used to benefit the individual.

SECTION THREE

Section Three, Constructing Relationships, moves to perspectives external to relationships *per se*, to focus on the extent to which relational meaning is created independently of the individuals concerned. We are stimulated to confront the sense in which the meaning of relationships, in spite of being characterized by privacy and individualism, comes from 'out there' and is not simply to be discovered phenomenologically. From the broader and more long-term angles of socially and academically constructed meaning, we see the formative function of language as its semantic and pragmatic uses dynamically evolve over time. The investigative lens enlarges, paling person to person issues, and extending to take in historical and intellectual representational and linguistic influences on relationship knowledge, understanding and process. From this wider angle, the distinctions between reality and myth become blurred, and a view of their overlapping similarity is gained. When relationship accounting is viewed panoramically, it is hardly relevant whether a person's reports about 'us' are false, exaggerated or insightful, whether they are representational and a route to underlying knowledge and how things are, as opposed to uncorresponding communications about relationships, designed, perhaps unwittingly, to achieve some extra-linguistic goal; rather it is the constructive function of accounting that becomes paramount, and the potency of this must be balanced against the microscopic creative potential of person doing and reacting to person.

In this section, linguistic issues – though they are not all – are central. Even if the whole volume had been devoted to the role of language in relationship accounting, the enterprise would be vast: 'To examine the use of words is to tackle the whole of psychology, sociology, cultural anthropology, and semantics combined' (Hudson 1972, p. 38). Questionnaires and experimental subjects in psychology laboratories have become remote! In contrast with other sections, the chapters here recede from the micro-scale problem of how you in particular understand me specifically, and my knowledge of your understanding of me, and away from how knowledge is applied in yours-and-my interaction so that it helps us to accomplish our goals. Whereas, previously, the concerns were primarily with understanding, and then with knowledge, here the foremost concern is the problem of meaning. Discussion of relationship meaning within historical and intellectual contexts raises implications for how research is conducted and the extent to which we are responsible for the nature of the relationships we lead. One theme in this last section concerns the truth value of accounts – whether there can be any such thing as an accurate account that can be taken as an objective index to the events it documents or whether it is a mistake to believe there is any single correct version. Shotter discusses some fallacies involved in relationship accounting. One person cannot arrive at a definitive account of an ongoing relationship, because the sense of it is not under any one individual's control, but rather is created jointly and carried along by 'passions'. To report on what happened retrospectively, therefore, inevitably involves imposing some after-the-event understanding that could not have been applied at the time because it had not been reached.

Another theme is the formal construction of meaning by relationship investigators. Duck deals with academic construction; he takes a lessons-of-the-past approach to show how the metaphors, concepts and methods investigators use contain implicit theories that send research in one direction rather than another, possibly creating false divisions, hiding connections and narrowing understanding. McGhee points out that personal relationship researchers lack a theory of what people are doing when they provide investigators with accounts, and argues for the socialization of method, and the treatment of accounts as 'situated conversation'. Shotter also touches on the academic's role in accounting for relationships with respect to the potential for shifts in morality arising from intellectual influences. An implication of his chapter is that it would behove academics to recognize the fallacies involved in their own supposedly objective relationship accounting, because of the potential for good in personal relationships, and because of the infiltration of academic versions of what happens into laypersons' plots.

Concern with the validity of accounting is raised from another angle by Livingstone in her critical discussion of theories and approaches regarding media representations of personal relationships. After reviewing different positions which have been adopted, and contrasting communications study approaches to representations with a key social psychological position, she puts forward the standpoint of 'conscious realism', to argue that media accounts have a creative role in the construction of relational meaning but that the extent and nature of this can only be understood by allowing for the interpretative role of the viewer. Television and literature present a special case, but the parallel with other less tangible cultural influences on understanding is clear. Gergen and Gergen look backward in time to put into a historical perspective the discourse by which relationships events are actualized. Arguments about reality-representation correspondence are besides the point, they suggest; what matters is the actions which follow from them.

The moral theme running through the chapters in this section has been indicated: i.e., the moral responsibility of those with a more powerful voice, once it is acknowledged that accounts from influential sources like academia, television and socially dominant groups are formatively involved in the sense people make of their encounters and resulting experience and action. Another recurring observation, discussed explicitly by Gergen and Gergen, is that relationship accounts (whether we call them representations, stories, narratives or conversations) are significant in pragmatic terms and so, by illocutionary effect, capture reality. It matters therefore which stories we find intelligible. The message here is not simply one about the moral responsibility of the investigator. As McGhee discusses in his Postword, our accounts are 'enabling', 'instructional' and 'empowering': in telling relationship accounts, alternative ways of being may be brought into view. Hence, the viability of exploring the nature and problems of accountability and in reflexively realizing what is involved in making relationships intelligible.

Thematically, this volume proffers some of the latest and arguably more exciting personal relationships work, filling a gap in the literature and pointing in valuable directions. Beyond the subject matter, it highlights new faces in social psychology. Some that have been in low profile for some time, though they have occasionally been more conspicuously evident, are here plainly noticeable; for instance, in the switch from individual to couple, from subject to participant, from content analysis to interpretation and implicature, from semantics to pragmatics, and from actor to story-teller. Investigators' accounts and lay persons' accounts are in some places analysed separately, but any boundaries between them are only for temporary use, and taken down in the over-arching look at *peoples'* discourses, reports, representations and so forth. Most of these chapters are rooted in a programme of empirical research, though in some cases it is not made prominent. We hope it will be taken as a sign of good health, following social psychology's sickness in the 1970s, that we have not made a fetish of data, though have welcomed it in places as a means of focusing and illustrating discussion. Some writers retrospectively review their work or field of interest, linking programmes with new developments, whilst other chapters are critiques in which the authors share their philosophies of the moment.

Its scope and perspective, the originality if not reputation of its contributors, and the general applicability of its subject matter, make this a volume that should appeal to others in addition to the students and investigators of personal relationships for whom it is principally intended. We suppose that undergraduates whose courses include a 'personal relationship' component will make most use of it; however, as participants in relationships, of course, everyone is a potential student and investigator of this subject, and we trust that its contents will not be beyond the reach of interested non-specialists. A measure of a psychological work's merit is if its contents can be applied reflexively to the people and processes involved in its making. In this respect, we ourselves have been able to draw from it in a non-academic sense, as human beings with our own hot and cold, up and down relationships. During times of disagreement and division, chapters within were useful towards making sense of difficulties, and while we may sometimes have been unmotivated to let the contents guide us back to harmony, we did not doubt the enabling relevance contained there.

REFERENCES

Antaki, C. and Fielding, G. (1981) 'Research on ordinary explanations'. In C. Antaki (ed.) *The Psychology of Ordinary Explanations of Social Behaviour.* London: Academic Press.

Berger, P.L. and Luckmann, T. (1966) *The Social Construction of Reality: A Treatise in the Sociology of Knowledge.* Harmondsworth: Penguin.

Duck, S.W. (1984) 'The field of personal relationships'. *The New Psychologist,* February, 32–5.

—— and Perlman, D. (1985) 'The thousand islands of personal relationships: a prescriptive analysis for future explorations'. In S.W. Duck and D. Perlman (eds) *Understanding Personal Relationships: An Interdisciplinary Approach.* London: Sage.

Gilligan, C. (1982) *In a Different Voice: Psychological Theory and Women's Development.* Cambridge, Massachusetts and London: Harvard University Press.

Hudson, L. (1972) *The Cult of the Fact.* London: Cape.

Interpersonal understanding: emotion, construal and reflection

1 Emotion, decision and the long-term course of relationships

David D. Clarke

People's accounts of their relationships are clearly important as research material, even though the nature of their importance can be seen in two different ways. On one hand, as Shotter (Chapter 13) argues in this book, they can be regarded as important in their own right, as a special reality that calls into being its own social world – a special activity or discourse that may be taken, not as describing some extra-linguistic domain, but rather as creating a domain of belief and experience in which what is so is what the account constructs to be so. This might be called the rhetorical position.

On the other hand, when viewed in a different way, accounts can be important sources of information about the thoughts, actions and feelings they purport to account for (even though the wisest interpretation of them may not involve taking them at face value). It is one of the greatest follies of many branches of psychology, and one of the greatest sources of its alienation from the public, that it assumes ordinary people have nothing informative to say about their own lives and actions. The respectful use of accounts as evidence in appropriate kinds of research may go a long way towards restoring the good faith of the social sciences in the eyes of the public, redefining the researchers' role as that of appreciating and supplementing lay knowledge, rather than dismissing and replacing it. I will call the view that accounts may be taken as (provisional) descriptions of their subject matter and legitimate means of investigating it, the representational position.

In this chapter people's accounts of close relationships, and of salient life choices, will be used in this latter mode to investigate an issue of general importance for psychology, within and beyond the study of relationships, namely the guiding principles of action, and particularly the role of the emotional system in directing the course of events. As Berenson argues in the next chapter, emotions are an essential and often neglected ingredient of our humanity, supportive of our rationality and not opposed to it, and essential driving forces in our dealings with one another.

The relationship accounts that formed the basis of the following studies took a variety of forms, from passages of narrative, through the ordering of pre-ordained descriptive terms, to the making of realism ratings for alternative representations of the course of relationships. But throughout, the point was the same, to examine people's own representations of their thoughts, decisions and actions for evidence that their emotional lives had played a central organizing role in the resulting relationships (or if you prefer the rhetorical position, that people had used the constructs of emotion in a particularly crucial way in securing the coherence of their subjective reality). The results may be interpreted in either way, but certain empirical checks and balances have been included so as to make the former and stronger interpretation at least a viable possibility.

As Berger points out, a crucial role for the mental system is that of action planner and co-ordinator, and much emphasis has been placed on the *cognitive* aspects of this process, while 'affective factors are not generally considered in the planning literature' (Berger, this volume, p. 169). Planalp, too, deals with the cybernetic properties of relational knowledge schemata in the governance and co-ordination of events and discourse, while conceding that 'relationships ... are inextricable from emotion' (Planalp, this volume, p. 187).

In some recent publications (Clarke 1983a; Harré, Clarke and De Carlo, 1985) I suggested that the control of action, and psychological processing more generally, are carried out by a hierarchy of cybernetic units operating simultaneously on a number of different levels. More particularly, though, the suggestion was that this hierarchy does not just consist of two major parts: high-level cognitions exercising overall control, and lower-level fine-grained sensory-motor co-ordination routines executing and fine tuning the strategies from the higher level. On the contrary it seems likely that conscious cognition and deliberate rational decision-making do not constitute the upper half of a two-level control system, but the middle third of a three level one. In other words there seems to be a third class of control system, which is superordinate to cognition in just the same respects that cognition is superordinate to sensory-motor control, that is it exerts a more global and more compelling influence and generates longer-term activity patterns and strategies than cognitive processes do. It was further postulated that the *affective* system and its systematic modulation of affective states play an important role in this third level control system, and that the long-term, affectively based patterns it produces can operate interactively between people over long periods of time, effectively generating and directing the course of the relationship between them.

Although largely a matter of conjecture at the moment, there are precedents for most of the major points in this argument. The multi-level, hierarchical nature of the structure of action and its underlying control systems has been described repeatedly (Broadbent 1977; Clarke 1983b; Craik 1966; Dawkins 1976; Michie 1976; Miller, Galanter and Pribram 1960; Powers 1973; Welford 1951). Heise (1979) extended Powers's (1973) hierarchical theory of action control by suggesting that the highest levels of control are exercised by the affective system. Recently a number of authors have been suggesting that affect exercises control over cognition, or is in some other respect the primary psychological system, with cognition playing a secondary role (Abelson *et al.* 1982; Bower 1981; Johnson and Tversky 1983; Tomkins 1981; Zajonc 1980, 1984). The importance of emotion and the effective communication of emotion for the success of close relationships has been stressed by Gottman (1980) and by Noller (1981, 1982, 1984). Clarke, Allen and Dickson (1985) found that seven classes of interpersonal relationship could be distinguished with 79 per cent accuracy by their affective tone alone, while Gottman (1979, 1982) showed the importance of 'temporal form' or the systematic progression of events and stages in the understanding of marital relationships.

The purpose of this paper is to explore the properties of various relationship and life-choice accounts, using this theory of hierarchical action control with affective primacy as a conceptual framework.

The first idea to be explored is that the choices people make between different courses of action will, for major choices at least, be more influenced by emotional than cognitive considerations, and will therefore be more comprehensible given an understanding of the actors' emotional states, than from their beliefs about the material circumstances of their decisions, opportunities, costs, benefits and so on. This idea also touches on the nature and conduct of psychology as a whole, since at present so much emphasis is given to the study of cognitive processes. If this conjecture proves to be correct, then the cognitive revolution in psychology, which has brought experimental work on information processing so much to the fore, will turn out to be at least partly mistaken, and will have taken us in the wrong direction to the extent that it has placed the greatest emphasis for research and teaching on those aspects of psychological processing that are not of the most fundamental importance. The use of accounts may help to remedy this imbalance since, in spite of their apparently cognitive origins, their content and purpose in research can range over emotional, motivational, historical, circumstantial, behavioural, contextual or for that matter cognitive factors, with greater ease and flexibility than any other single research method. It is especially in the content and construction of people's life accounts that the relative *unim*-portance of cognitive factors in their affairs may be shown. In the first of the experiments described below, the hypothesis is tested that the affective background to a decision is a better basis for predicting the outcome than the cognitive background.

Turning to the implications of the theory for the understanding of relationships *per se*, it suggests that at the core of any salient, close, interpersonal relationship, such as marriage, there will be a 'dialogue of the emotions', a reciprocal exchange of emotional states and influences, which over the long term makes up the essential 'story-line' or time course of that relationship. One of the particular merits of accounting research here is the emphasis it allows us to give to the form of relationship over time as a diachronic structure, a plot, a narrative or trajectory, whereas other research methods tend to treat relationships as states of affairs, static conditions that either prevail or do not amongst a given group of people.

A 'dialogue of the emotions' may go something like this. A man's declining love for his wife may cause her great anguish, which leads him to feel more guilty and thus more estranged from her, and so on. The form these events may take is infinitely variable, and as far as the people's essential dilemma, and their similarity with countless other couples is concerned, quite irrelevant. To ask whether his neglect takes the form of forgotten anniversaries or impatient words on the telephone; whether her misery finds expression in sobbing interludes in the bathroom when no one is there to hear, or in pessimistic conversations with her friends, is to obscure the essence of their plight rather than to reveal its essential details. A turnabout in their fortunes would not come in the thoughtful selection of an unexpected gift, or a friendly hug over the washing up, any more or less than in any other gesture that carried the same message, that he still felt (at least something of) the old warmth and concern for her. What counts is the feelings each has for the other, and the feelings they evoke in return, whether positive or negative, not the signs and tokens in which the feelings find expression.

The theory thus implies that this affective 'story-line' will be detectable and intelligible quite independently of the details of particular thoughts, events, actions and circumstances that might appear at first sight to make up the substance of the relationship, and to which most attention has been directed in research on relationships. The second study suggests that there *is* such a system of affective interdependencies, making up a complex network of possible pathways and progressions through the course of a marriage, and that this seems to have a structure that is independent of the specific events by which it is mediated and signalled.

The third implication of these ideas is that the 'dialogue of the emotions' running through the long-term course of a relationship such as marriage will have a definite stochastic structure with an identifiable order. That is, it will form a system of sequential dependencies where each event is influenced by only the preceding one or two or *n* events, where the resulting pattern is called a first or second or *nth* order structure respectively. This kind of analysis, deriving from the applied mathematics of Markov chains, has been used to study the sequential structures of sentences (Miller and Selfridge, 1950) and of dialogue (Clarke 1981, 1983b; Pease and Arnold 1973). The third experiment will investigate the order of the sequential interdependencies between the partners' affective states during marriage, and thus aim to characterize the general organization of the 'dialogue'.

THE FIRST STUDY

Six post-graduate students and post-doctoral researchers from Oxford University, aged 24–39 years old, took part in the first stage of this study. Two of them were men and four were women. Each subject was asked to recall a significant choice or dilemma from the past in which they could have taken one of several courses of action which it was up to them to decide. They were then asked to write two accounts of the events leading up to the choice, one of which was to emphasize their feelings and play down the material circumstances of the decision, and the other was to stress the logical and material factors in the decision, and to omit any mention of emotional considerations as far as possible. There was a control for order effects, half the subjects being asked to write the emotional version first, and half to write the factual/cognitive version first. Both versions were supposed to contain equivalent amounts of information. The subjects were then asked to describe the course of action they had chosen, and two others they might have taken but did not. The two versions of each problem were then typed onto separate pages, followed by the three possible outcomes in random order, with no indication of which had been the real outcome. The possible outcomes were listed in the same order on both versions of the problem.

As a manipulation check to ensure that the 'emotional' versions of the problems differed from the 'cognitive' versions in the way they were supposed to, but nevertheless had equivalent amounts of information overall, the twelve problem descriptions were rated without the lists of possible outcomes by ten subjects from the subject panel of the Oxford University Department of Experimental Psychology. There were five males and five females, aged 22–43, from middle-class backgrounds and occupations. The twelve vignettes were presented in random order, and each was rated on three five-point scales for emotional content, factual content and overall amount of information. As expected the six emotional vignettes were rated as having more emotional than factual content ($t = 4.88$, $df = 9$, $p < 0.001$), and the cognitive vignettes the reverse ($t = 10.07$, $df = 9$, $p < 0.0001$). Furthermore, the 'emotional' vignettes had more emotional content than the 'cognitive' vignettes ($t = 10.16$, $df = 9$, $p < 0.0001$) and the 'cognitive' vignettes had more factual content that the 'emotional' vignettes ($t = 3.97$, $df = 9$, $p < 0.0003$). However the 'emotional' versions were *not* more informative overall than the 'cognitive' versions, having a mean rating of 3.2 on the five-point scale of information content as opposed to 3.3 for the six 'cognitive' accounts. This difference is insignificant and conservative, operating *against* the demonstration of the hypothesis being explored here ($t = 0.42$, $df = 9$, $p < 0.687$).

Fifty-two new subjects then took part in a second stage of this study,

Table 1.1   Number of correct and incorrect judgements based on affective and cognitive information

Information given	Judgements	
	Correct	Incorrect
Affective	96	60
Cognitive	80	76

twenty-six males and twenty-six females, aged 19–54. Each subject was given a booklet consisting of their instructions for the experiment and one version of each of the six problems, together with the listing of its three possible outcomes. Unknown to the subjects there were two versions of this booklet, one containing three of the problems described in their cognitive form and the other three in their affective form, and the other booklet being the other way round, that is having the affective versions of the three problems that appeared in the first booklet in their cognitive form, and vice versa. The task for the subjects was to read each vignette and to make a first and second choice from the list of three outcomes for each, to show which outcome they thought had been the real one, and which the second most likely.

As a supplementary task the first twenty subjects in this part of the study (ten males and ten females) were asked to rate the confidence with which they made their choices of outcome, on a scale from 1 (definitely did not happen) to 5 (definitely did happen).

Table 1.1 shows the number of correct and incorrect first choices of outcome based on the emotional and cognitive descriptions of the six problems, and Figure 1.1 shows the results diagrammatically.

Affective vignettes produced significantly more selections of the correct outcome than did cognitive vignettes ($z = 1.82$, test for the difference of two proportions, $p < 0.05$, one-tailed).

Comparing the affectively based judgements and cognitively based ones in turn with the level of performance that could have been attained by guessing at chance, it turns out that both are considerably better than chance, but that the affectively based judgements exceed chance by a larger margin ($z = 7.39$, binomial approximation corrected for continuity) than the cognitively based judgements ($z = 4.67$). Both results are highly significant in their own right ($p < 0.00003$ in both cases). Chance performance was taken to be one correct answer in every three, as in each case there were three alternatives to choose from, of which only one was correct.

There was no difference in the confidence ratings for choices based on affective or cognitive vignettes, but, strangely enough, incorrect decisions were made with greater confidence overall than correct decisions. This effect was more pronounced for the affectively based choices than the cognitively based ones.

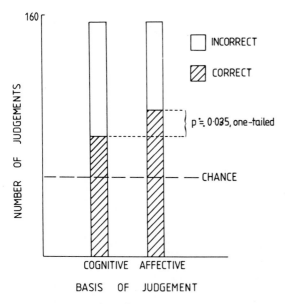

Figure 1.1   Number of correct judgements based on cognitive and affective information

One possibility may be that cognition and affective procedures are involved to different degrees, not only in the making of behavioural choices, but in the interpretation of them. Just as the cognitive system seems to be less influential in determining action, it may, when used interpretatively, give less accurate but clearer and more confident pronouncements, while the affective system delivers intuitions and hunches that are a more accurate guide, but less likely to be trusted. If this is the case it supports the point made in the introduction about the nature and role of contemporary psychology, that the over-cognitivization of its subject matter has misled us into placing greatest reliance, and undertaking most research, on aspects of human nature that are *less* important than the ones it encourages us to neglect. Alternatively, on the rhetorical view of accounts, it may be that the original story writers in this study recall or invent more intelligibly in the emotional than in the cognitive domain, and so the coherence of the resulting text is more useful to the subsequent judges in this condition. In other words it may be that they can justify their actions better with emotional than cognitive language, rather than that they necessarily build their actions at the time on emotional as opposed to cognitive foundations.

THE SECOND STUDY

Nine men and eleven women took part in this study, drawn from the subject panel of the Oxford University Department of Experimental

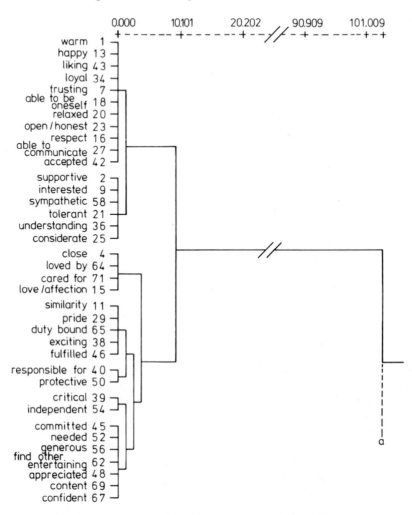

Figure 1.2   Cluster structure of feelings over seven relationship types

Psychology. They were aged 21–70 with a mean of 44, and all were married.

The materials for the study had been generated during a previous experiment (Clarke, Allen and Dickson 1985), in which ninety-two subjects had rated seventy-two emotions for their prevalence in seven classes of interpersonal relationships, such as marriage, friendship, siblinghood and with colleagues.

A cluster analysis was carried out on these ratings, which produced nine clusters of emotions, shown diagrammatically in Figures 1.2 and 1.3.

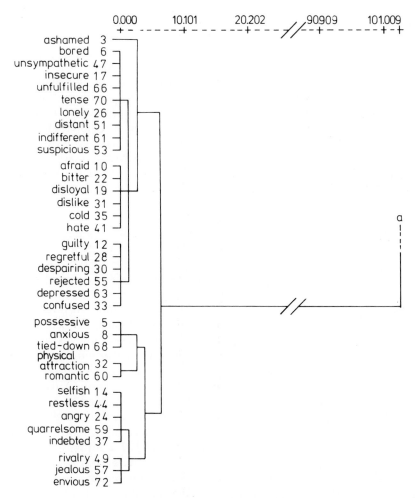

Figure 1.3   Cluster structure of feelings over seven relationship types (continued)

Each of the nine clusters was assigned a letter of the alphabet at random. The nine clusters of emotions and the code letter for each are listed in Table 1.2. These clusters and their code letters were typed out on nine large cards, and each of the code letters was imprinted on ten smaller cards using a commercial lettering set, making a deck of ninety small cards of nine types, one type for each code letter, with ten copies of each type.

The subjects, who were all married, were then told that we were interested in the feelings married people had for one another and the way these change over time, particularly over the long term. The subjects were asked to think of the emotional progressions and sequences they found to be typical of marriage, drawing on their own marriage or their knowledge of other people's as they chose. It was stressed that the sequences they should consider should be those occurring over the months and years of a relationship, not over the minutes and hours of a particular interaction or encounter, for example. Furthermore they should concentrate on the reciprocity of emotion, and report the sequences they thought of in terms of the feelings of first one partner and then the other in strict alternation. In this task we did not allow them to report two consecutive feelings or emotional states for the same person without reporting the partner's state in between. This is not a very great restriction, however, as the sequence 'partner 1 moves from state J to state G, while partner 2 remains unchanged in state A throughout' can be represented faithfully as 'A, J, A, G, A', starting with partner 2.

The subjects were asked to build a representation of the sequences they had in mind by selecting from the nine piles of small cards to represent the nine clusters of emotions, and arranging them across the table in a row from left to right. Each subject was asked to produce five different sequences.

The sequences were analysed by casting them into a 10×10 transitional frequency matrix, of which nine rows and nine columns represented the nine emotion clusters that appeared in the sequences, one extra row was used to tabulate the start of each sequence and its sequiturs, and one extra column was used to record the end of each sequence and its antecedents. One cell was empty by logical necessity, the transition from sequence start to sequence end with no intervening events, and so the table was treated as having only eighty degrees of freedom instead of eighty-one, in recognition of this constraint. There was a clear interaction between rows and columns ($\chi^2 = 346.7$, $df = 80$, $p < 0.01$) indicating that there was a regular sequential structure present in the data, and that in any consecutive pair of reported emotional states the antecedent was likely to have a significant effect on the nature of the sequitur.

To examine the contribution of each cell to the overall χ^2 value for the table, the standardized residual was calculated for each cell (see Colgan and Smith 1978). This is $(O - E)/\sqrt{E}$, where O and E are the observed and expected values for the cell. An informal procedure for judging which cells have disproportionately large residuals is to pick out those that are greater than the square root of the upper 5 per cent point of the appropriate chi-square distribution divided by the number of cells. This procedure was applied, and it showed twenty-two of the ninety-nine possible transitions to be remarkably common and twenty-nine to be remarkably uncommon. This is quite a surprising proportion, since a table of only weakly sequenced data would have the majority of transitions occurring with about chance frequency (which is of course not to say with the *same* frequency in all cases, as the chance frequency of two events occurring in succession depends on their individual frequencies of occurrence) and only a few

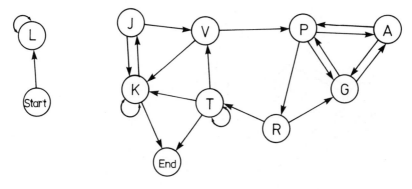

Figure 1.4   Positive transitions

transitions being significantly more or less common than one would expect by chance. In this case 52 per cent of the transitions are singled out by the normal residuals criterion as being remarkably frequent or remarkably infrequent. The positive, that is over-represented transitions, are shown diagrammatically in Figure 1.4, and the negative, that is under-represented transitions, are shown in Figure 1.5.

Table 1.2 showing the constitution of the nine clusters can be used as a key to Figures 1.4 and 1.5.

The point was again supported that emotional patterns can stand as a system or story-line in their own right, without the addition of the matters of detail to which psychological studies more commonly attend. This is not to claim that subjects do the task without making circumstantial, be-havioural or cognitive attributions to the actors, but only that the affective information they are given suffices on its own to specify all the other particulars they may need to invent.

Furthermore the reported structural dynamics of marriage that Figures 1.4 and 1.5 represent, has a number of interesting features. The map of positive transitions is in two apparently unconnected parts, showing that after an initial period of romantic attachment the relationship moves into other states, but at no particular time and with no particular next state. There were, of course, many transitions from romantic attachment to other states in the raw data, otherwise the remainder of the map would never have come into being, but no particular transition was outstandingly common. Of those which occurred, the one which came nearest to passing the criterion of normal residuals for inclusion on the map, was the transi-tion from romantic attachment to state K (being close, loved, caring for the other, love and affection). After that the next commonest transition was from romance to state T (warmth, happiness, liking, loyalty, trust, etc.).

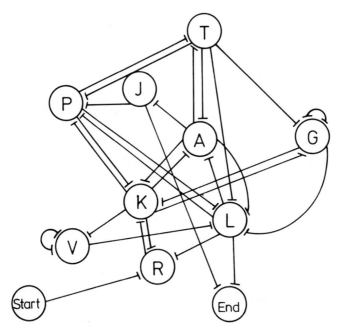

Figure 1.5 Negative transitions

However, the news is not all good. By far the most interesting feature of the map is the maximally connected subgroup of states P, A and G on the right-hand side. These are all negative states, and the richness of their interconnections suggests that once a couple gets into any of them they are likely to move around in that sub-system for quite a while, finding it difficult to escape. This sub-system functions like an 'absorbing state' in a Markov analysis, a kind of 'fly-paper' in the system, to which couples are not necessarily drawn by any particular process, but from which it is so hard to escape if they should fall into it by chance, that it accounts for a relatively large proportion of couples for a relatively large proportion of the time.

Note that because all the transitions in this map are reactive, this negative sub-system is not just a representation of monadic depression. It is a dyadic sub-system into which a *couple* gets drawn, and in which they hold one another. According to the map in Figure 1.4, however, there is one way out, by way of state R (and even that may lead back into the trap again). State R has only one label from the cluster analysis – 'ashamed'. Likewise there is only one way into the problematic sub-system, that is from state V, which includes a number of feelings that might add up to

Table 1.2 The nine clusters of emotions

Cluster A
Selfish, restless, angry, quarrelsome, indebted, rivalry, jealous, envious.

Cluster G
Passive, anxious, tied down.

Cluster J
Similarity, pride, duty bound, exciting, fulfilled, responsible for, protective.

Cluster K
Close, loved by, cared for, love/affection.

Cluster L
Physical attraction, romantic.

Cluster P
Bored, unsympathetic, insecure, unfulfilled, tense, lonely, distant, indifferent, suspicious, afraid, bitter, disloyal, dislike, cold, hate, guilty, regretful, despairing, rejected, depressed, confused.

Cluster R
Ashamed.

Cluster T
Warm, happy, liking, loyal, trusting, able to be oneself, relaxed, open/honest, respect, able to communicate, accepted, supportive, interested, sympathetic, tolerant, understanding, considerate.

Cluster V
Critical, independent, committed, needed, generous, find other entertaining, appreciated, content, confident.

---

complacency and neglect of a relationship, such as feeling content, confident, critical and independent.

The negative transition map (Figure 1.5) shows the state-to-state progressions that tend *not* to occur. These too are reactive, so when a state is shown not to be followed by itself this means that it is one that is not reciprocated within couples, such as state V, mentioned above, and state G, which is part of the negative sub-system and consists of the feelings 'passive', 'anxious' and 'tied down'. An interesting property of the negative sub-system is that it does not seem to halt with both partners reciprocating the same feelings. Rather it seems to generate constant motion with each negative state producing a *different* negative reaction in the partner. This may be a hopeful sign, as movement can be channelled into movement towards improvement in a way that complete stasis cannot.

The study does not attempt to distinguish the marital roles of husbands and wives. The subjects were not asked to designate the two people in their original portrayal of typical sequences as 'husband' and 'wife' and may not even have been thinking in these terms. This was for two reasons. A previous study (Clarke, Allen and Dickson 1985) had shown the feelings of husbands for wives to be virtually identical with those of wives for husbands *in aggregate*, although of course not necessarily in each couple considered separately. Therefore I did not feel that I was dealing with two separate emotional repertoires or systems for the two sexes. Secondly, I believe that while there *may be* systematic sex differences in emotional experience and reaction, the commonalities are more interesting and more important. The first priority in my view is to discover how people relate to other people in salient, if not always happy and close relationships, regardless of their sex or other roles. Scientific understanding and therapeutic intervention seem to have more to gain from the discovery of common ground between people than from the emphasizing of differences and divisions. I take it to be a positive result of this study, and the one which follows it, that so much of the pattern of emotional life can be made intelligible in material that does not distinguish the contributions of men and women to this shared pattern.

This experiment only uses a first order sequential analysis, that is one in which each event is related to its immediate antecedent alone. This may be to miss some of the more elaborate contingencies which higher order analyses can reveal. However the results of the next experiment vindicate this decision and suggest that affective sequences in marriage are predominantly first order. Furthermore a higher order analysis was contra-indicated as it increases the amounts of data required geometrically, and in this case seeks out elaborations of pattern that would probably go beyond the accounting capabilities of the original subjects from whom these data were obtained.

The unusual clarity with which the sequential patterns emerged, with over half the possible transitions being significantly over-represented or significantly under-represented, may be for a mixture of two reasons. This particular sequential pattern probably is very highly regular, but its regularities are also likely to be over-reported and enhanced by subjects giving their accounts of marriage in stereotypical form.

THE THIRD STUDY

Ten subjects, all of whom were native speakers of English, were recruited for the first stage, again using the subject panel of the Oxford University Department of Experimental Psychology. There were three men and seven women, aged 23–70 with a mean age of 52.4.

The ten subjects were seen individually and contributed in turn to fifteen lists of emotion words and phrases depicting the long-term emotional progression of a marital relationship. The fifteen lists, which were presented to each subject in a different random order, were built up in such a way as to give them different orders of sequential structure. Five of the lists had a first order structure, five were second order and five were third order. To generate a list or sequence of *nth* order, each subject would be shown only the last *n* items from the list so far, and would be asked to add the next item. This procedure would continue from subject to subject until all ten subjects had contributed, and the list was ten items long. The resulting list would then be an *nth* order structure throughout, since each of the ten items would have been chosen in a knowledge of the preceding *n* only.

In order to start off the procedure at the beginning of each list, fifteen three-word sequences were obtained in a pilot experiment to serve as a 'context' for the first few subjects. Examples of these three-state sequences were 'content–dissatisfied–worried' and 'doubtful–encouraging–confident'. These fifteen three-word contexts were assigned at random to the fifteen sequences to be generated. In all cases it was stressed to the pilot and main subjects that the emotional progressions they were to construct were to be (a) representative of marriage as they understood it, (b) entirely reactive, that is consisting of the states of the two partners in strict alternation and (c) long term, that is dealing in the course of events as it might be from month to month and year to year of a marriage, not from moment to moment during an individual interaction, since the underlying theory suggests that the emotional system makes its greatest contribution to the structure of the *long-term* course of events.

Lastly a group of five zero order sequences was produced by taking the fifteen lists obtained by the procedure above, extracting fifty items at random, and assembling them in random order to produce five further lists of ten items each. The zero order sequences were therefore representative of the other experimental materials in the type of items listed and the frequency with which they occurred, but not the sequential relations between them.

The fifteen three-word starter lists that had been used to initiate the procedure were omitted from all further listings of the sequences once they had served their purpose.

In the second part of this study, ten Oxford University undergraduates from a second-year psychology practical class were asked to rate the twenty sequences. There were seven women and three men. An experimental booklet was presented to each subject consisting of the twenty emotion-word sequences, in a different random order for each person, and identified only by randomly assigned letters of the alphabet. The subjects were told that these lists were meant to represent long-term reactive emotional progressions in marriage, but no mention was made of different orders of approximation. The subjects were then asked to give each sequence a rating from 1 to 7 to indicate how realistic they thought that sequence was.

As an example of the kind of material generated in this study, one of the

Table 1.3 Example of first order sequence of feelings in marriage

A. Contempt
B. Anxious
A. Worried
B. Puzzled
A. Inquisitive
B. Defensive
A. Annoyed
B. Misunderstood
A. Guilty
B. Bewildered

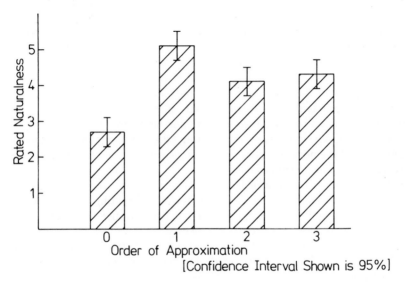

Figure 1.6 Perceived naturalness of emotional sequences as a function of orders of approximation

first order sequences is listed in Table 1.3. The mean ratings of realism for *zero, first, second* and *third* order sequences are plotted in Figure 1.6.

This study again showed that the diachronic structure of emotional life can be reproduced and recognized in the absence of specific details. The first, second and third orders of approximation are not significantly different in their rated realism, but they are all clearly seen as more realistic than the zero order sequence. This suggests that to be recognizable and familiar, affective patterns representative of marriage have to consist of more than the appropriate feelings in the appropriate proportions. There is a sequential regularity that has to be present too. However, this regularity appears to be first order only, consisting in the emotional reaction of each partner to the prior affective state of the other, and the addition of more complicated sequential dependencies does not make the representation recognizably more realistic. This is perhaps surprising, as it suggests that each partner's next emotional state is determined by the prior state of their partner, and is uninfluenced by their own prior state. If the prior states of both partners had an independent effect, then the resulting sequences would be second order, and there is no evidence in this study to show that second order sequences are seen as more realistic. This may be because the subtleties of a second order pattern were lost to the subjects, either at the stage of generating the sequences or of judging them; or it may be that marriage is really a matter of such close emotional bonding that each partner is more affected by the other than by their own past history, at least in regard of their feelings for one another.

CONCLUSIONS

In general the accounts that were collected, and the procedures they were subjected to, fit in quite nicely with the view that emotion provides an underlying theme to the course of action and relationship in the long term, which can be understood and characterized even in the absence of the details of cognition and behaviour whether recounted or observed, which for many investigators make up the essential substance of the subject.

Of course these results and conclusions are only tentative. Corroborating evidence would be required before the suggestions made here about the real nature of action, decision and relationship could be seen as firmly established. All three studies rely to an extent on the representational view of accounts being accepted, although not merely on trust. None are based on accounts taken at face value. In each case the pattern that has been reported was built up through the shared and agreed knowledge of subjects describing experiences, together with others recognizing true from false versions for example. As far as possible the studies were designed so as not to rely on subjects' reports *per se*, but rather to pose them with tasks that were only possible to do correctly in so far as they had systematic, consensual and correct beliefs about the structure of the phenomena being studied.

Some of the studies could be modified for use with more directly gathered observations and case materials, and this is one form corroboration might take, or alternatively the findings may be viewed according to the rhetorical view of accounts, as demonstrating no more than the role of people's conceptions of emotion in their attempts to present their social world as orderly, explicable and humane. In any case these generalizations about emotion, decision and relationship may be too sweeping to be substantiated or refuted as they stand. The next stage of this research as I envisage it will be to seek further support for these ideas but only as a by-product of the detailed characterization of the psychological processes that run and make up the affective system, so as to determine not only how emotional life proceeds and how it affects action and relationship, but also by virtue of what underlying mechanisms it operates in just the way it does.

ACKNOWLEDGEMENTS

I am most grateful for the financial support of the Economic and Social Research Council in carrying out these studies, and the help of Robert McIlveen in computing some of the statistical results. Special thanks are due to Dr Giovanni Carnibella for his extensive and expert help with the collection and analysis of data, and to Jill Crossland who played a major part in developing the materials and collecting data for the first study.

REFERENCES

Abelson, R.P., Kinder, D.R., Peters, M.D. and Fiske, S.T. (1982) 'Affective and semantic components in political person perception'. *Journal of Personality and Social Psychology*, 42, 619–30.

Bower, G.H. (1981) 'Mood and memory'. *American Psychologist*, 36, 129–48.

Broadbent, D.E. (1977) 'Levels, hierarchies and the locus of control'. *Quarterly Journal of Experimental Psychology*, 29, 181–201.

Clarke, D.D. (1981) 'Orders of approximation to English dialogue'. *Language and Communication*, 1, 207–36.

—— (1983a) 'Emotion and personality'. In R. Harré and R. Lamb (eds) *The Encyclopedic Dictionary of Psychology*. Oxford: Blackwell.

—— (1983b) *Language and Action: A Structural Model of Behaviour*. Oxford: Pergamon.

—— Allen, C.M.B. and Dickson, S. (1985) 'The characteristic affective tone of seven classes of interpersonal relationship'. *Journal of Social and Personal Relationships*, 2, 117–20.

Colgan, P.W. and Smith, T.J. (1978) 'Multidimensional contingency table analysis'. In P.W. Colgan (ed.) *Quantitative Ethology*. New York: Wiley.

Craik, K.J.W. (1966) *The Nature of Psychology*. Cambridge: Cambridge University Press.

Dawkins, R. (1976) 'Hierarchical organisation: a candidate principle for ethology'. In P.P.G. Bateson and R.A. Hinde (eds) *Growing Points in Ethology*. Cambridge: Cambridge University Press.

Gottman, J.M. (1979) *Marital Interaction*. New York: Academic Press.

—— (1980) 'Consistency of nonverbal affect and affect reciprocity in marital interaction'. *Journal of Consulting and Clinical Psychology*, 48, 711–17.

—— (1982) 'Temporal form: towards a new language for describing relationships'. *Journal of Marriage and the Family*, 44, 943–62.

Harré, R., Clarke, D.D. and De Carlo, N. (1985) *Motives and Mechanisms: An Introduction to the Psychology of Action*. London: Methuen.

Heise, D.R. (1979) *Understanding Events: Affect and the Construction of Social Action*. Cambridge: Cambridge University Press.

Johnson, E.J. and Tversky, A. (1983) 'Affect, generalisation, and the perception of risk'. *Journal of Personality and Social Psychology*, 45, 20–31.

Michie, D. (1976) 'An advice-taking system for computer chess'. *Computer Bulletin*, 10, 12–14.

Miller, G.A. and Selfridge, J.A. (1950) 'Verbal context and the recall of meaningful material'. *American Journal of Psychology*, 63, 176–85.

—— Galanter, E. and Pribram, K.L. (1960) *Plans and the Structure of Behavior*. New York: Holt, Rinehart & Winston.

Noller, P. (1981) 'Gender and marital adjustment level differences in decoding messages from spouses and strangers'. *Journal of Personality and Social Psychology*, 41, 272–8.

—— (1982) 'Channel consistency and inconsistency in the communications of married couples'. *Journal of Personality and Social Psychology*, 43, 732–41.

—— (1984) *Nonverbal Communication and Marital Interaction*. Oxford: Pergamon.

Pease, K. and Arnold, P. (1973) 'Approximations to dialogue'. *American Journal of Psychology*, 86, 769–76.

Powers, W.T. (1973) *Behavior: The Control of Perception*. Chicago: Arnold.

Tomkins, S.S. (1981) 'The quest for primary motives: biography and autobiography of an idea'. *Journal of Personality and Social Psychology*, 41, 306–29.

Welford, A.T. (1951) *Skill and Age*. Oxford: Oxford University Press.

Zajonc, R.B. (1980) 'Feeling and thinking: preferences need no inferences'. *American Psychologist*, 35, 151–75.

—— (1984) 'On the primacy of affect'. *American Psychologist*, 39, 117–23.

2 Emotions and understanding persons

Frances M. Berenson

My main purpose is to bring out the central role emotions and emotion concepts play in both self and other understanding, thus attempting to argue that it is mistaken to treat emotions as purely or necessarily or essentially passive phenomena and therefore also irrational. Emotions are all too often seen as interferences with our reasoning powers or as Peters (1961/62, p. 119) puts it: 'They are mists on our mental windscreen.' This particular view is not, by any means, limited to philosophers; it is a part of our everyday lives, as in such commonplace remarks as: 'He is incapable of thinking objectively (rationally), he gets emotional.' The implication is clear – emotions overcome us, they are irrational, and they certainly have nothing in common with objectivity.

I shall try to show why I take emotions to have an essential role in person understanding and why I think that a general dismissal of the important place emotions have in our understanding on the grounds of their passivity and irrationality cannot be justified. The situation can be put in a very simplified way, as follows: the mind is sometimes active and at other times passive. Activity of the mind is associated with being rational, making choices, taking decisions, forming intentions, etc. Passivity of mind is associated with being passive in the sense of being caused by various phenomena and thus the opposite of active and rational – being irrational. Activity of mind is closely related to rational decision-taking whereas passivity, being independent of one's decisions, is irrational because caused independently of any deliberation on one's part.

I am not, however, particularly concerned here with this account of the dichotomy of mind. My concern is with the next step, which places emotions firmly in the latter category; all emotions are taken as passive and therefore irrational (Hampshire 1965a; Peters 1971; Taylor 1966). It is not at all clear why what is passive must also be irrational, nor is it obvious that emotions are necessarily passive. As important, I do not see why one should insist that emotions do not involve any rational thought. At the very least, they involve seeing things in a certain way and this requires the application of concepts or, more generally, thoughts, which to some extent enter into attitudes, feelings and emotions.

I said that emotions involve seeing things in *certain* ways. This is because I do not want to rule out altogether any suggestion that our feelings or emotions are often caused in the sense that we all have predispositions to certain feelings that have a causal background and that may influence how we see things, what attitudes we have and to what extent we feel about things. In such cases, however, feelings and emotions stand in an internal relation to the perception. All perception of persons involves some attitude towards the other, even if it is only an attitude of disinterest, and it is, therefore, impossible to construe the seeing of a person in a certain way, such that the perception is separated off from the attitudes and feelings; they are entirely interrelated. The notion of causation involved here will not serve to support the thesis that emotions are *necessarily* passive and therefore also irrational. Such an account does not cover all possibilities; it does not cover the ways in which our emotional attitudes, which are an essential part of our form of life, contribute to our understanding of central features of human life, features that could not be adequately understood independently of a connection with the emotions.

Persons, by virtue of being persons, stand in relationships with others and to understand a person is to understand something of the relationships in which s/he stands. The very nature of such relationships, which are rich in all kinds of emotional attitudes, is such that giving a purely intellectual account of them would be to blind oneself to important facts about our form of life.

We find throughout the history of philosophy, from Plato and Aristotle to Hegel and Popper, to mention but a few, a movement advocating the cultivation of purely rational, cognitive powers, this achievement being dependent on the suppression and eradication of the emotions as interferences or, at best, on ignoring emotions as irrelevant to the development of reason. But what is completely overlooked in advocating such a course is that human beings are subject to emotions in ways that influence how they see and understand the world, and other human beings in that world. To ignore this is tantamount to demanding something of which we, qua human beings, are quite incapable.

The notion that emotions are passive, that they flood over us, overwhelm us and so on, is nevertheless still strongly embedded in the Philosophy of Mind. It is difficult to see why this model of the emotions still has such a hold over various philosophers. Richard Wollheim, for instance, wonders why 'we are unaccountably transported by laughter' on seeing something foolish, 'and then, as unaccountably, we are thrown down'

(Wollheim 1968, p. 227). It seems to me very curious indeed that he should be so puzzled. Up to a point he has already accounted for the laughter and the let-down in the very way in which he presents it as a problem. On seeing something funny or foolish, people, at least those with a sense of humour, will laugh but then there comes a point where, as we often say, enough is enough. This is just something that people do, amongst things like speaking, sleeping, smiling at someone, and so on. It is as *a result* of our perceiving (understanding) something as funny that we laugh. We are not unaccountably transported by laughter for *no reason*. People who laugh for no reason (unaccountably) are people we begin to worry about. What we laugh at (or cry at) is in itself very revealing about ourselves. Wollheim's example is just one vivid consequence of building a theory of emotions on their 'essential' passivity. We are at the mercy of what is capricious and irrational. Given this view it is, perhaps, no wonder that the role emotions play in our understanding of others and of ourselves has largely, though not altogether, escaped philosophical scrutiny.

One reason for the neglect is a lack of awareness of the complexities involved in individual human emotions, a lack that is exhibited revealingly in the rather simplistic dichotomies thought to be appropriate in this context, dichotomies like active/passive and rational/irrational.

Thalberg (1978) in his article 'Mental Activity and Passivity', discusses several well-known philosophers who cling to this traditional imagery of the emotions. He asks whether emotions are passive and whether they indeed operate like surging floodwaters, ferocious winds, uncontrollable flames, unruly saddlehorses, or citizens rebelling against their government. He offers a strong argument against the very possibility of categorizing emotions as passive. He asks us to suppose that we are either victims or bystanders (the only two possible alternatives for a passive state) when emotions like shame, rage, lust or embarrassment invade our mind. He then poses the important question: 'What could it possibly mean to say that these happenings constitute *our* shame, *our* fury, *our* craving ... ?' He concludes that the bystander and victim models are useless for a very strong and clear reason. If someone is drenched by a cloudburst or kidnapped we would never say that it was the person's downpour or the person's kidnapping. These events have no owner since the individual's role in them is entirely passive. Thus, if I am a victim or a bystander when an emotion 'occurs' or comes over me, it could not make sense to call it mine, inasmuch as I just happen to be 'in the way' or 'in its vicinity'. It becomes clear that neither of the two models make sense of the passivity of the emotions let alone of the central role that emotions play in our lives. In his summary, Thalberg (1978, p. 395) writes:

> The 'passivity' thesis in question seemed empty, since we could suggest nothing in the mental arena which might act upon us, in the clear-cut way that kidnappers act upon their prey. ... Moreover, if we have a merely bystanding relationship to our emotions ... we

shall be at a loss to explain what makes them 'ours'. . . . Overall, we discovered no 'way . . . of determining the passivity or otherwise of our inner life'. . . . So until we encounter more compelling arguments for this distinction within the psychological realm, I think we would avoid gratuitous mysteries if we confine activity and passivity to the physical world.

Thalberg is very aware of the point that emotions never *just* happen to us. They are connected with how we see things, what we care about, what matters to us; in short, there is a strong and necessary relation between our emotions, *ours* in the strongest sense, and the kind of individual each of us is. It is for this vital reason that any attempt to give an account of persons and person understanding independently of the emotional dimension must result in a distorted picture of what human beings essentially are. Collingwood's (1960) chilling and frightening description of the state of affairs depicted in Eliot's *Wasteland* dramatically underlines the consequences on the lives of human beings who no longer feel emotions.

The picture of a human being that emerges from this long-established view of the emotions seems fraught with serious conceptual difficulties. On this view we are asked to regard emotions as something that happens to a creature who would be intelligible to us as a *human agent* quite independently of his or her emotions. This, however, is to presuppose that emotions are somehow not a part of what we take a person 'really' to be. I suggest, on the contrary, that such a view is based on a profound misunderstanding of the concept 'person'. Our reflections upon our past and present activities, involvements and reactive attitudes such as remorse, embarrassment, shame, regret, anger, love, satisfaction, joy and perhaps pride, are necessary for the conception of oneself as a person. Similarly, the understanding of other persons, without taking into account their historical background of this kind, would be extremely difficult.

Without the above considerations it would be well-nigh impossible to come to grips with what would amount to an understanding of a particular person as a person of a certain kind. The development of one's understanding is at the same time very much a development in oneself of the person one is, and this kind of understanding is not simply reducible to the perfection of a specialized skill. We have to look to the role of emotional reactions in the context of the whole network of human activities and reactions, and the role they play specifically in our understanding of others towards whom they are directed. It is on the strength of the above considerations that we can be in a position to decide and make judgements about the respect in which emotions belong to the subject's passivity and the respect in which they possess an active character. This way of going about deciding the issue highlights these notions as important aspects of our thoughts about persons and how we see persons in situations.

Shared practices and shared activities are basic and necessary to the development of human powers and to the development of rationality. We can only understand what it is to be involved in a given practice or activity via the conceptual network that has been developed within the framework of interpersonal influences (Berenson 1984). It is through such influences that we also come to care about certain activities more than others; they become more personally important. We develop loyalties, we feel contempt for others who only dabble in them and fail to realize their importance so that our whole understanding of what is going on is largely dependent on our feelings, our degree of caring about a given activity. Our understanding here cannot be separated from emotional factors.

A strict dichotomy between our concepts and beliefs about the world and our interests and ways of living in it is mistaken because the two are generally inseparable where our understanding is concerned. There is an all-important connection between a person's passivity and their activity. This can be characterized in terms of the way in which a person's feelings and emotions are interconnected with the *kinds* of activities and relationships he or she engages in and that provoke his/her growth of understanding of these. To what extent a person becomes involved in his/her activities and relationships depends, in large part, on the kind of emotional responses s/he will have to them. This is important both for other and for self-understanding.

What I am suggesting here is that a person's understanding of his/her activities and of others is largely dependent on the kind of emotional responses s/he has to them and that these points are equally important to the understanding of the self. This implies that there is no significant dichotomy between the understanding of the self and the understanding of others; it seems to me that this implication is correct. In both self and other understanding the power to provoke understanding is an emotional power that provokes questions leading to a deeper understanding in the same way that one of the powers of art is to reveal to us what lies hidden in our emotional life. Here again art and music provoke questions about the emotional content of one's aesthetic experience – questions about why one is moved by a particular passage in a way that may lead to a deeper understanding of aspects of the work of art. The same applies to situations in which one finds oneself with others.

One may try to understand one's attitudes in terms of what it is about the person towards whom one feels drawn, or in whom one becomes interested and so on, and, further, why one finds certain features of a person's way of living attractive or repulsive, which may in turn reveal to our understanding something of our own dispositions. There is much that manifests itself about a person and s/he can reveal it to him/herself by such questioning. In becoming aware of the need for questioning of his/her responses, s/he begins to learn to understand important things about him/herself.

Hegel (1971) draws our attention to the relation between self and other understanding in a most interesting way. He opens the Introduction to the *Philosophy of Mind* with the following paragraph:

The knowledge of Mind is the highest and hardest, just because it is the most 'concrete' of sciences. The significance of that 'absolute' commandment, *know thyself* – whether we look at it in itself or under the historical circumstances of its first utterance – is not to promote mere self-knowledge in respect of the *particular* capacities, character, propensities, and foibles of the single self.

In his *Phenomenology of Mind* (1949) he says that the other self is the only adequate mirror of my own self-conscious self; the subject can only see itself when what it sees is another self-consciousness. This is the point of his famous 'Master/Slave' example. What we have here is a profound insight in that Hegel recognizes a very significant point about self-knowledge – namely that self-knowledge cannot be achieved through mere introspection into my own (I take this to be the significance of the 'single self') feelings, foibles, habits, likes and dislikes, etc. I cannot examine the single self and reach any *important* conclusions because I do not exist in isolation from other selves and my introspection must of necessity be based on an examination of my relationships with others.

Hegel can be taken, at this point, to be drawing attention to the importance of others in any serious understanding and knowledge of the self. I am here ignoring difficulties that subsequently arise from Hegel's account of the self and the other. His account is primarily metaphysical and emotions play no part in it. Nevertheless his insistence that knowledge of the self is necessarily dependent on knowledge of the other is of the greatest importance. For a detailed discussion see my paper 'Hegel on Others and the Self' (Berenson 1982).

In both self and other understanding emotions are inseparable from the growth of such understanding in that emotional attitudes, attachments and involvements are among the circumstances that enable situations to occur and to aid such growth or development of understanding and, further, that those situations and the way a person deals with them must themselves be characterized in terms of some relevant emotion concepts; such concepts, in turn, have to be understood in terms of what their role is in the life of a human being who is both rational and capable of feeling emotions.

We are often afraid of showing our emotions precisely because we do not want to give ourselves away, to expose to others our subjective aspects of whom or what it is that we really care about. This is very revealing in that such cases underline the importance of emotions in our understanding of others in terms of their attitudes, of what is important to them, why they react in the way they do and what makes them vulnerable. Personal relationships of certain kinds that encourage the growth of understanding, often encourage it by making the persons concerned less inhibited, less afraid or hesitant about revealing their feelings, all of which really amounts to a preparedness to give oneself away, to allow oneself to be oneself by getting involved in personal relationships. Merleau-Ponty's (1962, pp. 156ff.) discussion of the well-known Schneider brain-damage case is very relevant:

Schneider, and the majority of impotent subjects, 'do not throw themselves into what they are doing' ... and in so far as the subject coolly perceives the situation, it is in the first place because he does not live it and is not caught up in it. ... Faces are for him neither attractive nor repulsive ... sun and rain are neither merry nor sad; his humour is determined by elementary organic functions only, and the world is emotionally neutral. Schneider hardly extends his sphere of human relationships at all, and when he makes new friendships they sometimes come to an unfortunate end: this is because they never result, as can be seen on analysis, from a spontaneous impulse, but from a decision made in the abstract.

It might be objected that my use of this example is not very illuminating because Schneider, by virtue of his brain damage, may also have been inhibited in his powers of reasoning and this was the reason for his inability to form any relationships; that is why, in an important sense, he could not be reached. But this objection, as it stands, misses the point of the example, namely that people's powers of reasoning generally involve some connection with spontaneous impulses tinged with emotional tones of interest, enthusiasm, warmth, responsiveness and the like; considerations that in Schneider's case were not simply inhibited but absent altogether. It is because of such considerations that our conception of a person *as agent* with intentions, motives and desires becomes blurred unless we admit that allowance should be made for emotional factors. If we take as an example the detached man or woman who *never* loses his/her calm, in certain circumstances we would have grave doubts as to whether s/he really understood what was going on around him/her or happening to him/her; his/her calm might be grossly inappropriate to the situation. Such iron control, if it is control, on every occasion, is difficult to conceive in *human* terms.

It is also important to note that we can and do make judgements about the rationality or irrationality of emotions. We do have standards of appropriateness in this context and we know what would count as a departure from such standards. An irrational emotional response is judged as such in terms of its being an inappropriate reaction to an emotional situation that reveals an inability to cope with the situation. The response becomes *over-emotional* to an extent where a breakdown of rational thinking is clearly detectable. On the other hand, the man or woman who *never* responds in any emotional way, or spontaneously, to any situation confronting him/her can also be seen as lacking something in an important sense, such that the lack raises serious doubts about whether s/he really understood the circumstances in which s/he finds him/herself. Thus it would follow that we have to allow both for the rationality and irrationality of emotions because we do have standards of appropriateness arising from the former, standards that enable us to make judgements about mistaken or inappropriate emotional responses that may, and often do, cloud our understanding. Where our understanding is so clouded we need to take a more detached view but this does not, or need not, imply a completely unemotional view.

In addition, to really understand a given person's response that seems at first glance out of proportion in some way, one has to understand the person him/herself before one can make any judgements. When I speak of standards of appropriateness, I do not wish to imply that we have generally agreed criteria for *the* appropriate emotion and, as important, *the* appropriate intensity of the emotion, in general. What a person is capable of seeing in a situation and how s/he sees it is informed by his/her past history and thus the kind of understanding s/he brings to it; what s/he will consider relevant will stem from the understanding s/he has developed, from his/her past experiences, from the ways s/he has of thinking about the world and his/her particular human relationships. It follows that notions of appropriateness/inappropriateness in this sense involve more than judgements based on applying general principles. Legitimate individual variations have to be allowed for based on one's knowledge of the particular individual in question (Berenson 1981).

That we need some degree of involvement, interest in, enthusiasm for or caring about our activities is directly related to the meaningfulness human activities have; our interests, enthusiasms, etc. act as a spur or motive for actions, but what endows actions with meaningfulness, in this sense, is the recognition of the fact that all these spurs or motives are to varying degrees emotion impregnated and not at all just exclusively rationally decided upon. This kind of engagement stands in sharp contrast to activities stemming from indifference or prudence. Activities stemming from the latter are most often described as 'mechanical', implying mere automatic movement, almost like physical occurrences that are in an important way external to the agent.

Our emotions often arise from the way in which we see a given person in a situation, how we understand the situation in terms of what confronts us. All these factors are to a large extent based on rational considerations but the degree of caring or involvement will influence our judgements about the person's response to the situation and our feelings about his/her response may produce valuable insights. This is important both for other and for self-understanding. It is a fact that very often persons will not allow themselves to act on immediate generous impulses, following instead what might be termed a policy of non-involvement, through a cool calculation of advantages and disadvantages, of what can reasonably be expected of them, of the outcome of their actions or the possible degree of success.

I do not wish to deny that such considerations are extremely important. What I have been disputing is the view that such actions are necessarily *always* more appropriate. Cases where such actions are, on the contrary, inappropriate cover a wide range of human situations. To what extent is it appropriate, for instance, to stop or control an inclination to help or relieve someone's suffering by allowing the intervention of deliberations based on considerations that one does not want to get involved, etc.? One cannot always follow the inclination, however strong, to act spontaneously because this would demand a degree of involvement that would seriously interfere with the viability of one's own life; but at the same time too much deliberation accompanying every wish to act would result in an inability to take any decision in extreme cases. People often use this kind of prevarication as a substitute for action, quite deliberately, hoping that if they do it long enough, the time for acting will pass; they opt out.

Those kinds of cases are also extremely important within personal relationships, where, say, as a result of the way one sees a given relationship, one approaches one's best friend for advice or help and is met with a reaction that involves a hesitation instead of an immediate response. The failure to respond provokes questioning and reflection. There may, of course, be many various reasons for this failure but such emotion-provoked reflections may revise one's conception of the relationship, the need for the revision being prompted by one's emotional reactions, which, if ignored, may lead one to self-deception or complete misunderstanding. One comes to understand that the hesitation was a response that is not appropriate to a close friendship or that one's understanding of it was mistaken. The fact that the response was not what was expected may result, in certain cases, in a breakdown of the conception of that relationship. Typically, people who are unable to respond spontaneously in certain situations are people whom we see as incapacitated in an important way, in a way that prevents them from forming personal relationships.

The important aspect of understanding here is one's realization that it is not simply one's intentions and conscious decisions that reveal the sort of person one is but those involvements that go contrary to or are independent of one's conscious decisions and intentions, those not necessarily under one's control.

Similarly, the way one feels in the presence of another may be an important factor in understanding that person and oneself better. Such feelings again raise questions about what it is that makes one react in such a way thus enabling one to understand something about the other, some aspect which causes this reaction; one tries to arrive at a more detailed and precise description of what is going on. A blush often causes amusement and leg-pulling but on a different level I actually know of a man who fell in love with a woman when he saw her blush at a specific remark because it revealed to him much about her character and personality. The point I am making here is that our reactions and attitudes towards others, although emotional, are in an important way thought-provoking and thus belong centrally to the understanding persons have of each other and of the self. Far from being seen as disruptions, a person's emotions should rather be seen as revealing in all kinds of ways; emotions often provoke deeper understanding.

I have discussed the role emotions play in our understanding in terms of trying to answer the question whether a person *qua decider* can be separated from and be independent of his/her attachments, attitudes, relationships and the emotions that enter into these. Emotions, although not themselves something that are decided upon, do illuminate, in the sorts of ways discussed, our decisions on how we are to act and when the need to act arises. They influence our decisions about how we are to understand or see the world and the persons we come into contact with. The power that provokes real understanding is the emotional power, which illuminates and reveals to our understanding what may otherwise remain hidden. In effect, I have argued that the growth of understanding within personal relationships is not and cannot be solely intellectual growth; it is also strongly related to emotional growth. Much of the understanding we have of ourselves and of others is an understanding of the emotions and their role as springs of our actions. Understanding another's emotions and feelings is a part of understanding him/her. Emotions of all kinds act as an essential spur to our understanding of others. One's concern for understanding is intimately related to the concern for the person one is attempting to understand. These sorts of considerations are inextricably bound up with human relationships in general.

This brings me to the vital notion of context. Personal relationships provide the context within which one is enabled to understand a person's intimate springs of action in their widest sense. The notion of context is crucial and cannot be separated from understanding. This point can be made clearer by an example. Let us consider the example of a man in love – such a man has to be understood in the context of this love. His love is bound to influence his other activities and relationships. It may be decisive for what sort of other attachments he is prepared to form, the way he acts towards others, what other things he gets involved in and, perhaps, most importantly, it may greatly influence how he views the world; a view that may have altered radically in respect of the sort of attitudes he held previously. His relationship is now a vital part of his situation, the context within which he is to be understood.

One's emotions, whatever they are, carry with them most important ramifications for other aspects of one's life. Our understanding of others and of ourselves depends on our understanding of this crucial connection. Real understanding involves understanding of the person's emotional life, how this affects him/her as a subject, his/her wants, desires, what really matters to him/her and why. These aspects manifest themselves within a relationship.

In order to show what this kind of understanding amounts to, what it 'concretely' consists in, examples from literature are rather helpful in serving as illustrations. Examples from such works can be used to convey what is involved in the deep understanding two people have of each other within a personal relationship, as the crucial context within which such understanding develops and manifests itself is to a large extent supplied for us. What one is trying to understand here is the expressiveness people have for each other that literature also can manifest. By using examples from literature I hope to show, in detail, both what personal understanding consists of and how it is that emotions supply the all-important context in which one's understanding develops.

To begin with, let us take as our example George Eliot's *Middlemarch* (1959). Dorothea is a character who wants to do great things in the world and in an important way is most emphatically not a feminist. She has a set of principles she tries to live up to – to develop to the full her natural feminine capacity for devotion and submissiveness. In the first chapter she thinks: 'The really delightful marriage must be that where your husband was a sort of father, and could teach you even Hebrew, if you wished it' (p. 5). Her complete lack of feminine frivolity, her need for spiritual sacrifice, are facts of her character that prepare us admirably for what is to come. On meeting Casaubon, Dorothea decides that she has met the right man for her. She does not see him so much as a husband but as the ideal man, and as a result her feelings for him are predominantly those of daughter to father.

Casaubon finds that he is incapable of real love for anyone. Dorothea is completely self-deceived about the importance of her personal desires *vis-à-vis* her principles, which she has decided upon as most suitable for a worthwhile life. An example of this is her trying to explain to herself that she is not really bitterly disappointed at Casaubon's insistence that she take a companion on their honeymoon so that he can 'feel more at liberty' to pursue his research. She tries to subdue her annoyance: 'Surely I am in a strangely selfish weak state of mind', she said to herself. 'How can I have a husband who is so much above me without knowing that he needs me less than I need him?' (p. 89).

This passage shows her determination to remain convinced that she has done the right and noble thing in marrying Casaubon. Casaubon is re-vealed to the reader as one of Eliot's most interesting characters. He behaves and sees the world as solely scholarly. He is incapable of imagina-tion and feeling, the kind of feeling essential to understanding something of people different from himself. Thus his courtship of Dorothea is not one that arises from his feelings for her but one he constructs out of his literary memory of what courtship ought to be. This is not deliberate on his part, he just cannot do otherwise. Eliot writes: 'He determined to abandon himself to the stream of feeling, and perhaps was surprised to find what an exceedingly shallow rill it was . . . he concluded that the poets have much exaggerated the force of masculine passion' (p. 62). Casaubon wants very much to do the right thing but he just does not know how. He also begins to realize his failure as a scholar. A passage which follows here is most revealing: 'She was as blind to his inward troubles as he to hers' (p. 62).

We have here a relationship that is in a significant way impersonal; it lacks any real feeling. Both see each other as objects but not as objects of real emotions in that we come to understand that they are impersonal objects to each other. When Casaubon questions his lack of feeling, his answer takes the form of an assurance that it is not Dorothea's fault as he cannot think of any other woman who would please him better. Dorothea, we feel, would also be just as happy with any other scholarly person, perhaps happier. Dorothea's chief attraction to Casaubon amounts to her capacity to believe in him and worship him, or rather his intellect. When Ladislaw enters into the situation Casaubon feels threatened in this respect; he fears that Ladislaw may get Dorothea to see him as he really is. Eliot describes this as a strange kind of jealousy: 'There is a sort of jealousy which needs very little fire: it is hardly a passion, but a blight bred in the cloudy, damp despondency of uneasy egoism' (p. 225). But, however egoistic the jealousy, he really *feels* for the first time and this enables him to sharpen his awareness. His feeling himself threatened forces an insight into Dorothea's thoughts he was previously incapable of: 'there had entered into the husband's mind a certainty that she judged him, and that her wifely devotedness was like a penitential expiation of unbelieving thoughts' (p. 448).

It is important to see here that his understanding of Dorothea is limited to his understanding of her thoughts; he is still incapable of understanding her feelings. His jealousy has nothing to do with the possibility of a relationship developing between Dorothea and Ladislaw; on the contrary, the possibility that they are or will become lovers does not even occur to him.

Dorothea finally comes to understand Casaubon as a person when she is moved by pity towards him during his illness. She very gradually begins to see him as he really is and her pity grows to profound compassion for him which makes her realize that she has to give the promise he demands of her (to complete his work after his death). She expresses it thus:

> Neither law nor the world's opinion compelled her to this – only her husband's nature and her own compassion, only the ideal, and not the real yoke of marriage. She saw clearly enough the whole situation, yet she was fettered and she could not smite the stricken soul that entreated hers. (p. 515)

It is not until Dorothea is able to feel a personal emotion towards Casaubon that she begins to achieve an understanding that is personal, in complete contrast to the impersonal understanding of him as an object – as a suitable object for a husband. It is not until disillusion with her ideas and principles sets in, not until she gives up her fight to sustain her self-deception that she becomes aware of Casaubon as a person in his own right – a real person not an imaginary object of intellect worthy of her devotion. It is not until she feels deep pity for him that she is finally capable of a genuine act of devotion, involving genuine sacrifice, when she is ready to give her promise entirely for his sake. The contrast in, or change in her understanding can best be illustrated by the relevant quotations:

> We are all of us born in moral stupidity, taking the world as an udder to feed our supreme selves: Dorothea had clearly begun to emerge from that stupidity, but yet it had been easier to her to

> imagine how she would devote herself to Mr Casaubon, and become
> wise and strong in his strength and wisdom, than to conceive with
> that distinctness which is no longer reflection but feeling – an idea
> wrought back to the directness of sense, like the solidity of objects –
> that he had an equivalent centre of self, whence the light and the
> shadows must always fall with a certain difference.   (p. 225)

When the change comes it results in a qualitative change of her understanding:

> She was no longer struggling against the perception of facts, but
> adjusting herself to their clearest perception; and now when she
> looked steadily at her husband's failure, still more at his possible
> consciousness of failure, she seemed to be looking along the one
> track where duty became tenderness.   (p. 390)

Now Dorothea is able to realize that her understanding of Casaubon must
not be merely intellectual but must go through a crucible of feeling before
she can form a proper relationship with him, not as a strong man and a
scholar, but as a *person*, weaker than herself. She is now able to see their
life together with a new insight, from a different point of view and the
situations of life take on a new meaning.

Middlemarch is rich in subtleties of descriptions of personal relationships in which the understanding manifests itself. To see fully how the
understanding develops and what it amounts to, it is necessary to take into
account the accumulative perceptions of all the subtle issues, which is
impossible for me to do here. My aim was to convey the necessity of real
personal relationships within which this kind of personal understanding
and the understanding of self develops; to stress what is involved in the
transition from an impersonal to a personal understanding, which requires
a complex context and is inspired by emotions.

My choice of example involved relationships built on compassion, affection and love. I do not wish to imply that it is only emotions of this kind
that enable one's understanding to develop. The emotions of fear, hate or
envy may have the same sort of effect on our understanding. So, finally, I
want to turn to Shakespeare's *Othello*, where we are given a masterly
example of understanding based on hatred. Iago states his hatred and the
reasons that inspired it at the beginning of the play, in his first speech. He
also makes quite clear his overwhelming wish for revenge:

> In following him, I follow but myself.
> Heaven is my judge, not I for love and duty,
> But seeming so, for my peculiar end;
> For when my outward action does demonstrate
> The native act, and figure of my heart,
> In complement extern, 'tis not long after,
> but I will wear my heart upon my sleeve,
> For doves to peck at: I am not what I am!   (1.1. 58–65)

Shakespeare builds up a vivid picture of Iago, such that his actions are a progression of steps in the development of his thinking, most revealing of the man himself. At first Iago is bent merely on making mischief but soon finds that Othello's prestige and qualities of character can overcome slanders which Iago tries to perpetrate. He now realizes that the attack must be more direct, he must work on Othello himself; Iago's understanding becomes, accordingly, more acute. Thus, when Othello is confronted by Desdemona's irate father, Iago is there to learn what he can from the situation. After Othello's passionate declaration of love for Desdemona, when Brabantio says

> Look to her, Moor, have a quick eye to see:
> She has deceiv'd her father, and may do thee   (1.3. 292–3)

Iago remembers the words and although at the moment he does not realize their full significance and power, the time comes when he sees them as the potentially deadly weapon against Othello's weakest spot.

Iago now makes a conscious effort at understanding Othello. He knows that this is the only way in which he can be effective in devising means to his destruction. He is constantly inspired by his hatred and driven by it. Thus:

> The Moor is of a free and open nature too,
> that thinks men honest that but seem to be so:
> And will as tenderly be led by the nose...
> as asses are,
> I ha't, it is engender'd; Hell and night
> must bring this monstrous birth to the world's light.
>   (1.3. 397–402)

He spends his time listening, observing, feeling his way in almost constant proximity to Othello until his plans materialize. In act 3, he finally judges the scene set to bring out his strongest weapon:

> *Iago:*   She did deceive her father, marrying you; ·
>   And when she seem'd to shake and fear your looks,
>   she loved them most.
> *Othello:*   And so she did.
> *Iago:*   Why, go to then,
>   She that so young could give out such a seeming,
>   to seal her father's eyes up, close as oak,
>   He thought 'twas witchcraft   (3.3. 210–14)

We see here a significant change in Iago's understanding of Othello. At the beginning of the play he offers us a description of Othello that is little more than a caricature and Iago's attempts against him are at this stage on par with this shallow understanding. Gradually, as his hatred grows stronger so his understanding develops and with it his imaginative approach to ways of achieving his purpose. His hatred, far from preventing him seeing Othello as he really is, on the contrary sharpens his awareness to the extent where he is able to realize that Othello is of a constant, noble, loving nature and that his marriage is of the happiest: 'I dare think he'll prove to Desdemona a most dear husband' (2.1. 285–6).

The tragedy is that Othello does not really understand Iago; he knows and understands him only in his role of an honest, courageous soldier, not as a person. He has no feelings towards Iago. He does, however, apply this understanding to Iago's every action. Iago, by now, realizes all too well this gullibility on Othello's part, his 'free and open nature', and makes full use of it. The important point to note here is that Iago's hatred makes his understanding as acute as it is possible to a man of his natural limitations; his hatred enables him to realize to the full his potential for understanding. What is, perhaps, interesting is that Iago's limitations are due, in large measure, to his inability to comprehend love. For him love is 'a mere lust of the blood and permission of the will'. Thus he perceives jealousy in relation to his definition and is, therefore, genuinely frightened at Othello's display of passion, his depth of feeling, his uncontrollable fury. But yet, when Othello says 'Yet she must die, else she'll betray more men' (5.2. 6) he shows us that Iago has succeeded, he has compelled Othello to rationalize in the same way that he does. Iago's success reveals to us how wholly he has 'placed' Othello. What better proof of this than the fact that he succeeded in compelling Othello to act strictly within Iago's own field of understanding – suddenly Othello is behaving exactly as Iago thinks men should behave.

I have argued that the kind of understanding persons can achieve within personal relationships is made possible by what can be summed up as the expressiveness or significance persons possess for each other. This includes the variety of emotions, attitudes, feelings and interactions that take place within personal relationships. Much of the interaction and responses are spontaneous and this feature of spontaneity, with its quality that is akin to impact, is essential, as I have tried to show.

By contrast, lack of spontaneity, of impact and, often, lack of any feeling or emotion elicits lack of response and thus the power which provokes understanding is lacking. An excellent example of how such a lack completely inhibits any possibility of understanding is given by Virginia Woolf in *Mrs. Dalloway's Party* (1973). She describes two people at a party who have reached the stage of running out of small talk:

> So things came to an end. And over them both came instantly that paralysing blankness of feeling, when nothing bursts from the mind, when its walls appear like slate; when vacancy almost hurts, and the eyes petrified and fixed see the same spot – a pattern, a coal scuttle – with an exactness which is terrifying, since no emotion, no idea, no impression of any kind comes to change it, to modify it, to embellish it, since the fountains of feeling seem sealed and as the mind turns rigid, so does the body; stark, statuesque, so that neither Mr. Serle

nor Miss Anning could move or speak, and they felt as if an enchanter had freed them, and spring flushed every vein with streams of life, when Myra Cartwright, tapping Mr Serle archly on the shoulder, said: 'I saw you at the *Meistersinger*....' And they could separate.

(pp. 54–5)

This is a most striking example of what can happen when one is required to be on certain terms with another person and finds it is impossible. Lack of response and feeling can result in a paralysing blankness and thus blankness where understanding is concerned. Most of us have experienced the sheer agony of such a paralysis.

I have been particularly concerned in this chapter to show that emotions, far from being unwelcome disruptions to objective thinking, play a central and active part both where our actions are concerned and, as important, they are the revealing power that provokes real understanding of others and of oneself. Emotions cannot therefore be treated as purely or necessarily passive phenomena that are also irrational. A human being could not be intelligible to us *as an agent* independently of his/her emotional life; it is the emotional component behind our motives that endows human activities with meaningfulness. The very intelligibility of persons as agents is dependent on our recognizing the fact that without some emotional involvement of caring, interest in, and so on, there would be no strong motive to act. The decision to act is not simply based on finding rationally acceptable and appropriate objects of activity, concern, interest or involvement; this amounts to finding good reasons for one's actions but, as it stands, it is not enough without the spur to such well-considered actions that emotional involvement provides. The emotional dimension enables us to come to see activities in a different light, to care enough *to want* to do them in addition to having good reasons for doing them, although I strongly suspect the 'good' here may already be loaded with all sorts of emotional considerations.

To what extent a person becomes involved in his/her activities and his/her relationships depends in large part on the kind of emotional responses s/he will have to them. I spoke earlier of the man or woman who never loses his/her calm in various situations as someone who gives rise to grave doubts as to whether s/he really understands what is going on and that such iron self-control, if it is control, *on every occasion*, is difficult to conceive in human terms. A much more likely explanation is that s/he is unable to respond in any emotional way. It is very important not to confuse a lack of emotions with attempts to control emotions. The failure to feel an emotion in certain circumstances may reveal an absence of interest, insensitivity or callousness. All these considerations stress the given person's passivity. S/he is a passive bystander as a *direct result of the lack* of any emotion; she doesn't care to act.

If we accept the importance of these considerations then emotions cannot be seen simply as exclusively and essentially passive phenomena. At best, it could be maintained that they possess a passive aspect in that we cannot command ourselves to feel or cease to feel an emotion. The same applies to the view that emotions are essentially irrational. It has, I hope, been shown that they are irrational only in so far as they are tied to the uncontrollable aspect of passivity just mentioned; they may, therefore, be irrational in some cases but not in those I have discussed, where they lead to deeper understanding. The view that ties certain or all emotions to some necessary interference with reason stems from a decision to give an account of emotions in terms of their necessary characteristics. But emotions include such a varied assortment of feelings that to speak in terms of some essential characteristic is quite misguided. We get a mistaken view of their essential characteristics by selecting homogeneous examples of emotions and this practice is, to say the least, grossly misleading.

The understanding achieved within personal relationships is intimately related to and dependent on the interactions taking place. The persons concerned are participants in personal relationships which to a lesser or greater extent are unavoidably emotionally tinged in all sorts of ways. For this reason our theoretical reflections separated from feelings arising from these interactions are not, by themselves, adequate for either self or other understanding. There is a significant difference between understanding *that* another feels a certain emotion and understanding *how* s/he feels and why s/he feels that way. How persons react to the hopes, feelings, successes and failures of others forms a crucial part of understanding them. Without these emotional factors there would be nothing of importance or interest left to understand. Introspection or reflection that relies on taking a detached view, in the sense that involves stepping back from the relationship, as opposed to thinking about reactions that arise within it during a lived and felt experience, cannot yield real understanding. Detached thinking implies seeing the self and others as objects of contemplation and this leaves out of consideration vital emotional responses arising from live activities and reactions.

Personal relationships, which provide the vital context in which deep understanding can take place, also serve to underline the main difference between what is involved in our understanding of objects as opposed to our understanding of persons – persons are unique in having emotions and in forming personal relationships; and any understanding of persons is dependent on our understanding of what this crucial fact involves. Without the emotional dimension none of us would be persons.

REFERENCES

Berenson, F.M. (1981) *Understanding Persons: Personal and Impersonal Relationships*. Brighton: Harvester Press and New York: St Martin's Press.
—— (1982) 'Hegel on others and the self'. *Philosophy*, 57 (219), 77–90.
—— (1984) 'Understanding art and understanding persons'. In *Objectivity and Cultural Divergence: Royal Institute of Philosophy Lectures*. Cambridge: Cambridge University Press.

Collingwood, R.G. (1960) *The Principles of Art*. Oxford: Oxford University Press.

Eliot, G. (1959) *Middlemarch*. Oxford: Oxford University Press.

Hampshire, S. (1965a) *Freedom of the Individual*. London: Chatto & Windus.

—— (1965b) *Thought and Action*. London: Chatto & Windus.

Hegel, G.W.F. (1949) *Phenomenology of Mind*. London: Allen & Unwin.

—— (1971) *Philosophy of Mind*. Oxford: Clarendon Press.

Merleau-Ponty, M. (1962) *Phenomenology of Perception*, trans. C. Smith. London: Routledge & Kegan Paul.

Peters, R.S. (1961/62) 'Emotions and the category of passivity'. *Proceedings of the Aristotelian Society*, 62, 117–34.

—— (1971) 'Reason and passion'. In *The Proper Study: Royal Institute of Philosophy Lectures*, 4, 1969/70. London: Macmillan.

Taylor, R. (1966) *Action and Purpose*. New Jersey: Prentice Hall.

Thalberg, I. (1978) 'Mental activity and passivity'. *Mind*, 87 (347), 376–95.

Wollheim, R. (1968) 'Expression'. *Royal Institute of Philosophy Lectures*, 1, 227–44. London: Macmillan.

Woolf, V. (1973) *Mrs Dalloway's Party*, ed. by S. McNichol. London: Hogarth Press.

3 Explorations of self and other in a developing relationship

Sue Wilkinson

The focus of this chapter is the role of impression formation in its usual social context: the early stages of a developing relationship. It considers how, in the context of such a relationship, impressions of self and other both continuously evolve and are inextricably interlinked. Furthermore, the central thesis of the chapter is that impressions and relationship are reciprocally interdependent: the changing impressions affect the nature and course of the developing relationship; and the characteristics of the relationship, in turn, affect the content and evolution of the impressions. Such a view suggests (at least) two major corollaries: the necessity of studying impression formation in a radically different way from traditional studies; and the necessity of working towards a reconceptualization of the process, i.e. one that adequately represents its role and function within social relationships.

Using the distinction favoured by Antaki and Fielding (1981), current research in 'cognitive' social psychology (cf. Eiser 1980) seems to be balanced between work conducted within an 'information-processing' mode (exemplified by recent, extensive research in the area of attribution theory, e.g. Hewstone [1984]) and work conducted within a 'representa-tional' mode (exemplified by work on social representations, e.g. Farr and Moscovici [1984], and the present volume). However, within the area of impression formation the dominant research paradigms are determinedly within the information-processing mode, and many of these are not sub-stantially different from those used, for example, in Asch's (1946) studies of trait centrality. Then, laboratory 'subjects' were required to make judgements (within a specified format) about hypothetical people on the basis of a limited amount of highly controlled stimulus material; now social psychologists have moved out of the laboratory and ask for free descriptions of real people (e.g. Bromley 1977, 1986; Butterworth 1985), but they still elicit descriptions from single individuals at one point in time, and employ reductionistic forms of data analysis. This generally entails first content analysing the descriptions into units, which can then be classified and used as the basis for nomothetic statements (e.g. Bromley 1977); or cast into a matrix of people × descriptive units, which is completed by applying each descriptor to each person, in the manner of a repertory grid (e.g. Rosenberg 1977). All sense is lost of impression formation as a dynamic, social process, which normally takes place within the context of a developing relationship.

Of course, simply to acknowledge the social nature and context of impression formation is to increase dramatically the complexity of what needs to be studied. Even the simplest consideration of its implications must accept impression formation as a two-way process: as A forms impressions of B, so B forms impressions of A; both sets of impressions being in a continual state of flux. A more sophisticated analysis will need to take metaperspectives into account (following Laing, Phillipson and Lee 1966): i.e. that A's impression of B will be influenced by A's view of B's view of A; meta-metaperspectives may even be a possibility! In addition, the study of impression formation in its social context must recognize that both content and dynamics of the impression formation process will also influence, and be influenced by, the relationship between the two individuals: whether it appears to be deepening, deteriorating or relatively stable, for instance. A and B may have differing perceptions (and differing perceptions of each other's perceptions) of the relationship, of course, and these may feed back differentially into their changing impressions. Heyman and Shaw (1978) suggest a limited typology of 'constructs of relationship'.

Apart from a possible unwillingness to take all this on board, a further explanation for the manifest limitations of most research on impression formation to date may be the traditional subdivision of social psychological research into conceptually (and often methodologically) distinct areas. In this case, research on 'impression formation' or 'person perception' has remained almost entirely separate from research on 'social relationships' or 'friendship formation'. One exception is the work of Steve Duck, some of whose early studies – e.g. 1977 – attempted both to span these two fields and to look at change in impressions over time. However, impression formation was subsumed within friendship as merely an early stage of the acquaintance process: there was no consideration of the interplay between impressions and relationships, nor of the reciprocal perspectives and metaperspectives of the individuals involved.

INTO THE BREACH

My own work in this area began from the theoretical standpoint of Personal Construct Theory (Kelly 1955; Maher 1969), which provides both a strong rationale for idiographic investigation (Individuality Corollary [Kelly 1955, pp. 55–6]) and a theoretical basis for the way impression formation operates, emphasizing its necessarily social and, particularly, reciprocal nature (Sociality Corollary [Kelly 1955, pp. 95–7]). As an explicitly reflexive theory (see e.g. Bannister and Fransella 1980, pp. 179–81), Personal Construct Theory also has implications for the role of the researcher. In its emphasis on the essential similarity of layperson and scientist, it suggests a dissolution of traditional 'subject' and 'experimenter' roles (see Wilkinson 1978), and, following the Sociality Corollary, the necessity for the psychologist to enter into 'role relationships' with those s/he studies (see Stringer 1979). Some theoretical input was also derived from Ethogenic Theory (Harré 1979, 1983; Harré and Secord, 1972), which also shaped the methodology: i.e. the collection of accounts from research participants. For further details of the theoretical background, see Wilkinson (1981).

The methodology was developed and refined over four sets of studies (the data presented here will be drawn largely from the final set). It entails, essentially, case studies of pairs of individuals (of the same sex), conducted during the early stages of their developing relationship. The pairs are asked to monitor both their impression formation and the relationship. Initially, participants were university students who responded to an advertisement offering 'an opportunity to study in some depth how you see others and form relationships', but through their friends and acquaintances, a fairly broad pool of people was eventually tapped. I included myself in the pool, as having the same status as any other participant. Participants in the later stages were strategically selected (see Glaser and Strauss 1967) from those who had been involved earlier; the criteria for selection being introspective awareness and, to a lesser degree, ability to articulate such insights. The early sets of studies thus provided experience and training in the monitoring procedure and also provided the opportunity to study a number of the participants (including myself) in more than one relationship. The ratio of male to female pairs (representing willing volunteers) in the first stage was 2:3, but this decreased in later stages, with final stage participants being exclusively female. In common with Burnett (this volume), I found that male participants appeared less prepared to accept the time commitment, were less willing (or able) to be introspective about their relationships, and (not unexpectedly) there was also evidence from their accounts that they found the research experience less rewarding than did female participants.

Participants were first given an extensive briefing on the rationale behind and objectives of the research, which included an invitation to comment on it at any stage. They were then assigned (simply on the basis of a mutually convenient first meeting time) and introduced to a 'partner'. Pairs were requested to monitor their impression formation whilst getting to know each other over a period of (at least) 4–6 weeks. They were free both to determine the parameters of their meetings: time, place, activity, length, etc., and to decide if and when to terminate meetings (or monitoring of meetings) – although it was requested that this should be, as far as possible, at what seemed a 'natural' point in the relationship to do so. A reasonably 'homely' (but private) room with coffee-making facilities was made available, and most participants made use of this. They were asked to provide, as soon as possible after the first meeting, a minimally structured account of what had taken place. It was suggested that the account might include the following information: description/evaluation of meeting; initial impression of partner, including the basis for it if possible; partner's likely initial impression of oneself, including the probable basis for it; any sense of a relationship being formed; how partner might view this. Following subsequent meetings, participants were asked to record changes in both sets of impressions and in the relationship, and to note whether these seemed to be linked in any way. They were also asked to keep a note of any 'processing' of information (e.g. 'replaying' of or reflection on meetings) that appeared to take place between meetings. Such a procedure was not intended in any sense to be a real-life analogue: rather, a particular research context designed to facilitate individuals in the exploration of their own impression formation; a context of unusual safety, permission and encouragement to do so.

On terminating their sequence of meetings, participants were asked to summarize and reflect on the proceedings, in terms of what they felt they had learned about their own impression formation in the context of this particular relationship. They were also asked for an evaluation of the research and its methodology and extensively debriefed regarding my assessment of it. In addition, an extensive range of 'contextual' data was collected – again via minimally structured accounts – to supplement the data from the actual meetings, which were regarded only as the 'core' of each case study. This 'contextual' data consisted of biographical information, a self-characterization, an outline life history, and details of past and present social networks, with particular emphasis on key relationships.

My analysis is conducted on three levels. First, each individual within the pair is considered as a 'sub-case', relating her/his meeting data to contextual data. Then each pair is considered as a separate single case, which entails analysis of the perspectives and metaperspectives of both participants, including how these interact, primarily within the context of their particular relationship, but also in relation to the sub-case analysis for each participant. An important feature of the research is that my analyses of case and sub-case data are taken back to the participants themselves for comment and critique. It seems particularly important to negotiate my 'outsider's' perspective with the 'insiders'' views in the pairs where I am not a participant member. This level of communication maximizes the feedback available to participants, consistent with a view of the research as a learning process for everyone involved in it. At the third level of analysis, abstractions are made at the level of process: i.e. in terms of the nature and function of impression formation within the context of a social relationship, and of the ways in which impressions and relationship demonstrate their mutual interdependence. This third level of analysis entails both the establishment of commonalities between cases and the systematic comparison and contrast of cases.

WHAT I FOUND THERE

In presenting some of my findings here, I will focus primarily at the level of process. However, my second order abstractions will be grounded (cf. Glaser and Strauss 1967) in accounts data from both individuals and pair relationships, extracts from which will be provided in illustration.

Self and other

Probably the single most striking feature of the accounts of impression formation was the extent to which individuals referred impressions of their partners back to their own self-impressions: explicit reflections on self-knowledge were demonstrated to some degree by virtually all participants, and the overall amount of self–other comparison was remarkable (particularly given the fact that views of self were not amongst the 'suggestions' for the content of accounts). Thus, for example, one participant said:

> Looking at A, watching her face, the way she talked, the way she was sitting, I felt I had been wrong about my being more aggressive, or whatever, than her. Now I felt inadequate beside her. I could not sit in the chair with such ease and grace; my voice was grating whereas hers was mellifluous; she talked with ease, I talked in spurts. Then again she made one of those self-deprecating little gestures – she put her hand over her nose – one that I recognize because I do it myself. She is like me, I thought again.

This extract also illustrates particularly clearly the degree of flux in the impression formation process: not only do impressions change and develop from meeting to meeting (and, indeed, in reflection between meetings), they may evolve quite rapidly within the space of a few minutes during a single encounter.

In addition, it is also apparent from this extract that an important feeling behind the process of self–other comparison is an uncertainty about the self, a need both to explore and to attempt to define it. An account extract from another participant reveals this even more strongly:

> Difficult to admit, but I think that someone as collected as B appeared to be on the first meeting (and the fact that she's pretty, intelligent) makes it more difficult to empathize. If one feels self-

conscious (which I did on the first occasion) there is a greater tendency to hold oneself up as some kind of mirror to the other person. If one is feeling very together then, even with strangers, the self-image matters less (ideally, not at all, but!). . . .

Of course, it is possible that self – other comparison is particularly marked in the very early stages of a relationship, when the individual has relatively little information about, and thus may be more likely to project self-knowledge onto, her/his partner. I found some evidence that self–other comparison decreases somewhat as a relationship progresses, although still retaining considerable importance. Partner's similarity to self generally appeared to be emphasized if the relationship was going well; if not, the difference between self and partner was more likely to be given particular emphasis. I will return to this, with examples, a little later.

Elaine and Karen

In order to examine how such extensive reflections on self might contribute to the developing relationship, we need to move to the case study level, and consider the perspectives of both participants. The following extended example is taken from accounts of a first meeting between 'Karen' (a 'mature' student in her early forties) and 'Elaine' (a lecturer in her early thirties):

> Karen (describing her impression of Elaine): I was impressed – both by her academic subject background and by the careful, articulate way she expanded on her field of interest (problem-solving, lateral thinking, concept formation, etc.). Somewhere around this point I began to feel over-awed by Elaine's obvious ability and very conscious of the gaps in my own knowledge/ability. My own self-image embodies the idea that I am below average where rational, analytic thought is concerned. Consequently, I am impressed by this ability in others.

> Karen (describing Elaine's likely impression of her): Of course, I admitted I was backward where Maths/Philosophy are concerned. She then said something to the effect that some psychologists, biologists, etc. say they 'can't do Maths' as though they are quite proud of it – and that she thought this was regrettable. I remember falling over backwards to correct any impression she might have had that I was like that! I think I rather overdid this part of the conversation and began to feel embarrassed. I suppose that this amounts to a suspicion that I 'put myself down' in a way which affected her perception of me.

The second of these two paragraphs is a particularly interesting extract in that it reveals something of the 'mechanics' by which perspectives (Karen's view of herself) and metaperspectives (Karen's view of Elaine's view of her) are interlinked. Karen tries to bring the two types of impression together: she does not want Elaine to see her as 'proud' of her 'backwardness'. In her concern she 'overdoes' the correction, leading to embarrassment as she perceives that Elaine perhaps now sees her as too self-effacing. It is evident just how delicate and finely judged that process of attempting to 'adjust' the other's impressions of you (as you perceive them) really is.

In fact, Karen need not have worried, for in Elaine's report of the same meeting it appears that she has actually formed a positive impression of Karen, and is more concerned with whether she and Karen are similar and with reflecting on her own weaknesses:

> Elaine (describing her impression of Karen): Her humility began to come out as we talked about maths and how she couldn't do it. It wasn't the arrogant, self-satisfied 'Oh I've always been hopeless at maths' that I hear so often. It was more a concerned piece of self-appraisal and criticism, so I thought, Yes, she is a bit like me. But she talked about it more than I would. I would feel it's giving too much away to concentrate so much on my weakness, so I felt she probably wouldn't push herself or be as conscious of giving an impression of intelligence and competence as I know I am. So then I felt she is after all a bit less aggressive.

> Elaine (describing Karen's likely impression of her): I have very little idea of what she thinks of me. She makes me feel stronger than her, a feeling I often have with women, and not one I like very much. I feel much more at home with people who are very aggressive, who make me feel I have to struggle to compete. It's a lot more uncomfortable, but I prefer it somehow.

In the second of these extracts we can see an example of another particularly striking feature of participants' accounts: the frequent attempt both to define the relationship they are experiencing and to fit it into the context of others they have or have had. Again, they were not asked to consider other relationships when providing accounts of their meetings (although this was included amongst the 'contextual' data requested afterwards). As with the process of self–other comparison, it seems that the central aspect of this comparison process is a consideration of the role of their relationships in their self-definition. In this context we might return to the sub-case level (i.e. focusing on the individual) to examine in more detail Elaine's representation of self within the range of her relationships; this is particularly interesting in that it is also crucially related to her gender identity.

In the second of the two extracts from Elaine's transcripts given above, we can see that she is posing the questions 'Who am I, in relation to Karen?' and 'Who is Karen in relation to me?', not only in terms of her other relationships, but in gender-related terms: reflecting on her relationships with women in general, and on how these affect her self-image. In her account of her next meeting with Karen, she returns again to this particular line of exploration:

> Elaine: There was one point, when Karen mentioned that she is doing Citizens' Advice Bureau [CAB] work, when I started thinking about 'women's roles' again. Up till then I had been conscious that our chat was really a kind of interview that wasn't quite sparking . . . I was wondering could we be friends, and I was contrasting our chat with how I imagined two blokes might be. Wouldn't they be entertaining each other more, finding points that interested them both so that their relationship suddenly took off. This is the kind of thing I've wondered about before occasionally. I have a suspicion that men make closer men friends than women do women friends. It's something I would never admit in public because I'm slightly ashamed of it and do not like to admit any sexual differences except for the obvious physiological ones. So there I was with these thoughts drifting through my mind when Karen mentioned the CAB. Then I thought, How typical. Women do exactly that kind of thing, it's a caring, serving role, quite obviously she enjoys it and I can imagine would be marvellous at helping people in trouble. A man in her position wouldn't be doing that – is this a real sexual difference? Now I was conscious that we were two women talking and remembered that I am often uncomfortable in such situations.

This extract not only reveals Elaine's rather stereotyped view of sex roles; it appears that Karen's 'caring' work at the CAB, which personifies women's role for Elaine serves to remind her again of her discomfort in relationships with women (see her previous extract). However, this relationship is going well, and, as the closing sentences of Elaine's account of this meeting reveal, the possibility is there of a genuine friendship developing:

> Now I want to get a little bit closer to Karen and find out how deep she goes, and how far I can go with her – in the sense that we have shared a few interests and got closer, how many others are there? Could we take continued, indefinitely continued delight in each others' company as friends would? It's possible.

Perhaps in view of this, Elaine continues to expend a great deal of effort in trying to understand the ambivalent feelings her relationship with Karen produces in her. After their next meeting she says:

> Elaine: We talk about all sorts of things, from the emotional to the scientific, concrete to abstract and back. I'm not conscious of holding anything back. But I feel somehow that something is missing. Thinking about the close friendships I have, first of all they're mostly with men. Secondly the women I have as close friends are very aggressive

and pride themselves on their intellect. Neither of these statements are true of Karen. But what is the implication of that for the closeness of the relationship? Another point is that all the men I have as close friends have both female and male qualities. They too are aggressive, but they are also emotional, interested in the human condition and all of that. So obviously I feel drawn towards people who span a wide range of responses, interests, characteristics, etc. Where Karen doesn't quite fit into all of this is in the fact that she is very female. She's not aggressive – all her extroversion is manifested in her friendliness, caring, interest in others, relaxed manner. She is outgoing, but in no way seeks to conquer. I am attracted by that, I like it. I think I would like to have a mother like her. But in a friend I want the masculine dimension as well. It's something to do with the way I feel when I'm with her. I think I don't feel challenged. I'm not really learning anything. On the other hand, I would like to have her accomplishments at things feminine, so one might expect that I could learn that from her.... Maybe my feeling of uncertainty about our relationship comes from the fact that her femininity makes me take a more masculine role.

Now some of her conflicts become more understandable, as Elaine continues to explore her gender identity within the context of her relationships with both men and women. She notes that most of her close friendships are with men, and she construes these men as androgynous. On the other hand, she construes her close women friends as generally possessing 'masculine' characteristics: they are aggressive and pride themselves on their intellect (i.e. they are like herself, as described in her first extract). Elaine then construes Karen in comparison with both types of friend (and, by implication, with herself), and finds her manifestly different: she is not aggressive; she does not pride herself on her intellect. (N.B. Some of the evidence for this can also be seen in Elaine's first extract: Karen 'gives too much away' regarding her weakness.)

Although Elaine is able to admit that she likes Karen's 'feminine' characteristics (and in her second extract she even admires them), she is unable to accept them in a potential female friend: because of how she herself feels in relation to Karen. (N.B. She refers to this in three of the four extracts quoted above.) This is linked, too, with what Elaine wants from a friend (cf. also her second extract): she feels she is not being challenged and not learning anything. She notes that she could learn 'things feminine', but seems reluctant – perhaps this would threaten the impression of 'intelligence' and 'competence' she strives to maintain? This very impression – of intelligence and competence – creates for Elaine a definite 'masculine' role. She can accept this in her relationship with men (because she construes it as 'competing' on their own terms), but Karen's 'femininity' throws it into relief, and with her Elaine feels definitely 'stronger': too 'masculine' (cf. also her second extract). This suggests that a 'feminine' female friend may pose a threat to Elaine's sexual identity as a woman – despite her carefully cultivated 'masculine' characteristics.

Unfortunately (and frustratingly!) these participants were unable to continue meeting, so it is not possible to say whether Elaine would have resolved these apparent conflicts in her relationship with Karen. It is valuable in this instance, however, to be able to supplement Elaine's accounts of her meetings with Karen with some of the 'contextual' information she also provided.

Elaine is a first-born child – the elder of two sisters. She notes in her summarized life history that when her sister was born, she had to 'look out for (her)self' and 'find (her) own way'. She blamed constant parental quarrels on her mother's repeated emotional demands on her father, and notes: 'I determined not to make her mistakes, to be more cool and impersonal and also not to get married.' It could be suggested that this kind of childhood and stated resolve (whenever it actually dated from) contribute substantially to Elaine's public persona. Elaine sought to escape from 'small-town provincial life' by going to university and then very much 'made (her) own way' through a variety of jobs and experiences. It was some years before she began to work in a professional capacity: coming to this rather belatedly she felt she had to 'slog' to match younger people in the same position. It appears that this experience dashed her 'high hopes of an outstanding career', and the way she dwells on it suggests that it may underpin her lack of confidence, and have contributed in a major way to the development of her self-doubt and self-deprecation.

In recent years Elaine has worked hard to develop a group of close friends, of whom she says: 'All of them are entertaining, multi-dimensional people, very often living slightly eccentric lives (few are married, none have children).' She notes that she finds it 'a constant struggle' to keep up with these people and is often uncertain of her own contribution to the group. (Again, she is extremely self-deprecating.) This social group, which is predominantly male, is entirely separate from her work friends and colleagues – all of whom are female, and mostly married with children. This situation would seem to provide some clues as to how Elaine's polarization of masculine and feminine characteristics has developed – or at least is sustained: i.e. it reflects the nature of her social network. It is also clearer why the loss of her 'masculine' characteristics and/or the assumption of feminine characteristics may pose a threat to her: Elaine may well feel that such a change would jeopardize her position in her valued social group (already shaky, in her eyes), and involve her in becoming more like her work colleagues, and, by implication, like her mother.

Let us now return to the case study level, and add in Karen's changing impressions of Elaine, and her view of the developing relationship. I want to emphasize, particularly, the ways in which this relationship is a successful one, in order to contrast it with one that deteriorated rapidly.

Throughout their series of meetings, it is remarkable how 'in tune' the two women's perceptions are. Following their second meeting, Karen's account indicates how her changing impression of Elaine has affected the impression of herself that she is able to project, and how both have altered the nature of their relationship:

> Karen (describing her impression of Elaine): By the end of the session, the sense of deference I experienced last week had been reduced. Last week I think I was overawed by Elaine: she seemed cool and intellectual. There seemed very little about her as a person to which I could relate. As the session progressed, Elaine provided opinions and instances of activity with which I could identify.

> Karen (describing Elaine's likely impression of her): Last week I felt very conscious that I may have been giving the impression that I was lacking in confidence. This week I was less self-conscious. In part, this must have been due to the perception of Elaine as much warmer and more friendly. She smiled more and we were in accord on the subjects discussed. I am conscious, however, that we are proceeding quite carefully. We haven't for example, touched on socially sensitive areas of opinion. I wonder if we will?

> Karen (describing the relationship): Last week respect/awe got in the way of considering Elaine in terms of liking/not liking. Elaine is an interesting person. The fact that her company was enjoyable this week and that I could relate to much of what she had to say, has altered the relationship.

In particular, Karen's speculation as to whether they will move on to discuss 'socially sensitive' topics seems to echo Elaine's musings about the possibility of a deep friendship developing, following this particular meeting.

At the following meeting, the topic of Karen's CAB work comes up again, and it is interesting to note that Karen displays an awareness that this has some particular significance for Elaine (although, of course, she is not aware exactly what this is). In reporting on this section of the meeting, she notes: 'I began to be aware that Elaine was sensitive and perceptive about the "how and why" of her own behaviour and that of others.' This is the meeting where Elaine has described the flowing conversation (see extract beginning: 'We talk about . . .'), and Karen, too, sees this as having contributed substantially to their developing relationship: 'I think there was quite a marked change in our relationship this week. Conversation was fluent and relaxed: I experienced considerable rapport with Elaine during this session.'

A week later, too, her assessment of their relationship seems to square remarkably well with Elaine's (again, see the 'We talk about . . .' extract):

> Although there were aspects of Elaine's personality about which I was still curious, I was more content to take a passive role . . . I respect Elaine's intellect but am no longer overawed by it. Now, I am at the

stage where I feel her intellect is stimulating, interesting, and that I could learn from it. With this in mind, the suggestion is that, in a subtle way, she is the dominant partner in the interaction.

Note, in particular, how each is aware of her role in the relationship relative to the other – and yet both feel they could learn particular things from each other.

Elaine and Dawn

Next, we might look at the early stages of a relationship between Elaine and 'Dawn' (a post-graduate student, in her mid-twenties): a series of meetings that took place earlier in the research project, and that did not go particularly well for them. This sequence is of interest both for the additional (and largely confirmatory) perspective it provides on Elaine's view of her gender identity, and for the contrast it provides with her relationship with Karen. In this relationship there is a greater status difference between the participants, perceived by both of them, but whereas their initial perceptions of each other are congruent, these rapidly diverge. One participant fails to realize this, which, in turn, is associated with a deterioration in the relationship. Again, the changes in the relationship are crucially interlinked with the changing impressions.

After their second meeting, Elaine describes her impressions of Dawn, and their relationship, as follows:

> Elaine: [Dawn] gives the impression of not being particularly clever (relative to other university people, that is) by the way she talks ... – accent – it is the same kind of voice that goes with the stereotype of an unthinking, silly, scatter-brained woman. Also she is a little hesitant, not forceful; inclined to agree with me rather than find points of conflict; doesn't give me many new ideas ... I feel I am being a bit superior in all this. It comes from the fact that I feel completely at ease with Dawn, that I can handle anything that might occur, and that she is less sure about it all.

We see that Dawn, even more strongly than Karen, falls into Elaine's female stereotype, and that (despite her statement that she feels 'completely at ease'), Elaine is again uncomfortable in the contrasting role she has assigned herself. Dawn sees Elaine (and herself) in very similar terms; and in her case, as with Karen, again we see the anxiety about the impression of self that is being projected (metaperspective level):

> Dawn: Throughout this session, I got the impression that Elaine was a fairly dominant person – perhaps because she took the lead in conversation. I also felt a little bit small – even though more relaxed this time. Elaine had a very superior air about her – I found myself backing out from arguments which I don't usually do, but only because her arguments seemed much more forceful than mine and I

didn't want to carry on and look silly in case it turned out I really was wrong.

However, as their meetings progress, Dawn's views begin to change: as she is able to distance self and other, she gains in confidence, feeling she no longer suffers in the comparison (or, indeed, that it is necessary to make such a comparison all the time). This, in turn, enables them to establish a more friendly relationship – with talk of more personal activities – and produces a considerable revision in her impression of Elaine:

> Dawn: I felt more friendly altogether towards Elaine and thought that she seemed more open and less determined to put forward her views, and try to get me to accept them. She wasn't at all dominant as I had thought from last time. Perhaps this was also because I felt confident expressing my views this time – I feel I know enough about my own hobbies to talk about them ... it didn't seem to matter whether she had different approaches or different hobbies. I just realized that Elaine was a person and different from myself – not 'better' or 'worse' than me because I'm no longer judging her on myself in all aspects. I enjoyed our conversation – perhaps this is why I gained the overall impression that Elaine is a nice person, if a little serious at first meeting.

In contrast, Elaine's view of Dawn does not change: it becomes more entrenched:

> Elaine: The talk about hobbies and collecting things made me feel she might be a bit kind of fussy and narrow-minded, collecting all those things, having all those hobbies. Also the fact that she goes from one to another sounds a bit undisciplined and scatter-brained. A number of things are coming together this time ... and slot into a kind of stereotype of feminine, wanting to be protected, delighting in pretty things. This is what makes me feel distanced, and inevitably like her somewhat less.

Thus, not only does Elaine's perception of Dawn remain unremittingly negative (with Elaine maximizing the differences between them), but Dawn fails to see that this is the case, being caught up in her own impressions of Elaine. (In Kellian terms, with particular reference to the Sociality Corollary [see p. 42] Dawn fails to construe Elaine's construction processes and so ceases to be in a role relationship with her.) This failure at a metaperspective level can be identified as the point at which the relationship begins to founder: in fact, Dawn and Elaine meet only on one further occasion.

Mismatches and plateaux

Broadening the discussion again to the level of process, I would tentatively suggest a mismatch at the metaperspective level as one major indicator of incipient relationship breakdown. (That such a mismatch provides considerable pressure for change is also acknowledged by Heyman and Shaw [1978].) Certainly it is possible to see such processes at work in a number of other cases, although sometimes it appears to be a failure or breakdown in one individual's representation of the other's viewpoint (as in the case above), while in others it appears that reciprocal metaperspectives never develop. For example, compare these extracts from the accounts of another pair of participants:

> I sense there is a barrier of some sort between C and myself but can't quite place it. Although we superficially talk as equals there is somehow something extra on her side – is it she treats me or I feel she treats me a bit as one would a child? – listening, nodding and feeding back some points. I can't quite fix it.

Her partner is quite unaware of F's perception of her attitude:

> My first impression that I could make a friend of F has not changed.... My basic requirements for friendship are sense of humour, integrity/dependability, interesting ... I judge that F meets these requirements. (We are) two people with mutual interests who like to talk.

Not surprisingly, this relationship never really 'takes off'.

Often, one participant would be convinced that s/he had insight(s) into her/his partner, or even that reciprocal metaperspectives had been developed, while the other had no sense of this. For example:

> The relationship had progressed and seemed to be less tentative. I began to feel that I knew her and she knew me and that a relationship had been established ... I see her as quietly confident and very capable ... she is not someone you feel you know 'on sight' but is at the same time easy to talk to.

Her partner said:

> I keep changing my mind about this relationship – although realize it's steadily settling (sinking?) into a static pattern (possibly because I'm disappointed it hasn't turned out better) ... it's pretty superficial and impersonal, with repeat topics of common concern. When conversation dries up it feels awkward (our communication difficulties again – neither of us over-good at 'patching' – though I've learnt something of how to do this by practising!). Basically, I find G a bit boring (middle-aged housewifeish) and I suspect she's lodged rather uneasily between seeing me as a daughter ... and seeing me as [a] lecturer.

This last extract is of additional interest in that in it this participant refers to the relationship 'settling into a static pattern'. This seemed to be an alternative course to relationship breakdown when reciprocal metaperspectives had not been established, and was one aspect of the

research that I felt could have been influenced by its 'demand characteristics' (Orne 1962), i.e. that participants, regarding the research as a project
of limited duration and being keen to provide me with data, did not
choose to terminate unsuccessful relationships as promptly as they would
have done in 'real life'. (Of course, the request for participants to be deeply
introspective and analytic about their impression formation can itself be
regarded as a demand characteristic.)

Participants often referred to relationships as being 'stuck', or of being
aware of a definite 'transition point' at which they 'took off'. There was
sometimes an element of choice here:

> Feel relationship has now reached something of a plateau – easy and
> relaxed conversation.... Very aware that we were talking on an
> 'implicitly agreed' (and not very deep) level of intimacy ... neither of
> us attempted to violate this at all.... Feel as though this brings us to
> a choice point – will we stay on this level, or 'deepen'? Would
> speculate that we will stay on this level.

(Interestingly, this participant's partner also uses the word 'plateau' at a
similar time – but sees more potential for relationship development.)

CONCLUSIONS: ISSUES AND INSIGHTS

Finally, I would like to address several broader questions. First I will
consider some of the potential strengths and limitations of this research,
and second, the kinds of conclusions it is possible to reach from this very
detailed personal data, including, in particular, how such conclusions
might contribute to our understanding of relationships.

One kind of question that may be asked regarding the limitations of this
work is how far my findings from the early stages of relationships compare
with impression formation and modification in continuing and later stages.
The answer to this is, of course, dependent on the extent to which
individuals actually continued to monitor (and report on) their impressions
and on the relationship. My perception is that impression monitoring
remained vigorous, thereby suggesting that the changes in impressions
were salient, until the frequently identified 'transition point' referred to
above. After this, if the relationship was 'stuck' or deteriorating, the
individuals lost the energy and/or enthusiasm to continue their monitoring.
If, on the other hand, the relationship was 'taking off', individuals often
reported that they 'forgot' to monitor their changing impressions, or that
impressions no longer seemed so important to what was taking place: it
was as if the relationship developed a momentum of its own that blunted
the importance of 'person phenomena' (or at least individuals' ability/
willingness to pay continued attention to these). This could be interpreted
as providing a measure of support for Clarke's theory of hierarchical
action control (1985, and this volume), in that it may represent the
operation of an 'affective control system', which is regarded as superordin-

ate to cognition. However, these comments must necessarily be regarded as rather tentative, because relatively few pairs did continue meeting beyond a period of 6–8 weeks.

The question is also likely to arise of the generalizability of findings from this type of data, and, in particular, from this highly selective group of introspective participants (who may, for example, be contrasted with the individuals studied by Burnett [this volume] in terms of the effort they are prepared to expend in thinking about relationships). While these issues deserve consideration, I regard the case study framework of the research (and the insights of the participant group with whom it was conducted) to be its particular strength.

With reference to case study data in general, Honess and Edwards (1985), following Campbell (1984), point out that despite the fact that the criticism of limited generalization is so often levelled at case study work, it is simply not appropriate – because it confuses 'analytic' and 'statistical' inferential procedures. Case study research rests on the former type of procedure so cannot validly be criticized for failing to meet criteria associated with the latter. Further, individual cases must be judged in terms of their explanatory power, not in terms of 'typicality' (in fact the search for a 'typical case' further confuses the two modes of inference). Paradigmatic statements of case study methodology often refer to a process that Bertaux and Kohli (1984) call 'saturation': where the researcher or team move(s) from case to case, modifying questions along the way, until eventually it is found that subsequent cases 'confirm' the particular interpretation (cf. also Allport 1942; Herbst 1970). Thus, regarding my own data, it is possible to look for similarities in process between individuals (sub-cases) or pairs of participants (cases), in that patterns found in one person/couple may be duplicated, and hence confirmed, in others. A further way of proceeding may be to focus on comparisons and contrasts between individual cases, in order to establish a body of 'case law' (see Bromley [1977; also 1986] for a more detailed discussion of many of these issues). The results of this process may be regarded as essentially very similar to Sloman's (1976) suggestions as to the 'aims of science': the delineation and exploration of human possibilities – although unless communicated (such that an actuality for one person becomes a possibility for another [see Mair 1970]), they do not go as far as to extend the range of possibilities open to individuals. (I hope that my research, construed as a learning experience, can begin to do this.)

With regard to my 'selected' group, I would argue that this need not prove unacceptably restrictive if one focuses on processes rather than personal characteristics. There is no reason why these should not begin to be established in this kind of group (i.e. particularly introspective), using this kind of research technique (i.e. particularly intensive), and then cases involving different types of people/relationships (perhaps studied using different techniques), be 'added on', in the quest for 'saturation'. In that, at least to date, I have only conducted intensive case studies of introspective individuals, I am not in a position to speculate on the likely outcome of this endeavour, however. Alternatively, if it feels more comfortable for the traditional researcher to regard analytic inference procedures as the first stage in an inductive–deductive cycle of research, there is no reason why s/he should not test out the generalizability of such processes using a large, representative sample and statistical inference procedures. In fact, Robert Neimeyer is intending to conduct a study of this type, using my framework of a 'diary' of meetings, but structuring the data obtained by using a questionnaire format (1985, personal communication). However, it does need to be realized that this is a fundamentally different type of research (both procedurally and epistemologically).

Some case study researchers are likely to regard the quest for general theory as antithetical to this mode of research, or alternatively to argue that social processes such as those involved in impression formation and relationship development are highly specific in social, cultural and historical terms. (There is an interesting parallel here with recent developments in feminist research [see e.g. Kitzinger 1986; Stanley and Wise 1983; Walkerdine 1985].) Others may argue the particular benefits of case study work (again, see Bromley 1986). With particular reference to the study of impression formation within social relationships, I believe that the most comprehensive insights are likely to accrue from research conducted in an intensive case study mode. These may be maximized when the participants are committed to what is essentially collaborative research, working together as 'experts' in their own impression formation and relationship development (with the psychologist perhaps regarded as 'facilitator' of the investigation). In this way, all participants will have an investment in the research and all will be beneficiaries of it, in the sense of gaining an increased understanding of the dynamics of their own impression formation within their own relationships.

What of the conclusions that can be drawn from this kind of data? First, it is evident that these individuals are indeed capable of monitoring and reporting on their impression formation processes within this specialized (albeit relatively narrow) social context. Furthermore, the way in which participants responded to my invitation to explore their impression formation and relationship development provided considerable validation for the Kellian model of 'person-as-scientist'. It was evident on many occasions that participants were actively experimenting in the research, using their behaviour to pose questions and to test out specific hypotheses about their partners (see, in particular, Elaine's and Karen's speculations about the future of their relationship). Some experimented on a number of different levels: deliberately focusing on different kinds of cues at different times, for example, or trying out different ways of organizing and structuring their accounts. It is also evident that participants did, indeed, find the research of value to them, and feel they had learnt from it (see, for example, the penultimate extract, above). This is also borne out by many of their comments on and evaluations of the research. (A number of participants also commented on what 'hard work' the research was.)

Second, it appears that the insights gained from studying impression formation in this way suggest the need for a very different view of the process from the traditional information-processing one, a view that gives due regard to its place and purpose in its usual social context of a developing relationship. Having seen that individuals use their behaviour to conduct personal experiments, and the extent to which these experiments entail the comparison of self and other, I would argue that impression formation could be reconceptualized as an instrumental activity; as a means by which one's self can be construed – in relation to your construction of the other, and your construction of the other's construction of you. This person and this relationship can in turn be construed relative to others in your past and present social network, which will also reflect back on the construction of self. In short, when involved in the early stages of developing relationships, we are conducting experiments in self-exploration and definition and our impressions are our hypotheses. Whether these hypotheses (and thereby our views of self) are validated or thrown into question is likely to be critically linked with the likely future of the relationship.

Third, the degree of interdependence between impressions and relationships revealed in this data is of particular interest in the study of relationships, not only because it is so extensive, but because it would seem to be possible to delineate specific ways in which certain types or sequences of impressions contribute to rapid relationship development or breakdown; and also to identify particular points at which such change is likely to occur. In particular, I have suggested that a lack of congruence between participants' metaperspectives is one index that a relationship is likely to fail, either because one individual is unable to construe the other's perspective from the outset, or because a 'mismatch' in metaperspectives develops. However, in that my research has largely been confined to a study of 'person phenomena' in the early stages of relationships, and also within a restricted range of relationships, it must be acknowledged that such an analysis can only be regarded as a first step. Nevertheless, I hope I have been able to demonstrate something of the value of such an approach, which I regard as constituting a particularly promising line of enquiry for the future development of our knowledge and understanding of relationships.

ACKNOWLEDGEMENTS

I am grateful to the Social Science Research Council (now the Economic and Social Research Council) for financial support. I would also like to thank Peter Stringer for helpful discussion, Jonathan Potter for pointing out the importance of Aaron Sloman's analysis, and David Fisher for drawing my attention to the work of Heyman and Shaw.

REFERENCES

Allport, G. (1942) *The Use of Personal Documents in Psychological Science*. New York: SSRC.

Antaki, C. and Fielding, G. (1981) 'Research on ordinary explanations'. In C. Antaki (ed.) *The Psychology of Ordinary Explanations of Social Behaviour*. London: Academic Press.

Asch, S. (1946) 'Forming impressions of personality'. *Journal of Abnormal and Social Psychology*, 41, 258–90.

Bannister, D. and Fransella, F. (1980) *Inquiring Man: The Theory of Personal Constructs*, 2nd edition. Harmondsworth: Penguin.

Bertaux, D. and Kohli, M. (1984) 'The life story approach: a continental view'. *Annual Review of Sociology*, 10, 215–37.

Bromley, D.B. (1977) *Personality Description in Ordinary Language*. London: Wiley.

—— (1986) *The Case Study Method in Psychology and Related Disciplines*. London: Wiley.

Butterworth, A. (1985) 'Content and Context of Pupils' and Teachers' Mutual Perceptions in Three Junior Schools'. Unpublished PhD thesis, University of Liverpool.

Campbell, D.T. (1984) 'Can we be scientific in applied social science?' *Evaluation Studies (Review Annual)*, 9, 26–48.

Clarke, D.D. with Crossland, J. (1985) *Action Systems: An Introduction to the Analysis of Complex Behaviour*. London: Methuen.

Duck, S. (1977) *Theory and Practice in Interpersonal Attraction*. London: Academic Press.

Eiser, J.R. (1980) *Cognitive Social Psychology*. London: McGraw-Hill.

Farr, R.M. and Moscovici, S. (1984) *Social Representations*. Cambridge: Cambridge University Press.

Glaser, B.G. and Strauss, A.L. (1967) *The Discovery of Grounded Theory: Strategies for Qualitative Research*. Chicago: Aldine.

Harré, R. (1979) *Social Being*. Oxford: Blackwell.

—— (1983) *Personal Being*. Oxford: Blackwell.

—— and Secord, P.F. (1972) *The Explanation of Social Behaviour*. Oxford: Blackwell.

Herbst, P.G. (1970) *Behavioural Worlds: The Study of Single Cases*. London: Tavistock.

Hewstone, M. (1984) *Attribution Theory: Social and Functional Extensions*. Oxford: Blackwell.

Heyman, B. and Shaw, M. (1978) 'Constructs of relationship'. *Journal for the Theory of Social Behaviour*, 8 (3), 231–60.

Honess, T. and Edwards, A. (1985) 'Case studies and applied social research'. Paper presented in the symposium *Methodological Problems in Applied Social Research*. British Psychological Society Social Psychology Section annual conference. Clare College, Cambridge. September.

Kelly, G.A. (1955) *The Psychology of Personal Constructs*, 2 vols. New York: W.W. Norton.

Kitzinger, C. (1986) 'Introducing and developing Q as a feminist methodology: a study of accounts of lesbianism'. In S.J. Wilkinson (ed.) *Feminist Social Psychology: Developing Theory and Practice*. Milton Keynes: Open University Press.

Laing, R.D., Phillipson, H. and Lee, A.R. (1966) *Interpersonal Perception*. London: Tavistock.

Maher, B. (ed.) (1969) *Clinical Psychology and Personality: The Selected Papers of George Kelly*. New York: Wiley.

Mair, J.M.M. (1970) 'Psychologists are human too'. In D. Bannister (ed.) *Perspectives in Personal Construct Theory*. London: Academic Press.

Orne, M.T. (1962) 'On the social psychology of the psychological experiment; with particular reference to demand characteristics and their implications'. *American Psychologist*, 17, 776–83.

Rosenberg, S. (1977) 'New approaches to the analysis of personal constructs in person perception'. In A.W. Landfield (ed.) *1976 Nebraska Symposium on Motivation*. Lincoln, Nebraska: University of Nebraska Press.

Sloman, A. (1976) 'What are the aims of science?' *Radical Philosophy*, Spring, 7–17.

Stanley, L. and Wise, S. (1983) *Breaking Out: Feminist Consciousness and Feminist Research*. London: Routledge & Kegan Paul.

Stringer, P. (1979) 'Individuals, roles and persons'. In P. Stringer and D. Bannister (eds) *Constructs of Sociality and Individuality*. London: Academic Press.

Walkerdine, V. (1985) 'On the regulation of speaking and silence: sexuality, class and gender in contemporary schooling'. In C. Steedman, C. Urwin and V. Walkerdine (eds) *Language, Gender and Childhood*. London: Routledge & Kegan Paul.

Wilkinson S.J. (1978) 'Disrupting the subject–experimenter dichotomy'. Paper presented in the symposium *Knowledge for Whom?* British Psychological Society Social Psychology Section annual conference. UWIST, Cardiff. September.

—— (1981) 'Personal constructs and private explanations'. In C. Antaki (ed.) *The Psychology of Ordinary Explanations of Social Behaviour*. London: Academic Press.

4 Remembering relationship development: constructing a context for interactions

Dorothy Miell

Over the course of a relationship's development, new information about both the partner and the relationship is continually being acquired; thus the store of information and beliefs that comprise the relational history will need to be updated and possibly amended if the individual is to maintain a coherent and accurate context against which later events can be interpreted. This chapter reports a study that examines part of this process of building up a unique relational context by investigating the gradual evolution of the personal history of a relationship during the early stages of its development.

THE RELATIONAL LEVEL OF ANALYSIS

Although there has been a considerable body of research dealing with how individuals acquire and process information about their partners, as Wilmot (1980) observed, the variety of methods by which people acquire information about their *relationships* has not been investigated and little work has been focused on the ways in which individuals remember and structure such information (but see Planalp [1983] and this volume for a welcome exception to this observation) or how they use this information in interactions.

Some evidence for the way in which stored relational information serves as a context for behaviour in affecting interactions comes from a previous study (Miell 1984) of the conversations of eighteen couples. The reliance of strangers on very general, cultural rules about appropriate behaviour, where a particular relational context was missing, was evidenced in their impersonal, difficult and highly structured conversations. The general rules for polite interaction with a stranger allowed conversation to take place, but meant that it never became too involving or personal. In the interactions between friends, however, a very different pattern emerged, with easy, personal and unstructured conversations that broke many of the generally agreed rules of polite conversation by the use of interruptions, unanswered questions and metacommunications. These friends seemed to have developed, and relied on, a much more personal set of rules for appropriate conversation than the strangers, and their abbreviated communication required a unique shared context for interpretation; it was much less easily understood than that of the strangers, where every utterance was complete and structured and the meaning was explicit.

These findings suggested that a developed relationship provides a unique context for interaction as it both furnishes a personalized set of rules for appropriate behaviour, which has been built up by negotiation in many previous encounters, and it provides a rich store of shared personal knowledge. However, this is not a static context for current interactions, it is amended as partners gather information about each other and about their relationship; being extended, corrected and reorganized to assimilate the latest relevant details (and this process never ceases), it is continuous throughout the life of the relationship. Even when the relationship is stable and well-established, a novel event, a crisis for one partner they discuss, or even an 'out of character' remark or look, will cause the individual to check his or her picture of the relationship and to update it if necessary (Davis 1973; Planalp and Honeycutt 1984). Even once a relationship has ended, individuals still have to construct an acceptable version of the history of the relationship, and how and why it ended (Duck 1982; McCall 1982), and the accounts they offer are likely to be influenced (as are all accounts of previous developments in a relationship) by their current knowledge of the relationship, their theories of why it took the path it did and their desire to maintain a level of self-esteem (Scott and Lyman 1971).

These attempts to make sense of past events have however tended to be viewed merely as a methodological problem in using retrospective self-report data (as Christensen, Sullay and King [1983] do) where individuals are presumed to be 'misrepresenting reality' by using processes of inference and recasting (Ericsson and Simon 1980). Yet, rather than viewing such restructuring of the story of the relationship as a peculiar, problematic bias found particularly after relationships have broken down, it would perhaps be more fruitful to see it as a normal and continual process – a natural and necessary part of an individual actively constructing, interpreting, predicting and ultimately understanding the development of his or her relationships (Duck and Miell 1982). The constant restructuring of the story, or history, of a relationship's development need not be viewed as a methodological problem if it is better understood. Including an understanding of this restructuring process in our analysis of personal relationships would provide a richer, rather than a methodologically cloudier, picture of how relationships are conducted. Such a task is, however, a complex one as until recently there has not been a suitable method for use in studying this process. The study reported here addresses this by developing an entirely novel method and set of analyses to investigate just this process of retrospecting about a relationship's development over the course of that development in an attempt to elucidate some of the influential variables affecting recall of the path of development.

MEMORY FOR RELATIONAL INFORMATION

The model of behaviour in relationships adopted here is one that sees the individual actions and exchanges, and the strategies and tactics employed in these interactions, as being guided by a set of higher order beliefs and intentions for the relationship in which the interactions take place, and which give particular exchanges their meaning (Miell 1984). This set of intentions is developed partly from *general* beliefs about different types of relationship (e.g. friend, colleague); beliefs such as what are appropriate behaviours in these relationships, what developmental trajectories they generally follow and what might constitute 'taboo' conversational topics in each type; and partly (increasingly, as the relationship develops), from the *unique* store of information gathered over the course of this particular relationship, determining appropriate behaviour and the probable future development of the relationship.

This model of an organizing set of beliefs and intentions being developed and elaborated with available information, whilst also in turn guiding the gathering and interpretation of new information, bears many similarities to existing models of the development of cognitive schemata, which process material by selecting items for attention, gathering information about the items and storing this information for use later as a basis for action. Although this schematic processing has mainly been studied when it is involved in logical and perceptual categories of thought and action, the concept can also be applied to the processing of social information.

Research on social schemata has focused on several aspects of the schematic processing of social information, and these can be grouped into general classes of schemata, such as 'event' schemata, 'role' schemata, 'person' and 'self' schemata (Taylor and Crocker 1981). The first, event schemata, can be seen as guiding rules for appropriate behaviour at particular, well-defined social events such as a cocktail party, wedding, or staff meeting. In these situations, an appropriate schema can be employed that has been built up from previous experience or from explicit instruction, similar in many ways to Schank and Abelson's (1977) well-practised behavioural scripts. A second class is that of role schemata, which include the schema we may evolve to guide behaviour in and understanding of social roles such as parent, friend, or boss. The third and fourth classes of schemata, of person and self, approach more nearly the concern of the present argument as they deal with specific individuals, rather than with generalized roles or social events. Person schemata include prototypical notions such as introvert and extravert (Cantor and Mischel 1977) and representations of particular individuals (Hamilton, Katz and Leier 1980) and self-schemata involve the various conceptions held by an individual about him or herself in relation to both the physical and the social world (Markus 1977).

These schemata share certain important features in the way in which they deal with social information; essentially they *structure* the perception of this information, by both simplifying and categorizing complex and otherwise disjointed information, and by allowing the individual to fill in gaps in the information available, allowing him or her to go 'beyond the information given' (Bruner 1957). Where information is missing, schemata also play an important role for the individual in providing material consistent with the available information and expectations to fill the gaps.

What, however, of truly relational schemata? Although the schema for 'a friend' embodies a relational *principle*, and has thus been called a relational schema by some theorists (e.g. Housel and Acker 1979; Winograd 1977), it is too much a general, relationship-as-state label. As Wilmot and Baxter (1983) found, these types of schemata are of a lower level than *truly* relational schemata which embody 'relationship-as-process' principles. In the Wilmot and Baxter study, subjects found information about the *dynamics* of a relationship's development more useful as a means of structuring and interpreting information about a particular communication episode than information about the *state* of the relationship (i.e. as 'friend' or 'lover'). It would seem consistent with existing theories of schema development that just as a particular person schema is evolved for use with a partner as more information is gathered about them as individual people, so might a particular *relational* schema evolve as more information is gathered about the unique relationship between the 'self and partner'. This schema can then provide a basis for evaluating experiences, anticipating the future, structuring information, and setting goals and intentions relevant to the higher order level that is the relationship between the two particular individuals. This level is of higher order to other schemata both in that it is more elaborated and complex than role schemata loosely based on relationship labels (such as 'friend'), and in that it transcends the individual person and self schemata. In other words a particular relationship (and the relevant schema) can be seen to be more than just a sum of the two individual partners involved (McCall 1984) with a character of its own.

The study to be discussed here was designed to examine the workings of these hypothesized relational schemata, focusing on one aspect of them, the evolution of a personal history of the relationship as it is influenced by everyday events occurring in interpersonal encounters. In particular it was hypothesized that, during the early stages of relationship development, where we would expect the acquisition of particular relational schemata to be most rapid (and hence most readily observable), we should be able to detect a noticeable fluctuation in the personal histories of relationships as positive and negative events occur week by week. Further, it was hypothesized that none of the various relational histories constructed need follow a 'true' course of the relationship (such as could be assessed by traditional 'objective' measures of relational development), since the 'reality' to which relational schemata accommodate is one whose only existence is that determined by the developing relational schemata themselves (see Weber, Harvey and Stanley, this volume).

To examine these hypotheses, participants were asked to assess four of their personal relationships each week for ten weeks, in each week recording graphically their current feelings about the strength of these relationships as well as their retrospections about previous weeks' feelings and prospections about future feelings. In this way the links between the evolving history of the relationship (evidenced by the various retrospections about the relationship's development) and the beliefs about current events could be explored in some detail.

ASSESSING KNOWLEDGE OF RELATIONSHIP DEVELOPMENT

Forty individuals (twenty males and twenty females) were recruited to take part in this study, although over the course of the ten-week measurement period there was a high drop-out rate, and at the end of the study there were complete data from sixteen individuals (ten females and six males). This drop-out rate is similar to that in other longitudinal studies (e.g. Burnett, this volume; Duck and Miell 1982; Wilkinson, this volume) where a high level of commitment is required from participants. It is of course possible that those who stay in the study are more introspective, or more reflective than those who drop out – and thus the results may unduly emphasize this aspect of relational understanding. However, it is difficult to avoid such a problem in a longitudinal design.

The participants were asked to draw a series of graphs recording the developments in the strength of four of their relationships (a male and female close friend and a male and female acquaintance) each week for a period of ten weeks during the study. These graphs represented the strength of each relationship (0–100 scale), and subjects were asked to consider the overall strength of the relationship, not just particular aspects such as intimacy, empathy, etc., and to mark the current state of the relationship that week, then to mark in appropriate scores for previous weeks, and finally to predict future scores representing the later development of the relationship (Figure 4.1 shows a sample graph). Each week the subjects completed one graph depicting the development of each of the four relationships over the ten-week period of the study, without referring to the previous graphs, each having been returned on completion each

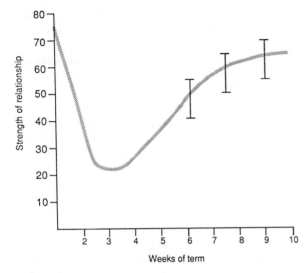

Figure 4.1   Example of a completed graph used in the study – chart of MH's relationship with female friend (drawn in week 5)

Comments: 'Our relationship is generally improving, but at the moment not very smoothly. It suffers from serious lack of understanding of each other at times and misinterpretation of each other's motives for doing things and the way we act towards each other. At the moment I feel that ultimate progress of this relationship is not guaranteed; it will only get considerably better if we are both determined that it will.'

week. Each of the ten graphs drawn by subjects for each of their four relationships yielded ten scores (one for each week of the period of the study).

A major problem for this type of research using repeated measurements with the same scale is that subjects may or may not be using the scale in a consistent fashion each week. It would not have been feasible to allow subjects to keep records of previous evaluations, as this would have influenced their current evaluations of the relationship and obscured the focus of the study: any *changes* in recall of a relationship's development over the weeks of development. As a result, a standardization procedure was devised that allowed comparisons to be made both between and within the sets of weekly evaluations provided by subjects. This procedure thus overcame the problem of consistency in using the scale as it allowed all the original relative differences between scores within any one week's set of scores to be maintained, whilst making comparisons between weeks possible.[1]

1 The calculations involved in this standardization method are too detailed to include in this chapter, but the author would be pleased to forward the details of these and other analyses mentioned here on request.

Analysis proceeded by making comparisons between the participants' memories of the relationship's development and the 'actual' path of development (as assessed by tracing the sequence of scores made each week for the feeling about the relationship that week). Preliminary analyses suggested three major observations could be made about the data. First, there were no significant differences between any of the scores from male and female participants. The second observation was that there were no significant differences in the accuracy of retrospections made about the four different relationships sampled (male and female friends and acquaintances). Thus the later findings of the study can claim to be generalizable to more than a limited range of particular relationships; they reflect some underlying process of thinking about and remembering relationships. Differences in the types of relationships studied might have been more exaggerated, however, had all the relationships here not been in such early stages of development. Although there were strong reasons for looking at the early development of relationships (when, as argued earlier, schematic processing of information might be at its most evident) relationships which have been established longer, or which are stable or even declining, may have revealed different patterns in the retrospections made about them, but only further research can address this speculation.

The third observation made from the preliminary analyses was that retrospections were most accurate when the relationship had been most stable in its path of development. This is as would have been expected, and turns the attention of all further analyses to the less accurately remembered, unstable relationships. The study was attempting to establish what processes underlie the memory for a relationship's development, suggesting that recall was based at least as much on current feelings and events as on actual events in the past, and hence that 'accurate' recall of the path of development (as assessed by comparison with the evaluations recorded earlier) was not to be expected. *How* the current events might affect recall was not, however, predicted, although two major analyses have suggested some of the processes at work in this reconstruction.

THE 'EXTENSION MODEL'

The first major analysis concerned what can be called the 'extension model' of memory for relationship development, where retrospections were hypothesized to be constructed with no reference to specific actual scores recorded in earlier weeks, but only from the recent changes in the relationship's development and a general feel for the overall path of previous development. The model was supported by the results of two analyses, which established that retrospections were nearer to an extension of the line drawn back from the developments between that week and the previous one than they were to the actual course of the relationship's development. Thus, individuals tended to construct retrospections which have smoother curves than the actual course of the development of their relationships, as they are apparently not recalling specific values week by week, but generalizing or 'extending back' more recent developments, especially when the relationship has been developing in an unstable way.

However, the test of accuracy of retrospections employed in these initial tests of the extension model was a strict one: retrospective evaluations of each week had to be within 5 points of the actual evaluation made in the appropriate earlier week to be considered 'accurate'. A final test of the extension model adopted a less stringent test of accuracy, calculating whether the *gradient* of the final week retrospection was nearer to the gradient of the extension or to that of the actual course of the relationship. On this criterion, the retrospections were not significantly closer to the extensions of the last week's development than to the actual course of development. This analysis suggested that individuals were using more information about previous development in the relationship than *only* the most recent changes, as the extension model had suggested. Instead, it seems that individuals had a fairly good recall of the pattern of earlier development, that is, of the previous changes in the strength of the relationship, although for some reason they were not accurate in recalling the absolute levels of the range of this pattern.

THE 'RECENCY EFFECT'

The second major analysis concerned what was labelled the 'recency effect', which explored the *ways* in which recent events affected the absolute values given to previous weeks' evaluations. This concerned the exaggeration of recent changes in the relationship when constructing a retrospection of the previous development. An examination of one particular relationship from the sample illustrates this tendency influencing the pattern of recall. Figure 4.2 depicts the retrospective and actual course of development of person VP's relationship with her close male friend. In each of the eight graphs shown in Figure 4.2, the horizontal axis represents the ten weeks of the study. The vertical axis represents the strength of the relationship as assessed by VP on the 0–100 scale. The eight graphs show the development of the relationship from weeks 3–10 inclusive. Each graph indicates (a) the present state of the relationship, (b) the actual course the relationship has taken up to that point and (c) the retrospection about that previous development made at that point.

In this example, we can see that until week 6 the retrospections remain fairly close to the actual course of the relationship's development. This is unsurprising, according to the extension model, as the actual development is an almost linear increase over these early weeks. In week 6 however, there is a sharp increase in the evaluation of the relationship which appears to have resulted in a corresponding underestimate of the previous strength of the relationship, thus having the overall effect of *exaggerating* this most recent event. In week 7, the rate of increase is less and correspondingly the retrospection appears to exaggerate the effect of this most recent

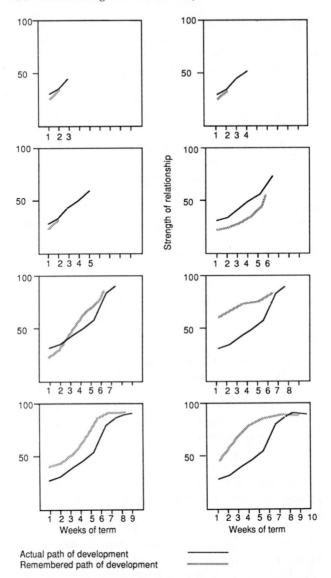

Figure 4.2   Example of a relationship's actual and remembered path of development – person VP's close male friend

development, displacing in both time and magnitude the recall of the increase which occurred in week 6. This effect continues in week 8, which sees only a slight reduction in the rate of increase of week 6 having been either forgotten or recalled as having occurred prior to the onset of the testing period. In week 9 the curve has levelled out and the recalled increase reappears, but still displaced in time owing to the exaggeration of this most recent event of the rate of increase dropping to zero. A continuation of this curve (very slightly decreasing) in week 10 exaggerates the horizontal character of the retrospection even more noticeably.

The recency effect thus concerns the tendency for the most recent changes in the strength of the relationship to be exaggerated in the overall retrospection – either increasing or decreasing the majority of retrospective values. An analysis of retrospections revealed that clockwise changes in the recent development of a relationship led to an overall increase in the values allocated to the previous weeks of development, anti-clockwise recent changes led to an overall decrease, and any other types of changes (e.g. linear increase or decrease, no change) did not increase or decrease the absolute levels of the values recalled for previous weeks. This is illustrated in Figure 4.3 by means of three examples. In the first, the shift in actual scores between two weeks, a and b, is anti-clockwise and increasing. If this most recent event is exaggerated, say by one week, the overall retrospection is decreased for all its values even though its relative shape may be otherwise unchanged. The second example shows that a clockwise increasing shift in the actual score produces an overall increase in retrospection values. The third and final example on Figure 4.3 is included to show that no change in the overall values of the retrospection need follow a linear increase (or decrease) in the actual development of the relationship.

Analyses suggested that at least two-thirds of all changes in retrospections conformed to this model, and thus it appears to be a useful and an important finding. It begins the process of describing some regular pattern of 'bias' in retrospective reports, rather than continuing to view memories of relationship development as error prone in an unpredictable, haphazard and methodologically problematic way, as many researchers have done.

The regular biases in retrospective reports established by the present study are very largely those that were predicted by an analysis of schematic processing and, in particular, by the hypothesized 'relational schemata' which guide the gathering, processing, storage and retrieval of information about social relationships. The schemata operate, as do other types of schema, by *structuring* information, allowing decisions to be made about what is and is not relevant information, enabling inferences to be drawn about missing information and that implied 'between the lines' of existing information, and acting as a prompt for retrieving previously stored information.

This structuring is achieved primarily by the simplifying and categorizing of relevant information, both of which processes were in evidence in the retrospective evaluations made by individuals in the present study. The process of simplification of information about the relationship's development was seen most clearly here in the 'smoothing out' of the course of development illustrated by the extension model. Clearly, individuals simplified the previous development of the relationship, but in a manner

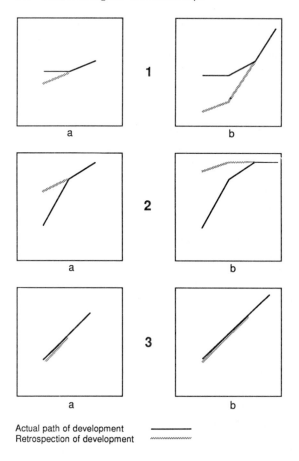

Actual path of development   ————
Retrospection of development   ∿∿∿∿∿∿

Figure 4.3 Examples of the recency effect on recall

consistent with their current schema for that relationship, rather than in any random way. Individuals seemed to assess the current state of the relationship and its most recent changes (if any) and then simplify the path of previous developments in line with this assessment. They appeared to smooth out those particular features that were less relevant to the current state of the relationship, whilst maintaining some level of accuracy in their recall for the general pattern of development. Information about the relationship's development as a *process* (i.e. as progressing, declining or stable) was clearly influential in the construction of their retrospections, as indeed Wilmot and Baxter (1983) had suggested it would be.

The categorization of relevant information as another means of structuring it is seen in the processes of 'filling in' missing information and in the alterations made to previously stored information in line with current feelings. Both of these processes were also evident in the retrospections made by individuals in the present study, as revealed in the 'recency effect' analyses. As predicted, individuals constructed complete retrospective reports based on recent changes and current feelings, even although the actual values associated with previous weeks' ratings were not recalled. Instead, retrospective ratings consistently reflected a general tendency to be increased or decreased as a result of particular changes in the most recent stage of the relationship's development.

The results of this study thus clearly support the view of memory for relationships proposed at the outset of this chapter as being an active, interpretative process, where the events of the past are *reconstructed*, rather than reproduced, in the context of current events, i.e. of schematic processing at a relational level. However, although the results suggest that indeed some form of relational schemata may bé employed by individuals, the details of this schematic processing have only begun to be uncovered. Many questions have been raised and yet remain to be answered by future work. For example, the influences on the recall of significant features in a relationship's development, such as peaks and troughs, have not been clearly described or explained by this study, as there were insufficient examples in the sample. In order to gather more examples of these features in future studies, it might be necessary to examine relationships that are more established or to consider an alternative design for the study. It might, perhaps, be possible to ask individuals to fill in a graph each time they perceived a change in their relationship (rather than every week), for a necessarily limited data collection period. In this way, it might be possible to extend the data collection period without increasing the work-load for an individual, making the likelihood of collecting data on significant features greater and focusing on these features more directly.

A further issue which remains to be addressed is that of the nature and influence of *prospective* reports of relationship development. With partners who know each other better than the individuals in this study, who have more relevant information on which to base these 'guesses' at the rela-tionship's future form, some very interesting and important findings might emerge about how they are influenced by, and in turn influence percep-tions of current and previous events in the relationship. Is it the case that prospective reports are categorized and simplified in the same ways as retrospective reports, or are particular events and their effects on the relationship anticipated, perhaps themselves influencing the interpretation of recent events in the relationship? This is obviously a rich, untapped area for future enquiry.

Perhaps more difficult to investigate would be the *level of agreement* between the histories of a relationship's development provided by both partners in that relationship. Although the present study began with sever-al pairs of friends in the original forty participants, in none of these pairs did both partners continue all through the ten-week data collection period, and therefore no adequate comparisons between their histories could be made. The data would be interesting, not to establish how 'accurate' either partner was (as true psychological accuracy is determined by reference to the person's own history as perceived at the time and not to another person's view of the events however closely involved that other is), but to illustrate the variety of truths that can exist and interact successfully. If partners view their relationship very differently, how do they co-ordinate their shared understanding and definition of the relationship, or is this unnecessary because they assume they see their relationship in the same way? The role of multiple levels of understanding in relationships, and how these are negotiated by partners, is an area of research that is very much in need of a suitable method of enquiry (Miell and Miell 1986), and this type of data could be of great value here.

These and many other questions remain. However, this study has made an important and necessary step in developing a workable method, procedures and a number of analyses that can be used to further investigate them. The present study has not only begun to shed light on the reconstructive process of memory for relationships, but also has uncovered regularities in retrospective reports that indicate they are not as unreliable and full of unpredictable error as some previous researchers had suggested. In remembering, people are not simply reaching with partial success into a decaying store of old information. Rather, the process is one of constructing and restructuring a view of a relationship which is creating the reality of that relationship.

REFERENCES

Bruner, J.S. (1957) 'On perceptual readiness'. *Psychological Review*, 64, 123–52.

Cantor, N. and Mischel, W. (1977) 'Traits as prototypes: effects on recognition memory'. *Journal of Personality and Social Psychology*, 35, 38–48.

Christensen, A., Sullay, M. and King, C.E. (1983) 'Systematic error in behavioural reports of dyadic interaction: egocentric bias and content effects'. *Behavioural Assessment*, 5, 131–42.

Davis, M. (1973) *Intimate Relations*. New York: Free Press.

Duck, S.W. (1982) 'A topography of relationship disengagement and dissolution'. In S.W. Duck (ed.) *Personal Relationships 4: Dissolving Personal Relationships*. London: Academic Press.

—— and Miell, D.E. (1982) 'Charting the development of personal relationships'. Paper presented to International Conference on Personal Relationships, Madison, July.

Ericsson, K.A. and Simon, H.A. (1980) 'Verbal reports as data'. *Psychological Reviews*, 87, 215–51.

Hamilton, D.L., Katz, L. and Leier, V. (1980) 'Organizational processing in impression formation'. In R. Hastie, T.M. Ostrom, E.B. Ebbesen, R.J. Wyer, Jnr, D.L. Hamilton and D.E. Carlston (eds) *Person Memory: The Cognitive Bases of Social Perception*. Hillsdale, NJ: Lawrence Erlbaum.

Housel, T.J. and Acker, S.R. (1979) 'Schema theory: can it connect communication's discourse?' Paper presented to the Interpersonal Communication Association Convention, Philadelphia.

McCall, G. (1982) 'Becoming unrelated: the management of bond dissolution'. In S.W. Duck (ed.) *Personal Relationships 4: Dissolving Personal Relationships*. London: Academic Press.

—— (1984) 'The organizational life cycle of relationships'. Invited address, 2nd International Conference on Personal Relationships, Madison, July.

Markus, H. (1977) 'Self-schemata and processing information about the self'. *Journal of Personality and Social Psychology*, 35, 63–78.

Miell, D.E. (1984) 'Cognitive and communicative strategies in developing relationships'. Unpublished PhD thesis, Lancaster University.

Miell, D.K. and Miell, D.E. (1986) 'Recursiveness in interpersonal cognition'. In C. Antaki and A. Lewis (eds) *Mental Mirrors: Metacognition in Social Knowledge and Communication*. London: Sage.

Planalp, S. (1983) 'Relational schemata: an interpretive approach to relationships'. Unpublished PhD dissertation, University of Wisconsin-Madison.

—— and Honeycutt, J.M. (1984) 'Events that undermine conceptions of relationships'. Paper presented at the 2nd International Conference on Personal Relationships, Madison, July.

Schank, R.C. and Abelson, R.P. (1977) *Scripts, Plans, Goals and Understanding*. Hillsdale, NJ: Lawrence Erlbaum.

Scott, M.B. and Lyman, S.M. (1971) 'Accounts'. *American Sociological Review*, 46–62.

Taylor, S.E. and Crocker, J. (1981) 'Schematic bases of social information processing'. In E.T. Higgins, C.P. Herman and M.P. Zanna (eds) *Social Cognition: The Ontario Symposium*, vol. 1. Hillsdale, NJ: Lawrence Erlbaum.

Wilmot, W. (1980) 'Metacommunication: a re-examination and extension'. *Communication Yearbook*, 4.

—— and Baxter, L. (1983) 'Reciprocal framing of relationship definitions and episodic interaction'. *Western Journal of Speech Communication*, 47, 205–17.

Winograd, T. (1977) 'A framework for understanding discourse'. In M.A. Just and P. Carpenter (eds) *Cognitive Processes in Comprehension*. New York: John Wiley.

5 Reflection in personal relationships

Rosalie Burnett

> Why he ought to have confidence – in other words, a full and firm
> conviction that his young wife would always love him – he never
> stopped to ask himself.... With his habitual mental control, having
> once deliberated these matters to do with his wife, he did not let
> his thoughts stray further in regard to her. (Leo Tolstoy, *Anna
> Karenina*)

It is not uncommon to hear people in a broken or failing relationship
confess to not having thought much about their situation and therefore not
having noticed problems developing. Similarly, many couples who, though
remaining together, lament the 'loss of sparkle' or 'meaningful connection'
between them may observe that they have fallen into an unthinking
routine in which they take each other for granted. It takes a crisis perhaps
before partners begin to reflect on what is happening, and to become
analytically curious about the complexities involved, and perhaps sensi-
tized to scope for change. The implication here, and in the quotation
above, is that more 'relationship mindfulness' (ongoing awareness, attention, reviewing events, reflective activity) would be constructive.

Yet reflection about relationships is rated low or negligibly in popular
estimation; at least, serious thought or discussion about relationships is
not sanctioned in a way that is true of other topics, such as politics,
religion and literature. Personal relationships – certainly in particular,
but also in general – are ineligible as a subject for public discussion or
shared appraisal. At best, everyday conduct and talk reveals a negligence
of serious thoughtfulness about relationships. While it is acceptable to
make an in-depth analysis of the latest sport event, commendable to make
detailed work plans, and desirable to be intelligently aware of the latest
world events, people do not 'set out' to reflect on their relationships in the

same way; relationships seem to be but a matter for passing thought and casual comment. In so far as it may be evaluated, thinking about relationships (perhaps more so than relationship talk) does not have a good public image. It is liable to be viewed with bemusement or disparagingly, conjuring up images of teenage girls lost in daydreams about romance, bored housewives with nothing more intellectual to engage their minds, or deserted husbands ruminating about what went wrong. According to such stereotypes, having relationships on the mind is an indication of intellectual limitation and narrowness, and a distraction from other more worthwhile pursuits and thoughts. There is some basis for consigning relationship reflection to the level of a time-wasting preoccupation, as with any mental distraction that may intrude into other business, but in doing so there is a danger of assuming that relationships are not worthy of concentrated thought.

The picture presented above of people as generally blank about relationships, and to some extent avoiding the subject, is contrary to the impression which might be gained from the literature on personal relationships. In the present volume, for instance, Weber, Harvey and Stanley are impressed with people's interest and ability in holding forth about their relationships; Livingstone refers to viewers of television soap operas as being knowledgeable about relationships; and Wilkinson's participants made penetrating appraisals of each other, sometimes theorizing in a way that is more subtle and insightful than that of many academics. These positive indications of relationship mindfulness fit with a general representation in the literature of laypersons performing a cognitively active role in their relations. However, I would like to suggest that this prevailing representation is an overestimation of relationship mindfulness; that subjective knowledge is applied superficially (Livingstone would probably agree that the interpretative role of the viewer could be more active and better informed); that willingness to discuss relationships may be the exception rather than the rule (the accounts Weber, Harvey and Stanley discuss were given by people obviously interested, in that they were enrolled on a course about relationships); and that analytical perceptiveness regarding relationships is a specialized interest and capacity (Wilkinson's participants were especially selected for the task). In this chapter, a main objective is to draw attention (in the face of much academic discussion about relationship knowledge) to the negative possibility that we are not particularly 'bright' when it comes to relationships, and to present a more sceptical perspective of mindfulness in relationships. Reflectiveness within and about relationships as an aspect of inadequate interpersonal awareness is discussed, and then consideration is given to how social values might be implicated in this superficiality.

The following is a preliminary look at aspects of relationship reflection: its incidence, its content and its social value, drawing from a project investigating personal relationship explanation and enquiry, and more broadly concerned with interpersonal awareness and understanding (Burnett 1986). Some modest empirical results will be mentioned to remove some of the openness of mere supposition, but the subject-matter presents methodological obstacles, not all of which were successfully surmounted, and therefore the temptation to offer more persuasive and intrinsically fascinating statistical analyses has been resisted. The cognitive activities of interest are grouped under the heading 'reflection' for want of one to serve better, and its usage will be defined for clarification, before going on to discuss whether and when people reflect on relationships; in other words, the incidence of relationship reflection. Next, the content of reflections will be explored; this is not easily separable from antecedent events and thoughts provoking reflection (heuristically labelled 'motivators' here) nor from the thoughts, insights and decisions that emerge (collectively described as 'conclusions' here). The direction of emphasis is away from detailed taxonomy and towards the more significant (socially and psychologically) quantitative and qualitative aspects of reflective activity, concentrating on gaps and inadequacies in reflection, and the implications in respect of mindfulness and awareness in relationships. The intention is to describe some small inroads into a neglected yet crucial area of personal relationship research (Duck 1980; Duck and Perlman 1985); it is hoped to stimulate interest in further investigation, particularly with regard to this as an area for research applications.

There is no single satisfactory term to describe the various cognitive activities I wish to imply. Some other possible labels suggest a process more calculating, detached and divorced from emotion than I intend to denote. As good as any is 'reflection' or 'reflective activity', which has been defined as 'individuals' time *out* of relationships, when they review, evaluate, interpret and assess' (Duck and Miell 1982, p. 238); although I would not want to exclude reflective activities *during* interaction, as a responsive commentary on relationship experience or stimulated by communicative exchanges. I refer essentially to 'thinking about' relationships, but would include here both lone musings and also the thinking that accompanies relationship talk. 'Reflection' is also intended to denote less serious and purposeful thoughts, like fantasies, 'reliving' of relationship experiences, or 'dwelling on' a specific memory linked to a relational encounter; not least because any and all of these may connect along the reflective process. What is required is a cognitive term that stretches from existential enquiry about the meaning of relationships to brooding in thought on a single moment or fixed image of relationship interaction, and is inclusive of a set of semantically similar concepts, more specific or slanted in meaning: pondering, considering, questioning, assessment, appraisal, evaluation, analysis, introspection, contemplation, meditation, and others. The common element is the lingering conscious attention given, but although the label 'reflecting' is being used in the following to cover all of these, a relevant distinction to be made will be between more conscious, searching and purposeful kinds of reflection and the more simple and less deliberate 'having relationships on the mind'.

Subconscious and 'passing' thoughts are excluded for practical investigative reasons, although it is not suggested here that they have no relevance for subsequent events. Rather, to borrow Antaki's categorization in Chapter 6, they belong under the heading of 'unperformable', are hard to reach, yet are 'inarticulately operative on the person's actions and feelings' (p. 98). To discover these and their import, investigation has to take a different route and look to the affective dimension of the mind (see Clarke, this volume; Harré, Clarke and De Carlo 1985). On another level, the practical orientation of this enquiry is such that the reflective activity of interest should be cognitively available – despite and not ignoring affective links – capable of being 'worked on' and extended as part of a person's resources.

THE INCIDENCE AND CONTENT OF REFLECTION

The potential relevance of reflective activity to the subjective creation of relationships is clear (Duck and Sants 1983). It may be that specific relationship experiences are shaped at least as much by participants' views of them as by anything they do, by extrinsic events, and (for which, see Section Three) by culturally constructed meaning in a wider context and over a longer term. A more extreme position is that a person's subjective reality is more creative of experience than objective facts; to argue that an inner view of 'how things are' is more significant than reality of a tangible, measurable kind is harder to dismiss with regard to the minutely eventful potency of some episodes in personal relationships. Even if this stronger line is not accepted, it is less easy to refute that individuals' ideas and theories about relationships in general, and their particular impression and assessment of their own relationships, have a formative role in the nature of events and experiences that follow. (In simple terms, if Jack's assessment of Jill shifts, he's likely to respond differently to her, and their lives could change.) Assuming, then, that a person's reflective activity is creatively involved in relational outcomes, it becomes relevant and important to question the amount and type of thinking people do.

There is however a question to be settled first: do people pause to reflect on relationships? Or, alternatively, does thoughtfulness accompany experience during interaction, such that some kind of accounting, self-reporting or knowledge use is going on all the time? If so, in either case, is such 'mindful' activity regular or rare? In this respect, there is a lesson to be learned from attributional researchers, who, throughout years of accumulating knowledge about attributional processes, neglected the meta-issue of the frequency of attributional activity in everyday life (Bond 1983; Manis 1977). In investigating cognitive processes, there is always a danger of building an image of people as more aware and mindful than perhaps they are, as a consequence of regarding the situationally stimulated and cooperative research subject as typical of the population s/he represents. It is important not to assume that mindfulness is a regular occurrence outside a research setting (Langer 1978), and to look to the possibility that thought-fulness of one type or another may require special circumstances before it is elicited (Lalljee, Watson and White 1982; Wong and Weiner 1981).

In the present research the incidence (the 'if and when') of relationship reflection has been regarded as not so much a meta-issue as a complementary issue to that of content ('how much', 'how thorough', as well as 'what'). In an overlapping way, incidence and content are treated as corresponding to the paired issues of quantity and quality. If it scarcely occurs at all, or only occurs in a limited context, then the implications of its absence or rarity could be more significant than content. Assuming that reflections could make some difference to relationships as lived, it is as important to investigate if and when, and also why, they occur as it is to investigate their nature. Incidence and content are also complementary in the sense that 'when' affects 'why' (incidence), and 'why' affects the content. Accordingly, the extent of reflection in terms of motives, impetus and context, and attitudinal issues in terms of 'why not' have been part of the present enquiry.

There are of course methodological problems, and a necessary tangent must be taken to note them and the limitations they impose on empirical investigation into the issues in question. By definition, unsolicited spontaneously occurring relationship reflections are not directly available to the investigator, and retrospective reports cannot be accepted without some degree of scepticism because of the likelihood that they have been influenced by memory (though see Miell's chapter for a way in which they are informative) and by self-presentational motives, such as a tendency to delete one's errors before recounting the story. The same and other problems apply to obtaining self-report data about context and motive; subjects cannot be expected always to recognize the rationale for their thinking even if they had one, and if they are able to identify *a* cause or *a* reason or relevant context, this does not negate the possibility of others. In research of this nature, it has to be borne in mind that people do not necessarily remember, or know how or want to answer questions truthfully about when and why they reflected on a relationship, except in a rough and ready way, and that they will tend to select only a single answer when perhaps multiple answers would be more correct. Further, as has been indicated, what they impart is a way of representing what they believe, hope or pretend is 'the truth'. Nevertheless, this does not mean that they will not succeed in identifying some authentic threads of thought and putting them into a meaningful context.

Allowing for these domestic truths of research regarding reflections, exploratory data were obtained in a self-report questionnaire study concerned with the incidence and content of reflections. Eighty subjects (forty men and forty women) from mixed social backgrounds and wide adult age-range, were asked which of nineteen personal relationships they had 'recently thought *a lot* about'. They were then directed to select the three (or up to three) best-remembered cases and answer open-ended questions about each:

1   Do you usually think a lot about this person?
2   Was there anything in particular that started you thinking about him
    or her?
3   What were you thinking with regard to him or her?
4   Did you reach any conclusions or make any decisions? If so, what were
    they?

The number of relationships subjects claimed to have thought 'a lot'
about, together with their answer to the first question give some indication
of actual or presented (probably something in between) extensiveness of
relationship reflectiveness. Answers to the other, more open, questions
were categorized. Results are set out in Figure 5.1.

The categorization of what for convenience has been labelled 'motivators', 'content' and 'conclusions' reveals the overlapping nature of each of
these. The division of reflections into this ordinal, linear sequence may
belie a more backwards and forwards loop-like or circular reflective process, with 'content' and 'conclusions' generating more motivating questions, emotions and associations. If the thinking is goal-directed, then the
'conclusion' or end-point may not be clearly separable from the 'motivator' or starting-point. In so far as the starting-point is related to incidence
of reflection, this connectedness of the reflection process is another way in
which content and incidence are complementarily interlinked. For example, imaginings in which the 'content' is about 'one's emotional and
physical desire to be with an absent loved one' could be motivated by the
same (the physical and emotional experience of desire), then lead to
conclusive thoughts about the same (the observation that one is experiencing physical and emotional desire for this person) with the possible result
of escalating or perpetuating those feelings, and thus leading in a circular
way to thoughts of a similar content. This separation of 'reflections' into
the equivalent of a beginning, a middle and an end, is therefore problematic in terms of obtaining data, but there are some different issues involved
and so the distinctions are valid.

It is fair to assume that the number of 'motivators' and 'conclusions'
supplied by subjects has been boosted. That there is a response bias in that
direction is indicated by the number of participants who answered with an
unsubstantiated 'yes' to questions 2 and 4, and by the low number who
gave 'I don't know' (only two) and 'I can't remember' (one) responses,
both of which seem plausible answers under the circumstances. Some
answers are likely to be in response to an unavoidable 'demand characteristic' of such a study; i.e. (however unslanted the questions might be in
favour of a positive or negative response), the possibility that they might
have been reflective in recent days about 'this or that' is raised for them,
and just searching to find out will lead participants to plausible thoughts
that might have accompanied recent events, and which they are then likely
to convince themselves indeed applied. This is perhaps especially true of
the conclusion: revisiting the thought-content may prompt a decision or
conclusive line of thought for the first time, though the participant may

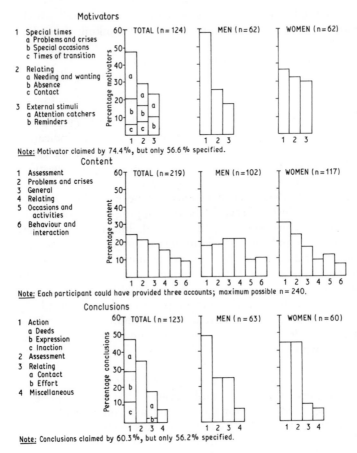

Figure 5.1   Incidence and content of relationship reflections

not recognize this. Thus, the exercise of completing a questionnaire becomes part of the reflective process (we are back with the problem of
investigation producing an enhanced representation of the spontaneous
thinking it wants to discover!).

Motivators

In 219 relationship accounts, 57 per cent were represented as having been
stimulated or motivated by something in particular (74 per cent, if unelaborated 'yes' responses are included, plus those where subjects claim 'I
think about him/her all the time', implicitly identifying the potential circu-
larity from motive for reflection to content of reflection to reflective
conclusion). To help identify the nature of motivators, these have been

organized into seven sub-categories, and then further amalgamated into three main groups (Figure 5.1). These are 'special times' (48 per cent) including negative life events like periods of illness, marital conflict, periods of transition and adjustment like settling into a new job or retirement, and special occasions such as birthdays and weddings; 'relating' (29 per cent), which contains items concerned with forming, renewing and maintaining relationships; and 'external stimuli' (23 per cent), which brings together items that are reminders of the other person, like a photograph or a song, and attention-arousing behaviour, such as the other person's bad temper. Further division of the seven sub-categories reveals that the other's ill-health (including illness during pregnancy and mental illness) is the most frequently mentioned motivator. This, together with most other items under 'special times', corresponds with the pattern, identified by Wong and Weiner (1981), of unexpected or negative events preceding attributional thinking. However, the sub-category of 'special occasions' (14.5 per cent), reverses this case, being mostly expected and positive events (e.g. Christmas, birthdays and anniversaries), though it could be maintained that these are infrequent enough to be regarded as novel (Lalljee, Watson and White 1982). Identification of attraction, loneliness and missing other's contact, as motivators, is relatively rare (22 per cent in combination); since these are the only items that focus on self, the 'motivators' group appear to emphasize, surprisingly maybe, a concern with other's needs.

The range of motivators is somewhat wider than previous studies in attribution research have suggested, not being confined to unexpected or negative events – though these are prominent. It is informative to note what is missing or not much in evidence among claimed reasons and provocations to reflect. More often it is the other's rather than self's predicament that leads to reflection, but the problems involved are problems of major proportions rather than the more transient troubles of day-to-day. Positive behaviour and actions are seldom identified: it is as if they are taken for granted, in keeping with the theory that events have to be unexpected or aversive before they are noticed. Similarly, in a study by Abele (1984) on social cognitions, subjects reported less thinking when events were going well or were normal; but, for them, it was subjectively important events – usually negative – that stimulated cognitive activity, rather than the unexpected. In the present analysis, there is no indication of the media, or educational discussion or any other more impersonal and objective sources acting as provokers of thought. One possible explanation for this is that these more extrinsic motivators are not among plausible causes and reasons for thinking about one's own relationships.

Content

Reference has already been made to the continuity between 'motivator', 'content' and 'conclusion'. In an obvious sense, all belong to content, and the separate questions invited an artificial division or the possibility of repetition. However, the 'content' section is in effect the 'central issue' of the account. The layout and relevant question ('what were you thinking about?') invited more detail than for other sections, and the responses were accordingly slightly longer, though certainly not as long as might be expected, the significance of which will be returned to later. The majority of participants confined themselves to bare statements; only 12.5 per cent gave accounts of more than twenty-five words.

The various subjects participants mentioned in response to being questioned about the 'content' of their reflections were classified into six groups (Figure 5.1). Longer accounts containing elements of more than one category were sorted according to the principal theme. In order of frequency, the six subject groups are: 'assessment' (25 per cent), 'problems and crises' (21 per cent), 'general' (19 per cent), 'relating' (15 per cent), 'occasions and activities' (11 per cent) and 'behaviour and interaction' (9 per cent). Many of the 'assessment' category are about the person (8 per cent) as opposed to the relationship, and usually take the form of bald statements of opinion or feeling about the other, e.g. 'How kind she is', 'I was thinking that he's unco-operative.' The largest sub-category for this group, and for content as a whole, concern assessment of the relationship (11 per cent), again usually unelaborated, e.g. 'about our friendship and where it was going'; 'just what a good wife and mother she is and that I couldn't do without her'. There were significantly more women than men making evaluative references of this kind. This will be returned to, together with other differences between the reports of men and women participants.

'Problems and crises' contains items comparable with the similarly named sub-category under 'motivators'. The largest sub-category here is ill-health (10 per cent). With respect to the group named 'relating', which is concerned with starting, sustaining and renewing relationships, 6 per cent referred to desired or anticipated contact, e.g. 'I was thinking just that I would like to see her more often.' 'Occasions and activities' nearly corresponds with the motivator sub-category 'special occasions', except that the former is more inclusive in the way suggested by the name. The 'behaviour and interaction' group primarily consists of references to either the other's negative behaviour (5 per cent) (e.g. 'about her taking my money'), or to conflict (2 per cent) (e.g. 'about why we can't get along better').

The variability in length of the 'content' section could be a function of presentational style or a strategy for participating in such a study, with the shorter contributions belying a possible depth and detail of thought that the longer reports begin to show. That is, the distinction may be simply a matter of styles of reporting and degree of willingness to disclose. Compare for instance 'I was speculating about the direction of the relationship', which may just be a caption for lengthy contemplation, with the following more revealing account:

This woman cohabits with a long-term friend of mine, so my first thought is that, if I were to have some kind of affair with her, I would be doing to my friend what my wife's lover did to me. Since I have suffered a lot as a result of my wife's lover's conduct, then surely I must nip in the bud all feelings that I have for this woman. Surely. And yet I am tempted to try to push things just a little bit further. Do I love her? I don't know. She's physically presentable, though not as attractive as my wife. What really attracts me to her is her mind, to which mine responds and we strike mental sparks off one another – that never happened with my wife. I admire the way she holds down a high-powered executive job; the way she paints and plays the violin; the way she copes with the demands of her family; her excellent cooking, her flair in entertaining, her linguistic skills, and many other talents. Even if I don't love her, she is more or less my ideal woman. But to attain her I would have to do the dirty on my friend. And this I cannot do. Or can I? What does she think of me, I wonder? I know that she likes me and enjoys my company, but since I have discovered that my feelings were more than friendly, we have not been alone together. There have, however, been special hugs and squeezes as well as kisses on meetings and parting.

Accounts were more typically (unlike the above) in the form of summary statements after the event, and so do not reveal anything of the stream of consciousness involved. Reports like that above may be a first verbalization of more abstract awareness of a situation or, like the usual more truncated responses, may themselves be summaries of much lengthier inner monologues. The problem here is in determining whether shorter responses were limited by a lack of original reflectiveness, or by other constraints. The methodology was conducive to more extended accounts; it is therefore fair to suggest that in general, despite other possibilities, relationship reflections are privately not well articulated and are unsustained. The lack of detail and explication found was despite the fact that participants were able to complete the questionnaire anonymously and unhurriedly in their own place and time. Some of the lack of detail must be attributable to unequal ability to communicate via the written word, but in addition, paucity of words indicates at least in some cases a tendency for reflections to be pre-verbal, superficial and lacking in complexity.

Conclusions

Of the 60.3 per cent of accounts for which 'conclusions' were claimed, 56.3 per cent were treated as valid. The rest were unsubstantiated 'yes' responses or a report of a concluding or next event, e.g. 'he's got a letter to go into hospital' as opposed to a finishing point to the matter of reflection referred to under 'content'. Again, in describing the types of conclusions mentioned, it is helpful to sort responses into groups. Those found lend themselves into three-way grouping (Figure 5.1): 'assessment' (35 per cent), 'action' (47 per cent) and 'relating' (18 per cent). Many of the items that make up the 'assessment' category (which is comparable to the same named category under 'content'), are statements of appraisal or evaluation regarding what the other person is like or might be feeling (15 per cent), e.g. 'She's very affectionate and outgoing'; 'She's never satisfied.' Less frequently (7 per cent), they comprised an evaluation of the relationship or mutual feelings, e.g. 'We love each other very much'; 'I felt we had a very safe and good friendship which would last a long time.' An equal percentage (7 per cent) are about self or other's view of self, e.g. 'I'm sure they are happy about what I'm doing.' Conclusions in this group are relevant to making sense and are self-directed, as distinct from action-oriented and other-directed, or else they affirm general appraisal of or feeling about the other or the relationship.

The 'action' category contains three subgroups, which are 'deeds' (23 per cent), 'expression' (21 per cent) and 'inaction' (11 per cent). 'Deeds' includes reports of what should be or has been done, e.g. giving money, advising, praying and, especially, some form of communication. Items in this category are usually positive and constructive, though by way of exception one refers to contemplated suicide, and another to taking violent action. A minority revealed a more detailed plan, revealing something approximating a problem-solving approach. An example is (to help a friend 'with a basic I'm not okay attitude'), 'Give him more responsibility; make him feel more part of his peer group; praise his work more often.' Another such example is (with regard to conflict between mother and daughter), 'Try not to lose my temper with her and keep my cool and keep a firm eye on her. Let her know who is boss, but at the same time let her know that I love her.' 'Inaction', in contrast to the above, consists of comments like 'decided there was nothing I could do about it', 'wait and see', 'keep up the same' or 'leave him to deal with it'. The 'expression' sub-category contains conclusions concerned with self-presentation and items that are more about emotional display towards other than about action, e.g. 'don't show feelings', 'smile more', 'be sympathetic and affectionate'.

The 'relating' category items are primarily about making contact with other and the form such contact should take, whether visiting, phoning or writing, e.g. 'decided to write but avoid meeting her', and, as such, this could have formed another subgroup of the 'action' category. This group is appropriately separated, however, because it corresponds with the 'relating' category among the 'motivators' group, and because the relevant items generally refer to doing something outside of or removed from action within a relationship – i.e. with making relationships or reforming them, e.g. 'I'm going to try and become friends with him.'

Content and conclusion link with each other in the case of problem-solving or goal-directed reflectiveness. However, there are other types of reflection that would not necessarily be intended to lead anywhere, such as fantasizing or reminiscing. Given that the majority of accounts (60.3 per cent) are reported as being conclusive (i.e. the conclusion question is answered) and, further, given that accounts are biased towards action and problem-solving, it would appear that people's relationship reflections are (a) not aimless, and (b) more practical than theoretical, more forward-looking than retrospective, and more pinned to reality than fantasy. There was a male–female differential in reported conclusiveness (men = 66.7 per cent; women = 54.7 per cent); similarly there was a greater percentage of motivators claimed by men (men = 82.3 per cent; women = 67.5 per cent). The impression to be gained from this result is that men are more rational and more decisive in their thinking. It is also possible that this effect is produced by a combination of the cultural expectation that men act decisively, and a 'demand characteristic' to resolve the issue when faced with a question about conclusion. Another artefact, which is an extension of that mentioned above, is relevant to useful implications rather than reliability of results. There is some indication that being directed to the possibility of conclusive or purposeful reflection may have a constructive value. Some subjects (4 per cent) answered 'no' to the conclusion question, but then nevertheless went on to supply a 'conclusion': asking themselves the question rounded off the reflection. Aiming for a tentative decision or resolution is likely to be of particular value where negative feelings are involved. A few participants, for instance, recognized the potential destructiveness of negative emotions which accompanied their reflections, as in the following case where some photographs of a boyfriend's ex-fiancée had aroused strong jealousy:

> I have to make myself think that it is not important and believe me I am trying very hard! I'm going to try and dismiss these jealous feelings, and think of what we have and tell myself that it is better than they ever had. I'm going to try and not take it out on him. Because I was, and I even started to dislike him – I am not fair to him sometimes. I am going to love him more.

Indications

The results of the reflection study suggest that personal relationships are thought about frequently but superficially. The nature of the analysis unavoidably leaves scope for alternative interpretations with regard to the incidence and content of relationship reflection. The possibilities, for instance, that participants were writing-shy or disclosure-shy or have short memories could each be relevant to the sparseness, in general, of reported thoughts, i.e. participants could be held back from showing just how thoughtful they are by these plus other obstacles and aversive factors (to be discussed). Conversely, the invitation to share reflections is an encouragement of *ex post facto* thoughtfulness, and few people would want to present themselves as not having thought about any of the relations listed. It could be argued, therefore, that these data *either* understate *or* overstate the extent of reflective concerns. On balance, it seems more plausible that the reports are an exaggeration of the case in the general population, in that participants, as volunteers, are motivated to perform positively – to 'come up with something'; in this respect they are not representative.

The indications for frequency are higher than for depth and length of content. According to self-report, the incidence is high; from the relationships they were asked to select from, subjects claimed to 'think a lot' about 34 per cent, and they claimed to 'often think a lot' about 68 per cent of the people/relationships they selected for accounts. Whatever the thoughts then, this suggests that our familiar others are frequently 'on the mind'. When considered against the nature of the reported 'content' though, this does not allay suspicions that much of this reflectiveness amounts to shallow musings and easily reached conclusions, in place of anything more contemplative or analytical. There are many petty and simple issues that are easily resolved, but it is not as if relationships are unproblematic! If people are as frequently but casually attentive to relationships as this study suggests, it may just be that their consciousness of these others is comparable to the kind of awareness we have for 'background music' – occasionally drawn to it but otherwise only appreciating it in a very limited way.

The content of most reported reflections is superficial and empty of detail. Given that there is an emphasis on unpleasant predicaments of 'other' and what action to take on their behalf on the one hand, but lack of detail on the other hand, people impress as thoughtful more in the caring sense of the word rather than the philosophical sense. Reflections are set in a framework of concern for others plus purposefulness (i.e. 'motivators' and 'conclusions'), but are apparently limited in complexity and length. As has been indicated, reflection can take numerous forms, including fantasy, reminiscing, replaying, planning, description, explanation, problem-solving and assessment, and there was some evidence of all of these, especially the last two. There are some notable sex differentials suggested by the results, but these can be most usefully addressed in the next section together with the implication of socialized attitudes and values. The overall indications are that, despite there being a general tendency to think a lot about people in relationship to oneself and about specific relationship matters, this thinking is not as inquisitive, sustained, substantial or as explicitly goal-oriented as it might usefully be. An attention to subtleties and detail is missing, yet it is these on a day-to-day basis that affect the quality of relationships and satisfaction with them.

MOTIVATIONAL AND AVERSIVE FACTORS

Why do relationship reflections tend to be impoverished and casual and mainly linked to major events, special times and generalized relationship wants and need? This general conclusion is supported by other analyses in the same research project (Burnett 1986). A step towards explaining this involves considering motivational factors as they relate to both participation in relationship research and to private and shared relationship reflections. Some insights regarding possible blocks or deterrents against thinking and communicating about relationships can be drawn from another linked study (Burnett 1984), and from looking at results regarding sex differences in reflection and associated attitudes in the context of relevant social values.

Attitudes to thinking and communicating about relationships

Follow-up data regarding attitudes to providing relationship accounts was collected in respect of seventy-seven participants, after they had been asked to write an account in the form of a simulated letter to a confidant about 'what your relationship with X is like'. An equivalent version of the same questionnaire was given to five participants (all men) who eventually declined to provide the account. The items and the resulting means from rating scales are shown in Table 5.1.

The three items participants rated most highly were 'difficulty of relationship explanation', 'effort in thinking of a reply' (i.e. to the general question about the relationship), and the view 'that relationships should not be discussed with outsiders'. The order was the same for both men and women, although men's ratings indicated that these were significantly more problematic for them. The first two of these items indicate the degree of difficulty in verbalizing and organizing views and knowledge regarding a relationship, perhaps being required to conceptualize about them in detail for the first time. 'Effort in thinking of a reply' can be distinguished from the effort involved in writing it, with the separate problems that comprises, because this was queried as a separate item. The third item suggests some sensitivity about communication in general, as opposed to about the specific relationship to be explained, but this sensitivity seems to be more related to respect for the other's privacy than a case of embarrassment on one's own behalf: ratings for embarrassment are lower. 'Disinterest in personal relationships in general' and 'embarrassment about the relationship in question' were the least applicable items.

There were some significant sex differences both in respect of this attitudes study (Table 5.1) and the reflection study (Figure 5.1). These are mutually informative, and are explicable with reference to cultural and intellectual values, which in turn inform the present enquiry about how much 'relationship thinking' people do. Men appear to be more reticent in respect of communicating and thinking about relationships. They rated all the attitude items more highly than did women; in other words, they indicate that they are less inclined to communicate and think about relationships than are women. (Both Wilkinson and Miell, this volume, evidently found women more willing participants in their studies.) The

Table 5.1 Means for men and women comparing inclination to think and communicate about personal relationships

Items	Men (n = 41)	Women (n = 36)	p (2-tail)*
Relationships in general (PRs)			
Rarely think about PRs	3.49	2.69	0.01
Prefer not to analyse PRs	3.67	2.81	0.005
Embarrassed writing about PRs	2.84	2.40	0.09
PRs are difficult to explain	4.43	3.46	0.001
PRs shouldn't be discussed with outsiders	3.80	3.07	0.02
Don't know much about PRs	3.21	2.77	0.09
Not interested in PRs	2.30	1.76	0.03
Not useful to analyse PRs	2.60	2.02	0.05
Own specified relationship (X)			
Prefer not to think about X	3.09	2.39	0.03
Embarrassed writing about X	2.32	1.71	0.02
Distressed writing about X	2.13	2.07	0.79
X is complicated	3.35	2.98	0.32
Very little to say about X	3.32	2.92	0.17
X is uninteresting	2.84	2.98	0.63
Task of writing about relationship			
Much effort to think of reply	3.89	3.12	0.01
Much effort to write reply	3.47	2.66	0.01
Uncomfortable in task	2.49	1.91	0.03
Bothered by write to confidant instruction	3.29	1.94	0.000

* Significance levels for *t*-values
Note: The higher the score, the greater agreement with item.
Rating scale 1–7 where 1 = in no way applies, and 7 = fully applies.

most significant differences are in respect of 'writing to a confidant', 'difficulty in explaining relationships', 'preferring not to analyse personal relationships'. Further, men are more silent with regard to relationship communication. The sex bias with regard to writing an account has already been mentioned. Male and female participants were drawn from the same source (psychology department subject panel), and could have been expected to be equally committed, yet the difference in return of accounts (or simulated letters in this case) is highly significant: thirty-seven women wrote seventy-five 'letters', i.e. 97 per cent of those requested, and forty-six men wrote fifty-six 'letters', i.e. 68 per cent of the total requested (the numbers of participants includes replacements for one female 'drop-out' and ten male 'drop-outs' in an extended study).

The same imbalance is evident in the reflections study; a variety of people participated drawn from different backgrounds and not connected with the psychology department. Females supplied 117 accounts, i.e. 97.5 per cent of those requested, and males provided 102 accounts, i.e. 85 per cent of those requested. The most striking sex differences to emerge from the reflections study, as can be seen in Figure 5.1, are that women are considerably more concerned with assessment (of both persons and relationships) than men, whereas men are rather more concerned with 'relating' – the business of forming, keeping and maintaining relationships in the basic sense of meeting and making contact. It could be said, in summary, that men are more bothered about the practical enabling aspects that make relationships possible regardless of what goes on within them, whereas women care more about monitoring and evaluating the intrinsic relationship events and experiences. In the reflections study, men presented themselves as more aware of where their reflections originated than did women, and the categorization indicated that men are more reflective about problems and crises, although overall women show more reflectiveness in relationships. The greater tendency of women to evaluate and assess is in keeping with the results regarding their more positive attitude to relationship analysis, and the extra thinking that they do about relationships in general. In a further study dealing with interests and concerns (Burnett, in preparation), women claimed to 'think' more, as well as 'know' and 'talk' more about their own closest relationship, although both sexes claimed to 'care' equally.

A reluctance or wariness on the part of men to engage in relationship talk has been noted by others (e.g. Hodson 1984); and explanations have been offered for masculine disadvantage with regard to intimate relationships (e.g. Miller [1983] with respect to male friendship) and emotional expressiveness (Naifeh and Smith 1985). At the same time, a number of studies have dealt with contrasts between concerns and philosophies of men and women, indicating the ways in which these are obstructive to harmonious intimate relationships (e.g. Eichenbaum and Orbach 1984; Gilligan 1982). The common view emerging is that the usual system of child care, being divided unequally between men and women, perpetuates differential effects on gender identity and also maintains the status quo regarding acceptable male and female qualities and values, and even their language (see Gergen and Gergen, this volume, for a fascinating discussion of a related theme). The question of differential reflectiveness and an unequal degree of readiness to communicate about relationships are presumably connected. If people are disinclined to discuss something, they may be similarly blocked in their thoughts about it. As Berenson suggests in her chapter, caring about something and arriving at an understanding are connected.

An explanation for the relatively low levels of reflection and relationship interest, especially amongst men, indicated by the present enquiry, can be summarized in terms of a cycle of devaluation–distancing–disregard concerning the subject. From a historical perspective (again see Gergen and Gergen), the separation of male and female concerns, and the construction of scholarship by men for men, has resulted in a strange anomaly whereby matters of personal relationship have been excluded, or have been re-formulated so that they are recognizable only under another heading. The separate aspects have all been the object of some school of thought, or division of science, but it is only now with the emergence of personal relationships as an academic discipline (Duck and Perlman 1985) that an integral subject can be seen. Thus for instance, it has been possible for psychologists, philosophers, anthropologists and the like to construct a science of enquiry into human nature whilst simultaneously leaving learn-ing about relationships (as we live them day by day) to chance. An intellectual tradition that has distinguished between 'soft' and 'hard' scien-ce (Hudson 1972) must be implicated in the neglect (avoidance?) of emotion by scholars (the chapters by Clarke and Berenson are both re-levant here). The academic edifice and the family socialization system referred to above have distanced people, especially men, from the more thought-provoking aspects of person-to-person affairs.

There is too, as another factor averting attention from relationships: the intrinsic emotional dimension, which, because it is so potentially revealing about the individual, threatens to expose the more vulnerable, less 'male' characteristics and lead to loss of face. Thus distanced, the 'curiosity motive' (Koestler 1978) has been directed elsewhere, and the value system with force has been one which has denigrated conventional female qual-ities and morality (Gilligan 1982), prohibited as unmanly a need for affec-tion, security and intimacy (Skynner and Cleese 1983), and shamed men into silence and unawareness about relationships. A passive approach to learning about relationships continues into adulthood and into effortless but often failing personal relationships. Now that it has become an academic discipline, the elevated status of 'personal relationships' as a subject to be taught and investigated will perhaps break into this devalue–disregard cycle, escalating the rebalancing of values that is threatening to take place (e.g. Goldberg 1983; Rubin 1983).

IMPLICATIONS AND APPLICATIONS

Some reflections accompany or become the topic of communication, but most reflective activity occurs in an unspoken dimension of relationship experience, where understanding (if it exists) is tacit, knowledge is intuitive and insights are felt rather than said. Baxter, in this book, holds that indirect cueing as opposed to explicit communication is functional, allow-ing individuals room for manoeuvre. Relationships are complex, uncertain things and have need for this openness. However, some inexplicitness may be attributable to an inability to articulate the relevant information, or restraint arising from attitudes hostile to bothering in any kind of deliber-ate way with matters of relationships. Not talking can be linked with not knowing, and the uncertainty that is met by indirectness and ambiguity may be thus increased, leading to more inexplicitness and ambiguity, and so forth. Lacking both the interest and the additional knowledge arising from discussion, the issues become difficult to conceptualize. The implications are that much of the relevant thinking is aimless and, like the interactions Baxter mentions, imprecise. A case can be made for more relationship mindfulness, even if it does mean (or perhaps partly because) that individuals may have to answer more for themselves.

Clearly, there are some kinds of relationship reflectiveness that are not to be advocated: no one profits from obsessional or depressed brooding or incapacitating preoccupation, and to be endlessly thoughtful without knowledge or awareness may lead to relationship failure just as effectively as thoughtlessness. However, the more constructive or purposeful kind of reflection (monitoring, noticing, reviewing, planning, etc. – not impressively in evidence in the present investigation), providing it is matched by a readiness to adapt and change, is a necessary accompaniment to relationship awareness.

At a time when people are expecting more from relationships, but simultaneously are increasingly more likely and more free to end them (e.g. Morley 1984; Rubin 1983), and given the evidence on benefits of good relationships to health and happiness (e.g. Gove, Hughes and Style 1983; Leavy 1983), the value of greater relationship awareness and appreciation is clear. A necessary and useful application of personal relationship research is indicated. It is timely to foster and encourage an interest in 'relationships' as a subject for basic yet more formalized education and learning. More specifically, a habit of being reflective, in the constructive way indicated, can be encouraged as part of this education, and in therapy groups. There may be a case for relationship-consciousness raising, literally. An increase in relationship knowledge and a change of attitudes to the value of personal relationship education will be likely to increase constructive thoughtfulness within relationships, providing useful information and insights and also the concepts to make explicit the understanding that is often only intuitive or tacit.

As an experimental project in the encouragement of relationship interest and self-critical reflectiveness, the author has recently provided relationship-understanding courses for probation and after-care service 'clients', selected for attendance because of their relationship difficulties. These courses were not especially demanding in terms of time or intellect, as befitted the educational and motivational level of most (mainly compulsory attendance) of the participants; however, merely attending stimulated what was claimed to be an uncustomary attentiveness and orientation of mind: 'Now that I come to think of it . . .' and 'I haven't looked at it that way before' were typical commentaries on the relationship observations made.

There is likely to be some scepticism about the idea of teaching or encouraging people to be more reflective in relationships (in the sense of monitoring, appreciating and being more consciously aware of daily relationship events) on the grounds that such reflectiveness would be disruptive, calculating and inauthentic. But we can find some basis for reassurance in the precedent of social skills training, the success and merit of which is now beyond question (e.g. Spence and Shepherd 1983). As with social skills training, concern about disruptiveness resulting from acting deliberately and calculatedly is only relevant to initial stages when new habits of mind are being acquired. But people can surely be taught to be more attentive and appreciative in relationships, just as they can be taught, say, to listen to and recognize more in music, thus in the long-term enhancing their enjoyment and understanding of it. And, just as newly learned social skills can become part of one's authentic response pattern, so an appropriate thoughtfulness can be learned and practised so that it becomes a characteristic way of responding in personal relationships.

The credo underlying this discussion is that interpersonal awareness could be heightened by an increase in thought, discussion and learning about relationships. To understand their own relationships individuals need detailed knowledge about each other (Peters 1974) at the same time as being emotionally responsive and emotionally aware (Berenson 1981 and this volume). Beyond one's own relationships, more formal learning and discussion about the nature of intimate interpersonal life in general is appropriate. The 'ups and downs' of relationships colour and define the quality of private lives and have shared public consequences; therefore the issues involved are profoundly serious – so long as they are regarded as 'soft' in the intellectual world, and in ordinary life are only to be found in the 'women's department', then we must expect to be often at a loss when attempting to account for relationships. A start is to appreciate and place value on the scope for more thought.

REFERENCES

Abele, A. (1984) 'Thinking about thinking: causal, evaluative and finalistic reasoning in social situations'. *European Journal of Social Psychology*, 15, 315–32.

Berenson, F. (1981) *Understanding Persons: Personal and Impersonal Relationships*. Brighton: Harvester Press.

Bond, M.H. (1983) 'Cross cultural studies of attribution'. In M. Hewstone (ed.) *Attribution Theory: Social and Functional Extensions*. Oxford: Blackwell.

Burnett, R. (1984) 'Thinking and communicating about personal relationships: some sex differences'. Paper presented at the Second International Conference on Personal Relationships, Madison, Wisconsin.

—— (1986) 'Conceptualisation of personal relationships'. Unpublished DPhil thesis, Oxford University.

—— (in preparation) *Intimate Awareness: Thinking, Knowledge and Understanding in Personal Relationships*. London: Methuen.

Duck, S.W. (1980) 'Personal relationship research in the 1980s: towards an understanding of complex human sociality'. *Western Journal of Speech Communication*, 44, 114–19.

—— and Miell, D. (1982) 'Towards an understanding of relationship development and breakdown'. In H. Tajfel (ed.) *The Social Dimension: European Perspectives on Social Psychology*. Cambridge: Cambridge University Press.

—— and Perlman, D. (1985) 'The thousand islands of personal relationships: a prescriptive analysis for future explorations'. In S.W. Duck and D. Perlman (eds) *Understanding Personal Relationships: An Interdisciplinary Approach*. London: Sage.

—— and Sants, H.K. (1983) 'On the origin of the specious: are personal relationships really interpersonal states?' *Journal of Social and Clinical Psychology*, 1, 27–41.

Eichenbaum, L. and Orbach, S. (1984) *What Do Women Want?* Glasgow: Fontana/Collins.

Gilligan, C. (1982) *In a Different Voice: Psychological Theory and Women's Development*. Cambridge, MA: Harvard University Press.

Goldberg, H. (1983) *The New Male–Female Relationship*. London: Coventure.

Gove, W.R., Hughes, M. and Style, C.B. (1983) 'Does marriage have positive effects on the psychological well-being of the individual?' *Journal of Health and Social Behavior*, 24, 122–31.

Harré, R., Clarke, D.D. and De Carlo, N. (1985) *Motives and Mechanisms: An Introduction to the Psychology of Action*. London: Methuen.

Hodson, P. (1984) *Men: An Investigation into the Emotional Male*. London: BBC, Ariel Books.

Hudson, L. (1972) *The Cult of the Fact*. London: Jonathan Cape.

Koestler, A. (1978) *Janus: A Summing Up*. London: Hutchinson.

Lalljee, M., Watson, M. and White, P. (1982) 'Explanations, attributions and the social context of unexpected behaviour'. *European Journal of Social Psychology*, 12, 17–24.

Langer, E.J. (1978) 'Rethinking the role of thought in social interaction'. In J.H. Harvey, W.J. Ickles and R.F. Kidd (eds) *New Directions in Attribution Research*. Hillsdale, NJ: Lawrence Erlbaum.

Leavy, R.L. (1983) 'Social support and psychological disorder: a review'. *Journal of Community Psychology*, 11, 3–21.

Manis, M. (1977) 'Cognitive social psychology'. *Personality and Social Psychology Bulletin*, 3, 550–66.

Miller, S. (1983) *Men and Friendship*. London: Gateway Books.

Morley, R.E. (1984) *Intimate Strangers: A Discussion of the Elements in the Generation, Preservation and Disintegration of Relationships and Marriage*. London: Family Welfare Association.

Naifeh, S. and Smith, G.W. (1985) *Why Can't Men Open Up?: Overcoming Men's Fear of Intimacy*. London: Muller.

Peters, R.S. (1974) 'Personal understanding and relationships'. In T. Mischel (ed.) *Understanding Other Persons*. Oxford: Blackwell.

Rubin, L.B. (1983) *Intimate Strangers: What Goes Wrong in Relationships Today – and Why*. Glasgow: Fontana.

Skynner, R. and Cleese, J. (1983) *Families and How to Survive Them*. London: Methuen.

Spence, S. and Shepherd, G. (1983) *Developments in Social Skills Training*. London: Academic Press.

Wong, P. and Weiner, B. (1981) 'When people ask "why" questions, and the heuristics of attributional search'. *Journal of Personality and Social Psychology*, 40, 650–63.

Section Two

Accounting in use: functions, action and communication

6 Performed and unperformable: a guide to accounts of relationships

Charles Antaki

Like most of the contributors to this book, my theme is people's own accounts of relationships. I want to see if there is a way we might catalogue the variety of things that go under the name of an 'account', and to see how we might catalogue the variety of uses to which psychologists put them. What I don't want to do is tackle the question (raised by Harré and Secord [1972]) of whether the accounts that people give ought to be used as the method of choice in investigating social action; instead I want to assume that the question is open, and discuss more neutrally the range of meanings of 'accounts' and the range of options open to the researcher. To stretch the two ranges out, I shall examine performable and unperformable accounts: by this I mean, on the one hand, the sort of account that is articulatable and can be examined as if it were a conscious social device, and, on the other hand, the sort of account that is unavailable for social performance, and needs to be examined as an inarticulatable mental representation. The contributions to this book range over quite a variety of 'accounts', as indeed is the case in the literature. Since there is such a great deal of ambiguity in researchers' use of the term 'account', I think it might be worth at least having two extremes clearly separated.

PERFORMABLE AND UNPERFORMABLE ACCOUNTS

If we stretch out the distinction, we have, on the one hand, a performable account that is a version of the relationship the person could choose to broadcast (say, the account an aggrieved spouse might give to friends). On the other hand, an unperformable account is one that exists quietly and is inarticulately operative on the person's actions and feelings. It is a mental representation of the relationship that is cognitively unavailable for public consumption.

The distinction is worth making, I think, even though one can press on very successfully with a definition of an account that amalgamates the two interpretations. Harvey *et al.* (1986), who give an excellent review of attributions in relationships (and see Weber, Harvey and Stanley's treatment of accounts in relationship decline in this volume), see accounts primarily as self-reports, but self-reports that have a variety of motivations, from the 'quest for understanding and control', through 'the presentational motive' to 'emotional release'. The reason why I want to separate out performable from unperformable accounts here in this chapter is because the eclecticism of Harvey *et al.*'s (1986) treatment is, compared with much of the literature on accounts, rather uncharacteristic. There is what looks like an unbridgeable gap between those who see an account as a social interaction (like, say, apologizing or promising) and those who see it as a private, unconscious cognition (like, say, recognizing a face or judging the length of a line).

The visibility and the symbolic role of performed accounts make them a prominent candidate for study in relationships; but, clearly, the hidden accounts, through their operation on the person's actions and feelings, are no less important for a full picture of what accounts mean in people's lives. Nevertheless there is a feeling in some quarters of social psychology that the hidden accounts are, since they seem to have no interpersonal context, somehow less social than the others; and, to return the compliment, there is a feeling on the other side that performed accounts – though anecdotally appealing – have a merely epiphenomenal reality with little to say in the prediction of behaviour.

I think both of these views are rhetorically useful in marking out territories of research, but both have an element of overstatement. Of course there are things about a performed account that are of little interest to the cognitive psychologist (in the sense in which the term is currently used), and there are things about the mechanics of information-processing that will not interest the person concerned with social performance and symbolic interaction. But there are things in the middle. It may be that a personal relationship of a certain intensity will bring hidden accounts to consciousness and, from there, to visibility; and it may be that what seems, on the face of it, to be a clear matter of automatic judgement turns out to be affected by such performance considerations as the audience, the respondents' mood, and so on. The sense that people make of the relationships in which they happily or unhappily find themselves is liable to a wide range of influence, and there is enough overlap for there to be some point in each camp's knowing about the other's work.

Harvey *et al.* (1986), in talking about accounts as reports of relationships, and specifically about attributional accounts of the end of relationships, comment that they 'provide clues about the individual respondents, the groups with whom they are involved, and the historical contexts surrounding them ... they also provide clues about the gamut of psychological processes attendant to the termination of close relationships' (p. 190). This is a very useful framework to adopt for accounts generally. Altering Harvey *et al.*'s emphasis slightly, and using the analogy of a performance, we can crudely say that there are three kinds of thing to talk about in accounts: first, the stage (things to do with the context in which the account is given); second, the actor (the giver of the account); and third, the audience (the receiver of the account). Note that this theatrical kind of language looks rather symbolic-interactionist, but I only mean it as one way of cutting up the account cake. There are other ways: one could cut it so that, for example, one face showed accounts as *reports* (truthful or otherwise) and another showed accounts as *justifications and excuses* (plausible or not). These are important distinctions, and we shall see more of them below.

THE CONTEXT OF ACCOUNTS IN RELATIONSHIPS – WHEN, WHERE, BETWEEN WHOM, AND WHY?

Asking questions about the stage on which the account is performed (its social and psychological context) tells us a good deal: an account given in a therapeutic context will be different from an account given to colleagues at work, an account given in the heat of the moment will be different from one given in affectionate reminiscence, and so on. The most obvious difference is between accounts as *reports* and as *justifications*: the context of the account will prompt the person to give either what is first and foremost a sense-making account – an account the psychologist can use to get at what was going on in the event being explained – or, on the other hand, an account that is first and foremost an interpersonal action in its own right (see Harré [1979, pp. 127–8] for discussion of this distinction in ethogenic terms). Reports and justifications crop up in different places and in different times, but no hard and fast rules are likely to be useful here. Instead we can try out three coarse-grained descriptions that match various treatments of accounts in the literature.

The clinical setting

A good place to start is with the distinction between those accounts that occur in interactions positively set up to elicit accounts (therapy sessions, research interviews, and so on), as opposed to those that appear in the course of some other activity. The role of accounts in such set-ups is dealt with in the clinical literature, especially in the work on the process of the clinical encounter. There is also a growing attributional literature (which we shall come to below) that uses what people say in clinical and quasi-clinical interviews to analyse their problems and make predictions about their situation. The difference between an account given in a context like this and one given in the course of normal life is that here the account is 'off-line', as it were; out of the heat of the relationship and in the retrospective cool of a supportive encounter between 'expert' and 'client'. The ostensible reason for the account is to analyse the client's problems. Broadly speaking, all this is liable to encourage an account as a report.

Of course there may be other, self-presentational aspects to it, and there is a very interesting body of work in the communications field (see e.g. Jacobs and Jackson 1982, 1983) which thinks of any conversational account as being an attempt made by one party to convince the other. In relationship accounts this has a very obvious application to the hidden self-presentational aspects of ostensibly neutral reports, and the analogy of an account as a persuasive interaction reveals very useful questions about accounts, such as the way they are ordinarily verified, accepted and negotiated (see Jacobs and Jackson 1983; McLaughlin, Cody and Rosenstein 1983).

The relationship setting

In the heat of the relationship kitchen, Duck comments that 'processes of judgment, attribution, communication, attempts at interpretation and evaluation of the partner and so on [are] ever-present in all relationship activity' (Duck 1984, p. 167). If he is right, then some kind of private, if not public, accounting is going on all the time. His proposal is that it is mostly an internalized and unperformed activity: 'Such activity is proposed to be largely conscious, private, evaluative' (Duck 1982, p. 11) although, as we shall see, the results of this activity can be shared – willingly or not – with the partner.

With specific reference to causal attributions, Harvey and his colleagues have been at the forefront of research into self-reports in relationships. Harvey *et al.* (1982) note that 'attribution may take many forms at different stages of a relationship' (p. 109). In the beginning, partners may be accounting – to themselves – for things like the attractiveness of the other person and so on. Later, when things start to go wrong (and, as Wong and Weiner [1981] and Lalljee, Watson and White [1982] point out, it is the novel and unexpected that prompts attributional work), the accounts begin to turn outwards. Partners may challenge each other and demand justificatory accounts, or they may use their accounts to broadcast their version of the relationship to their friends: 'Divergences in attribution about important matters (e.g. how much time each person devotes to the need of the other) may become more pronounced ... and these ... understandings may in fact be communicated to third parties who in turn may reinforce them' (Harvey *et al.* 1982, p. 109). Such an account can be done to help the person 'go back and "flesh out" the characters and events so that they can *predict* the outcome' (Harvey *et al.* 1986, p. 193). Equally, the account can break through to public performance, as we shall see below; consciously or not, the account can, like an aria in an opera, serve the function of moving the action along.

The public setting

Duck (1984, p. 169) gives us a useful diagram of the development and decline of a relationship. This paints perhaps too precisely rational a picture of what, to the actual participants, must seem like a rather messy process, but it serves us well here by capturing the role of accounts in the relationship's decline, showing the points when they may reach the public wavelengths.

You can see, from Figure 6.1, that partners will engage in account-giving at various points in their relationship – especially when the relationship has become critically unsatisfactory. Duck has picturesquely described five phases in the dissolution of a relationship: the breakdown period, when things carry on, but unhappily; the intra-psychic phase, where partners privately brood; the dyadic phase, where the brooding breaks out into open, confrontational (justificatory) accounting; the social phase, when accounts (this time accounts as reports) are shared and solicited from others; and, finally, what Duck morbidly but memorably calls the 'grave-dressing' phase. In this most public of report, 'the partners and their relevant networks construct publicly negotiable accounts of the course of the dead relationship and create an agreed history for the relationship and its demise' (Duck 1984, p. 167).

THE ACCOUNT-GIVER

The second thing we can think about is what goes into the actors' performance. Performing an account is no easy or trivial matter. To make sense, the accounter must respect all the rules common to any communication – especially what have come to be known as the Gricean maxims of co-operation, informativeness and so on (see e.g. Grice 1975). Refusing to give an account is no escape from the problem, since one risks looking stubborn or worse; Leudar and Fraser (1985) show some of the consequences (see also Baxter in this volume). Account-givers, whether in public performance or in their private reflections (for which see Burnett's chapter) are limited by the information available to them in particular, as individuals, or in general, as humans with cognitive limitations. Certainly there is a place here for experimental research of the type exemplified by recent anti-introspectionist writings, though perhaps not many social psychologists would go quite so far as to say, along with Nisbett and Wilson (1977) that people simply do not have any access to their higher cognitive processes.

Whether or not these cognitive doors are closed to them, it is certainly the case that people's access to ordinarily articulatable aspects of their lives is by no means reliable or uniform. People are limited by their degree of

Dissolution states and thresholds	Person's concerns	Repair focus
1. Breakdown: Dissatisfaction with relationship	Relationship process; emotional and/or physical satisfaction in relationship	Concerns over one's value as a partner; relational process
Threshold: I can't stand this any more		
2. Intra-psychic Phase: Dissatisfaction with partner	Partner's 'faults and inadequacies'; alternative forms of relationship; relationships with alternative partners	Person's view of partner
Threshold: I'd be justified in withdrawing		
3. Dyadic Phase: Confrontation with partner	Reformulation of relationship; expression of conflict; clearing the air	Beliefs about optimal form of future relationship
Threshold: I mean it		
4. Social Phase: Publication of relationship distress	Gaining support and assistance from others; having own view of the problem ratified; obtaining intervention to rectify matters or end the relationship	*Either*: Hold partners together (Phase 1) *Or*: Save face
Threshold: It's now inevitable		
5. Grave Dressing Phase: Getting over it all and tidying up	Self-justification; marketing of one's own version of the breakup and its causes	

Figure 6.1 A sketch of the main concerns at different phases of dissolution

Source: Duck (1984), p. 169.

insight; by their explanatory repertoires; and, as we mentioned above, by their reasons and motivations for giving an account at all. Reasons and motivations fall into various types, corresponding to various categories of explanation.

In categorizing explanations of social behaviour, Brewin and Antaki (in press), drawing on Antaki and Fielding (1981) and on Forsyth (1980), divide up reports and justifications into two further sub-categories each. Their four categories are: accounts of what happened (descriptive accounts); accounts of who caused it (agency accounts); and accounts of its propriety (moral accounts) which, in interpersonal situations, shade into accounts used for excuse or justification (self-presentational accounts). One account could be thought of as accomplishing each of the four functions together, depending on which aspect of its context one has in mind, so one should bear in mind that this section is not really separable from the section above.

Descriptive accounts

This sort of account sets the terms of what is going on – in a word, a phrase, a sentence or a book. It can appear as an explicit response to a question (like 'What is going on?', 'What are you doing to me?'). More commonly, it simply appears in the mundane terms someone uses to talk about an act, an event or a state of affairs. Jill may accuse Jack of having too many late nights. Jack may deny that they are 'late nights' and claim that he is (simply) 'down the pub' or 'in a bar'. Clearly the participants think that there is a world of difference between the two descriptions of the same activity.

We should acknowledge immediately that, to hark back to our first section, the context – especially the world-knowledge that the accounter assumes her or his audience shares – is crucial. Any description that an accounter gives is, as Gergen suggests (e.g. Gergen 1982) really best understood not as an empirical statement, but as the sense the accounter is making of an enigmatic and endlessly interpretable stream of events. If we are cautious, we shall treat people's descriptive accounts as being at least as likely to be a sense-making attempt at categorizing ambiguity – for which we need to know the accounter's context – as it is to be a clinically accurate representation of the truth about the event, whatever that may be. Of course, one might go so far as to say that, since there is vanishingly little chance of really knowing what the truth is about any state of affairs, one might as well take a completely relativistic approach and dismiss any description but the accounter's own. This galloping relativism has its attractions, but this is not the place to pursue the question of whether they outweigh the problems of arbitration and prediction. The discussion of descriptions of actions and psychological entities in general can be followed up in Gergen (1982, 1984) and, with respect to descriptions of personality in particular, in Hampson (1983). With respect to relationship accounts, Gergen and Gergen's chapter in this volume very neatly makes the case for seeing accounts as being bound far less by 'fact' than by linguistic, social and cultural convention. To make their argument crude, they argue that accounts are narratives; narratives are stories; and stories are, well, stories.

Let us carry on with the cautious feeling that there may be little the psychologist can do to verify, even at leisure and with documentary evidence and so on, people's descriptions. What we can see is that the position of someone actually inside the relationship must be still more difficult, especially if the partner holds to a different, rival description. Suppose partner A asks partner B 'What is going on?' B has been given a very strong card to play: the description of the event narrows the channels of discussion, and the explainer can find her- or himself heading in unintended directions. For example, B can say 'We are going through a bad patch'; if this is accepted by A then a co-operative causal analysis will seem to be worthwhile, and the transient nature of the circumstances will seem to suggest that transient causes are likely to be discovered – all prefiguring some kind of rapprochement. If, on the other hand, B more pessimistically says 'It's the beginning of the end', it will be all too clear to both parties that things are probably beyond help.

Talking about descriptive accounts this way suggests that their role is to be one of the many ways that people regulate and negotiate their relationships. While it is true that they are powerful agents of performed regulation (compare describing your absences from home as 'overtime at the factory' and 'getting away from the blasted kids' – both of which might be true), they also, obviously, play a part in automatic or unperformed accounts. Simply as a matter of logic, the person has to have some kind of working description of what he or she is doing, or what the other person is doing, to be able to make any causal sense of it. An automatic attribution for the cause of a partner's behaviour needs to be preceded by the person making a judgement about what it is that the partner is actually up to. It is true, though regrettable, that attribution workers have tended to ignore this axiom, and that most laboratory attribution research is done on events that are predigested by the experimenters and presented to respondents on an unnegotiable piece of paper. This too is something which, fortunately or not, we haven't the space to pursue here. (In parenthesis, it is very well worth noting the efforts of Newman [1981] to broaden the vocabulary here, and her paper is recommended reading.)

Accounts of agency

This has traditionally been the focus of attributional treatments, which, until comparatively recently, have tended to see accounts as being literal judgements of the causality of a given event. This has had to be liberalized, as we shall see in the section below, and more concern is nowadays taken with the interpersonal context of attributions. Intriguingly, this was the original intention of attribution theory's 'father', Fritz Heider. He had wanted, in his seminal book *The Psychology of Interpersonal Relations* (1958), to throw light on relationships, as the title shows; yet it was not until the work of Orvis, Kelley and Butler (1976) that an empirical study of accounts in relationships came through to catch attribution workers' attention. Orvis, Kelley and Butler found that when asked to comment on events that had led to 'attributional divergences' (times when they had disagreed about the cause of something), partners would explain the other person's behaviour relatively dispositionally, whereas they saw their own behaviour as comparatively situationally determined or amenable to some kind of justification. This actor–observer pattern was unusual in that it was found using people's verbatim accounts, rather than with more abstract rating scales common to the area (see Watson's [1982] review of the actor–observer difference). It is worth bearing in mind, though, that the underlying theme of the respondents' attributions, though ostensibly merely causal, may well have had distinctly moral overtones, given the nature of the interpersonal arguments they were explaining (ranging over 'nearly a complete summary of "ways to aggravate, frustrate, threaten, anger or embarrass your partner"' [Orvis, Kelley and Butler 1976, p. 370]). A similar study by Harvey, Wells and Alvarez (1978) looked at verbatim attributional accounts for more important conflicts in a relationship and here it was found that couples apparently don't know they have different causal attributions for events – a surprising finding. The examination of how partners attribute causality for events in their relationships is turning into a popular area for research. Attention is turning to attributions which more clearly pack a punch of evaluation and morality, as we shall see in the next section.

Accounts of morality

The account that someone gives when some kind of moral evaluation is being made (or might be made, unless the account neutralizes it) needs to be thought about in rather different terms from mere attributions of causality. After all, there are many ways of justifying oneself without actually making a causal statement. Sykes and Matza (1957), Scott and Lyman (1968) and, more recently, Schonbach (1980) and Tedeschi and Riess (1981) give lists of ways it might be done. Table 6.1 shows Semin and Manstead's (1983) typology of all of these plus one or two of their own.

Most of the entries in the table are clear enough. We need only pick out an example of an excuse and a justification. Suppose partner A has said something rude to partner B's best friend. Partner A might try the excuse that they didn't *mean* to be rude (A1: denial of intention). If the description of rudeness is undeniable, then partner A is driven back to try a justification: perhaps that the best friend deserved it (B2: appeal to principle of retribution). There is much to be thought out in this area of accounting, and the reader will find a great deal of interest in Semin and

Table 6.1 A synthetic typology of accounts

A   EXCUSES

A1 *Denial of intent* ('I did not intend to produce these results')
    Accident
    Unforeseen consequences, due to:
    – lack of knowledge
    – lack of skill or ability
    – lack of effort or motivation
    – environmental conditions
    Identity of target person mistaken

A2 *Denial of volition* ('I did not want to perform this act')
    Physical causes:
    – temporary (e.g. fatigue, drugs, illness, arousal)
    – semi-permanent (e.g. paralysis, blindness, deafness)
    Psychological causes originating in:
    – self (e.g. insanity, overpowering emotion)
    – others (e.g. coercion, hypnotism, brainwashing)
    Lack of authority ('I would like to help you, but I do not have the authority
        to do so')

A3 *Denial of agency*
    Mistaken identity ('It wasn't me, honest')
    Amnesia ('I can't remember anything about it')
    Joint production ('It wasn't only me who did it')

A4 *Appeal to mitigating circumstances* ('I am not entirely to blame')
    Scapegoating – behaviour in question was a response to the behaviour or
        attitudes of another or others
    Sad tales – selected arrangement of facts highlighting dismal past

B   JUSTIFICATIONS

B1 *Claim that effect has been misrepresented*
    Denial of injury (no harm done)
    Minimization of injury (consequence only trivially harmful)

B2 *Appeal to principle of retribution*
    Reciprocity (victim deserving of injury because of his/her actions)
    Derogation (victim deserving of injury because of his/her qualities)

B3 *Social comparison*
    (Others do same or worse but go unnoticed, unpunished or even praised)

B4 *Appeal to higher authority*
    Powerful person(s) commanded
    Higher status person(s) commanded
    Institutional rules stipulated

B5 *Self-fulfilment*
    Self-maintenance (catharsis, psychological or physical health)
    Self-development (personal growth, mind expansion)
    Conscience (acted in accordance with)

B6 *Appeal to principle of utilitarianism*
    Law and order
    Self-defence
    Benefits outweigh harm

B7 *Appeal to values*
   Political (e.g. democracy, socialism, nationalism)
   Moral (e.g. loyalty, freedom, justice, equality)
   Religious (e.g. charity, love, faith in deity)
B8 *Appeal to need for facework*
   Face maintenance ('If I hadn't acted like that I would have lost credibility')
   Reputation building ('I did that because I wanted to look tough')

Source: Semin and Manstead (1983).

Manstead (1983) and the other sources mentioned above. S/he may also like to browse through the very interesting but more technical literature on legal and jurisprudential treatments of such accounts (a good place to start is with Hart and Honore's magisterial book [1959], and, for a more social-psychological treatment, Lloyd-Bostock [1983] is an excellent source).

In the attribution literature, conceptions of mere causal attribution are, as we noted above, being liberalized to cope with the obvious importance of moral evaluations in accounts. Blame, rather than causal agency, is the key here; an important treatment of this theme is given in Fincham and Jaspars (1980).

For our specific concerns, the changing times are captured by Fincham (1985), who takes the bold line that 'attributions of fault or liability are pivotal in relationships' (p. 212). He suggests that we consider the degree of satisfaction in the relationship and exactly what kind of attributions the partners are asked to make. With these guiding principles, we can make sense of a number of intriguing findings. For example, Fincham and O'Leary (1983) found that distressed spouses rated causes of negative behaviour as more global, while non-distressed spouses considered causes of *positive* behaviours as more global. Other findings indicate that these attributions have a behavioural effect, and are not merely leisured armchair retrospections: Doherty (1982), for example, found that newlywed wives' tendency to attribute their husbands' behaviour to unpleasant intentions or traits also tended to be seen to criticize him more often and to respond angrily to his coercive statements. The reader is referred to Fincham (1985) for an up-to-date review.

THE AUDIENCE

The third question is: what can we learn about accounts from how audiences receive them? We noted above that the giving of an account is inseparable from the context, and the same applies to receiving one, so all that was said in the first section bears on what will be said here. It is also the case that all four types of explanation (description, agency, morality and self-presentation), which we used to catalogue what the accounter did, apply equally well to what the audience has to do. Let us assume that what we said about context and type of explanation applies here, and turn in this section to consider how accounts are decoded.

The audience is assumed by the accounter to be able to decode what the account means and, routinely, audiences manage to interpret accounts as acceptable or unacceptable, complete or incomplete, serious or sad, intelligible or unintelligible. But this is by no means an easy matter; apart from all the communicative skills the audience has to have (to which we referred above), the audience has to know all pertinent strands of the relationship's history, and all the personal as well as the general criteria by which the account could be judged sensible. The prime thing I want to stress in this last section is that partner A has to make guesses – perhaps quite sophisticated ones – at what partner B thinks, and about what partner B thinks that partner A thinks.

This kind of metaknowledge quickly gets confusing, so let's take a look at a couple of concrete cases from two very different domains corresponding to the difference between a justificatory context and a reporting context. In the first, the account the person gives is meant to smooth over a hiccup in his (professional) relationship; in the latter, the context is a friendly one in which the account is meant to explain something about the person's relationship. The extracts below are from Svartvik and Quirk's (1980) corpus of surreptitiously recorded conversation. In the first one, A, a senior academic, demands an account from his junior, B.

A(1):   ... I'd like to be frank with you ... since you were here last
B(1):   erm
A(2):   when you were interviewed for a job here
B(2):   hm hm
A(3):   I've heard from a number of sources that you have said in a [3 or 4 syllables unintelligible] that you think that you did not get the job because of me
B(3):   Oh, no, I have never said that .... In fact I went to great pains ... will be perfectly frank with you: I went to great pains to put it about quite publicly that you were the one who was in fact supporting me in the interview with Professor Pitt
A(4):   I find it very strange that, er, people
B(4):   No, I have certainly not. That is one, that is one charge on which I am absolutely not guilty
A(5):   well I'm very glad to hear it because ... you are
B(5):   Absolutely not guilty
A(6):   you are absolutely right saying that
B(6):   you
A(7):   I was the one who supported you I was
        (Svartvik and Quirk 1980, pp. 374–5, punctuation added and phonological information omitted)

The interaction goes smoothly on after that. Note how the challenge was led up to, A(1), expressed, A(3), vociferously denied, B(3), half-repeated, A(4), redenied, B(4) and finally accepted, A(5). This is a very compact and neat version of an account interaction (see Schonbach [1980] for a full description of the ramifications it can get into). Its clarity is perhaps unusual: the challenge in A(3) is direct, and the account in B(3) is an equally direct denial. Examples of accounts like this make it look almost redundant for the psychologist to say anything. But we can point out a couple of things that will help us when we turn to a less obvious case. Look at A(4) and B(4). B has just expressly and fulsomely denied the charge, but A rather ambiguously says: *A(4): I find it very strange that, er, people.* To which B replies: *B(4): No, I have certainly not. That is one, that is one charge on which I am absolutely not guilty.* What B says seems an over-emphatic reply to what, out of context, is just a report of A's state of mind. Presumably B has to know something like this: that A knows that his report of his puzzlement would be understood by B as revealing that B's initial denial was insufficient to set his (A's) mind completely at rest. With this appreciation of what A has in mind, B can and does proceed with more proof of his case (actually, he just repeats his denial, but this seems to work). There is more to it than that, perhaps; e.g. A might have wanted to retreat a little from the outright challenge he gave B, and A(4) may be intended to emphasize A's reliance on other people as the source of the accusation. In any conversational exchange there is a great deal beneath the surface, as of course ethnomethodologists and sociolinguists have been telling us for decades.

Gergen and Gergen, in their fascinating structural treatment of relationship narratives (Chapter 15), make the point that an account *counts*. Accounts can be performed in order to take someone somewhere; to paraphrase Austin, the Gergens suggest that people 'do things with accounts': the narrative form can amuse, implicate, propagandize and everything else, not just inform and excuse, as was the case in the example above. 'Narrative accounts are more like invitations to a dance than mirrors of reality' (p. 274), as they put it; and the following example shows the neat synchrony – and sidestepping – in accounts that the simile suggests.

In this conversation between two women, A has the occasion to give an account of the state of her relationship with a man with whom she went to a play:

> A(1): I said nah, let's go and see it ... and it was quite funny, we really quite enjoyed it in fact
> B(1): oh Time Out's [a review magazine] never right
> A(2): No
> (Both laugh)
> A(3): we .. we had already agreed that it wasn't a good thing to go by, but ...
> B(3): yeah .. so you've been seeing him a lot
> A(4): (coughs) No, about once a week

B(4): Is it all sort of fast and furious?

A(5): No, it's definitely not fast and furious. He's the laziest bugger I've ever come across, I think

B(5): (laughs)

A(6): whenever we do anything, I have to go and meet him at the pub outside the hospital, and I hate meeting people in pubs .. and even more, I hate walking into th.. hospital one

B(6): mm ... yeah

A(7): four thousand people all watching who you're meeting

B(7): yeah

A(8): and then we went for this .. went to the theatre .. we went for a meal afterwards at .. erm .. oh, place in Baker Street
(Svartvik and Quirk 1980, pp. 693–4, punctuation added and phonological information omitted)

From there, the narrative turns to restaurants and then to other matters. The account that B casually asks for, *B(3): yeah .. so you've been seeing him a lot*, is met initially by A cooling it down somewhat: *A(4): (coughs) No, about once a week*. But B presses on with a more direct question: *B(4): Is it all sort of fast and furious?* A has to make a direct reply to this. The account she then gives – very much a narrative, in the Gergens' sense – is emphatic, and raises a laugh from B; from then on, A is allowed to move smoothly into her feelings about pubs in general and this pub in particular, evading any detailed answer to the question. Yet one has the feeling that B will have picked up a working idea of A's relationship with the fellow about whom she is so affectionately abusive. A presumably knows this, and feels able to move on to other matters; she has some idea of what B will accept as an intelligible and satisfactory account.

Now clearly this kind of analysis is highly subjective, and it is difficult to know how we could ever validate the kind of interpretations I have made of the participants' metaknowledge; working with verbatim accounts is not easy. Nevertheless, if we attend to the kind of metaknowledge that seems to be necessary for the interaction to proceed, we can make one or two stabs at understanding how the account is decoded. We unfortunately have no space to look into this question here, but you may like to have a look in Antaki and Lewis (1986) for more on the subject.

CONCLUDING COMMENTS

I've clambered up various hillsides to take a look at the terrain of 'accounts', and to see how the crowd of people interested in accounts forms into various groupings on it. The map I've drawn is dominated by the fissure between performed and unperformed accounts, but this is partly a rhetorical divide, and researchers on either side have – or ought to have – much in common, as I've tried to point out. The map is partial and bound to be incomplete in various ways, and the reader may want to go to the various sources I've mentioned and check for herself or himself how the land lies. In addition to other chapters in this book itself, which should be primary reading, I would particularly recommend Harvey *et al.* (1986) and Fincham (1985), for excellent sources on the attributional perspective, and Semin and Manstead (1983), and perhaps Antaki (1981), for more general views about accounts.

REFERENCES

Antaki, C. (ed.) (1981) *The Psychology of Ordinary Explanations of Social Behaviour*. London: Academic Press.
—— and Fielding, R.G. (1981) 'Research into ordinary explanation'. In C. Antaki (ed.) *The Psychology of Ordinary Explanations of Social Behaviour*. London and New York: Academic Press.
—— and Lewis, A. (eds) (1986) *Mental Mirrors: Metacognition in Social Knowledge and Communication*. London and New York: Sage.
—— and Naji, S. (1985) 'Because ... in conversations'. Paper presented to BPS Social Psychology Conference, Cambridge, September.
Blumstein, P.W. (1974) 'The honouring of accounts'. *American Sociological Review*, 39, 551–66.
Brewin, C.R. and Antaki, C. (in press) 'An analysis of ordinary explanations in clinical attribution research'. *Journal of Social and Clinical Psychology*.
Doherty, W.J. (1982) 'Attribution style and negative problem solving in marriage'. *Family Relations*, 31, 23–7.
Duck, S.W. (1982) 'A topography of relationship disengagement and dissolution'. In S.W. Duck (ed.) *Personal Relationships 4: Dissolving Personal Relationships*. London and New York: Academic Press.
—— (1984) 'A perspective on the repair of personal relationships: repair of what, when?' In S.W. Duck (ed.) *Personal Relationships 5: Repairing Personal Relationships*. London and New York: Academic Press.
Fincham, F.D. (1985) 'Attributions in close relationships'. In J.H. Harvey and G. Weary (eds) *Attribution: Basic Issues and Applications*. New York: Academic Press.
—— and Jaspars, J.M. (1980) 'Attributions of responsibility: from man-the-scientist to man-the-lawyer'. In L. Berkowitz (ed.) *Advances in Experimental Social Psychology*, vol. 13. New York: Academic Press.
—— and O'Leary, K.D. (1983) 'Causal inferences for spouse behaviour in maritally distressed and non-distressed couples'. *Journal of Social and Clinical Psychology*, 1, 42–57.
Forsyth, D.R. (1980) 'The functions of attributions'. *Social Psychology Quarterly*, 43, 184–9.
Gergen, K.J. (1982) *Towards Transformation in Social Knowledge*. New York: Springer-Verlag.
—— (1984) 'Aggression as discourse'. In A. Mummendey (ed.) *The Social Psychology of Aggression*. New York: Springer-Verlag.
Grice, H.P. (1975) 'Logic and conversation'. In J.L. Morgan (ed.) *Syntax and Semantics*, vol. 3. New York: Academic Press.
Hampson, S. (1983) *The Social Construction of Personality*. London: Routledge & Kegan Paul.

Harré, R. (1979) *Social Being*. Oxford: Blackwell.
—— and Secord, P. (1972) *The Explanation of Human Behaviour*. Oxford: Blackwell.
Hart, H.L.A. and Honore, A.M. (1959) *Causation in the Law*. Oxford: Clarendon Press.
Harvey, J.H., Wells, G.L. and Alvarez, M.D. (1978) 'Attributions in the context of conflict and separation in close relationships'. In J.H. Harvey, W.J. Ickes and R.F. Kidd (eds) *New Directions in Attribution Research*, vol. 2. Hillsdale, NJ: Lawrence Erlbaum.
——, Weber, A., Yarkin, K. and Stewart, B.E. (1982) 'An attributional approach to relationship breakdown and dissolution'. In S.W. Duck (ed.) *Personal Relationships 4: Dissolving Personal Relationships*. London and New York: Academic Press.
——, ——, Galvin, K.S., Huszti, H.G. and Garnick, N.N. (1986) 'Attribution in the termination of close relationships'. In R. Gilmour and S. Duck (eds) *The Emerging Field of Personal Relationships*. Hillsdale, NJ: Lawrence Erlbaum.
Heider, F. (1958) *The Psychology of Interpersonal Relations*. New York: John Wiley.
Hinde, R.A. (1979) *Towards Understanding Relationships*. London and New York: Academic Press.
Jacobs, S. and Jackson, S. (1982) 'Conversational argument: a discourse analysis approach'. In C.A. Willard (ed.) *Advances in Argumentation Theory and Research*. Illinois: Southern Illinois University Press.
—— and —— (1983) 'Strategy and structure in conversational influence attempts'. *Communications Monographs*, 50, 285–304.
Lalljee, M., Watson, M. and White, P. (1982) 'Explanations, attributions and the social context of unexpected behaviour'. *European Journal of Social Psychology*, 12, 17–24.
Leudar, I. and Fraser, W.I. (1985) 'How to keep quiet: some withdrawal strategies in mentally handicapped adults'. *Journal of Mental Deficiency Research*, 29, 315–30.
Lloyd-Bostock, S. (1983) 'Attributions of cause and responsibility as social phenomena'. In M. Hewstone (ed.) *Attribution Theory and Research*. New York: Academic Press.
McLaughlin, M.L., Cody, M.J. and Rosenstein, N.E. (1983) 'Account sequences in conversations between strangers'. *Communication Monographs*, 50, 102–25.
Newman, H. (1981) 'Interpretation and explanation: influences on communicative exchanges within intimate relationships'. *Communication Quarterly*, 123–32.
Nisbett, R.E. and Wilson, T.D. (1977) 'Telling more than we can know: verbal reports on mental processes'. *Psychological Review*, 84, 231–59.
Orvis, B.R., Kelley, H.H. and Butler, D. (1976) 'Attributional conflict in young couples'. In J.H. Harvey, W.J. Ickes and R.F. Kidd (eds) *New Directions in Attribution Research*, vol. 1. Hillsdale, NJ: Lawrence Erlbaum.
Schonbach, P. (1980) 'A category system for account phases'. *European Journal of Social Psychology*, 10, 195–200.
Scott, M.B. and Lyman, S. (1968) 'Accounts'. *American Sociological Review*, 33, 46–62.
Semin, G.R. and Manstead, A.S.R. (1983) *The Accountability of Conduct: A Social Psychological Analysis*. London and New York: Academic Press.
Stratton, P., Heard, D., Hanks, H.G.I., Munton, A.G., Brewin, C.R. and Davidson,

C. (1986) 'Coding causal beliefs in natural discourse'. *British Journal of Social Psychology*, 25, 299–313.

Svartvik, J. and Quirk, R. (1980) *A Corpus of Conversational English*. Lund, Sweden: Gleerup.

Sykes, G. and Matza, D. (1957) 'Techniques of neutralisation: a theory of delinquency'. *American Journal of Sociology*, 22, 664–70.

Tedeschi, J.T. and Riess, M. (1981) 'Verbal strategies in impression management'. In C. Antaki (ed.) *The Psychology of Ordinary Explanations of Social Behaviour*. London and New York: Academic Press.

Watson, D. (1982) 'The actor and the observer: how are their perceptions causally divergent?' *Psychological Bulletin*, 92, 682–700.

Wong, P. and Weiner, B. (1981) 'When people ask "why" questions, and the heuristics of attributional search'. *Journal of Personality and Social Psychology*, 40, 650–63.

7 The nature and motivations of accounts for failed relationships

Ann L. Weber, John H. Harvey and Melinda A. Stanley

An account is like a story that contains a rich array of plots, characters, and patterns of interaction (Harvey *et al.* 1986). These stories were first referred to as accounts by Robert S. Weiss (1975) in his well-known work on marital separation. More recently, Harvey *et al.* have theorized that accounts are especially developed or disclosed surrounding the loss of close relationships. Accounts are believed to be important because they may help people make better sense of the loss of these relationships. They also help people to achieve a greater sense of psychological control regarding the loss, and they serve as a pathway for emotional release. Accounts develop over a period of time, are rehearsed and periodically elaborated, and probably stay with us to our graves, although we at times may forget portions of them which then recur in our thoughts when triggered by various stimuli.

The concept of accounts is valuable for psychological research because it involves the examination of real people's self-representations of their real relationships. The study of accounts can be a relatively non-reactive process and it can be undertaken by examining both the written and the oral reports of respondents. Specific examples of written material containing accounts include newspaper articles, musical lyrics, and diary entries.

EXAMPLES OF ACCOUNTS

Diary entries form the basis of Paul C. Rosenblatt's *Bitter, Bitter Tears* (1983), an analysis of nineteenth-century diaries in the light of twentieth-century grief theories. In his book Rosenblatt examines diary entries recounting relationship loss, in an attempt to assess how people coped with grief in the last century, and how that coping process was similar to the coping process employed in grieving experiences of contemporary people. The following account, taken from Rosenblatt's book, illustrates the immediacy of the diarist's pain as she reflects on the death of her husband eighteen months earlier:

> This night finds me solitary and alone in my room, a boarder in my own house. How strange and lonely everything is! ... how I miss the dear, good husband that left me over a year ago for his home with Jesus, but the days are passing swiftly on when I shall meet him there. Happy meeting, blessed day. I have been very busy these holidays arranging my house ... putting away & fixing up my things so I have not lived over & dwelled upon the past so much as usual.
> (Entry of December 31 1874) (Rosenblatt 1983, p. 22)

If the death of a partner provokes acute grief, separation and divorce likewise appear to fuel grief themes in the accounts of modern individuals. Robert Weiss reviews such themes in *Marital Separation* (1975), an analysis of the feelings and behaviors revealed in the testimonies of participants in Weiss's seminars for the separated. The following example captures the intensity of separation distress reported by one seminar participant in his own diary:

> My hands are shaky. I want to call her again but I know it is no good. She'll only yell and scream. It makes me feel lousy. I have work to do but I can't do it. I can't concentrate. I want to call people up, go see them, but I'm afraid they'll see that I'm shaky. I just want to talk. I can't think about anything besides this trouble with Nina. I think I want to cry.
>
> I just went to make myself some coffee. I hardly knew what I was doing. I tried to drink it and couldn't ...
>
> The only thing I seem to be able to do is to write this. As long as I'm concentrating on how I feel, I feel almost all right. I wonder why. I'm scared. I feel almost hunted. (Man, mid-40s) (Weiss 1975, p. 48)

Another seminar participant's account documents the vigilance and insomnia characteristic of reactions to recent separation:

> I am having the most vicious time, not because of anything going wrong in my life especially; there seems to be no problem, except I can't sleep. I can't sleep, and it keeps building and building until I feel really absolutely devastated. I function all right in my job. And I try to schedule things every evening, social things, things like that. But even when I think I've done well, I still can't sleep at night. And I feel awful .... It just shows the power that your mind has over your body.   (Weiss 1975, p. 50)

While account themes may indeed be inspired by intense feeling and recent loss, by death or separation, account-making is a process that continues throughout one's life and relationships. Accounts are formed and used long after grief is spent and loss is "gotten over." Years and years after a loss, a person appears able and quite ready to compose and relate a story of the lost relationship. Perhaps the emotional intensity of the story has faded somewhat over the years, but the poignance and power of the account appears to remain intact.

For this chapter, we solicited accounts, in written form, from older adults who participated in a short course on personal relationships as part of an Elderhostel (older adult continuing education) program in the Southeast US. Volunteers from this program completed surveys of their memories of past relationships, many of their stories reaching back several decades into personal experience. In the following examples culled from our respondents' submissions, note that these accounts may seem less "traumatized" than the "younger" examples above, but they nonetheless show no lack of detail, imagery, or personal meaning.

One respondent, asked to describe her recollection of the final interaction in her lost relationship, said that it was still

> Too painful to remember – the anxious days and nights of intensive care at the hospital.   (Woman, early 70s)

Another recalled with vivid detail her first meeting with her now-deceased husband:

> I met my husband at a Halloween dance. I was with someone else but was introduced to him. Didn't know what he looked like (because of his costume), and when he asked me to dance I kind of didn't want to. During the dancing, he joked some and I thought he was too young. Actually he was two years older. I soon found out that one cannot go by the first meeting. When I met him a week later at another dance, was I ever surprised! We decided in two weeks we'd marry and so we did within four months.   (Woman, mid-60s)

Though an account may be based on an old, long-stored memory, it nonetheless can recall and preserve much of the emotional intensity and immediacy of a very recent experience. The following account seems both to recall and to attempt to explain those early but enduring feelings:

> I was not particularly attracted to him in the beginning. However, as I sat in the car with him along with other students, my palms were sweaty! My heart was pounding. I was confused and didn't understand my reaction, since he had not even touched me or held my hand.... Thinking back on this relationship, (I think) perhaps the flame of love and devotion for one another and the intense sexual desire was more intense due to my husband's travel and long periods of separation. We cherished the time we had together.
>   (Woman, late 60s)

We might expect the memories of lost loves to fade somewhat over time, yet account-making seems to keep alive and revitalize recollections in defiance of the years. One respondent found this to be true of her reminiscence about a relationship that had ended many years ago, before her second marriage:

> (I did feel) tremendous loss when the relationship wavered earlier; when it finally ended, I was already planning to marry someone else. It seems now as I write this that time has magnified, perhaps, my feelings for this man, as happens with women sometimes about their late husbands. I feel softer toward this man than towards my second husband. And it was a good marriage.   (Woman, late 60s)

Sometimes an account of one relationship is hard to separate from another; one story seems to flow into the other, either in chronology or in the tangle of emotions stirred by recall. The following account illustrates how reminiscences about lost loves revives related memories and conflicting emotions:

> When I first met (this young man, almost 50 years ago), I thought he was the best looking man I ever saw . . . . He was so handsome – had a mustache – when he took me out to dinner, I was so proud of him . . . I was nervous . . . (But) he just wasn't interested in a lasting relationship. As I think about it now, he got what he wanted – sex – and nothing more . . . (When the relationship ended) I thought it was the end of the world . . . . . I have never told anyone I had sex before I was married. In those days, you just didn't do things like that . . . . (Later) I was married to the most wonderful man, handsomest man, gentle, kind, loving. We had (many) romantic and wonderful . . . years together. He has been dead (several) years, and I miss him every day – it does not get easier, only harder.
>
> (Woman, early 70s)

Accounts, as we shall further examine, can serve to *explain* recalled events – for the account-maker as well as for the audience. The account-maker can adopt a more understanding perspective when looking back on recalled relationships. Several respondents to our survey felt it necessary to point out the historical context of their remembered loves, by way of explaining the choices they had made and the events they experienced:

> I'm sure I and my contemporaries married on a far different basis than couples do today. Physical attraction was not enough. What were his parents like; what kind of manners did he have; what were his likes and dislikes? It was important, because this was a life-time contract. Mistakes were made of course. However, among the couples I know of my age, I can probably count the divorces on the fingers of two hands. At this point, death is a more likely end to a relationship.   (Woman, mid-70s)

> In a college setting during the great depression years (1931–5), I and most of the men and women I knew were seriously training for a career. With very limited job prospects we did not allow our relationships to develop toward marriage. In those days, living together – "shacking up" – was not accepted behavior in a college town.
>
> (Man, early 70s)

These "explanations" for recalled relationship events point to the usefulness of accounts in providing rationalizations of recalled actions and events. By far the most frequently sounded theme among our survey respondents' stories was justification or clarification of past choices and actions. Some of this takes the form of bitter but resigned balancing out of the costs and benefits of the relationship's end:

> I feel cheated. I put in the hard years of helping a man get ahead, bore his children, raised them, and then find myself alone and unable to enjoy the fruits of my efforts. On the other hand ... I am financially independent, free to do what I want to do. Still I miss the social life, the summer house, the VIP trips, and a central home for the children to come to on holidays instead of splitting their time between two houses.   (Woman, early 60s)

> I had a feeling of utter failure as a wife but could not manage to be happy in the circumstances, i.e. insecurity, particularly economic. I could not reconcile myself to what seemed to be poverty. ... I suppose I rationalized that this was the only way it could have ended, and further events seemed to justify my earlier actions.
>
> (Woman, late 60s)

Sometimes the justification theme of an account focuses on the lessons learned, both from the relationship itself and from its loss:

> (He) worked for a prominent designer in the next office. I never noticed him much till our first date. (He) taught me to be uninhibited, see myself honestly, appreciate my sense of design. (He) made me feel special – kissed me on the street in downtown Detroit (unheard of in those days). He encouraged me to openly express feelings ... I learned (that) I was a separate entity, to be forthright, and have courage of my own convictions. ... I would not have missed it for the world – nor would he.   (Woman, mid-60s)

Sometimes the account-maker states the lesson or rationalization for ending one relationship and moving on quite succinctly:

> I always wanted a husband and family, so I was willing to take second-best.   (Woman, early 70s).

A further observation we can make about the accounts gleaned by our survey is that while, in general, they are somewhat less emotionally "immediate" than the accounts of the more recently bereaved or separated, they are nonetheless cognitively clear and useful. The survey responses also confirm an aspect of accounts important to interested investigators: people are generally very *ready* and able to relate accounts. Oral and/or written relations are provided so promptly and thoroughly, that it seems the respondent was only waiting to be asked – this account along with many others was right there, just below the surface, poised for practical use. People's personal relationship stories – details and conclusions – are apparently maintained *in* memory though not necessarily comprised exclusively *of* memory. As we shall develop further, accounts seem to be composed of motivation and exposition as well as elements of recall.

THE ROLE OF ACCOUNTS

Harvey *et al.* (1986) discussed the inherently social role of accounts. Accounts are about others, and they are discussed with others. Even in our private ruminations, in our playing back of material and explanations, we review and analyze as if we were making cases to others. In the study of accounts it is not really important whether or not accounts are "accurate" rather it is the *role* played by accounts in the functioning of the individual who uses them that is of primary importance to the psychological researcher. Specific topics of interest include *when* accounts are used, *why* they are used, and the particular *content* of accounts. One can assume that there is a degree of truth in accounts, but their major merit as a psychological concept is in the role that the account plays in psychological experience and functioning. Is this role primarily an expository one? Are accounts defensive? Are they plaintive? These and other roles may be served by account-making. (See Antaki's chapter in this volume for a thorough and inviting analysis of the nature of accounts.)

Harvey *et al.* (1986) link the concept of accounts to Weiss's (1975) reports of people who were in the process of marital separation, as noted above. They also noted the important work of Hunt (1969) concerning records of accounts given by persons reflecting on extramarital affairs in which they had been involved. In the present chapter we will extend the linkage to more recent work that we believe also shows the merit of the account approach. One is Rosenblatt's *Bitter, Bitter Tears* (1983), already noted above, especially in regard to the role of accounts in expressing and working through grief. We also will extend our analysis to another 1983 book, *Excuses: Masquerades in Search of Grace*, by C.R. Snyder, Raymond Higgins, and Rita Stucky. In general, in this chapter we hope to present an overview of the meaning of accounts: their nature, the motivations that give rise to account-making, how an understanding of accounts may be useful to relationship participants, and how accounts may be found and studied.

MEMORIES AND ACCOUNTS

We will begin by examining some components of accounts. Of what are accounts exactly comprised? What are they to the individual who is the account-maker? What characterizes the telling of the account, and what does an account contain? Probably the easiest characteristic of an account to recognize is that accounts are generally based on *memories*. While accounts may be initially *based* on memories, they do not necessarily restrict themselves to memories. They require considerable embellishment, emotional revival, and, of course, inference. We take accounts to be a form of causal thinking and speculation. They seek to explain, but they seek to do so based on what may be inexplicable experiences, so that an individual making an account initially relies on memory, perhaps builds on memories as a beginning base for the account. The memories that make the best accounts, that are easiest to explore and expand upon are those which are vivid. So to some extent, a good account requires a vivid imaginal memory – one that can be recalled, experienced and reviewed in detail in some sensory capacity. There is a good deal of work in the cognitive literature on qualities of vivid memories, "flashbulb" memories, bizarre images, and whether or not images are truly analogous internal representations or essentially propositional in nature. We will assume that a good vivid memory for forming the basis of an account would have to have some kind of emotional and sensory imagery qualities (Harvey, Flanary, and Morgan, in press).

Even though an account may be based on a memory that has some accuracy or some basis in fact, memory being essentially a human, private, intra-psychic process, is constructive and malleable. This means that what one remembers as having happened and what actually happened may be quite different. Over time the memory may take on new qualities, nuances, colors, and refined fabrications, basically because the memory has even new meaning for the individual who is forming the account. Essentially, accuracy is not an issue for the account-maker. We cannot judge an account in terms of how accurate that memory is. Account-accuracy is not an issue of self-deception or other-deception. Rather, the account has a purpose to the account-maker that may or may not require that the account reflect accurately on the individual's true experience. What the account-maker relates and ultimately forms as the account becomes the psychological reality for that individual. Accounts are also steeped in nostalgia; they may reflect on not only an existence that is remembered in somewhat distorted ways, they may even reflect on something that never really happened – a "reality" that never really quite was. Human memory itself does not function simply as a videotaped transcription of an actual event, but rather something that is called up in the mind of the remem-berer for a purpose. It has to serve some sort of function!

ACCOUNTS HAVE CAREERS

Accounts probably are formed over the life of a close relationship. One of the reasons why individuals in a relationship will choose to engage in certain shared actions is so that they will develop a certain shared history.

They can then reflect on their shared experiences, or have mutual stories to tell about the same kinds of events. To some extent a lot of relational activity then might be undertaken by partners for the very purpose of creating a story the partners can share later – an attitude that is reflected when partners say to each other, "Some day we'll look back on all this and laugh," or "Won't this be an interesting thing to tell our grandchildren about?" or "I wonder what we'll think about this years from now when we look back on it." In many activities in a relationship one might just assume that at some point one is going to be engaged in relating the tale of that experience, and that perhaps that is one of the main reasons to undertake the experience in the first place.

By extrapolation, the foregoing reasoning is consistent with Baxter's thesis (this volume) and Sillars and Scott's (1983) argument that disparities in partners' accounts, or perceptions about critical relationship events, may not necessarily lead to an erosion of the relationship. As these theorists conclude, one vital factor in determining whether or not divergencies in accounts are harmful is the degree to which such divergencies undercut each partner's construction of social reality. If they do undercut such central patterns of cognitions (e.g. accounts about the importance of one's devotion to his/her parents or close relatives), their role may be devastating to the relationship.

If two partners in a relationship undergo similar experiences, or undergo experiences at the same time and are ongoingly aware that they are to be formulating some story or way of relating this episode later, does it matter that partner accounts agree with each other? In other words, is the discrepancy of accounts an important issue? It has been noted, for instance, that it can be very upsetting for an individual emerging from a now-ended relationship to comment, "It appears we've had different perspectives on our experiences for a long time," or "It looks as though she/he and I never really did see eye-to-eye," or "It looks like the breach between our points-of-view has been growing for quite a while." It might be very important for partners in a relationship not only to share experiences of which they can then develop shared accounts, but that their accounts not be too discrepant. It may be that the degree of discrepancy between accounts at all stages of a relationship is some sort of index about the quality and real intimacy of the relationship. It might be as close as we come to "accuracy" as a valued feature in account-making. It is not so important that the account be an accurate reflection of reality, but rather that one's *own* account be confirmed or validated by *another* individual, most especially by the partner in the relationship. As long as the relationship is to continue, then the partners should have mutually validating accounts. If the relationship is over, and the individuals involved have parted ways, then it is not at all surprising for one partner to discover that the other's version does not validate his/her particular recollection of relationship experiences.

Apparently, when partners in a relationship share experiences, or at least share some memories of their joint experiences, this can be a way of validating the one-time existence of their relationship. One popular song from the 1970s contains the following lyrics: "Don't say you don't remember – I'll never love anyone else. If you say you don't remember, how can I go on living with myself?" The singer in that tale is telling us essentially that the most important thing to retrieve, or to preserve, now that the relationship is over, is the sanctity of the memory – that it should remain intact, that her partner at least remembers having been involved once with her, and that he at least remembers some of the things they shared. As long as one's partner remembers as well as oneself, one can be content that the relationship was real and that it had meaning for one's life.

STORY-TELLING AND SOCIAL VALIDATION

Another quality that characterizes the nature of accounts is that accounts are a form of story-*telling*. Accounts are told, they are related, whether to an external audience or privately to oneself. They are typically constructed as a tale or narration, so that they can be related perhaps as a form of self-presentation or background, a kind of résumé for other people's and potential partners' information. This story-telling characteristic of accounts can take either an oral or written form. In the more common oral form, it can be a kind of informal self-presentation: "This is what I've been doing with my life, this is where I've spent my time, these are the people I've been involved with." As such, an oral account or story must have an audience. It may be tailored to the particular audience hearing it, and customized to the circumstances surrounding its narration.

Besides consideration of the audience or staging, another story-telling quality of accounts is that they relate a particular *chronology* of relationship experiences: a beginning, a middle, and an end to the story. Even if those experiences did not seem to mean a "beginning," "middle," or "end" *at the time they happened*, nonetheless in the relation of the account, and in the chronology that is reviewed, this temporal "packaging" becomes a very important feature of the story's structure. It has to make sense, it has to be a sort of summation of one's experiences, and it has to have, frequently, a lesson or "moral." The accounts related by Weiss in his book (1975) typify these story-telling qualities, as do the reports we received from our Elderhostel participants.

SYNTHESIS

In our close relationships, we may deliberately "store" events and ideas away in memory for later retrieval and review, saving memories up for a quiet moment that permits self-analysis, or until a crisis point necessitates our obsessive review and search for meaning. Even as we share experiences with our partners, we know we are adding elements and episodes to our relationships histories, which can be pulled out of the file later in reminiscences with our partners, or woven into final accounts of how and why the relationships ended. The story-line of the account is ongoing through the life of the relationship. If the two partners agree with each other in the versions they construe and compare, they validate their accounts as well as their relationship. "We're seeing things the same way, so our relationship must be 'real.'" The story is, however, always private and intra-psychic; we cannot read our partners' minds nor "check" their stories for honesty. Thus an account can be developed even of a *non*-relationship, as in a case of unrequited love or asymmetric partnership.

Koller (1981) touches on this tragic "privacy" of relationship account-making in an insight reached in her own poignant self-analysis:

> If I'm not loved when I love, the lack can't be repaired by any action of mine or repented by the person who doesn't love me. It's all right to cry when the thing is over, but after that you have to let your reaching-out wither away by not feeding it. Which I never understood before.
>
> Or am I simply getting around to noticing that loving is something shared, and that one person loving without return is telling *herself* a story? (pp. 244–5; emphasis added)

The goal of the story-telling is meaning, sense, understanding. Another observation we can make about accounts is that accounts may serve to reveal recurrent themes or patterns in one's relationship experiences. These patterns should be recognizable, they should strike a familiar chord. When one relates an account, one is frequently leading up to a concluding statement that summarizes an experience other people can share or recognize, and in which others can see themselves. The lesson or moral that an account relates ultimately can be something that is even recognizable in popular music or the melodramatic plot-lines of movies or books. An account may conclude that a relationship was "wrong from the start" or that a relationship was a matter of "the right person but the wrong time" or that a relationship was a matter of "fate – it wasn't meant to be." The account-maker may relate his/her story as though the lesson were now clearly recognizable and easily understood, and even hinted at when these experiences were first undergone by the account-maker. Nonetheless, what it really represents is the account-maker's *quest for meaning*. Perhaps in retelling his story, the account-maker might think to him/herself, "I can figure out what was going on with me and why things were happening to me in the way that they were. Maybe if I tell someone else what happened to me, it will be clearer to me how it all makes sense – why it all had to happen in the first place."

THE MOTIVATIONS FOR ACCOUNT-MAKING

Why do people form and relate accounts? Accounts are characteristically a matter of memories, some dredged up, some haunting. Accounts also are a matter of story-telling, and of recurrent, familiar themes. We as researchers can describe accounts to some extent, we can even find examples that parallel our descriptions, but it may be harder to understand why people undertake account-formation and relation in the first place. There are, in fact, several motivations underlying account-making. We shall look at six such motivations here, and consider the various forms that accounts might take to serve each of these motivations.

Self-esteem

First of all, accounts are a way of preserving and protecting *self-esteem*. Probably one of the best examples of this is reviewed in the recent work by Snyder, Higgins, and Stucky, entitled *Excuses* (1983), who relate several forms of excuses, examples, and purposes that excuses serve for those who tender them. Probably the category of excuses that best characterizes the purpose of account-making is the category that Snyder *et al.* refer to as "retrospective excuses." These are "masquerades for the past." The excuse-maker is trying to retell or reshape the past in order to present him/herself in a more acceptable, socially approvable way. Retrospective excuses are essentially a matter of "reframing performances." Snyder *et al.* offer several examples of the need to reframe one's performances. They cite, for instance, the dilemma of the witnesses to the Kitty Genovese murder, who had to come up with some explanation about why they did not report the apparent crime under way. Other kinds of performance-reframing take the form of blaming the victim, or de-escalating the harm one has perceived in the situation, in general trying to make one's behavior in retrospect appear more acceptable. In a relationship, one probably undertakes performance-reframing excuses in order to explain why a relationship ended or why conflict was experienced. Sometimes, for instance, the person who left the relationship may have to explain to him/herself and others why the relationship was left. The leaver has a certain amount of guilt with which to deal. The person who was left, the "leavee" in the relationship, has to manufacture some sort of explanation about why such rejection was even possible. "What kind of person must I be if my partner could so easily leave me?" the leavee might have to explain. Reframing performances might be a characteristic quality of retrospective relationship accounts. We make excuses by saying that "what happened to me could have happened to anybody," or "what I experienced was not that unusual," or "I'm not the one who was at fault." In general, then, one purpose of account-making is the preservation of self-esteem, and this may take the form of excuses, especially the form of excuses in which we reframe past performances.

Emotional purging

A second motivation for accounts may be a simple emotional purging: that is usually the experience of grief. The best recent example of account-making in written form is to be found in Rosenblatt's *Bitter, Bitter Tears* (1983). Rosenblatt extends the accounts literature by examining descriptions of grief experiences recorded in personal diaries kept throughout the nineteenth century. Rosenblatt's analysis contributes to the accounts literature both by supplying methodological procedures, which prove fruitful in developing a theory of grief reaction, and by reviewing common reactions to grief experienced following loss, separation, or death. These analyses may contribute to our understanding of accounts regarding failed relationships.

The content of Rosenblatt's analysis of grief experience contributes ideas that may be useful for future work on accounts of failed relationships. As Rosenblatt asserts, a variety of losses in addition to death can produce grief responses; in fact as mentioned earlier Rosenblatt's analysis included examination of separation from loved ones in addition to loss of loved ones by death. Although separation during the nineteenth century occurred as a result of searches for better farmland, or visits with distant relatives, similar processes likely occur as one attempts to deal with thoughts and feelings resulting from marital separation, divorce, or the ending of any close relationship. In all situations involving loss of a loved one, an individual must experience the work of *detaching*. Part of this work includes creating explanations for the loss, i.e. accounts.

As a result of examining variables associated with grief reactions, Rosenblatt identifies a number of variables that also might influence the accounts one develops following the failure of a close relationship. For example, following a separation the respective reactions of the "leaver" and the "leavee" sometimes differ, with the "leavee" experiencing greater grief. Differences in accounts developed by the leaver and the leavee following dissolution of a close relationship would be a useful avenue of study given that such roles can be identified. Rosenblatt further argues that one's hopes for another (e.g. one's child), or for one's relationship with another may influence the severity of one's grief following death or separation from the other. Similarly, one's hopes for a close relationship most likely would influence the story that one creates to explain the failure of that relationship. Finally, Rosenblatt argues for the significant role played by co-residence in grief reactions: grief reactions are not so severe when a lost other has lived far away. Grief is protracted and more involving over the loss of a co-resident or close colleague. The influence of co-residence even seems to overpower the effects of the length of time two people have known each other, or the complexity of their relationship. The significance of this variable seems to involve the disconnecting that occurs along with non-co-residence. Such a variable might influence also the accounts developed about failed relationships – cohabitation may influence the accounts made, and the required continued associations that sometimes follow the dissolution of today's relationships (e.g. continued working relationships after break-up), although not cohabitation *per se*, may affect the nature of accounts.

An extension of Rosenblatt's discussion of grieving and mourning can be found in the discussion by Sheldon Kopp of the refusal to mourn (1971). Kopp looks at the experience of a patient in therapy who has a difficult time accepting that parental love might have been inadequate or even nonexistent. This painful experience, even though it occurred in childhood and long ago, cannot be rationalized; it cannot be denied. It somehow has to be accepted and worked through:

> All he can do now is to try to face how really bad he feels, and how stuck he is with it. Then he may turn to others in his life, and try to be open enough so that they may get to know him. ... Perhaps someone else will love him. But in any case, no one can take anyone else's place. It will never be made up to him. He will just have to do without, like it or not, and face his losses and his helplessness to change them. He must weep, and mourn and grieve them through. He must unhook from the past to make do with the rest of the world. ... Not such a bad trade after all.   (p. 152)

As mentioned earlier, perhaps one of the most important experiences one can undergo in the process of getting over a relationship is the process of *detaching*. An account, in a sense, can become a means of detaching or putting the relationship behind oneself. In another sense, however, a relationship is never abandoned, the relationship is never over. The grieving quality and motivation in accounts probably explains why many accounts are characterized by bitterness, sorrow or other vivid kinds of emotional qualities (Harvey *et al.* 1986). At times it may seem as though the process of getting over a broken or lost relationship is chaotic and out of control, suggesting yet another motivation for one's developing an account.

Establishing a sense of control

A third motivation for account-making then becomes this very issue of *control*. When one relates an account, after all, it is one's *own* account, one's own story, one's own special version of the events that transpired in the conflict or breakdown of a relationship. When one tells one's own story, perhaps for the first time, aspects of the relationship that seemed out of control at the time can seem to be more under one's control now. We can after all retrospectively understand and make sense out of an experience that at the time must have seemed very senseless and ridiculous. A very painful experience can in retrospect be seen as one that has provided a valuable lesson or important moral. This control aspect or motive of account-making is illustrated explicitly in a recent book by humorist Nora Ephron, entitled *Heartburn* (1983). In this story, Ephron tells a fictionalized account of the break-up of her own marriage to journalist Carl Bernstein. In the book, Ephron changes her own character's name and that of her ex-husband, but (according to reviews) essentially preserves the important details of her own non-fictional experiences in this fictionalized format. Throughout the book she relates funny, satirizing anecdotes about what went wrong in the fictional characters' marriage, and seemingly makes light of the very tragic events surrounding her real-life break-up. As she closes the book, Ephron relates a revealing explanation about this flippant approach to recalling the circumstances of her own break-up. In the story, Ephron's persona has been seeing a therapist named Vera:

> Vera said: "Why do you feel you have to turn everything into a story?"
> So I told her why:
> Because if I tell the story, I control the version.
> Because if I tell the story, I can make you laugh, and I would rather have you laugh at me than feel sorry for me.
> Because if I tell the story, it doesn't hurt so much.
> Because if I tell the story, I can get on with it.   (pp. 176–7)

That passage from *Heartburn* neatly summarizes the important control features of a good account. When you relate an account, you are not only revealing what you experienced and what you wish you had experienced in the break-up stages of your relationship, you also are making those rather out-of-control events once more your own. Once again, you are in charge of the relationship; in fact, you are in charge of aspects of the relationship you never before felt you had in your charge.

The search for closure

A fourth motivation for developing an account is the search for *closure*. The importance of closure cannot be underestimated in terms of psychological comfort. Closure, an important Gestalt principle, suggests that we cannot stand to have a story left unfinished. This principle is of course the Zeigarnik effect. In the late 1920s Bluma Zeigarnik discovered that individuals who were unable to finish reading stories had a greater and more detailed recall of those stories than individuals who had been allowed to finish reading (Zeigarnik 1938). In essence, those who finished their stories mentally filed them away and forgot about them. According to the Zeigarnik effect, we are bothered by loose ends; we do not like not knowing how something has turned out. Developing and relating our own accounts of our relational experiences gives us a chance to tie up those loose ends that might have been left hanging. Closure in accounts may provide the stability we need and seek, which proves so elusive in relationships themselves. Closure in our accounts may be the only kind of closure we can successfully obtain and realize at the time. Closure becomes a sort of Holy Grail: we always seek it; we're not satisfied until we have reached it in some form. Perhaps in some ways, aspects of account-making are even more satisfying than certain aspects of the real relationship. An account gives us closure not only in pointing out *how* a relationship ended, but in fact *that* a relationship ended.

The search for understanding

A fifth general motivation for account development is that accounts are a part of ongoing attributional activity in relationship development. A good example of this is shown in the work of Lloyd and Cate (1985) whose discussion suggests that partners develop accounts *throughout* the life of a relationship, yet become focused and particularly poignant in their account-making at specific points of conflict in the relationship, and especially at the point of break-up. Lloyd and Cate note that partners are *in* a relationship, not analyzing it from the outside, and as a result their versions of the psychological reality of the relationship may be very different from that of investigators studying the nature of the relationship. In reviewing major work on relational explanation, Lloyd and Cate note,

> when describing the forces that affected their relationships, partners rarely spoke in terms of "dyadic crystallization" or "role fit." Rather, partners in close relationships offered descriptions that centered around explanations and causal attributions as to the reasons why their particular relationship developed in the manner in which it did.
>
> (p. 2)

This ongoing attributional activity is particularly triggered by the need to answer "Why is the relationship changing?" And of course, given that a break-up may be the most significant change to be experienced in a relationship, at that point both partners are going to feel the greatest need to engage in attributional activity; hence, the development of an account.

Accounts as ends in themselves

A sixth motivation for account development is really a sort of disclaimer about the motivational quality of accounts: accounts are in many ways, as we have cited, the means to an end. Accounts help us to achieve a sense of closure, control, and engage in ongoing attributional activity, to answer the "whys" of relationship conflict and breakdown. Accounts also help us to come up with excuses to preserve our self-esteem. Accounts constitute a form of grieving or mourning activity, a purgative emotional experience. However, accounts are not only a means to an end; they are also an *end in themselves*. Accounts are, after all, the lone vestige of the close relationship now gone. All we have left are our stories; perhaps all we ever had are our stories (see Koller 1981). Harvey *et al.* (1982) argue that relationships *do not end*; they rather continue, though only at the cognitive and emotional level, no longer in day-to-day experience:

> Relationships are as much symbolic events and images to the involved parties as they are interactional episodes or histories. We may put space or time or other people between ourselves and formerly significant others, but we maintain the relationships in our mind.
>
> (p. 119)

Why do we continue relationships in our minds? Why is it so hard to accept at some point that a relationship is really over? Perhaps it is true of human nature that relationships cannot genuinely be ended, although time, circumstances, and distance may interfere with continuing relationships in a real world setting. Because our minds grasp so tenaciously at memories and because we have such capacity for vivid recall, flexibility, and reframing our own experiences, it may indeed be that much of relationship experience is sought and undertaken primarily to construct just these sorts of cognitive and emotional accounts in the first place. We promise to be true to our partners in the good days in our relationships. We promise that we will always be in love, that we will always cherish, that we will never become tired of the other individual. We promise always to maintain the same standard of commitment that we feel so strongly and almost naturally today. Over time, however, something goes wrong with our plans and promises. There are a thousand reasons why people might in fact end up parting ways. It might be very hard for us to accept, on a cognitive and emotional level, that we *have* in fact parted ways. What about our promises? What about our commitment to some romantic notion that when we say "always" or "never," we really mean it? This is in fact a very idealistic romantic notion, and yet our society supports just that kind of romantic mythology. We feel we should be able to say to a partner at some point, "I will always love you," and really mean it and in fact devote a lot of our life's energy to fulfilling and completing that promise. When a relationship has ended, in terms of day-to-day contact and real world experience, all that we have left are these vestigial attributions that gradually take the shape of a story, a beginning–middle–end account. It may be that all we have left of the relationship is this mental scrapbook. The account becomes a way of first exhuming and then reviving the relationship, or aspects of the relationship, from time to time. It turns out that by reviving these accounts, by embellishing them, by continuing to save and cherish them – whether they recur spontaneously or we deliberately trigger them by reviewing souvenirs – it may be that the account is our only way of keeping our long-ago promise. A good deal of social value is placed on this romantic myth that we be able to keep these promises of "always" and "never." Somehow this romantic myth, this personal commitment to always, has to be sustained, it has to be approximated. By recalling and cherishing and embellishing, and relating again and again, in many different circumstances, our personal accounts of the tragedies or comedies that were our actual relationships, we are being true to our original promise. It's a way of protecting our self-esteem as well as convincing ourselves that real commitment, real closure, is possible in a relationship: "I am being true in the only way that I can be true; I'm not being true to you as a living partner, I'm being true to my memory of you, and my recollection, my version of the story of our relationship. It's all that I can do, and I'm doing all that I can do."

To reiterate, then, accounts are in many ways means to the ends of closure, control, and so on. But accounts are also an end in themselves. Perhaps we undertake account-making because we essentially seek to have just that end-product – the account itself. It satisfies a need to have explanation, to have meaning, and to maintain some otherwise unmet need. We are unable to be true and maintain that commitment while continuing in the relationship. The account enables us to keep those promises and commitments.

The utility of accounts

It may be, as some researchers and theorists suggest, that only after we have formulated some kind of satisfactory account, however skeletal or embellished it might be, can we truly move on and pick up and continue our lives, as Ephron's character suggests in the quote from *Heartburn*. To quote from Sheldon Kopp (1971) about the importance of the mourning experience: "By mourning our losses and burying our dead, in therapy and in the rest of our life, we open ourselves to the only real contact we can have with others ... touching now, standing in the rubble of the past" (p. 5).

Are accounts useful? Can understanding the importance and the details of account-making be applicable and practical for participants in relationships themselves? It is possible that one way an understanding of an account can be useful is in looking at the overall process of interpersonal *attraction*. Psychologists have reiterated for decades now that one of the most important ways that two people can find themselves attracted to each other is to discover some basic *similarity* between themselves. Traditionally, this kind of research has focused on attitude similarity, even similarity of physical characteristics such as height, and similarity of basic background experiences and values. Another important quality in which two people might be similar, and might seek similarity from the very beginning, is in ways and processes by which people make accounts. It is important, therefore, not only that two people share experiences and have similar account contents, but that people have similar ways of formulating accounts. It can be very distressing toward or after the end of the relationship to discover that you and your partner never really were in synch, or for a long time have formed dissimilar accounts. Partners may apply an understanding of accounts then at the outset of a relationship, to an examination of how they form their stories and how they tell their stories. Accounts may also be a way of informing each other about one's own past. An individual may, for instance, want to relate a sort of "relationship résumé" to a new acquaintance in order to summarize his/her past experience, and also to show his/her account-making style: "This is how I view the relationship experiences I have had."

ACCOUNT-GATHERING METHODS

Given the importance of accounts in relationships and in individual partners' ideas about what is important in relationships, where do investigators find accounts and how can they be studied? We have already suggested and demonstrated the availability of accounts in oral or written self-reports. This can take the form of a survey or questionnaire, or, over a longer time period, of a journal. In fact, it appears that people have a relatively easy time answering questions, particularly questions about memories and conclusions drawn about these memories. Our own work with Elderhostel volunteer respondents illustrates the effectiveness of this approach. Another way of uncovering self-report accounts might be examination of people's diaries and stories, as in the work of Rosenblatt.

Although Rosenblatt acknowledges the limitations of examining diary entries (e.g. the rarity of useful diaries and the possible resultant restricted sample of diaries; absence of entries relevant to grief may not be indicative that certain reactions did not occur, etc.), he makes the case that diaries are extremely useful research material. In particular, Rosenblatt argues that diaries provide records of reactions uncontaminated by a researcher's questions and/or reactions. Also, despite evidence that diaries were not always completely private, the use of personal diaries permits examination of more private disclosure than might be obtained in a research setting. Rosenblatt also utilizes quantifiable measures of grief expressed in diary entries (e.g. proportion of monthly entries that contain mentions of the lost person, proportion of monthly entries that contain grief for the lost person) and attempts modest statistical analyses (primarily descriptive statistics are provided along with correlational analyses) that add significantly to development of a theory based on anecdotal evidence. Such procedures should prove useful in the further development of theories regarding accounts of failed relationships.

People often have recorded diary accounts without any expectation that these would be reviewed by investigators. Therefore, lessons and themes may be harder to sift and pluck out of the diary format. We have found that literature can yield a number of "accounts," in poetry, in fiction, or in autobiography. Music and lyrics also can suggest various themes and shapes of accounts currently popular or "fashionable," either in the archives or again in people's self-reports.

The methodology of studying accounts continues to be broadened. A recent study by Lloyd and Cate (1985) provides another illustration of this approach. These investigators asked people between eighteen and thirty-two years of age who had had a break-up in a "significant" relationship during the last twelve months to trace the development and dissolution of the relationship via the retrospective interview technique. This technique involves the respondent's indication on a graph of "chance of marriage" and of turning points in commitment over the time-frame of the relationship. Also, Lee (1984) developed a combination questionnaire–

interview technique to test his predictions about the sequences of events involved in separation. Based upon the subjects' descriptions of their break-up, Lee asked raters to construct independent "maps" of the dissolutions specifying all of the parameters of his model. The research was successful in showing that raters could make discriminations so as to reflect Lee's multidimensional conception.

Finally, in terms of new methods, Baxter and Wilmot (1985) reported a study using an ethnographic interview to solicit informant accounts of topics that were "off limits" in the context of an opposite-sex relationship in which they were involved. Open-ended interviews were used to obtain the accounts, and Bulmer's (1979) method of analytic induction was used to develop basic categories of taboo topics from 172 topics generated in the interviews. This work provided insight regarding the topics that were considered to be taboo and the informants' reasons for so considering these topics. Most account-gathering methods seem to rely quite comfortably on various forms of self-report. Inferences must be cautious but are not impossible nor always difficult. The stories are right there; it seems as though people are very ready to relate their accounts, which may be right at the front tip of their minds. They need not be sought or fabricated, they may be altered slightly in the telling and re-telling, and yet the narrator readily recognizes what an account is and why it is important. The hardest decision an account-maker may have to make is *which* account to tell, and about *which* relationship.

CONCLUSION

Accounts are so important that they become spontaneous and accessible. They are reworked and refined with time and experience. As we have argued here, they serve several purposes to the account-maker: control, grieving, self-presentation, even to the point of excuse and masquerade. As we have noted, they are also an end in themselves. They represent an essential psychological reality to the account-maker. These stories we tell are all we have of past relationships and our idealized liaisons. They are scrapbooks of mental photographs for which we wish we had posed. They allow us the indulgences of nostalgia and self-expression, the creation of our own relational reality. They also teach us and remind us of lessons we might have learned. They are useful and practical, bridging the gap between the real and ideal, the fantastic and pragmatic. They truly merit the increased attention of the corps of researchers who share a fascination with the dynamics of close relationships.

REFERENCES

Baxter, L. and Wilmot, W. (1985) "Taboo topics in close relationships." *Journal of Social and Personal Relationships*, 2, 253–69.
Bulmer, M. (1979) "Concepts in the analysis of qualitative data." *Sociological Review*, 27, 651–77.

Ephron, N. (1983) *Heartburn*. New York: Alfred A. Knopf.

Harvey, J.H., Flanary, R. and Morgan, M. (in press) "Vivid memories of vivid loves gone by." *Journal of Social and Personal Relationships*.

——, Weber, A.L., Yarkin, K.L. and Stewart, B.E. (1982) "An attributional approach to relationship breakdown and dissolution." In S. Duck (ed.) *Dissolving Personal Relationships*. London: Academic Press, 107–26.

——, ——, Galvin, K.S., Huszti, H.C. and Garnick, N.N. (1986) "Attribution and the termination of close relationships: a special focus on the account." In R. Gilmour and S. Duck (eds) *The Emerging Field of Personal Relationships*. Hillsdale, NJ: Lawrence Erlbaum, 189–201.

Hunt, M.M. (1969) *The Affair*. New York: World.

Koller, A. (1981) *An Unknown Woman: A Journey to Self-discovery*. New York: Bantam.

Kopp, S.B. (1971) *Guru: Metaphors from a Psychotherapist*. Palo Alto, CA: Science and Behavior Books.

Lee, L. (1984) "Sequences in separation: a framework for investigating endings of the personal (romantic) relationship." *Journal of Social and Personal Relationships*, 1, 49–73.

Lloyd, S.A. and Cate, R.M. (1985) "Attributions associated with significant turning points in premarital relationships: development and dissolution." *Journal of Social and Personal Relationships*, 2, 419–36.

Rosenblatt, P.C. (1983) *Bitter, Bitter Tears*. Minneapolis: University of Minnesota Press.

Sillars, A. and Scott, M. (1983) "Interpersonal perception between intimates: an integrative review." *Human Communication Research*, 10, 153–76.

Snyder, C.R., Higgins, R.L. and Stucky, R.J. (1983) *Excuses: Masquerades in Search of Grace*. New York: John Wiley.

Weiss, R.S. (1975) *Marital Separation*. New York: Basic Books.

Zeigarnik, B. (1938) "On finished and unfinished tasks." In W.D. Ellis (ed.) *A Sourcebook of Gestalt Psychology*. London: Routledge & Kegan Paul.

8 Friendship expectations

John J. La Gaipa

INTRODUCTION

Role schema are social schemata used to process information pertaining to such social roles as friendship (Taylor and Crocker 1981). The friendship expectancies activated by these role schema provide the perceiver with hypotheses about expected behavior from friends. These expectations are intrinsic to the accounting and mapping of what friendship is all about. The nature of the friendship expectancies, however, is not determined solely by socially imposed constraints. Personal experience is also relevant, and therefore it is useful to differentiate prescriptive from predictive expectancies. Prescriptive expectations are the normative expectations acquired during socialization: the normative quality implies that people "ought" or "should" do certain things. In contrast, the predictive aspects emphasize the anticipatory quality of friendship expectations, the likelihood that certain activities will occur.

When a person, then, is located within a social category, certain inferences are made as to what can be expected. The personal experiences as well as the social context influence the attributions that are made. It is important to note that these two kinds of expectations are often highly related. They share common ground in that both aspects serve as interaction guides. The main difference is that the predictive expectations lack the obligatory flavor of the former.

The "rules of friendship" are receiving increasing attention. This notion focuses on the prescriptive aspects of friendship expectations in specifying the cultural notions about correct and incorrect ways of doing things. Argyle and Henderson (1985) define a rule as behaviors that most members of a group think or believe should be performed or not performed. An essential element of a rule, like a prescriptive expectation, is that there is a shared belief about the importance of doing something. Argyle and Henderson (1984) have identified the "rules of friendship" that are part of a package of universal rules. The friendship rules, in particular, show the importance of the rules of reward – giving emotional support, offering help when needed, and repaying debts and favors.

Bigelow and associates have focused on the developmental aspects of rule acquisition as they apply to different kinds of relationships. Bigelow (1986) conceptualizes friendship expectations as being at a higher level of abstraction than social rules, which are viewed as operational definitions of social strategies making up expectations. Social rules are used also in the break-up of a relationship to maintain a positive social image of self in the social network (La Gaipa 1982).

This distinction between prescriptive and predictive expectations can be incorporated within a systems approach that employs a hierarchical level of analysis: a lower level cannot be fully understood apart from the higher level (see La Gaipa 1981b). From a cultural level, the normative aspects of friendship expectations are most salient. They also tap some of the ideals of interpersonal relationships that guide and direct friendships. From a behavioral level, expectancies are defined in terms of their predictive quality, that is the subjective probabilities that certain kinds of friendship activities will occur. Contextual factors are important moderators of such anticipated qualities. From an individual-psychological level, the focus is on individual differences along these prescriptive and predictive dimensions. Developmental and personality factors are relevant here.

This chapter is about studies on friendship conducted as part of a research program that draws on both approaches. Research on the growth, maintenance, and termination of friendship draws more heavily on prescriptive expectations. In such research we have examined the degree to which each party have had their expectancies confirmed or disconfirmed. The research paradigm regarding predictive expectancies draws more heavily on a social perception paradigm, and focuses on the attributions and inferences made on the basis of social category information. The procedure is more experimental involving the manipulation of member category information.

In this chapter I will present the results of studies generated by a research program on friendship initiated in 1969. The first characteristic of this program is its reliance on a multi-dimensional approach to friendship reflected in the friendship scales developed. A second characteristic is the interest in the influence of life stages on conceptions of friendship, and age-related changes in social knowledge. A third characteristic is the search for individual differences in how individuals think about friendship. A fourth characteristic is the interest in the possible influence of multiple category membership on the perceiver and the perceived. A fifth characteristic is the focus on a systems approach to friendship, in particular, on the importance of social context, and the interface of friendship and kinship in the larger social network.

MULTI-DIMENSIONAL APPROACHES TO FRIENDSHIP

Several multi-dimensional models of friendship have been developed to understand the growth, maintenance, and termination of friendship. Researchers (e.g. Davis and Todd 1985; La Gaipa 1977b; Wright 1985) have also constructed instruments for studying and measuring relationships. A key notion is the concern with the values and expectations of friendship, as operationalized in terms of the importance assigned to different rewards of friendship.

Wright (1984, 1985) was the first to develop both a model and a procedure for operationalizing friendship variables. The final form of the Acquaintance Description Form has 13 five-item scales, including measures of interdependency, favorability, interpersonal rewards or values, (e.g. utility, ego support, and stimulation), aspects of the self and relationship differentiation. Wright (1984) contrasts his self-referent model with the social exchange models (La Gaipa 1977a), in focusing on the intrinsic end-in-themselves quality of friendships. The rewards of friendship are viewed in terms of their significance to the self. In order to evaluate oneself in a positive way, it is helpful to have friends who provide one with ego support, self-affirmation, stimulation, and security.

Davis and Todd (1985) have developed a descriptive psychology approach to personal relationships based on the notion of relationship prototypes. Love involves fascination, exclusiveness, and a desire for sexual intimacy, whereas these are not essential to friendship (Davis and Todd 1982). In love there is a higher expectation of loyalty and mutual assistance than in friendship. When expectations are not met in a love relationship, there is a sense of personal betrayal, whereas in friendship such violations are more likely to count as disappointments.

Development and validation of Friendship Inventory for adults

The motive underlying research on friendship expectations was part of a quest for understanding the meaning of friendship (La Gaipa 1977b). In the initial study, 150 university students asked their peers to think of a friend (at a specific level of friendship) of the same sex. They were asked to describe critical incidents that showed why they chose this person. From the over 1,800 friendship statements, 80 items covering four levels of friendship were administered to 1,167 students. Each subject read the four definitions of friendship: best, close, good, and social acquaintance, and then rated each of the items in terms of its importance for that level. A series of factor analyses were done. Finally, a 35-item Friendship Expectancy Inventory was developed that measures seven dimensions. This inventory was administered to nearly 5,000 individuals as part of the standardization study.

Description of friendship scales

The following is a summary of the scales.

(a) *Positive Regard:* shows appreciation; enhances self-worth; makes me feel worthwhile; thinks my ideas are important.
(b) *Authenticity:* can be open and honest, real, genuine, and spontaneous; no need to "keep up a front."
(c) *Helping and Support:* helps promote my welfare; does things willingly; gives help readily.
(d) *Self-disclosure:* free to express inner private feelings; can reveal secret hopes and ambitions; can reveal what I am ashamed of.
(e) *Acceptance:* acknowledges my identity and individuality; shows unconditional positive regard; don't let differences come between us.
(f) *Similarity:* possess similar points of view, similar attitudes and interests, compatible personalities.
(g) *Strength of Character:* evokes admiration because of character, achievement, and social responsibility.
(h) *Empathic Understanding:* interprets accurately the feelings of another; understands how one really feels; listens to what one has to say.

The empathy scale was not in the original form of the inventory. The acceptance scale was eventually combined with authenticity because of the high correlations between them.

The friendship scales are presented in a variety of formats depending on the purpose of a specific study. In the friendship values format, the subjects rate each item on a five-point Likert scale from "slightly important" to "extremely important." In the friendship expectancy format, the subjects rate each statement in terms of the expected probability of occurrence from 50 per cent of the time to 90 per cent of the time. In the friendship behavior format, the subjects use a seven-point scale and describe a specific friend in terms of how often the behavior has occurred from "never" to "always." In another format, each friendship statement is presented three times with instructions including (a) how important is this to you; (b) how much do you think you should receive; and (c) how much do you actually receive. This format provides measures of need fulfillment and expectancy confirmation. Various simple and complex scoring systems have been developed, the usefulness of which appears to vary with the content of the scale and contextual variables of the study.

Early validation studies

An early study assessed the relationship differential potential of the friendship inventory. Wegreniuk (1971) instructed subjects to use the scales for describing their most and least preferred friends in terms of what they expected from them. The degree of discrimination from the most to the least were as follows: helping, authenticity, similarity, positive regard, acceptance, self-disclosure, and strength of character.

The standardization study (La Gaipa, 1977b) indicates that the same dimensions are not involved as an individual moves from one level of friendship to the next. Movement from social acquaintance to good friend probably can occur along any of the dimensions. Movement from good friend to close friend is most pronounced on two dimensions, self-disclosure and helping. A change from close friend to best friend is most evident on self-disclosure. Authenticity is fairly important at all levels. The dimension showing the least change across levels is strength of character.

In a second series of studies, each of the friendship items was responded to in terms of two rating scales: what they expected to receive and what they actually received from their friends. In an experimental study of fraternity students (La Gaipa, 1972a), evaluative anxiety did not affect expectations of support, but did lower their appraisal of the amount of support provided by the group and the perceived similarity with the group members. Somewhat different results were obtained in a "field study" in which an unobtrusive measure of cohesiveness was used. Friendship expectations were higher in the high cohesive norms than in the low cohesive norms. But the fulfillment of expectations did not differ by level of cohesiveness, suggesting that expectations rose faster than need fulfillment in the more cohesive residents. In a further study involving alcoholics in group therapy, a follow-up was conducted as to the success of the program (La Gaipa and Uriel 1974). The best predictors of remission occurred when the alcoholics thought they received more support than they had expected with regard to self-disclosure and helping. In a study of conformity in adolescent years, an intimacy deficiency score was computed from scales measuring authenticity, intimacy, acceptance, and positive regard. The disparity between expectancies and fulfillment decreased with age. Sex differences were also found. When expectancies were confirmed, males had a higher conformity score, but females had a lower conformity score.

Research was also done in a Roman Catholic convent. The sisters apparently are more attuned to the spiritual world than the social world of the convent. As compared to laywomen, the sisters assigned lower ratings as to the importance of authenticity, positive regard, openness, and sensitivity. A composite score of humanitarian warmth also differentiated sisters from laywomen, though in an unexpected direction. The sisters valued it less, aspired for it less, and received it less than laywomen. The sisters expected to receive more support but received less of it than the laywomen.

Longitudinal studies

Several studies have assessed the predictive validity of the friendship scales. The first study (Lischeron and La Gaipa 1971) involved administering the friendship scales to seventy-six male university room-mates at the beginning and end of the school year. Expectancies were measured while the room-mates were still relatively unacquainted. What each party believed they received was measured at the completion of the year. Expectancy confirmation was predictive of changes in the level of friendship. The poorest predictor was self-disclosure, with a nonsignificant r of 0.17. The best predictor was perceived as similarity, with an r of 0.46. The actual similarity of friendship expectancies was not predictive of friendship change ($r = 0.04$).

In a second major longitudinal study a total of 446 incoming university students were administered a long questionnaire that included the friendship inventory. At the end of the academic year, 350 again filled out the questionnaire (Howitt 1976). In the third phase of the study a total of 102 subjects remained. Heilbronn (1975) analyzed the data on these subjects across all three points in time, covering a two-year period.

The importance of the level of the relationship for changes in the friendship schemata was examined with reference to attributions regarding reward outcome and equity. In time one, the best predictor of friendship was the desire or motivation to form a close relationship. At time two, six months later, the best predictors were assessments of companionship as measured by the mutual activities checklist, and effort given to the other person. With regard to interpersonal rewards, he/she judged the quality of the relationship from the amount of reward given other as compared to what was received. The more given to other, the closer the relationship. At time three, a year later, the focus is on how much was received from the room-mate. If the individual believes that other gave less than he/she received, then the relationship is problematic. There is a shift then, in the comparison made with regard to equity from: "the more I give, the closer the relationship" to "the more he/she gives, the closer the relationship." It is not clear why this change occurs. Perhaps the individual has more information about other after two years, while after one year more information is available about self.

This longitudinal study of relational changes in friendship suggests that the schemata undergo changes with the stage of the relationship. After knowing each other for six months, six of the seven friendship dimensions were about equally predictive of the level of friendship; the correlations were in the 0.50 to 0.70 range. After a two-year period of acquaintance, more differentiation was obtained. "Self-disclosure" becomes one of the poorer predictors of friendship growth. "Helping" becomes one of the best. "Authenticity" is also predictive, but particularly of the break-up of a relationship. Accounts of the termination of the relationship, particularly by females, focus on the loss of trust and "phoniness" of the former friend.

Personal accounts of changes

We have used the essay format to study conceptions of friendship of adolescents as well as children. In one study we asked adolescents to tell us about their expectations, as well as to describe personal experiences regarding the growth and decay of friendship (Bigelow and La Gaipa 1980). Few differences were found between early and late adolescence. The main change was that intimacy was cited more often, a shift from 15 per cent to 50 per cent. Sex differences were not dramatic with the exception of "Self-disclosure." A number of researchers have noted that females are more concerned with this dimension than males (cf. Miell, Duck, and La Gaipa 1979). We found that in early adolescence 23 per cent of the females and 9 per cent of the males mentioned intimacy. In late adolescence, the figures are 61 per cent as compared to 40 per cent, respectively. In late adolescence, females are also more attuned to the need for loyalty: 75 per cent of the females as compared to 52 per cent of the males.

Growth and decay are generally not described in terms of the same dimensions. For example, common activities is often cited as promoting the growth of a real friendship, but decay is seldom described in terms of a decrease along this dimension. Moreover, "strength of character" is seldom cited as a factor in the growth of a friendship, but actions indicating low morals or weak character are the second most often given reasons for decay. "Loyalty and commitment" is fairly important for growth but the most important reason for decay. "Positive regard" is a reason for both growth and decay, whereas "Helping" is mentioned for growth, but rarely for decay. A social exchange interpretation may explain growth, but breakdown is less easily explained. Less than 1 per cent of the subjects made such statements as "he stopped helping me" or "she stopped sharing intimate information."

AGE-RELATED CHANGES IN SOCIAL KNOWLEDGE

A cognitive-developmental approach

Several friendship theorists view friendship expectations as similar to general cognitions in becoming more abstract and less egocentric with increasing age (Bigelow and La Gaipa 1975; Damon 1977; Selman 1980; Smollar and Younnis 1982). The nature of changes is posited to be shaped by the child's level of cognitive functioning. These theorists acknowledge the influence of Piaget (1965) who has mapped changes in cognitive functioning from egocentric and concrete stages to empathic and abstract stages.

Selman (1980) has constructed a developmental stage model that has received much attention. The structural analysis makes use of the organizing concept of "perspective taking." In the Momentary Playmate stage (ages 3–7), friends are defined by proximity, and the child does not easily separate his/her viewpoint from others. In the One-way Assistance stage (ages 4–9), there is growing awareness that other children have different perspectives, but friends are still largely valued in terms of their usefulness. In the Fairweather Co-operation stage (ages 6–12), co-operation really begins, but friends are still viewed as serving self interests. It is not until the Intimate-Mutual Sharing stage (ages 9–15) that there is awareness that co-operative behavior can be mutually beneficial. Finally, in the Autonomous Interdependent stage (twelve years and older), the child realizes that some interests are unshared and must be satisfied in autonomous behavior by each person.

We have been influenced also by Piagetian theory of social development. But the notion of stages has not been central to our research. Instead, greater priority has been given to the construction of a taxonomy of friendship expectations, an essential step in the identification and consequences of friendship expectations. In the original study, 480 children from grades one through eight were asked to write a short essay describing the qualities and behaviors they expected from a best friend (Bigelow and La Gaipa 1975; La Gaipa and Bigelow 1972). The content analysis used a coding schema containing twenty-one dimensions. The data were analyzed in terms of when dimensions emerge, and change in frequency, by grade level. Bigelow (1977) replicated the study in Scotland, as well as looking at some of the implications of changes in social cognitions. Bigelow also identified nine dimensions that showed change over time and constructed a developmental scale.

Bigelow and La Gaipa (1980) proposed a three-stage developmental theory of friendship expectations on the basis of the age-related changes observed in their studies. This "stage theory" is additive rather than hierarchical and stresses the sequential invariance aspect of the development of friendship cognitions. In the first stage the child is highly reward-oriented, and is concerned with the expectation that friends will "play with them and be nice to them." Mutual activities is a major feature of friendship (see Furman and Bierman 1984). In the second stage, during the fourth or fifth grade, other elements are added, in particular, a concern with conventional morality. Friends are expected to follow moral rules. This is similar to what Kohlberg (1968) refers to as the "good-boy, good-girl" phase. In the third stage, during the sixth, seventh and eighth grades, loyalty and empathic understanding influence the preadolescents' thinking about friendship. In this stage common interests also become more important. The preadolescent turns to friends to share secrets, and is concerned that such confidences are not violated. A number of researchers have replicated various aspects of this general progression from concrete to abstract expectations using similar research paradigms (Hayes 1978; Reisman and Shorr 1978; Sharabany, Gershoni, and Hofman 1981).

The basic assumption underlying this research is untested, namely, that the emergence of friendship conceptions is related to cognitive development. Kerr and Hiebert (1984) recently examined the relationship between children's friendship expectations and their performance on Piagetian cognitive tasks measuring perspective-taking and conservation. A card sort task of twenty-three cards was constructed that contained statements pertaining to friendship categories derived primarily from Bigelow and La Gaipa (1975, 1980). The friendship stage scores were significantly related to performance on the cognitive tasks. Children that had achieved concrete operational functioning were found to rate the abstract concepts of friendship as more important than did children still at the preoperational stage.

The Children's Friendship Expectancy Inventory (CFEI)

Wood and La Gaipa (1978) applied more traditional psychometric procedures to construct an inventory similar to the adult form. More than 500 friendship essays written by children, collected earlier by La Gaipa and Bigelow (1972), were examined for ideas for items. Experimental items were administered to nearly 1,000 children. The final inventory contains twenty-eight items. The instructions are to rate each item in terms of their importance in choosing a best friend. The responses are marked on vertical ladders and are scored in terms of the four dimensions isolated by factor analytic studies. The first expectancy dimension, "conventional morality," focuses on the character traits of a friend as an individual, instead of the quality of the relationship. Friends should not lie, cheat or say mean things, or get others into trouble. The second expectancy dimension, "mutual activities" focuses on the stimulation value of a friend in games and sports. Friends are expected to participate in the same sports, games, and other activities. "Empathic understanding," the third dimension, refers to a set of expectations that a friend is sensitive, warm, reassuring, and trustworthy. One can share sensitive information with such a person who is a confidant. "Loyalty and commitment" describes a friend who remains a friend in spite of the cost or sacrifice involved. This dimension taps the strength of the relationship or its resistance to disruption.

Each of the variables seems to meet a different function (La Gaipa 1981c). "Conventional morality" appears to serve a screening function by avoiding children as friends that have negative qualities. "Mutual activities" serve as a reinforcing function insofar as pleasant associations facilitate bonding. "Loyalty and commitment" serves a testing function regarding the limits or intensity of the relationship. "Empathic understanding" serves a growth function: mutual understanding and a shared perspective facilitates the upward movement of a relationship.

Ayers (1985) has dealt with the difference between the "theory" and "practice" of friendship among adolescents. Is there a relationship between what they expect from a friend and how they assess their real-life friends? Using a modified form of the CFEI, Ayers found a positive association between what people expect from friendship and how they actually rate the friendship behavior of their real friends. In addition, a measure of satisfaction with their existing friendships was obtained. For the total group, the assessment of empathic understanding best predicted friendship satisfaction ($r = 0.46$). For individuals involved in reciprocal dyads, friendship satisfaction was best predicted by a combination of empathic understanding and conventional morality ($r = 0.61$). For individuals in non-reciprocal dyads, there were no successful predictor variables of friendship satisfaction. For males, friendship satisfaction was best predicted by the mutual activities scale. For females, empathy and conventional morality were the best predictors. Loyalty is related to satisfaction, but added little beyond the predictions obtained with empathy.

Youth and adulthood

Much of the interest in children's conceptions of friendship is based on the idea that problems in adult friendship can be traced to this life period (see Erikson 1963; Sullivan 1953). Cross-sectional research is the main research paradigm because of obvious costs in conducting longitudinal studies. Macfarlane and La Gaipa (1985) retrieved the original children's essays collected by La Gaipa and Bigelow in 1970. Some of the children had signed their names to the essays. Fifty-nine still resided in the same city, and all but three agreed to participate in a taped, telephone interview. The children were now between twenty-two and twenty-six years old. The same question was asked regarding what they considered important in a close friend of the same sex. Additional questions were asked to obtain a more comprehensive view of their current notions of friendship.

The relationship between the social cognitions of youth and adulthood was not strong, and varied with the nature of the specific dimension. Adolescent conceptions of friendship were more predictive of the affective than the cognitive aspects of adult friendships. Focus on propinquity is later associated with the view that friendship has a potential for harm, and an emphasis on acceptance is later associated with a negative image of friendship. Perhaps looking for persons that are accepting of one's idiosyncrasies leads to disappointments later in life. In sharp contrast, early adolescent males that give priority to loyalty later tend to have positive views of friendship.

Adult intimacy status was measured through the use of the Erikson Psychosocial Inventory Scale (Rosenthal, Gurney, and Moore 1981). Neither identity nor intimacy status of adulthood appear to be dependent upon the establishment of intimacy in early adolescence. Adolescent intimacy, however, was related negatively to the support dimension of instrumental aid. Adolescents focusing on intimacy are less likely to look for instrumental aid in friendship as adults; an early focus on the expressive aspects carries over into adulthood. It appears, then, that pre-adolescents that talked about the importance of "acceptance" in friendship were particularly concerned with "identity confirmation" and "self-worth" in adulthood. Earlier concerns with "propinquity" and "common interests" were related to later concerns with personal qualities of a friend that could be admired. It should be noted that "acceptance" was the only variable that was correlated with itself in 1985. Although sex differences were considerable in early adolescence, by adulthood most of these differences have disappeared, even on the dimension of intimacy.

The majority of participants in this study had progressed to higher levels of friendship conceptions as adults, at least two-thirds of the sample. The data suggest that many adults are capable of maintaining relationships characterized by intimacy regardless of the developmental level in childhood. These results support La Gaipa's (1979) contention that different social experiences beyond preadolescence are more relevant to the progression of friendship expectations than cognitive developmental factors at this time. The direction of growth, then, is not rigidly determined, but dependent upon varying experiences.

Some differences were found between the friendship expectations of the subjects in their early twenties and late twenties. Two age samples, 22–23 and 24–26, were taken, corresponding with 9–10 and 11–13. The younger adults were less likely to cite "strength of character" (admiration) as important in their friendships and more likely to cite the importance of "intimacy" than were older adults. It appears that intimacy drops off from the early to later twenties, and strength of character gains in importance. Perhaps the older participants were more established in terms of career and family, and felt less compelled to discuss personal matters.

Developmental studies with the FEI

The FEI has been used to study age-related changes, particularly in adolescence and old age. Changes in the meaning of friendship during adolescence were examined in a study of 4,400 adolescents ranging in age from twelve to twenty years (La Gaipa 1979). The responses were separately analyzed by level of friendship over time. An unexpected finding was the trend toward assigning less importance to the friendship dimensions with age. The most dramatic decreases were found for the lower levels of friendship, i.e. good friend and social acquaintance. "Self-disclosure," in particular, was rated as less important in these lower level friendships with increasing age. The only dimension that showed an increase in value with age was "authenticity." The results of this study suggest that social development during the adolescent years can best be explained in terms of social experiences. Cognitive developmental theories that focus on the role of maturational factors may be of less relevance after the onset of adolescence.

The friendship inventory was also administered to eighty seniors between the ages of sixty-three and eighty-seven (La Gaipa 1981a). Significant correlations were found between age and the friendship scales, the average being an r of 0.57. The positive correlations ranged from 0.70 for "acceptance" to 0.40 for "self-disclosure." It should be noted that this does not mean that there is a direct relationship between age and what individuals consider important in friendship. Rather, what is critical is the changing demands and contextual constraints. Within this sample of seniors, the changes were most dramatic after seventy-five years. We suspect that the high correlations with age of "acceptance," "authenticity" and "helping" reflect an increasing concern with vulnerability accompanying the aging process. As seniors become more dependent, they have an increased need for friends that will not exploit them, friends with whom they can be themselves, and that will give them the support they need. We suspect, then, that failing health has consequences on friendship expectations.

FRIENDSHIP EXPECTATIONS OF THE PERCEIVED AND THE PERCEIVER

Individual differences

Though most people are exposed to the same notions of friendship during the process of socialization, the interplay of contextual and personal factors leads to variations in friendship expectancies. Individual differences have been of special interest to us. Certainly, the same inferences are not made simply by the knowledge that a person is in the social category of friendship. The inferences concerning another, moreover, may reveal more about the perceiver than the perceived (Kelly 1955).

Different research tools have been used to study individual differences in friendship expectations: self-report inventories, psychiatric classifications, and demographic variables. The use of personality questionnaires has not proved very fruitful (see Howitt 1976; La Gaipa 1977b; La Gaipa and Howitt, 1975). Statistically significant but not very meaningful relationships have been found. Here are some examples.

Individuals that perceive themselves as responsible and dependable are likely to expect more from their friends than individuals that view themselves as otherwise. The higher the social maturity of an individual, the higher the perceived level of rewards obtained from others. Individuals with a high sense of well-being are more likely to emphasize "authenticity" and "empathic understanding" than persons with a low sense of well-being. Persons who are inflexible, deliberate, and cautious are more likely to value "self-disclosure" than those that are not.

Psychiatric types

The friendship inventory was administered to 174 psychiatric patients (Engelhart, Lockhart, and La Gaipa 1975). The female schizophrenics differ from normals in placing more value on the importance of the character traits of the potential friend, whereas the male schizophrenics differ from normals in placing less value on similarity. Perhaps paranoid females feel safer with a friend with strength of character, whereas the paranoid male may not feel comfortable with a person having a similar problem.

The profile of friendship expectations of the neurotic males looks like the profile of normal females, whereas the profile of the neurotic females is like that of the normal males. The neurotic males appear to have feminine-like receptivity, while neurotic females de-emphasize the importance of friendship-type behavior and focus on their own self-sufficiency and independency. The cognitive structure of the social knowledge of neurotics appears to be dominated by acceptance–authenticity, whereas the major dimension for the psychotics was intimacy, much like the normals.

Neurotics and introverts

Eysenck (1953) has proposed a fourfold classification of extroversion–introversion and neuroticism–stability. La Gaipa and Engelhart (1978) used this classification system to identify four subgroups in a study that included self-reports and psychiatric diagnosis by staff. In the first phase, the Eysenck Personality Inventory (EPI) was used to identify 111 extreme scorers out of a total of 300 subjects. In the second phase, forty-six neurotic patients were identified that were under psychiatric treatment. Most of these patients were diagnosed as depressives or in anxiety states. Staff ratings were also obtained on introversion–extroversion differences within this neurotic group. Essentially the same kind of results were obtained with the personality inventory and the diagnostic classifications. The results varied by gender. Females indicated they were more likely to engage in self-disclosure than males, regardless of stability–neurosis. Extroversion–introversion is more critical within the introverted group, neurotic females have a greater tendency to disclose than neurotic males, but no sex difference was found for the extroverted group. It would seem that no simple relationship exists between gender, neurosis, and introversion.

Aggressive and withdrawn girls

A multi-assessment approach was used to study the conceptions of friendship (La Gaipa and Wood 1985). A Behavioral Description Form was used by teachers to identify popular, aggressive and withdrawn girls (La Gaipa and Wood 1981). A TAT-type projective test evaluated psychosocial adaptation on five ego stages as posited by Erikson (1963). Significant differences were found. Popular vs. Withdrawn: empathy is twice as important as loyalty. The Withdrawn place much less emphasis on empathy than the popular girls, and, somewhat surprising, more emphasis on loyalty. Popular vs. Aggressive: the aggressives assign more value to loyalty. Aggressive vs. Withdrawn: the aggressives value empathy more than the withdrawn, who, instead, assign higher priorities to loyalty and lower priorities to conventional morality. Erikson views trust as a cornerstone of social development. We found that the trust variable did not differentiate quality of peer status. Low trust plays a somewhat different role in choosing friends by type. Aggressive girls low on trusting look for friends that are warm and understanding. Withdrawn girls who have low trust look for good companionship. For the popular girls, low trust is associated with feelings of inferiority and alienation.

MEMBER CATEGORY INFORMATION

Experimental studies of social perception

Research on social perception is concerned with the use of social category information in making inferences. Ethnic and racial stereotypes have been studied extensively from this perspective. Information-processing regarding individuals located in a category does not occur piecemeal; the information is integrated. Some kind of information, e.g. a dominant trait, may help to structure the image of the stimulus person. La Gaipa (in press) found that the stereotypes of many ethnic groups are structured by the occupation associated with the ethnic name. A major research strategy is to present member category information in a vignette form either separately and/or in combination with other information to assess the relative impact of the content of the information.

In an impression-formation study, vignettes were developed on the basis of behavioral checklists used to identify popular, aggressive and withdrawn children (La Gaipa and Wood 1974). The friendship expectations evoked by the image of the popular child were quite different from expectations for the aggressive and withdrawn child. The likelihood of such behavior was much stronger. Higher expectations were found for the Withdrawn than for the Aggressive on all dimensions, except on mutual activities. Knowledge about a peer's psychosocial problems is used to make inferences regarding what they can expect, as well as the desirability of the peer as a potential friend.

Friendship in disturbed adolescents

Emotionally disturbed adolescents often have few friends. The image of the disturbed adolescent was examined in a social perception study designed to assess acceptance–rejection, and the dimensions used (La Gaipa and Wood 1981). A vignette was presented to 105 university students in which an "emotionally disturbed" adolescent was described as being eighteen years old, still in school, of the same sex, and as under the care of a counselor. The instructions were to indicate the likelihood that the disturbed adolescent would behave the same as a non-disturbed adolescent. Only 20 per cent of the subjects said the likelihood of acceptance was the same.

The emotionally disturbed were perceived as less likely to provide social validation and identity confirmation, less likely to engage in reciprocal exchange; less likely to provide helping and support, and less likely to provide stimulation value. Not surprisingly, the likelihood of receiving these kinds of friendship rewards were strongly associated with acceptance–rejection of other as a potential friend.

Personality

A sample of 149 university students was administered the Jackson Personality Research Form (PRF) and an impression-formation questionnaire (Travis and La Gaipa 1974). Five stimulus persons were presented in the form of vignettes – impulsive, aggressive, autonomous, affiliative, and orderly. These personality descriptions were obtained from the PRF manual as characteristics of higher scorers on the PRF scales. Below each of the PRF vignettes was presented twelve friendship expectancy statements that were scored in terms of four scales: "positive regard," "authenticity," "intimacy," and "similarity."

The vignette with the personality description of the affiliative person activated higher levels of friendship expectations than the other four personalities. A person who comes across as affiliative is assumed to be the kind of person likely to behave as a "real" friend. On the other hand, aggressive types are viewed as least likely to engage in friendship behavior. Moreover, the affiliative type was perceived as showing the most promise as a potential friend, and the aggressive type as having the least promise.

These data were also analyzed in terms of the relationship between the personality needs of the subjects and the corresponding personality descriptions in the vignettes. The use of personality descriptions in making inferences about friendship was found to vary with the actual similarity between the perceiver and the stimulus person. The need for order had the most powerful effect. The greater the need for order, the higher the friendship expectations evoked by information that the stimulus person was also orderly. This finding suggests that persons with a need for structure are likely to reject as friends persons that are disorderly. A few sex differences were found with regard to the desire to develop a friendship. Aggressive males indicated they have much in common with other aggressive persons and would like them as friends. Aggressive females, however, showed no such preferences. Females high in affiliation needs were most likely to expect authenticity from another female with the same need for affiliation.

A SYSTEMS APPROACH TO CLOSE RELATIONSHIPS

The notions of social network and systems are receiving increasing attention (cf. La Gaipa 1981b). Within this broad perspective friendships are viewed as part of a larger social system rather than as isolated dyads. The social context is viewed as essential for understanding such relationships as friendship.

Social context

A basic assumption that we have made in our research program is that the social context influences what is anticipated or expected from potential resource persons. When an individual needs support he/she scans different parts of the social network. Decisions have to be made regarding the choice of sub-system. Social knowledge about these different aspects of the social network is essential. The individual develops over time expectancies with regard to what kind of behavior is likely to occur as a consequence of trying to activate different parts of the social system.

Little information is available on what kind of social contexts have what kind of effects on what kind of friendship dimensions for what kind of individuals. Renwick (1985) has examined the impact of competitive situations on friendship expectations. She used an experimental design in which type of competition was manipulated using vignettes. The two categories of conflict of interest involved competing for academic grades within a university environment, and competing for the love and affection of a person of the opposite sex. The three levels of friendship were close, good, and social acquaintance. The La Gaipa Friendship Scales used included "authenticity," "self-disclosure," "positive regard," "helping and support," and "similarity."

It was found that competition does not destroy the relationship, but shifts the anticipatory aspects down one level. Nevertheless, even under strain, close friends are predicted to "come out ahead" of good friends or acquaintances.

The degree to which specific aspects of friendships are expected to change under competitive conditions varies with the stage of the relationship. The higher levels of friendship showed the most downward change. For close friends this "uneven effect" was most dramatic in competitive contexts involving the affection of a person of the opposite sex. If a close friend has to compete for such affection, this reduces the degree to which the competitor is expected to be genuine. Much less openness, spontaneity, and realness is expected from a person trying to take away the one you love. Considerable decline is also expected in positive regard. Changes in other dimensions are significant, but less dramatic. Close relationships are durable in spite of this competition, but less intense.

The findings for "self-disclosure" are of particular interest in view of the attention this variable has received in prior research. Of the five dimensions examined by Renwick, "self-disclosure" was judged to be least likely behavior. This was found for all levels of friendship. The effect of competition served to decrease the likelihood of occurrence still further. Under competitive conditions, however, "self-disclosure" continued to differentiate level of friendship, anticipated to occur more often, the higher the level. Renwick found few main or interactive gender effects. One interaction was with regard to the dimension of "helping and support" from a close friend. Under competition for affection, females anticipate a greater decline in support than do males.

The family as a support system

The behaviors that are expected from friends are common to other close relationships (Argyle and Henderson 1985). In my personal interviews regarding friendship, a common response was "My sister is my best friend." Clark and La Gaipa (1979) administered two forms of the interpersonal relationships scales to 213 subjects, aged 10–19, in a rural village in southern England. One form was the friendship inventory, whereas the other form contained the same items but oriented in terms of their siblings. For females, no significant difference was found with regard to what they expect from their sisters and their close friends in terms of "positive regard," "helping," and "similarity." But females expect more from their friends with regard to the expressive dimensions of "authenticity," "empathy," and "self-disclosure." Males make much less of a difference between their brothers and close friends. Younger boys expect more "help" from their brothers than their friends. Older boys think "similarity" is more important with regard to their friends than for their brothers. This study suggests that siblings are an important support system in adolescence, particularly for females.

Development of a social support inventory

The observation that there are some basic interpersonal dimensions common to different close relationships led to the construction of a new social support inventory (La Gaipa 1984). Four dimensions found to recur in various studies include instrumental aid, identity confirmation, emotional expression, and empathic understanding as basic support dimensions. Several factor analytic studies were used as a basis for the final selection of items. The alpha reliabilities were: Instrumental Aid (0.88); Identity Confirmation (0.81); Emotional Expression (0.79); and Empathic Understanding (0.82). Each scale contains five items for a total twenty-item inventory.

Instrumental Aid includes much of the content from the helping and support scale but with more focus on the attitude behind the giving, including spontaneity and the motive of not getting something in return. Identity Confirmation is similar to the "positive regard" scale. The key notion in this dimension is that of helping other to view self as worthwhile and competent, and to have more confidence in one's self. Emotional Expression is similar to the "intimacy/self-disclosure" scale. The focus is on helping other to be open about his/her fears and anxieties. Empathic Understanding is a revision of the "acceptance" and "authenticity" dimensions, and the addition of items on accuracy. Such a person really listens; tries to see things through the other's eyes, and accurately interprets how other really feels.

A study was done to compare friendship and kinship in crisis situations (La Gaipa 1984). The kind of chronic condition did not make much difference with regard to the expected behavior they would receive. If the patient has cancer, the immediate family is assumed to provide more empathy than relatives, but no difference was found between friends and family. More instrumental aid and understanding was specified for cancer patients than heart patients. Overall, across health conditions, the immediate family was perceived as more likely to provide support than friends, in particular with regard to instrumental aid and identity confirmation – to help a sick person feel worthy and competent.

Long-term chronic conditions accentuate the differences between friends and kin in the support perceived to be provided. In the non-crisis, day-by-day interactions, few differences were found between friends and kin with regard to helping, identity, or empathy. Under crisis situations, families and relatives provide much more help, identity confirmation, and somewhat more empathic understanding than friends. Situational pressures are not believed to increase the support that friends are likely to provide. Instead, the trend was downward with less support provided. In particular, emotional expression, listening, showed a significant decrease from "normal" to "crisis" situations.

Most of the research on friendship in disciplines, outside of psychology, treats it as one type of social support. Dunkel-Schetter and Wortman (1982), in a study on cancer, found that the more close friends, the fewer the symptoms. Negative emotions were related to having fewer close friends, whereas patients with more close family members had more problems in functioning. Weisman (1979) notes, however, that friends tend to withdraw from the sickbed, because their relationships to the patient are fairly circumscribed in time, depth, intimacy, and commitment. Newly diagnosed patients do not rank friends very high with respect to problems they are experiencing. He suggests that this indicates the limited expectations held about friends.

In a study on family and friends of cancer patients (La Gaipa and Friesen 1984), we sought to identify some of the basic dimensions underlying the various constraints or support problems. Factor analysis identified three dimensions: "affect arousal," "task ambiguity," and "personal cost." The difficulties of support persons center around negative emotional reactions to the situation, uncertainty as to how to give support and an assessment of the personal costs of involvement with the patients. Friends of the patients, in particular, felt the major problem they faced in dealing with the patient was "task ambiguity" – not knowing what to do. "Task ambiguity" was a more serious problem than "affect arousal" or "personal cost." A higher number of relatives and friends available in the patient's community was associated with more support problems particularly "task ambiguity" and "personal cost." And friends were found to report more problems in giving support than kin.

An unexpected finding was regarding advice-giving. The support persons, particularly friends and relatives, reported having considerable problems in this area. A task interpretation of this would be that advice-giving requires an understanding of the nature of the problem, and specific information and knowledge unlike the more "experiential" types of support. It should also be noted that advice-giving is not always appreciated by the cancer patient (Dunkel-Schetter and Wortman 1982). Reisman (1982) found that advice-giving is a very common form of friendship behavior, but one that is least desired by the receiver. People want others to listen, not to give advice. Advice-giving can be aversive. It can have detrimental effects on feelings of self-worth.

CONCLUSIONS

In this essay I have tried to show that an understanding of role expectations is a viable approach to accounting for relationships. The focus throughout has been on friendship expectations about the activities that are viewed as appropriate in the role category of friend. The notion that different activities are expected from friends and enemies is not really new. From the time of Aristotle, philosophers have made this observation. Our efforts were designed to identify a small number of variables that could explain much of friendship, to operationalize the variables, and to relate them to antecedents and consequences of such expectations on relationship changes.

The emergence of friendship expectations was of interest. The unfolding of these social cognitions in childhood was related first to the more general cognitive development, and then to the personal and social experiences of the child moving through the adolescent years. Reality testing leads to more realistic expectations, and there is growing awareness of the conditions that influence what can be expected.

Friendship expectations are not an isolated category of social knowledge. Rather, they are shaped by the experiences of the individual. Insofar as the expectations influence interpersonal behavior, there may be some side-effects on peer acceptance–rejection. Research reported in this paper has shown that preadolescents with behavioral problems, the emotionally disturbed, the neurotics and the psychotics tend to look at friendship in somewhat different ways than the more stable individuals. I have shown that such individuals are also expected to behave in somewhat different ways from the more normal, stable individuals. The data suggests, then, that multiple categories are involved in the inferences made. A friend with a psychological problem is not expected to behave according to the shared beliefs about a friend. Certainly, such information may distort what a specific individual is likely to do in a friendship relationship. But there is some evidence that a psychological problem is likely to have some impact on conceptions of friendship. Our findings do fit in with the old "kernel of truth" hypothesis regarding social stereotypes.

Dyadic relationships do not evolve to higher levels of intimacy simply because the two parties have similar ideas about friendship. The expectancies serve mainly as a guide, i.e. as part of the evaluative schema for assessing relational changes. What really matters is the behavior of the other party, interpreted as confirming or disconfirming the expectations. Social knowledge about friendship, then, has significance mainly insofar as it is translated into actions that are congruent with the recipient's cognitive framework.

The affective structure of friendship has been largely neglected in my research, as well as by other investigators of close relationships. The importance of affect, however, is evident in my research on persons with some kind of psychological problem. The neurotics and the psychotics, the withdrawn and the aggressive have problems in both cognitive and affect domains, each one probably having some kind of an impact on the other. The importance of the affect quality of relationships was quite evident in the over 1,000 accounts of friendship written by children and adolescents. To the youth, friendship is more than "fun and games." Friendship serves as a vehicle for navigating the difficult passage during this period of transition. But friendship is also viewed as making a person more vulnerable. Tensions and anxieties associated with friendship come through their personal accounts of the growth and termination of such relationships.

If friendship is such a fulfilling and wonderful experience, how come it is so uncommon? Many people have never had more than one or two close friendships in a lifetime, and these often represent fantasies going back to childhood. In a nation-wide survey of 40,000 individuals, mostly young adults, *Psychology Today* indicated that one-third of the respondents said they never had a close friend (Parlee 1979). Studies of the elderly provide similar results. For instance, Powers and Bultena (1976) found that two-fifths of elderly males and one-third of elderly females report they never had a close friend. Research studies vary somewhat on the number of close friends. Reisman and Shorr (1978) observed an average of six close friends in their sample. The problem of defining levels of friendship is a major problem. Moreover, it is quality rather than quantity that matters. But even this is difficult to measure. In my own research, I found that "self-disclosure" is the dimension that best discriminates close friend from good friend. The term "confidant" appears to signify what people mean by close friend. But a belief often expressed in interviews that I have done is that it is not easy to find confidants that can be trusted.

Most people can articulate the ideals of friendship quite readily. Knowledge of friendship expectations is widely shared. But when probed, cynicism is often expressed regarding the confirmation of expectations. We isolated a strong negative dimension in the factor analytic study of adult friendships (Macfarlane and La Gaipa 1985). A recurring theme was that friendship may make you vulnerable, and that it could be dangerous. So, a distorted view of what people really feel and think may result from simply looking at the positive side of friendship.

The affect side of relationships may turn out to be the central organizing and mobilizing force in interpersonal relations (Clarke, Allen, and Dickson 1985). The affect domain of friendship has its own structure that needs to be investigated. Accounting for the reluctance of some people to form close relationships requires understanding of the anxieties associated with this personal support system. When the likelihood of finding someone who can be a confidant is believed to be low, there may be little motivation to seek out such a person. The potential rewards from close relationships require understanding of the anxieties associated with this personal support system. The rewards may never be realized for large numbers of people.

My research has called attention to the significance of the social context with regard to the normative expectations and predictions made of persons in the social category of friend. In the real world, social ideals about this relationship are modified by the larger knowledge structure of which such cognitions are a part. The individual has to process information about other persons in the social network that may impact on friendship. Furthermore, the individual has to be cognizant of strategies used by self and others to achieve objectives that are independent of the relationship. As Renwick (1985) has noted, friendship may suffer when there is competition for a scarce commodity. Such competition may evoke negative affect, and even challenge some of the ideals or illusions about the sanctity and integrity of the relationship. Finally, recent research on friendship within the context of health psychology suggests that the conceptualization of friendship is situation-bound. Individuals do articulate quite readily the ideals of friendship, but acknowledge the greater reliability of the kinship network in hard times.

REFERENCES

Argyle, M. and Henderson, M. (1984) "The rules of friendship." *Journal of Social and Personal Relationships*, 1, 211–37.

—— and —— (1985) "The rules of relationships." In S. Duck and D. Perlman (eds) *Understanding Personal Relationships*. London: Sage.

Ayers, M.E. (1985) "Friendship expectations and real-life friendships." Unpublished master's thesis, Wake Forest University, Winston-Salem, NC.

Bigelow, B.J. (1986, July) "In search of children's social rules." Paper presented at the Third International Conference on Personal Relationships, Tel-Aviv, Israel.

—— (1977) "Children's friendship expectations: a cognitive developmental study." *Child Development*, 48, 246–53.

—— and La Gaipa, J.J. (1975) "Children's written descriptions of friendship: a multidimensional analysis." *Developmental Psychology*, 11, 857–8.

—— and —— (1980) "The development of friendship values and choice." In H.C. Foot, A.J. Chapman, and J.R. Smith (eds) *Friendship and Social Relations in Children*. New York: John Wiley, 15–44.

Clark, A.A. and La Gaipa, J.J. (1979) "Sibling rivalry: the friendly answer." Unpublished manuscript, University of Windsor, Windsor, ON.

Clarke, D.D., Allen, C.M.B., and Dickson, S. (1985) "The characteristic affective tone of seven classes of interpersonal relationship." *Journal of Social and Personal Relationships*, 2, 117–28.

Damon, W. (1977) *The Social World of the Child*. Jossey-Bass: San Francisco.

Davis, K.E. and Todd, M.J. (1982) "Friendship and love relationships." In K.E. Davis and T.O. Mitchell (eds) *Advances in Descriptive Psychology*, vol. 2. Greenwich, CT: JAI Press.

—— and —— (1985) "Assessing friendship: prototypes, paradigm cases and relationship descriptions." In S. Duck and D. Perlman (eds) *Understanding Personal Relationships: An Interdisciplinary Approach*. London: Sage, 17–38.

Dunkel-Schetter, C. and Wortman, C.B. (1982) "The interpersonal dynamics of cancer: problems in social relationships and their impact on the patient." In H.S. Friedman and M.R. DiMatteo (eds) *Interpersonal Issues in Health Care*. New York: Academic Press.

Engelhart, R.S., Lockhart, L.M., and La Gaipa, J.J. (1975, March) "The friendship expectations of psychiatric patients." Paper presented at the meeting of the South-eastern Psychological Association, Atlanta.

Erikson, E.H. (1963). *Childhood and Society*. New York: Norton.

Eysenck, H.J. (1953) *The Structure of Human Personality*. New York: John Wiley.

Furman, W. and Bierman, K.L. (1984) "Children's conceptions of friendship: a multimethod study of developmental changes." *Developmental Psychology*, 20, 925–31.

Hayes, D.S. (1978) "Cognitive bases for liking and disliking among preschool children." *Child Development*, 49, 906–9.

Heilbronn, M. (1975) "A longitudinal study of the development and dissolution of friendship." Unpublished doctoral dissertation, University of Windsor, Windsor, ON.

Howitt, R. (1976) "A self–other attributional model of friendship formation." Unpublished doctoral dissertation, University of Windsor, Windsor, ON.

Kelly, G.A. (1955) *The Psychology of Personal Constructs*. New York: Norton.

Kerr, M.K. and Hiebert, K. (1984, June) "The development of friendship and cognitive concepts." Paper presented at the meeting of the Canadian Psychological Association, Toronto, ON.

Kohlberg, L. (1968) "The child as a moral philosopher." *Psychology Today*, 2, 25–30.

La Gaipa, J.J. (1972a, May) "Comparison level and the evaluation of friendships rewards." Paper presented at the meeting of the Midwestern Psychological Association, Cleveland, OH.

—— (1972b, June) "Personality factors in friendship." Paper presented at the meeting of the Canadian Psychological Association, Montreal.

—— (1977a) "Interpersonal attraction and social exchange." In S.W. Duck (ed.) *Theory and Practice in Interpersonal Attraction*. London and New York: Academic Press, 129–64.

—— (1977b) "Testing a multi-dimensional approach to friendship." In S.W. Duck (ed.) *Theory and Practice in Interpersonal Attraction*. London and New York: Academic Press, 249–70.

—— (1979) "A developmental study of the meaning of friendship in adolescence." *Journal of Adolescence*, 2, 1–13.

—— (1981a) "The meaning of friendship in old age." Paper presented at symposium Friendship over the Life Cycle at the meeting of the Canadian Psychological Association, Toronto.

—— (1981b) "A systems approach to personal relationships." In S.W. Duck and R. Gilmour (eds) *Personal Relationships 1: Studying Personal Relationships*. London and New York: Academic Press, 67–89.

—— (1981c) "Children's friendships." In S.W. Duck and R. Gilmour (eds) *Personal Relationships 2: Developing Personal Relationships*. London and New York: Academic Press, 161–85.

—— (1982) "Rules and rituals in disengaging from relationships." In S.W. Duck (ed.) *Personal Relationships 4: Dissolving Personal Relationships*. London and New York: Academic Press, 189–216.

—— (1984, July) "A comparative analysis of friendship and kinship in crisis situations." Paper presented at the Second International Conference on Personal Relationships, Madison, WI.

—— (in press) "Stereotypes and perceived ethnic-role specialization." In W. Bergmann (ed.) *Psychological Research on Anti-semitism*, vol. 2. White Plains, NY: Aldine Press.

—— and Bigelow, B.J. (1972, June) "The development of childhood friendship expectations." Paper presented at the meeting of the Canadian Psychological Association, Montreal.

—— and Engelhart, R.S. (1977, May) "Extroversion–introversion, neuroticism and self-disclosure in friendship." Paper presented at the meeting of the Southeastern Psychological Association, Hollywood, FL.

—— and —— (1978) "Sex differences in self-disclosure and friendship." Paper presented at the meeting of the Southeastern Psychological Association, Atlanta.

—— and Friesen, N. (1984, July) "Burnout in the informal social network of cancer patients." Paper presented at the meeting of the Second International Conference on Personal Relationships, Madison, WI.

—— and Howitt, R. (1975, June) "The role of individual differences in an attributional model of friendship formation." Paper presented at the meeting of the Canadian Psychological Association, Quebec City.

—— and Uriel, M. (1974, June) "Psychosocial satisfaction and the effectiveness of group therapy for alcoholics." Paper presented at the meeting of the Canadian Psychological Association, Windsor, ON.

—— and Wood, H.D. (1974, June) "An approach to the study of friendship in terms of implicit personality theory." Paper presented at the meeting of the Canadian Psychological Association, Windsor, ON.

—— and —— (1981) "Friendship in disturbed adolescents." In S.W. Duck and R. Gilmour (eds) *Personal Relationships 3: Personal Relationships in Disorder*. London and New York: Academic Press, 169–88.

—— and —— (1985) "An Eriksonian approach to conceptions of friendship of aggressive and withdrawn preadolescent girls." *Journal of Early Adolescence*, 5, 357–69.

Lischeron, J.A. and La Gaipa, J.J. (1971, June) "The friendship expectancy inventory: prediction of the growth of friendship." Paper presented at the meeting of the Canadian Psychological Association, St John's, Newfoundland.

Macfarlane, V. and La Gaipa, J.J. (1985, June) "Friendship in youth and adulthood: a serendipitous longitudinal study." Paper read at the meeting of the Canadian Psychological Association, Halifax, NS.

Miell, D.E., Duck, S.W., and La Gaipa, J.J. (1979) "Interactive effects of sex and timing of self disclosure." *British Journal of Social and Clinical Psychology*, 18, 355–62.

Parlee, M.B. (1979) "Survey report on friendship in America: the friendship bond." *Psychology Today*, 13, 45–113.

Piaget, J. (1965) *The Moral Judgment of the Child.* New York: Free Press.

Powers, E.A. and Bultena, G.L. (1976) "Sex differences in intimate friendships in old age." *Journal of Marriage and the Family*, 38, 739–48.

Reisman, J.M. (1982) "Friendship and psychotherapy." *Academic Psychology Bulletin*, 4, 237–46.

—— and Shorr, S.I. (1978) "Friendship claims and expectations among children and adults." *Child Development*, 49, 913–16.

Renwick, R.M. (1985) "Competition with friends: perceptions, accounts and expectations." Unpublished doctoral dissertation, University of Lancaster, Lancaster, G.B.

Rosenthal, D.A., Gurney, R.M., and Moore, S.M. (1981) "From trust to intimacy: a new inventory for examining Erikson's stages of psychosocial development." *Journal of Youth and Adolescence*, 10, 525–37.

Selman, R.L. (1980) *The Growth of Interpersonal Understanding: Developmental and Clinical Analyses.* New York: Academic Press.

Sharabany, R., Gershoni, R., and Hofman, J. (1981) "Girlfriend, boyfriend: age and sex differences in intimate friendship." *Developmental Psychology*, 17, 800–8.

Smollar, J. and Youniss, J. (1982) "Social development through friendship." In K.H. Rubin and H.S. Ross (eds) *Peer Relationships and Social Skills in Childhood.* New York: Springer-Verlag, 279–98.

Sullivan, H.S. (1953) *The Interpersonal Theory of Psychiatry.* New York: Norton.

Taylor, S.E. and Crocker, J. (1981) "Schematic bases of social information processing." In E.T. Hoggins, C.P. Herman, and M.P. Zanna (eds) *Social Cognition: The Ontario symposium.* Hillsdale, NJ: Lawrence Erlbaum.

Travis, S.K. and La Gaipa, J.J. (1974, June) "Individual differences in the attribution of friendship traits to similar and dissimilar persons." Paper presented at the meeting of the Canadian Psychological Association, Windsor, ON.

Wegreniuk, K. (1971) "Friendship expectations in small groups." Unpublished manuscript, University of Windsor, Windsor, ON.

Weisman, A.D. (1979) *Coping with Cancer.* New York: McGraw-Hill.

Wood, H.D. and La Gaipa, J.J. (1978, June) "Predicting behavioral types of preadolescent girls from psychosocial development and friendship values." Paper presented at the meeting of the Canadian Psychological Association, Ottawa.

Wright, P.H. (1984) "Self-referent motivation and the intrinsic quality of friendship." *Journal of Social and Personal Relationships*, 1, 115–30.

—— (1985) "The acquaintance description form." In S. Duck and D. Perlman (eds) *Understanding Personal Relationships: An Interdisciplinary Approach* London: Sage.

9 Planning and scheming: strategies for initiating relationships

Charles R. Berger

Social cognition researchers have accorded such theoretical constructs as prototypes (Cantor and Mischel 1977, 1979), scripts (Schank and Abelson 1977), self-schemata (Markus 1977) and other schemata-related entities (Taylor and Crocker 1981) a central role in the processing of social information. In general, these constructs have been employed to explain how persons arrive at judgments of themselves and others. Well-formed schemata about persons, roles, and events promote faster information-processing and influence the complexity and direction of social and self-judgments. In addition to these functions, schemata are implicated in the production of social action (Taylor and Crocker 1981); however, since most social cognition research employs measures of such dependent variables as recall, recognition memory, reaction time, and judgment, the relationship between schemata and action in ongoing social encounters is not well understood. This state of affairs is reminiscent of the late 1960s when researchers (e.g. Wicker 1969) became concerned with the relationship between attitudes and behavior only after hundreds of studies were reported in which attitude assessment through the questionnaire was the sole method used to index persuasion.

The purpose of this chapter is to begin to redress this current imbalance by focusing attention on the links between *plans* as cognitive structures and social actions. The relationship between planning and social action will be discussed within the specific context of relationship initiation, i.e. asking others for dates. This particular context was chosen because it is one that is very salient to college students and is one domain in which some students are likely to be experts. These reasons obviate the often heard criticism of college sophomore subjects as unrepresentative of persons in the "real world;" wherever that is to be found. We will first consider some general issues with respect to plans as cognitive structures and then explore the relationship between plans and relationship beginnings.

PLANS AND SOCIAL ACTION

The idea that plans mediate between other cognitive structures and action is not new. Miller, Galanter, and Pribram (1960) argued that plans could be conceived of as Test–Operate–Test–Exit (TOTE) units arranged hierarchically. More recently, artificial intelligence researchers and cognitive scientists have designed and implemented planners to guide robot arms (Sacerdoti 1977), organize sequences of errands (Hayes-Roth and Hayes-Roth 1979), produce various speech acts (Cohen and Perrault 1979), and understand action sequences (Schank and Abelson 1977; Schmidt 1976; Wilensky 1981, 1983). In addition, Hobbs and Evans (1980) have argued that conversation can be viewed profitably from a planning perspective and Bruce (1980) has emphasized the importance to readers of goal and plan recognition for the successful understanding of stories.

In general, plans are believed to serve two principal functions (Wilensky 1983). First, the ability of a perceiver to recognize the goals others are seeking and the plans they are employing to achieve their goals aids in the process of developing explanations for the others' actions. Plan recognition is centrally implicated in action understanding. Second, plans are responsible for the production of goal-directed action. However, the two processes are quite different. The process of action generation entails either the instantiation of a stored plan or the fabrication of a new plan to produce the actions necessary to achieve a goal; while the process of action understanding works in reverse. The observer sees the actions being manifested in pursuit of a goal and must try to find planning knowledge that will explain the actions. Obviously, both of these processes are vital in the development, maintenance, and decay of personal relationships; however, the main focus of this chapter will be on plans and action generation in the relationship context.

SOME THEORETICAL CONSIDERATIONS

Planning may be viewed as a problem-solving process in which an initial state of the world is given and plans are developed to achieve a desired state or goal. Human planners have the capacity to monitor a number of aspects of this process; although, because of limited attentional capacities, they may not be able to monitor all of these aspects simultaneously. First, persons can monitor their progress toward the goal, i.e. they have a way of comparing their current state with both an initial state and a desired state. Second, persons have the ability to formulate plans and to anticipate the

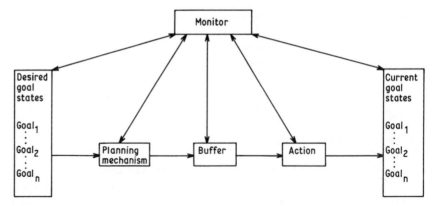

Figure 9.1   Action generation process

potential consequences of realizing their plans in action. However, unanticipated consequences can and do occur in the implementation of plans. Third, persons have the capacity to formulate and hold plans in a buffer during which time they can decide whether or not they wish to realize their plans in action. Again, however, there are some significant limitations to this monitoring capacity. Frequently employed plans that are stored in long-term memory can be enacted without conscious awareness or mindlessly (Langer 1978). Moreover, the fact that persons can express regret for the enactment of some behavioral routine (e.g. "I didn't mean to say that") indicates that monitoring and control of ongoing action is not perfect; assuming of course that the regret arises not because of another's reaction to the performed actions, but because of one's reactions to one's own actions. This process is depicted in Figure 9.1.

As the process shown in Figure 9.1 indicates, most social interactions involve a multiplicity of goals that may be explicit or implicit to the persons engaged in them. Thus, for example, an individual might have the goal of persuading another person to do or believe X but also be interested in preserving their relationship with the other whether or not the persuasion goal is reached. Goals related to relationship preservation or face-saving are frequently activated in parallel with other social goals like persuasion. In fact, most social interactions are multi-goal affairs. Most probably, however, these multiple goals are not equally important to the social actor in many situations.

Metagoals

In social interaction situations, there are certain metagoals that spawn metaplans that control in turn the development of plans to reach inter-action goals. Wilensky (1981, 1983) has postulated the metagoal of *effici-*

ency in plan development. This goal embodies the notion that one should develop plans that reach goals in the most efficient manner. A series of papers (Berger and Kellermann 1983, 1985; Kellermann and Berger 1984) has suggested that another important metagoal in social interaction contexts is *social appropriateness*. Persons formulate their plans such that they try to maximize the levels of social appropriateness of the actions they produce.

It is possible for the dimensions of efficiency and appropriateness to come into conflict with each other. For example, in one of our studies of information-seeking in initial interactions we found high efficiency in information-gathering to be associated with judgments of reduced social appropriateness of behavior (Berger and Kellermann 1983). Persons who were asked to seek as little information as possible from their partners were generally judged to be efficient but socially inappropriate; while persons instructed to seek as much information as possible received the opposite pattern of efficiency and appropriateness ratings.

The pursuit of other social goals may bring the efficiency and appropriateness dimensions into a consistent relationship with each other. For example, if one's goal is to ingratiate one's self to another, the most efficient way to do so would result in the production of socially appropriate actions. Even when persons attempt to achieve social goals where negative actions can be employed, e.g. persuasion, they may try to blunt the negative impact of these actions by acting in ways that make them more attractive to their partners. Mehrabian and Williams (1969) found that persons who were attempting to persuade others displayed more positive nonverbal behaviors than did persons who were not attempting to persuade their conversational partners. Thus, at times socially appropriate actions may be used to compensate for the potential negative impacts of more efficient actions.

The notion that the metagoals of efficiency and appropriateness guide the formation and alteration of planning activity is consistent with Baxter's discussion (Chapter 11 in this volume) of the role of cognition in relationship interaction. She points out that indirectness in communication between intimates may reduce threats to face that might arise if more direct talk were used. However, indirect talk might be somewhat less efficient than direct talk. Of course, in very well developed relationships, persons may know each other so well that even very indirect messages are rapidly and clearly understood; thus, the dimensions of efficiency and social appropriateness might well be maximized simultaneously in these situations.

Plan formation

At least two different conceptualizations of plan formation have been employed by artificial intelligence researchers who have implemented planning programs. Sacerdoti (1977) argues that planning begins at a high level of abstraction and proceeds in stages progressively to more concrete levels of action. His planner contains a number of critics that compare the desired state or goal with the alternatives that have been generated at each level of abstraction. These comparisons determine whether the plan as developed will lead to the desired goal. Hayes-Roth and Hayes-Roth (1979) have argued that while this top-down approach to planning may be appropriate for certain goals, planning is frequently an opportunistic process. Planning steps may not occur in a well-defined sequence and persons may formulate their plans by jumping from one possibility to the next in what may appear to be an almost random search strategy. Detailed examination of think-aloud protocols generated by persons planning a series of errands demonstrates that at least in this domain, a top-down approach is most probably not used.

Newell (1978) has contrasted open-loop and closed-loop views of human motor control. The open-loop view requires that initial plans be highly detailed and not subject to modification by the vagaries of environmental contingencies. A cue sets off the process and actions are directed by the detailed plan. This relatively rigid view of motor control can be contrasted with the more flexible closed-loop system. In such a system, initial plans are not as well formulated and can be modified as they proceed. Newell argues that this latter view of the relationship between plans and actions is probably a more realistic one in the domain of motor control. The same would seem to be the case for ongoing social interactions. As noted previously, persons do appear to have the capacity to monitor plan formation and deployment such that they can prevent fully formulated plans from being actualized in social actions and they can modify plans in response to environmental contingencies as the plans unfold.

Having argued that plan formation is to some degree event-driven, it should be pointed out that in ongoing social interactions, the degree of adjustment to environmental contingencies can vary depending upon the specific goals of the interaction. Thus, highly ritualized forms of social interaction like greetings may be produced by a top-down, open-loop planning system. Such a process might produce the following interaction sequence:

PLANNER: Hello, how are you this morning?
OTHER: Not so good.
PLANNER: Have a nice day.

In these kinds of interactions the planner does not process in any depth the response offered by the other. In this instance, the planner has reached his or her goal, i.e. greeting other. Although such extreme situations are relatively rare in social encounters, they do suggest that persons are capable of producing social actions that are driven by a top-down, open-loop planning mechanism. Ritualized conflict situations may also be motivated by such planning mechanisms. Nevertheless, the great majority of social interactions appear to be the product of an event-driven, closed-loop planning process that is opportunistic in nature.

Even though the planning processes involved in the production of social interaction are generally opportunistic, the metagoals of efficiency and social appropriateness maintain a regnant status in the face of environmental contingencies. Contingencies that arise during the course of goal striving are evaluated against these two metagoals and plans are modified or not modified accordingly. Thus, planning processes for the attainment of social goals exhibit flexibility within the constraints of efficiency and social appropriateness.

Contingencies that arise during the give and take of social interactions can affect the planning process in at least two ways. First, if persons are put into the position of entering their interactions without a well-formulated plan, they may employ events that occur during their interactions to direct the plan formation process. A second possibility is the situation in which persons have relatively well-elaborated plans with a number of alternative paths available for reaching their goals. In this instance, environmental contingencies might determine what specific paths are discarded or chosen rather than the shape of the overall plan itself. The availability of well-articulated plans in memory will determine, in part, the impact that environmental contingencies are likely to have.

Dynamic aspects of goals

Thus far, the flexible nature of the social interaction planning process has been emphasized. In addition, it has been argued that most social interaction situations involve the simultaneous striving for a multiplicity of goals. It is equally important to recognize that during the course of social interactions, the goals for which interaction participants strive can be modified in a number of ways. We will now consider some of these possibilities.

First, goals may *dissolve* during the course of interactions. By the end of a particular encounter, persons may actually forget or may not be able to articulate the reasons they began the encounter in the first place. This is little different from the situation in which persons go to a room for a given purpose but upon arrival to the room forget why they went to the room in the first place. Norman (1981) provides a number of examples of such action slips reported by individuals. Apparently, persons can carry on very articulate conversations with others but be totally unable to remember why they began the conversation; even though they consciously initiated the conversation for a given purpose. In encounters where goals have dissolved, persons may set new goals while in the process of conversing. These new goals may be unrelated to the initial goals of the interactants.

A second possible goal change that can occur is *parlaying*. Persons may begin an interaction with a particular goal in mind, e.g. develop a friendship, but because of information they derive during the interaction, they may change their goal to that of inducing their conversational partner into becoming a lover. Notice that if our example is turned around, we still have an example of parlaying. In the case of goal parlaying, unlike goal dissolution, there is some relationship between present goals and the previous goals of the interaction. Even in an instance where the progression of goal development seems to be unrelated, e.g. a person who asks a stranger for directions but ends up falling in love with the stranger, the fact that asking for directions brought the stranger and the direction-asker into contact with each other allowed for the satisfaction of potentially loftier interpersonal goals. In many instances goal parlaying would seem to be the product of a conscious intent to capitalize upon the achievement of a particular goal. The notion of goal parlaying has been introduced here in order to help capture the opportunistic nature of planning processes in ongoing social interactions. However, it is clear that not all social actors and actresses are equally sensitive to opportunities for parlaying that are presented during the course of their interactions with others. Why these individual differences exist is an interesting research question.

As their interactions unfold, persons who are attempting to reach goals may experience *thwarting* from at least two sources. First, the goals being sought by one party may be in conflict with those being sought by their interaction partner. A second and conceptually different problem is that of goal blockage. Goal blockage stems not from direct conflict between interaction partners' goals, but from the intervention of physical or social factors that prevent goals from being reached. For example, events may occur that interrupt conversations before persons can achieve their goals. The mere presence of other persons may constrain persons in such a way that goals must be abandoned. The distinction between goal conflict and goal blockage is an important one since goal conflict is more likely to have significant affective consequences with regard to one's interaction partner; while goal blockage is less likely to produce the same kinds of affective consequences.

In addition to potential differences in the affective consequences produced, goal conflict and goal blockage most probably have very different effects on the planning process. In the case of goal blockage, the fact that outside events interrupted an ongoing action plan may mean that the planner will simply reiterate the same plan. After all, the reason for goal failure was not a defective plan, but the "slings and arrows of outrageous fortune." In the case of goal conflict, however, the interactant obtains evidence that a plan is not working as it should; thus one might expect the planner either to terminate the interaction or fabricate a new plan. Of course, plans that work may require several reiterations before they are successful.

Berger and Kellermann (1986) examined the interaction consequences of goal conflict in a study in which interaction participants were given either compatible or incompatible interaction goals. Experimental participants were tested in dyads in which one person was given the goal of finding out as much as possible about their conversational partner (High Seeker). High Seekers were paired with persons who had been given one of three possible goals to achieve during their conversations. Some participants were told to reveal as much about themselves as possible during their interactions (High Revealers). Others were instructed to reveal as little as possible about themselves (Low Revealers); while others were told to have a "normal conversation" (Normals). Thus, the High Seekers paired with High Revealers and Normals were in compatible situations, whereas the High Seekers paired with the Low Revealers were in incompatible situations. The focus of this investigation was upon the verbal and nonverbal strategies that High Seekers employed to overcome the resistance offered by the Low Revealers. Importantly, the High Seekers faced with Low Revealers did *not* decrease the rate at which they asked questions over the course of their interactions. Question-asking rate showed no significant variation among the conditions over the five-minute interactions. However, High Seekers responded to the thwarting offered by their Low Revealing partners by increasing the rate at which they disclosed certain kinds of information about themselves. Most likely this adjustment was made on the assumption that the partner might reciprocate in kind the information offered by the High Seeker.

These findings led Berger and Kellermann (1986) to suggest that the process of plan formation in the face of failure to reach goals may not be a linear one in which old, ineffective plans are discarded for new ones. Instead, it was argued that plans may actually *accrete* over the course of an interaction, i.e. persons may continue to do what normally works with the hope that it will start to become effective at some point; however, they may also add new plans in order to cope with the failure they are experiencing. This accretion model is very different from a discrete, linear model of plan development and modification. Another important point made by the Berger and Kellermann (1986) study is that in order to understand the breadth and depth of persons' planning capabilities, it is necessary for them to experience plan failure in ongoing interaction situations. When individuals' plans are immediately successful in achieving goals, we gain little information about their planning capabilities. Goal conflict and goal blockage in a very real sense bring out the best (or the worst) in human planners and these situations inform us as observers about the number of alternative plans that persons have available to them and their abilities to formulate and deploy plans in ongoing situations.

Although the emphasis of this discussion has been upon goal conflict, goal blockage and the responses that these contingencies produce, it is important to recognize that the present analysis allows not only for goal conflict but also plan conflict. Persons who are attempting to reach the same or compatible goals in ongoing interactions, but who have very different plans for so doing, may disagree over the relative efficiency of plans or their social appropriateness. Interactants may have to come to an agreement on ways to assess the relative efficiency or appropriateness of each other's plans. Such agreement may rest upon the sharing of some kind of plan for evaluation. In the domain of personal relationships, plan conflict would appear to be a very important source of relational disruption.

PLANNING FOR ACTION: ASKING FOR A DATE

This section will focus upon the development of plans for the achievement of the specific social goal of asking someone out for a date. Given the methodology used to collect the data to be discussed, the plans that will be delineated here are those that persons have stored in long-term memory. These data do not bear on the process of plan formation and deployment during ongoing interactions; however, it is probable that the ability of planners to fabricate plans on-line is related to the store of plans they bring with them to interactions, i.e. the more alternative plans that persons have available to them in a particular domain, the more likely it is that they can construct new plans in the face of goal failure.

Our ability to test hypotheses concerning the planning process depends upon the development of ways to index the plans available to persons. As a way of beginning this process, students were asked individually to imagine themselves in a party situation where they saw an attractive person they wished to ask out for a date for the following Saturday night. Research participants were then asked to list the steps they would use to achieve this goal. Obviously, such a procedure indexes only that planning knowledge of which participants can be consciously aware. There is little doubt that a considerable amount of planning knowledge is tacit and not subject to access by introspection; even when participants provide think-aloud protocols in the process of reaching goals (Ericsson and Simon 1980). Moreover, although think-aloud protocols might provide more insights than the approach used here, it is difficult to imagine how persons could provide such protocols in the process of actually asking someone out for a date. In spite of the potential limitations of the approach used, these data provide a useful beginning to the study of the role that planning knowledge plays in relationship initiation.

The participants for this research were sixty-eight undergraduate students who were surveyed during class time. In addition to performing the listing task described above, they answered a number of questions concerning their current and past dating behavior. The final sample of persons contained thirty-three males and thirty-five females. Several coders examined the protocols and attempted to discern individually generic patterns that could be used to characterize the entire sample of protocols. We attempted to find a limited number of general procedures that were used by the participants. Individual summaries were then compared and compiled in diagrammatic form as shown in Figure 9.2.

Figure 9.2 shows a number of common planning paths that were prominent in the protocols. While the diagram displayed in Figure 9.2 looks like

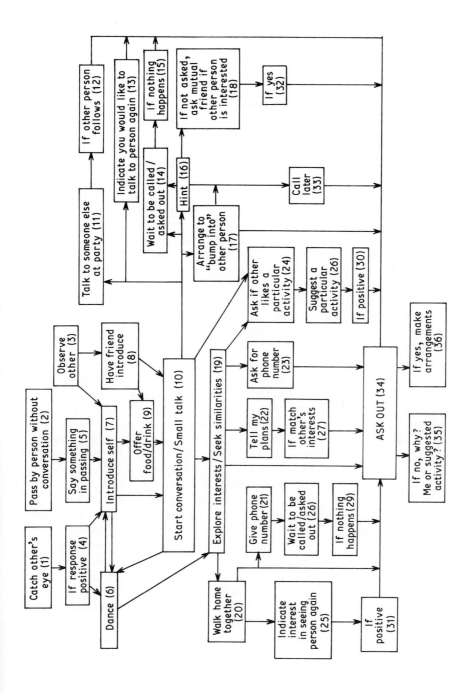

Figure 9.2 Alternative plan paths for date requesting

the kind of causal diagram associated with structural equation modeling, the arrows between the action boxes do *not* imply any kind of causal relationship between the various actions. Furthermore, the reader should keep in mind that a given individual might enter a planning path at its beginning or later in the sequence. For example, some persons might begin by catching the other person's eye (1) and then move through action boxes 4, 7, 10, 19, and end in box 34. Others might omit boxes 1 and 4 and begin with 7 or 10 and then progress toward 34.

There are a number of features of the planning path diagram that are especially important. First, some persons report that they would engage in activities designed to acquire information about the person through observation or to assess the person's level of interest before introducing themselves to the person. Paths, 1, 4, 6; 2, 5, 7; 3, 7 and 3, 8, 10 all represent these pre-interaction attempts at information-gathering and interest assessment. In addition, although analyses of the protocols did not reveal this path, it is reasonable to assume that some persons might begin in box 11 and then proceed to 7 or 10.

A second striking feature of the planning diagram concerns the degree of directness of the planning paths. Perhaps the most well-worn path for males is 7, 10, 19, 34, which is relatively direct. However, by comparison consider the 3, 8, 10, 16, 18, 32, 34; the 7, 10, 19, 20, 21, 26, 29, 34; or the 7, 10, 17, 34 paths. These options are considerably less direct and actually involve waiting for the other person to ask for the date first. These indirect strategies were more characteristic of the female protocols. In fact there were a few females who explicitly indicated that they either could not ask a male for a date because they would not know how to do so or they knew how to ask for a date but for reasons of social appropriateness would not. These gender differences were reflected in a structured item at the end of the listing task that asked the participants to indicate whether they were: (1) the one who usually asked for a date, (2) usually asked for a date by someone else, or (3) asked the other out about 50 per cent of the time. Of the male participants, 55 per cent indicated that they usually asked the other person; while 80 per cent of the females answered that they were usually asked. The difference between males and females on this item was statistically significant ($X^2 = 34.53$, $df = 2$, $p < 0.001$).

While the gender differences found in these data are interesting in themselves, it is more important to recognize that for some females planning knowledge is available to them but because of certain social constraints they will not realize this knowledge in their social actions. This fact highlights the control that such metagoals as social appropriateness can exert on the process of translating plans into actions. There is a related situation that did not appear in these protocols but is worth mentioning here. This scenario involves the person who knows very well how to ask for a date, but has great difficulty carrying out these plans in the social situation because of anxiety or other adverse emotional responses. This possibility suggests that affect can become attached to plans in some way and may facilitate or inhibit their implementation. Unfortunately, these affective factors are not generally considered in the planning literature.

A third facet of Figure 9.2 that is of interest is the action boxes that indicate contingency planning. Boxes 12, 15, 18, 29, 30, 31, 32, 35 and 36 represent this kind of planning activity. Although several of these boxes are tied directly to box 34, it is worth noting that there are differences in the contingencies they indicate. For example, box 29 implies that if something happens, in this case being called by the other, the date will occur. By contrast, boxes 31 and 32 imply that if the person is not interested, they will *not* be asked out and the date will not occur. Box 35 is a response to rejection. In this case the planner wishes to know whether the refusal was based upon dislike of him or her or the activity the planner suggested. Such information is vital for making a decision about continued interest in the other person.

A final characteristic of the planning paths depicted in Figure 9.2 is their positive nature. In essence, the sequences shown in the figure tell individuals what to do rather than what *not* to do. For example, it is easy to suppose that even before approaching a given person to ask for a date, an individual might have to test a number of hypotheses. Thus, if the target person is already involved with another person or if the target person may not find the potential asker attractive, the sequences shown in Figure 9.2 may *not* be executed; some of the pre-interaction action boxes give a hint that persons are sensitive to these possibilities. Furthermore, once a person is involved in the interaction itself, there are a host of actions that the person suppresses, i.e. things that should *not* be done. These "negative plans" do not appear in the protocols analyzed here. One potential reason for their omission is their sheer number. Nevertheless, a theory of planning must somehow explain how actions and action sequences that are parts of possible worlds are excluded from worlds of plausible social conduct.

The data displayed in Figure 9.2 represent conscious manifestations of the procedural knowledge that persons can provide concerning the date-getting goal. The protocols revealed at least two additional kinds of information that were not directly related to procedural knowledge. First, sometimes persons described specific classes of actions that they would perform during the entire course of the date-asking episode. For example, some males indicated that they would try to be humorous during the interaction, while some females indicated that they would show interest in their partners by maintaining eye contact with them. Other respondents said that they would be pleasant or smile a lot in order to increase their chances for a positive response. These kinds of actions were not part of the step-by-step accounts depicted in Figure 9.2 but were actions designed to create a certain atmosphere for the episode. These actions were labeled "atmospherics."

A second class of actions that deserve separate attention are related to what are labeled "tests." Tests are designed to determine whether partners are interested enough in the persons who are asking so that if they are asked, they are likely to say "yes." These assessments of interest are arrived at by monitoring the verbal and nonverbal action of the partner for signs of responsiveness and interest. If responsiveness and interest are sufficiently high, the person will ask the other; however, if some threshold is not reached, the person will not ask. In addition to this type of test, one person indicated that before asking for the date, he would reassess his own level of interest in his partner. While this would seem to be an obvious thing to do before asking, only one person explicitly mentioned it.

Males seemed especially prone to use tests in their protocols. This tendency is probably due to the fact that they employed relatively direct means for asking. Moreover, although no male *explicitly* mentioned the possibility that being refused a date might produce feelings of disappointment and loss of self-esteem, the inclusion of tests and the contingency contained in box 35 suggest that asking for a date involves the additional metagoal of not losing face by being turned down. Not only do tests hedge against this possibility, but the use of such atmospherics as humor allow the rejected date-seeker to write off the entire episode as "a joke;" thus lessening the blow to self-esteem. In short, males seem to be particularly sensitive to potential rejection in the date-getting context.

There is little doubt that when it comes to asking a person for a date, there is considerable individual variation in persons' abilities to reach this social goal. Informal discussions with students reveal that there are indeed expert and novice date-getters. It is tempting to speculate that experts in this domain are adept at getting persons to agree to go out with them because they use *the* "right approach." The implication of this speculation is that there is one best way to insure that a person will respond favorably to such a request. Most probably, however, the notion of optimality or efficiency of plans in this domain, as well as other social contexts, is somewhat broader than that of planning a sequence of errands in an optimal manner. As we noted earlier, persons may be able to think of very efficient ways of asking for dates but not be able to implement these plans because of constraints imposed by the metagoal of social appropriateness. In addition to these constraints, however, are those that are imposed by limitations in communication skills. Such skill deficits could undermine a very efficient and appropriate plan. Again we see that procedural knowledge is a necessary but not a sufficient condition for the achievement of social goals. Plans chosen for implementation must be compatible with the kinds of communication skills that a person possesses.

One way of trying to reduce the complexity depicted in Figure 9.2 is to resort to some kind of counting measure of plan complexity. For example, one might ask respondents to produce as many alternative plans as possible for achieving a particular goal and then simply count the number of alternatives generated as an index of "plan complexity." One might further reason that persons with a larger number of alternatives are likely to be more competent date-getters than those who have relatively few alternatives available to them. Such an approach to planning knowledge is probably overly simplistic. Most likely, some plans are better than others for some persons. Thus, persons who have relatively few close-to-optimal plan paths available to them are probably better off than persons who have many sub-optimal paths available for use.

At this point in time, the reduction of planning knowledge to some quantitative form is premature. Moreover, it is most probably the case that planning competence tends to be domain-specific so that the development of a general measure of such competence is likely to fail. While there are most likely general principles of planning, the use of such principles depends upon the acquisition of domain-specific knowledge. Without such knowledge, the general principles are not very helpful. Thus, a more useful approach to the study of plans would be to contrast the plans of experts in a domain with those of novices in order to see if there are general features of plans that differ across these groups.

While planning ability appears to be domain-specific, there are general action plans that are useful across a number of different interpersonal goals. For example, Rosenfeld (1966), Kellermann and Berger (1984), and Mehrabian and Williams (1969) found that persons seeking to achieve the goals of social approval, persuasion, and information acquisition respectively all tended to display similar patterns of nonverbal behavior. Persons seeking these goals tended to smile more, gesticulate more and be more attentive to the targets of their goal-seeking attempts. Thus, what appear to be diverse interaction goals may produce action plans that involve similar atmospherics. These findings suggest that some plans may consist of prepackaged sequences of actions that can be instantiated as a unit. These social action packets (SAPS) can be linked together in a variety of ways depending upon the particular goal sought. In the context of date-seeking, persons might be drawing their specific plans from a more general SAP concerned with request-asking. The request SAP provides the basic outlines for the date-asking plan; however, the particulars of the date-asking plan are filled in and modified as the interaction episode unfolds. The view espoused here is not incompatible with the notion that planning for social interactions usually involves a closed-loop, opportunistic process. Even closed-loop systems of planning carry with them the assumption that persons bring some kind of very general initial plan with them that can be modified as the action sequence unfolds. These very general plans are similar to the notion of SAPS.

If the above account has some degree of validity, then the differences between expert and novice planners in a particular domain may arise from several sources. First, there may be differences in the kinds of SAPS that the two groups bring with them to the interaction situation. Second, the SAPS of the two respective groups may be similar, but the translations of these SAPS into more specific plans may be different. The novices may have a translation problem. Third, the SAPS and their translations to more specific plans may be similar, but the novices may lack the communication skills necessary to implement the domain-specific plans they generate.

Fourth, when faced with goal failure, the novices may be less able to diagnose the reasons for failure. This alternative implies some kind of perceptual deficit in the novices. Finally, novices may be able to diagnose reasons for failure but be unable to formulate alternative plans for pursuing the elusive goal. Given this non-exhaustive list of possible reasons for performance differences between experts and novices, it seems unlikely that questing after general measures of planning competence is a wise course of action.

What is much needed in the study of plans is some way to represent them in a useful way. The system shown in Figure 9.2 represents a first attempt to accomplish plan representation in the context of social interaction. There is no guarantee that such an approach is the most useful one that could be used. Furthermore, this presentation has had little to say about the nature of interacting plans (Bruce and Newman 1978). Obviously, the ability of persons to achieve their interaction goals depends upon the plans of their co-actors' and interactants' abilities to understand the plans of their co-actors. These possibilities raise the complexity level of the analytic problem by several degrees of magnitude; however, in order to develop a complete theory of social interaction planning, this level of complexity will have to be considered.

The view of planning espoused in this presentation is one that is decidedly biased in the direction of cold cognition, although hot cognition did find its way into the discussion of atmospherics and tests. Nevertheless, the role that affect plays in planning processes was generally not considered. This is a serious omission, especially in the domain of interpersonal relationships, where affect plays a key role. Moreover, Clarke (in this volume, p. 3) has persuasively argued that the affective system may assume a regnant status in the control of social action. While affect or desire (Brand 1984) is critically important in the production of social action, social psychologists interested in the study of social cognition have paid very little attention to answering the question of what *procedural knowledge* social actors and actresses must have in order to accomplish various social goals. Clearly, it is not enough to want or to desire to accomplish a particular social goal. One must know how to do it. Thus, work that focuses upon the role that affect plays in relationships can be seen as complementing that which is concerned with aspects of cold cognition like plans and procedural knowledge.

There are two priorities that we are addressing in this line of research. First, attention is being paid to the development of a more formal theory of social interaction planning that is highly general. Second, interaction data are being collected in an effort to examine the relationships between plans and the verbal and nonverbal actions that persons generate during their goal-oriented conversations with others. Examination of such links should help to bridge the gap between cognition and social action that persists some twenty-five years after Miller, Galanter, and Pribram (1960) tried to fill it with their TOTE units.

ACKNOWLEDGEMENTS

The author would like to express his deep appreciation to Martha Mastin, Carol Miller-Tutzauer, Ann Obenchain, Renee Pearl, and Maria Vignali for their assistance in various phases of this research. Robert A. Bell and Kathy Kellermann provided valuable comments on an earlier version of this chapter. The idea of "negative plans" was suggested by Patrick McGhee whom I thank very much.

REFERENCES

Berger, C.R. and Kellermann, K.A. (1983) "To ask or not to ask: is that a question?" In R.N. Bostrom (ed.) *Communication Yearbook 7*. Beverly Hills: Sage Publications.

—— and —— (1985) "Personal opacity and social information gathering: seek, but ye may not find." Paper presented at the annual convention of the International Communication Association, Honolulu, Hawaii, May.

—— and —— (1986) "Goal incompatibility and social action: the best laid plans of mice and men often go astray." Paper presented at the annual convention of the International Communication Association, Chicago, IL, May.

Brand, M. (1984) *Intending and Acting: Toward a Naturalized Action Theory*. Cambridge, MA: MIT Press.

Bruce, B.C. (1980) "Plans and social actions." In R.J. Spiro, B.C. Bruce, and W.F. Brewer (eds) *Theoretical Issues in Reading Comprehension*. Hillsdale, NJ: Lawrence Erlbaum.

—— and Newman, D. (1978) "Interacting plans." *Cognitive Science*, 2, 195–233.

Cantor, N. and Mischel, W. (1977) "Traits as prototypes: effects on recognition memory." *Journal of Personality and Social Psychology*, 35, 38–48.

—— and —— (1979) "Prototypes in person perception." In L. Berkowitz (ed.) *Advances in Experimental Social Psychology*. New York: Academic Press.

Cohen, P.R. and Perrault, C.R. (1979) "Elements of a plan-based theory of speech acts." *Cognitive Science*, 3, 177–212.

Ericsson, K.A. and Simon, H.A. (1980) "Verbal reports as data." *Psychological Review*, 87, 151–214.

Hayes-Roth, B. and Hayes-Roth, F. (1979) "A cognitive model of planning." *Cognitive Science*, 3, 275–310.

Hobbs, J.R. and Evans, D.A. (1980) "Conversation as planned behavior." *Cognitive Science*, 4, 349–77.

Kellermann, K.A. and Berger, C.R. (1984) "Affect and the acquisition of social information: sit back, relax, and tell me about yourself." In R.N. Bostrom (ed.) *Communication Yearbook 8*. Beverly Hills: Sage Publications.

Langer, E.J. (1978) "Rethinking the role of thought in social interaction." In J.H. Harvey, W. Ickes, and R.F. Kidd (eds) *New Directions in Attribution Research*, vol. 2. Hillsdale, NJ: Lawrence Erlbaum.

Markus, H. (1977) "Self-schemata and processing information about the self." *Journal of Personality and Social Psychology*, 35, 63–78.

Mehrabian, A. and Williams, M. (1969) "Nonverbal concomitants of perceived and intended persuasiveness." *Journal of Personality and Social Psychology*, 13, 37–58.

Miller, G.A., Galanter, E., and Pribram, K.H. (1960) *Plans and the Structure of Behavior*. New York: Holt, Rinehart & Winston.

Newell, K.M. (1978) "Some issues in action plans." In G.E. Stelmach (ed.) *Information Processing in Motor Control and Learning*. New York: Academic Press.

Norman, D.A. (1981) "Categorization of action slips." *Psychological Review*, 88, 1–15.

Rosenfeld, H.M. (1966) "Approval-seeking and approval-inducing functions of verbal and non-verbal responses in the dyad." *Journal of Personality and Social Psychology*, 4, 597–605.

Sacerdoti, E.D. (1977) *A Structure for Plans and Behavior*. Amsterdam: Elsevier North-Holland.

Schank, R.C. and Abelson, R.P. (1977) *Scripts, Plans, Goals and Understanding: An Inquiry into Human Knowledge Structures*. Hillsdale, NJ: Lawrence Erlbaum.

Schmidt, C.F. (1976) "Understanding human action: recognizing the plans and motives of other persons." In J.S. Carroll and J.W. Payne (eds) *Cognition and Social Behavior*. New York: John Wiley.

Taylor, S.E. and Crocker, J. (1981) "Schematic bases of social information processing." In E.T. Higgins, C.P. Herman, and M.P. Zanna (eds) *Social Cognition: The Ontario Symposium*. Hillsdale, NJ: Lawrence Erlbaum.

Wicker, A.W. (1969) "Attitudes versus actions: the relationship of verbal and overt behavioral responses to attitude objects." *Journal of Social Issues*, 25, 41–78.

Wilensky, R. (1981) "Meta planning: representing and using knowledge about planning in problem solving and natural language understanding." *Cognitive Science*, 5, 197–233.

—— (1983) *Planning and Understanding: A Computational Approach to Human Reasoning*. Reading, MA: Addison-Wesley.

10 Interplay between relational knowledge and events

Sally Planalp

Social knowledge in any form – knowledge of ourselves, knowledge of other people, knowledge of social situations, or knowledge of relationships – is knowledge about something. There are links, to varying degrees veridical or spurious, complex or simple, between knowledge structures and observable phenomena. For example, knowledge of a close friend might include information about physical appearance, background, motivations, traits, or activities that are based on data such as eye color, place of birth, occupation, characteristic behaviors, etc. Similarly, new events (such as finding out that s/he betrayed a confidence) may alter one or more aspects of that knowledge (such as his/her trustworthiness or motivation to preserve your friendship).

While it is apparent that knowledge is grounded in reality (however tenuously), how a particular form of knowledge is grounded in what aspects of reality is not so apparent. Social knowledge is especially difficult. A person knows that his/her friend's eyes are blue because they consistently register a certain wavelength of light but how does s/he know that s/he is honest? This question has plagued personality research for almost two decades (Mischel 1968) and has been begged for much longer by considering traits the raw material of impression formation (Asch 1946) even though it is clear that they are not (e.g. Cantor, Mischel, and Schwartz 1982; Carlston 1980; Ebbesen 1980).

Precisely the same question plagues research on other forms of social knowledge, including research on knowledge of social and personal relationships. There is a constant interplay between knowledge of relationships and the interactions and events that occur between two relational partners. People approach others with some knowledge of what behavior is appropriate for the type of relationship they have (strangers, co-workers, future in-laws, etc.), they interact, use information from that interaction to corroborate, elaborate or change their working relational knowledge, interact again based on the updated knowledge, and so on throughout the course of their relationship. It is this interplay between relational knowledge and interaction that has been the guiding concern of the conceptual analyses and empirical research reported in this chapter.

RELATIONAL COGNITION

In investigating the interplay between relational knowledge and events, a social cognitive perspective has been adopted for several reasons. First, the most plausible, parsimonious, and fruitful assumption about relational knowledge is that it functions within the same cognitive system as other forms of knowledge, both social and non-social. A number of lines of research have found direct parallels between object categorization and person categorization (Cantor and Mischel 1979; Rosch 1978), self-knowledge and other forms of knowledge (Bobrow and Norman 1975; Markus 1977), political expertise and chess expertise (Chase and Simon 1973; Fiske, Kinder, and Larter 1983) and automatic and controlled processes in social and non-social realms (Langer 1978; Schneider and Shiffrin 1977). That is not to say that there are no important differences between our knowledge of people and pot roasts (not the least of which is that we assume that other people have knowledge of us but pot roasts do not) but rather that any differences must be incorporated into a unified information-processing system (Ostrom 1984).

A second reason to place the study of relational knowledge within a general cognitive framework is that it provides a common framework for studying diverse phenomena that must ultimately be integrated. Knowledge of relationships must be integrated with the domains of discourse, events, people, and emotion. A basic cognitive system that includes knowledge structures and the processes by which they are used (for overviews see Hewes and Planalp [1982; in press] and Planalp and Hewes 1982) has been used to study all four. For example, van Dijk and Kintsch (1983) have synthesized an enormous body of research on discourse-processing into a working model of how discourse is understood and Greene (1984) has outlined the components of a cognitive model of discourse production based on a variety of research at several levels of abstraction. Markus's (1977) and Hastie et al.'s (1980) work is representative of hundreds of studies done in the area of self and person cognition. Work by Bower, Black, and Turner (1979), Forgas (1982), and Schank and Abelson (1977) is also founded in a social cognitive perspective. Even emotion, a phenomenon that is sometimes considered antithetical to a cognitive framework (Zajonc 1980), has undergone extensive analysis from within that framework (Clark and Fiske 1982; Mandler 1984; Roseman 1984). Thus the social cognitive perspective provides a basis for exchange and synthesis among the different aspects and components of relationships.

Because of the common cognitive substratum, substantive and methodological developments in one domain can be applied to another, although not without reflection (Fiske and Taylor 1984, ch. 10). Of particular use in studying the interplay between relational knowledge and ongoing interactions and events are measurement techniques for studying knowledge structures and substantive findings concerning how knowledge influences the processing of events and vice versa, which will be reviewed later in this chapter.

Schemas, processes, and events

Isen and Hastorf (1982, p. 4) state that today's cognitive social psychology "is concerned not only with what you know or think about people, but with how you come to know what you know, the processes by which you make use of it, and those by which it comes to influence other knowledge and behavior." If "relationships" is substituted for "people," the concern with understanding the interplay between relational knowledge and ongoing interaction could not be stated more clearly. The three key elements are relational knowledge, relational events, and several different types of cognitive processes which link them.

Relational schemas   In the cognitive literature, knowledge structures have a number of aliases – schemas, scripts, frames, prototypes, and implicit theories – but they all refer to the same basic entity. All are coherent, organized structures of tacit knowledge that are distilled from experience to guide cognitive processes, and through them, behavior. They are forms of social knowledge, not in the sense of undeniable truth, but in the sense of beliefs assumed to be true and acted upon as it they were true (Wegner and Vallacher 1977, p. 21). The differences between the various forms have been articulated elsewhere (Hewes and Planalp 1982) and are largely a matter of emphasis due to associations between terms and lines of research. If one is concerned with how relationships are categorized, particularly by degrees rather than as discrete categories, the term prototype would be used to maintain consistency with other work on social categorization (Davis and Todd 1985). If one is concerned with the stages and expected sequences of relational development, one might speak of relational scripts (Bower, Black, and Turner 1979). In my research, I have used the term relational schema because it seems to be the most general and maintains consistency with other work that links knowledge structures to cognitive processes and observable events (Planalp 1985; Planalp and Hewes 1982).

Relational schemas have several important properties. First, they consist of abstract knowledge based on past experience (Bartlett 1932) which guide interpretations of events in the present and expectations for the future. Thus they provide the continuity among interactions that Hinde (1979, pp. 14–15) argues is an essential component of relationships. Second, they are made up of interconnected slots with constraints on the types of entities that can fill the slots (Minsky 1977). Obviously, men cannot be mothers and professors cannot be illiterate. But beyond the obvious constraints are more subtle ones that may have a great deal of impact on our interactions. For example, if one believes that lovers are of opposite sexes, a homosexual couple could render the "lovers" schema inapplicable, resulting in a situation that is literally "unthinkable." Third, the slots of the schema serve as a basis for interpreting incoming information. As information about a particular relationship is acquired, slots are filled, resulting in an instantiated schema. For example, a person's "marriage" schema might consist of a husband and wife who share love and intimacy. One instantiation of the marriage schema would be himself, his wife, and their particular ways of sharing love and intimacy. Fourth, when slots cannot be instantiated from incoming information, default values can be supplied. For instance, in the absence of knowledge about the living arrangements of married couples, one would probably assume they live together (although the prevalence of commuter marriages may be changing that default value). Thus relational schemas provide a mechanism for interpreting new information about a relationship in light of prior knowledge.

Relational events   If relational schemas are instantiated by incoming information, one must ask what the source of that information is. As stated earlier, relationships are grounded in patterns of interaction. Most theorists and researchers including Cappella (1984), Duck and Sants (1983), Hinde (1979), Kelley *et al.* (1983), and others have recognized the importance of studying interaction for understanding relationships and/or bemoaned its neglect. Certain events that would not be considered interactions in the typical sense also have great impact on relationships. The acts of signing a marriage license, making love, physically attacking one's spouse, or moving out of town are examples. Thus interactions and events seem to be the stuff of which relationships are made. That is, when we know about relationships we know about how people consistently act toward and interact with one another.

Interaction, unfortunately, is almost bafflingly complex and it is by no means clear which particular aspects of relational knowledge are linked to which aspects of interaction. For example, a wife might believe her husband loves her because he smiles at her, leans toward her, and looks into her eyes (Patterson *et al.* 1984), tells her or someone else so, puts up with her obnoxious behaviors (Baxter and Wilmot 1984), acts in her interests (Hendrick *et al.* 1984), or does any number of other things, all of which combine in some unspecified way. It is one thing to say that relational knowledge is grounded in patterns of interaction but quite another to specify how. That is one of the primary goals of research on relationships.

Cognitive processes

As is apparent in the examples above and as has been noted by a number of scholars (e.g. McClintock 1983), the events and interactions that make up relationships are seldom if ever "brute facts" (Searle 1969, pp. 50–3) or "undigested interactions" (Duck and Sants 1983, pp. 33–4). Rather, events and interactions are interpreted and produced through complex cognitive processes. To continue Duck and Sants's metaphor, cognitive processes might be considered the "digestive processes" that transform raw sense data into meaningful, useful forms and integrate them with pre-existing knowledge. To go beyond the metaphor, cognitive processes are involved not only in dealing with whatever information is presented but also in selecting relevant information and guiding behavior that might produce further information (Berger 1979).

The many cognitive processes that link incoming information to prior knowledge have been reviewed extensively elsewhere (Brewer and Nakamura 1984; Planalp and Hewes 1982). They include attention, information integration, inference, storage and retrieval from memory, and a number of judgmental and decision-making processes. Several studies are noteworthy because they have dealt specifically with cognitive processes and relational information. For example, Berscheid and Graziano (1979) investigated how expectations about future interactions influenced what information was selected and remembered from videotapes. Knowledge of social and personal relationships served as important bases for information integration and inference in Schank and Abelson's (1977) computer simulation of natural language understanding and Labov and Fanshel's (1977) detailed analysis of the meaning of a psychotherapeutic interview. Spiro (1980) demonstrated how a specific form of relational knowledge guided memory distortions of information about fiancés' relationships. The use of relational knowledge in choosing messages has been observed often among linguists (Fielding and Fraser 1978; Freedle and Duran 1979; Halliday and Hasan 1976, p. 22) and communication scholars (Miller *et al.* 1977; Sillars 1980; Tracy *et al.* 1984).

Links between schemas, processes, and events   The three major elements of relational cognition are inextricably linked both logically and empirically. Schemas are useless without cognitive processes and groundless without observable events. Cognitive processes have nothing to process without schemas and events. Events are uninterpretable, isolated phenomena without cognitive processes and schemas. In addition, as Anderson (1978) argued and Ebbesen and Allen (1979) illustrated, knowledge and processes can combine in any number of ways to produce the same empirical predictions. Knowledge structures must be fixed if their effect on processes is to be determined or, alternatively, processes must be fixed if the structure of relevant knowledge is to be determined. This is assuming that events are fixed as well, as they almost always are in strictly cognitive studies (i.e. the experimental stimuli are carefully controlled). In more naturalistic circumstances it is not always clear what events are being attended to, remembered, or judged, leaving another parameter free to vary. The upshot is that two of the three parameters must be fixed to study the third. This puts someone studying relational cognition in a precarious position because very little is known about relational knowledge and events. Yet by now enough studies have been done to have a good deal of confidence that basic cognitive processes do not differ substantially from one domain of knowledge to the next, making it possible to fix processes and either knowledge or events to study the third component.

Spiro's (1980) study of relational memory is a good example of fixing two of the three parameters. He cited evidence that balance theory (Heider 1958) was one knowledge structure that guided cognitive processes; i.e. people believe that agreement fosters positive feelings and disagreement fosters negative feelings. He also postulated that memory was reconstructive; i.e. people do not completely reproduce events of the past but also reconstruct what must have happened based on what they believe to be true. The test consisted of presenting subjects with fixed information about the opinions of two fiancés concerning their respective desires to have children and their ultimate marriage or break-up. Reconstructive memory was vindicated when memory for the original information was systematically distorted, primarily in the direction of balance theory. Thus by fixing knowledge and events, he was able to study reconstructive memory.

The same strategy was used somewhat differently to find out what form of relational knowledge makes it possible to choose remarks in conversations that are appropriate in terms of dominance (Planalp 1983, 1985). For instance, if a supervisor wanted something done a command would be in order, but if a subordinate wanted something done, a request would be more appropriate. What kind of relational knowledge do people draw on as the source of those intuitions? To find out, relational events and cognitive processes were fixed so that alternative knowledge structures could be tested.

Relational events were fixed by constructing three hypothetical conversations between professors and students and generating three alternative paraphrases for most remarks that varied along the dominance dimension. The key cognitive process was fixed by arguing that reconstructive memory is guided by relational knowledge as demonstrated repeatedly in a number of content domains (Bartlett 1932; Mandler and Johnson 1977; Taylor and Crocker 1981). With relational events and cognitive processes fixed, the correct form of relational schema could be inferred by analyzing influences on reconstructive memory for the set of remarks. Three different forms of relational knowledge were tested. The first was knowledge based on simple dominance; i.e. we know that professors are dominant (and so should produce dominant remarks) and students are submissive (and so should produce submissive remarks). The second was called situation-specific dominance; i.e. professors and students maintain levels of dominance that vary from situation to situation. For example, professors were expected to be more dominant when asked to change a grade than when asked to let a student add a course (Planalp 1985, p. 15). The third was called behavior-specific knowledge or knowledge that a specific behavior is expected in a specific circumstance. For example, when students want to talk to their professors they should say "I'd like to talk to you" rather than "I have to talk to you."

In the experiment subjects were asked to read one of the conversations between professor and student and to answer some distractor questions about it. A week later they were then asked to try to remember the conversation and to select the remarks they had read from the three alternative paraphrases. The results indicated that memory was strongly biased toward paraphrases that were most likely to occur (as judged by another group of subjects), regardless of which ones were actually read. This finding vindicated reconstructive memory, not only because memory errors were strong and systematic but also because they were based on knowledge of what is most likely to have occurred.

The results were more equivocal concerning what form of relational knowledge guided reconstructive memory. Neither simple dominance nor situation-based dominance accounted for the the pattern of memory errors but behavior-specific knowledge did. The problem was that behavior-specific knowledge predicted too many memory errors (79 of 95). It is unlikely that people could remember so many specific behaviors without some organizing principle. The most plausible candidate seemed to be a system of rights and obligations that guided appropriate levels of dominance. That is, professors did not have to be dominant all the time because their rights were recognized. Similarly, students were not always submissive because they had rights as well. Instead, professors and students chose remarks that reflected their knowledge of what to expect of others and what others expected of them.

SCHEMA USE AND CHANGE

There are two basic types of interplay between relational knowledge, cognitive processes and relevant interactions and events. The first occurs when knowledge of the relationship is used to interpret interaction (assimilation); the second occurs when actions or interactions produce some change in the person's knowledge of the relationship (accommodation). Both are necessary if relational knowledge is to be useful and accurate. Although very little is known about either in the domain of personal and social relationships, there has been research in related areas that is informative about how assimilation and accommodation operate.

A prior condition for either assimilation or accommodation to occur is that relational knowledge and events must be perceived as relevant to one another. Knowledge is used to interpret only relevant information and only relevant information has any impact on knowledge, by definition. In everyday interaction, people probably link up information to relevant relational knowledge both deductively and inductively. Sometimes the nature of the relationship is known in advance because of structural criteria (boss–worker) or prior experience (old friend) and relevant information about the relationship can be deduced. At other times, the relational definition is vague and cues must be used to infer the appropriate one. For example, my students report that they occasionally find themselves in the position of not knowing whether an engagement is a friendly gesture or a date. They turn to information such as how far in advance plans were made, the nature of the activity, and who pays for it as relevant cues and infer the nature of the relationship from them. Once the relevant knowledge (schema) is accessed, it serves as a framework to interpret incoming information and to guide behavior. There is ample evidence of schematic effects on several cognitive processes (Planalp and Hewes 1982, pp. 124–33). For example, schemas guide attention to relevant information (Taylor, Crocker, and D'Agostino 1978), enhance its storage and retrieval (Schustack and Anderson 1979), provide a basis for making inferences (Carlston 1980) and for selecting appropriate action, including action directed toward gathering further information (Snyder 1984). Processing of incoming information is usually enhanced regardless of whether that information is consistent with the schema or inconsistent, so long as it is relevant. For example, information that a friend betrayed a confidence or that s/he did you a favor would both be attended, remembered, and acted upon even though the first is inconsistent with people's schemas for friendship and the second is consistent (Davis and Todd 1985). Information that is irrelevant to friendship (that s/he is kind to his/her mother for instance) would not be processed as deeply (except by his/her mother).

It is primarily the degree of fit between incoming information and the relevant schema, however, that determines whether the new information will be assimilated into the schema or whether the schema will be accommodated to it. Consistent information is assimilated, moderately consistent information (especially ambiguous information) is likely to be assimilated, but inconsistent information has the potential to force accommodation in the schema.

Assimilation

Incoming information is consistent with a schema if it falls within the constraints of the schema's slots and so serves as an appropriate instantiation of the schema. For example, two siblings who call the same people "Mom" and "Dad," look somewhat alike, and get together for holidays probably fall within the constraints of the sibling schema and so are an appropriate instantiation of it. Their particular relationship will probably be assimilated or absorbed into the sibling schema so that it is indistinguishable from the typical sibling relationship. But for perfect instantiations the general and instantiated schemas are identical and it makes no difference which is used to interpret new information, remember old information, or guide action.

The more interesting case occurs when incoming information is partially consistent or at least not inconsistent with the schema. This is when schemas exert powerful assimilation effects. First, schemas guide how the new information is to be interpreted. If the new information is at all ambiguous, as much information in the social world is, the interpretation will be skewed in the direction of the schema. For example, if a remark could be taken as either an insult or a joke, it would probably be taken as the former if made by an enemy and as the latter if made by a friend. Goody (1978, p. 39) also observed that it is difficult to ask a purely informational question in relationships of clear authority. Questions from the person in authority may be taken as blaming or interfering; those from the person without authority may be taken as challenges. Second, schemas are the basis for inferences. For example, based on knowledge of divorced couples, one could infer that they probably would rather not be seated side-by-side at a dinner party (even though the conclusion is not strictly warranted and might be incorrect). Third, schemas produce strong effects on memory. If new information is interpreted as an instantiation of a schema, the memory trace of the event is made up of unique information about the event itself and additional information filled in from the schema (inferences produced by default values). As memory for the event decays, more and more unique information is lost and information from the schema supplied in its place. The result is memory errors that are systematically biased consistent with the schema, as found in the study of balance theory discussed earlier (Spiro 1980). In essence, what *was* becomes increasingly supplanted with what *must have been*.

The long-term result of assimilative interpretation and memory is a conservative bias in dealing with new information. As long as it is not blatantly inconsistent it is likely to be treated as if it were consistent. This may be one reason that definitions of relationships are relatively stable despite fluctuating patterns of interaction. Interactions are notoriously ambiguous and difficult to remember verbatim and so may be the ideal fodder for schema assimilation.

Accommodation

Nonetheless, there is a counterbalancing force that keeps people better in touch with reality – attention. Attention is triggered, not by expected, schema-consistent events but by unexpected, schema-inconsistent events (Brewer and Nakamura 1984, pp. 144–6). Because schema-inconsistent events cannot be fitted easily into the interpretative framework (by definition) they require more attention and deeper processing in order to make sense of them (Hastie and Kumar 1979). The conditions under which inconsistent information is confronted, however, may not lend themselves to increasing attention. If there is a great deal of inconsistent information, very little time to interpret it, or if attention is focused primarily on other matters (as is often the case in interaction), there may not be sufficient attention to allocate and the inconsistent information may be lost.

If sufficient attention can be allocated, attribution processes take over (Fiske and Linville 1980; Hastie, Park, and Weber 1984). The inconsistent information may be attributed to schema-irrelevant factors such as the situation. For example, if one's spouse is inattentive it might be attributed to his/her bad day or failure to recognize the importance of the specific issue at hand rather than to general lack of concern. The inconsistent information may also be given less credence than consistent information. As Nisbett and Ross (1980, p. 170) describe a study by Lord, Ross, and Lepper (1979), "Supporting evidence was handled with kid gloves; opposing evidence was mauled." It is not hard to think of examples in the interpersonal domain. People who like one's current amour may be credited with uncanny perceptiveness; those who dislike him/her may be accused of obtuseness, not knowing him/her very well, or having ulterior motives. Expertise and motivational factors also influence the degree to which inconsistent information is grappled with (Crocker, Fiske, and Taylor 1984). For example, if one has a lot of experience in a certain kind of relationship, deviations from expectations are more likely to be noted. Similarly, if one has a strong desire to be friends with someone, evidence indicating that the other person does not want to be friends would not be accepted as wholeheartedly as it would be if the desire were weaker.

If the inconsistent information survives as relevant and important, it may be linked to the schema but "tagged" as inconsistent. The "schema + tag" memory trace (Graesser, Gordon, and Sawyer, 1979; Graesser *et al.* 1980) has the dual advantages of being linked to the schema that can serve as a retrieval cue and receiving deeper processing through increased attention. This may explain why schema-inconsistent events are often remembered better than schema-consistent events, whereas both are remembered better than schema-neutral or irrelevant events (Hastie 1981). Tags provide a basis for modifications to schemas, although it seems likely that only recurrent tags would warrant changing schemas. For example, if a friend has been supportive except for one instance in which money was not lent it would probably not be necessary to alter one's perception of the friendship. If, however, s/he was supportive except for the multiple occasions when one asked for financial support, a scope condition on the friendship would be warranted. It is possible, however, that no modification of the schema would make it compatible with the inconsistent information; the two are simply inconsistent and one must go. If the inconsistent information cannot be explained away, the schema may be undermined. Examples of this sort of inconsistency may be events that violate the ground rules of relationships (such as infidelity or disloyalty).

Drawing on work by Rothbart (1981), Crocker, Fiske, and Taylor (1984) have suggested three models of schema change, all of which are plausible for relational schemas. The first, the bookkeeping model, accounts for gradual adjustments made in slot constraints and default values as anomalous information is incorporated (possibly through tags as discussed above). Relational examples are plentiful – the gradual evolutions from passionate to companionate marriages, from parent–baby to parent–adult child relations, from close friends to distant acquaintances. The second, the sub-typing model, accounts for change in which schemas are subdivided into types that are variations on the theme. For example, the prevalence of commuter marriages may produce a consistent sub-schema to cover them or opposite-sex friendships may become a special sub-type of friendship. The third, the conversion model, accounts for sudden, "all-or-none" changes such as violations of the ground rules of relationships discussed earlier.

Change by conversion has been investigated in studies by Davis and Todd (1985) and Planalp and Honeycutt (1985). Even though Davis and Todd were primarily concerned with how violations of expectations affected friendships whereas Planalp and Honeycutt were concerned with how events undermine conceptions of friendships and romantic relationships, the results were strikingly similar. First, many of the same types of events were interpreted as violations, including betrayal of confidences, betrayal of trust, and sexual malfeasance. Second, the effects of the violation permeated the relationship, leading to less positive ratings on a number of judgements (e.g. support, intimacy). Third, resolutions of violations were relatively rare but when they did occur the relationship often became even stronger.

The different ways in which relational schemas change in response to changes in interaction or events have received very little research attention. All three models of schema change may be appropriate under different circumstances and could be informative about schematic structure. For example, an event that produces change by conversion may be linked to an important or central characteristic of the relationship whereas one that only enters into the bookkeeping may be more peripheral. Similarly, events that produce different sub-types may give clues to optional configurations within the overall schema.

Investigations of the spread of change among different beliefs about the relationship may also provide information about schematic structure. In the study cited earlier Planalp and Honeycutt (1985) studied how unexpected events changed beliefs about different aspects of the relationship. They found, for instance, that deception most strongly affected beliefs about trust and competing relationships most strongly affected beliefs about exclusiveness, as one would expect. In addition, factor analysis revealed that change spread within three subsets of beliefs more than between them. The first set was labeled "trust" because of high loadings for honesty, trust, and willingness to confide in the other. The second was labeled "involvement" because of high loadings on closeness, companionship, and emotional involvement. The third was labeled "relational rules" because of high loadings on exclusiveness, freedom, duties, and responsibilities. The correlations between factors, however, ranged from 0.40 to 0.56 indicating that changes permeated the entire belief structure to some extent. The findings indicate that meaningful subsets of relational schemas can be found by studying the spread of change.

TERRA INCOGNITA

Research on schemas and the ways they influence and are influenced by incoming information has developed rapidly in the last decade and has yielded findings that are remarkably consistent across several content domains including linguistic materials, descriptions of people, and descriptions of social episodes. There is reason to suppose that the interplay between schemas for relationships and the interactions and events upon which they are based operates in much the same way, although it has received only minimal research attention compared to the work devoted to schemas–event links in other domains. In this paper, I have discussed general findings about schema–event links and have reasoned by analogy to the particular case of relational schema–events links in order to show that similar links are plausible and that positing those links provides useful guidelines for further research. Nevertheless few of those links have been investigated empirically in the relational domain, leaving much room for further speculation and investigation.

These are two properties of relationships that present additional challenges to research on relational schemas. The first is that relationships are dyadic by definition. Ultimately we must understand not only how each relational partner's schema develops, is maintained, or changes but also how the two are linked through interaction. If two people approach an interaction with different relational schemas, how are they brought into agreement, if at all? It would probably not give people enough credit to say that each person acts out of his or her own conceptions and that the joint product (the interaction) is the basis of agreement because their actions may be incompatible and lead to awkward situations. Instead, it is likely that metacognition plays a part. That is, each person has knowledge of the other person's relational knowledge that makes it possible to anticipate and explain the other's actions even if their relational knowledge is not in synchrony. Research on social perspective-taking (O'Keefe and Delia 1982), the adaptation of messages to the receiver's level of knowledge (Harris, Begg, and Upfold 1980) and cognitive biases (Hewes et al. 1985) indicates that this is not only possible but commonplace in everyday life. Yet despite the complexities that are introduced, there is no reason to suppose that metaknowledge is developed, maintained, or changed in ways that are different from other forms of knowledge.

The second property of relationships that must be considered is that they are inextricable from emotion. The connections between cognition, emotion, and interaction are important concerns for all domains of social science but they are crucial for understanding relationships. One perspective is that both emotions and conscious thought processes are outcomes of largely unconscious interpretations of interaction (Mandler 1984). Another clearly complementary perspective is that emotional states and cognitive processes (conscious or unconscious) guide interaction. A third perspective that is especially interesting for work on relational schemas is that emotions are just one aspect of interaction that is interpreted like the rest through conscious or unconscious cognitive processes. That is, people have beliefs about what emotions are appropriate to a relationship and use that knowledge to judge how they feel during interaction. For instance, strong feelings toward one's spouse may be interpreted as passion now that it is appropriate in marriage whereas in earlier centuries the same feelings might have been interpreted as lust or spiritual devotion (Gadlin 1977). People also take measures to enhance emotions that are appropriate to relationships and discourage those that are inappropriate (Gordon 1981) just as they do to interact appropriately. Certainly these and other links between cognition, emotion, and interaction must be studied before we can fully understand relationships.

SUMMARY

There is constant interplay between relational knowledge and events during social interaction but very little research has investigated that interplay directly. In this chapter I have argued that it is fruitful to look to literature on social cognition for research guidelines because relational cognition is a special case of social cognition and because knowledge–event links have been studied more extensively in other related realms of social cognition. A number of conceptual analyses and empirical findings concerning knowledge structures, cognitive processes, and observable events are directly applicable to the study of relational knowledge and events. In particular, research on assimilation and accommodation provides insights into how events are interpreted in light of relational knowledge and how relational knowledge changes in response to events. Finally, suggestions were made for studying how two relational partners' knowledge of their relationship is linked through interaction and how relational cognition is tied to emotion.

REFERENCES

Anderson, J.R. (1978) "Arguments concerning representations for mental imagery." *Psychological Review*, 85, 249–77.

Asch, S. (1946) "Forming impressions of personality." *Journal of Abnormal and Social Psychology*, 41, 258–90.

Bartlett, F.C. (1932) *Remembering*. Cambridge: Cambridge University Press.

Baxter, L.A. and Wilmot, W.W. (1984) " 'Secret tests': social strategies for acquiring information about the state of the relationship." *Human Communication Research*, 11, 171–201.

Berger, C.R. (1979) "Beyond initial interaction: uncertainty, understanding, and the development of interpersonal relationships." In H. Giles and R. St Clair (eds) *Language and Social Psychology*. Baltimore: University Park Press.

Berscheid, E. and Graziano, W. (1979) "The initiation of social relationships and interpersonal attraction." In R.L. Burgess and T.L. Huston (eds) *Social Exchange in Developing Relationships*. New York: Academic Press.

Bobrow, D.G. and Norman, D.A. (1975) "Some principles of memory schemata." In D. Bobrow and A. Collins (eds) *Representation and Understanding: Studies in Cognitive Science*. New York: Academic Press.

Bower, G.H., Black, J.B., and Turner, T. (1979) "Scripts in memory for text." *Cognitive Psychology*, 11, 177–220.

Brewer, W.F. and Nakamura, G.V. (1984) "The nature and functions of schemas." In R.S. Wyer, Jr and T.K. Srull (eds) *Handbook of Social Cognition*, vol. 1. Hillsdale NJ: Lawrence Erlbaum.

Cantor, N. and Mischel, W. (1979) "Prototypes in person perception." In L. Berkowitz (ed.) *Advances in Experimental Social Psychology*, vol. 12. New York: Academic Press.

——, ——, and Schwartz, J. (1982) "Social knowledge: structure, content, use, and abuse." In A. Hastorf and A. Isen (eds) *Cognitive Social Psychology*. New York: Elsevier.

Cappella, J.N. (1984) "The relevance of the microstructure of interaction to relationship change." *Journal of Social and Personal Relationships*, 1, 239–64.

Carlston, D.E. (1980) "Events, inferences, and impression formation." In R. Hastie, T.M. Ostrom, E.B. Ebbesen, R.S. Wyer, Jr, D.L. Hamilton, and D.E. Carlston (eds) *Person Memory: The Cognitive Basis of Social Perception*. Hillsdale, NJ: Lawrence Erlbaum.

Chase, W.G. and Simon, H.A. (1973) "The mind's eye in chess." In W. Chase (ed.) *Visual Information Processing*. New York: Academic Press.

Clark, M.S. and Fiske, S.T. (1982) *Affect and Cognition*. Hillsdale, NJ: Lawrence Erlbaum.

Crocker, J., Fiske, S.T., and Taylor, S.E. (1984) "Schematic bases of belief change." In J.R. Eiser (ed.) *Attitudinal Judgment*. New York: Springer-Verlag.

Davis, K.E. and Todd, M.J. (1985) "Assessing friendship: prototypes, paradigm cases and relationship description." In S. Duck and D. Perlman (eds) *Understanding Personal Relationships: An Interdisciplinary Approach*. Beverly Hills: Sage.

Duck, S. and Sants, H. (1983) "On the origin of the specious: are personal relationships really interpersonal states?" *Journal of Social and Clinical Psychology*, 1, 27–41.

Ebbesen, E.B. (1980) "Cognitive processes in understanding ongoing behavior." In R. Hastie, T.M. Ostrom, E.B. Ebbesen, R.S. Wyer, Jr, D.L. Hamilton, and D.E. Carlston (eds) *Person Memory: The Cognitive Basis of Social Perception*. Hillsdale, NJ: Lawrence Erlbaum.

—— and Allen, R.B. (1979) "Cognitive processes in implicit personality trait inferences." *Journal of Personality and Social Psychology*, 37, 471–88.

Fielding, G. and Fraser, C. (1978) "Language and interpersonal relations." In I. Markova (ed.) *The Social Context of Language*. New York: John Wiley.

Fiske, S.T. and Linville, P. (1980) "What does the schema concept buy us?" *Personality and Social Psychology Bulletin*, 6, 543–57.

—— and Taylor, S.E. (1984) *Social Cognition*. Reading, MA: Addison-Wesley.

——, Kinder, D.R., and Larter, W.M. (1983) "The novice and the expert: knowledge-based strategies in political cognition." *Journal of Experimental Social Psychology*, 19, 381–400.

Forgas, J.P. (1982). "Episode cognition: internal representations of interaction routines." In L. Berkowitz (ed.) *Advances in Experimental Social Psychology*, vol. 15. New York: Academic Press.

Freedle, R. and Duran, R.P. (1979) "Sociolinguistic approaches to dialogue with suggested applications to cognitive science." In R.O. Freedle (ed.) *New Directions in Discourse Processing*, vol. 2. Norwood, NJ: Ablex.

Gadlin, H. (1977) "Private lives and public order: a critical view of the history of intimate relations in the United States." In G. Levinger and H. Rausch (eds) *Close Relationships*. Amherst: University of Massachusetts Press.

Goody, E.N. (1978) "Towards a theory of questions." In E.N. Goody (ed.) *Questions and Politeness*. Cambridge: Cambridge University Press.

Gordon, S.L. (1981) "The sociology of sentiments and emotions." In M. Rosenberg and R. Turner (eds) *Social Psychology*. Basic Books: New York.

Graesser, A.C., Gordon, S.E., and Sawyer, J.D. (1979) "Recognition memory for typical and atypical actions in scripted activities: tests of a script pointer + tag hypothesis." *Journal of Verbal Learning and Verbal Behavior*, 18, 319–32.

——, Woll, S.B., Kowalski, D.J., and Smith, D.A. (1980) "Memory for typical and atypical action in scripted activities." *Journal of Experimental Psychology: Human Learning and Memory*, 6, 503–15.

Greene, J.O. (1984) "A cognitive approach to human communication: an action assembly theory." *Communication Monographs*, 51, 289–306.

Halliday, M.A.K. and Hasan, R. (1976) *Cohesion in English*. London: Longman.

Harris, G., Begg, I., and Upfold, D. (1980) "On the role of the speaker"s expectations in interpersonal communication." *Journal of Verbal Learning and Verbal Behavior*, 19, 597–607.

Hastie, R. (1981) "Schematic principles in human memory." In E.T. Higgins, C.P. Herman, and M.P. Zanna (eds) *Social Cognition: The Ontario Symposium*, vol. 1. Hillsdale NJ: Lawrence Erlbaum.

—— and Kumar, P.A. (1979) "Person memory: personality traits as organizing principles in memory for behaviors." *Journal of Personality and Social Psychology*, 36, 25–38.

——, Ostrom, T.M., Ebbesen, E.B., Wyer, R.S. Jr, Hamilton, D.L., and Carlston, D.E. (1980) *Person Memory: The Cognitive Basis of Social Perception*. Hillsdale, NJ: Lawrence Erlbaum.

——, Park, B., and Weber, R. (1984) "Social memory." In R.S. Wyer, Jr and T.K. Srull (eds) *Handbook of Social Cognition*, vol. 2. Hillsdale, NJ: Lawrence Erlbaum.

Heider, F. (1958) *The Psychology of Interpersonal Relations*. New York: John Wiley.

Hendrick, C., Hendrick, S., Foote, F.H., and Slapion-Foote, M.J. (1984) "Do men and women love differently?" *Journal of Social and Personal Relationships*, 1, 177–95.

Hewes, D.E. and Planalp, S. (1982) "There is nothing as useful as a good theory ...: the influence of social knowledge on interpersonal communication." In M.E. Roloff and C.R. Berger (eds) *Social Cognition and Communication*. Beverly Hills, CA: Sage.

—— and —— (in press) "The place of the individual in communication science."

In C. Berger and S. Chaffee (eds) *Handbook of Communication Science*. Beverly Hills: Sage.

——, Graham, M.L., Doelger, J., and Pavitt, C. (1985) "'Second-guessing': message interpretation in social networks." *Human Communication Research*, 11, 299–334.

Hinde, R.A. (1979) *Towards Understanding Relationships*. New York: Academic Press.

Isen, A.M. and Hastorf, A.H. (1982) "Some perspectives on cognitive social psychology." In A. Hastorf and A. Isen (eds) *Cognitive Social Psychology*. New York: Elsevier.

Kelley, H.H., Berscheid, E., Christensen, A., Harvey, J.H., Huston, T.L., Levinger, G., McClintock, E., Peplau, L.A., and Peterson, D.R. (1983) "Analyzing close relationships." In H.H. Kelley, E. Berscheid, A. Christensen, J.H. Harvey, T.L. Huston, G. Levinger, E. McClintock, L.A. Peplau, and D.R. Peterson (eds) *Close Relationships*. New York: W.H. Freeman.

Labov, W. and Fanshel, D. (1977) *Therapeutic Discourse*. New York: Academic Press.

Langer, E.J. (1978) "Rethinking the role of thought in social interaction." In J. Harvey, W. Ickes, and R. Kidd (eds) *New Directions in Attribution Research*, vol. 2. Hillsdale, NJ: Lawrence Erlbaum.

Lord, C., Ross, L., and Lepper, M.R. (1979) "Biased assimilation and attitude polarization: the effects of prior theories on subsequently considered evidence." *Journal of Personality and Social Psychology*, 37, 2098–109.

McClintock, E. (1983) "Interaction." In H.H. Kelley, E. Berscheid, A. Christensen, J.H. Harvey, T.L. Huston, G. Levinger, E. McClintock, L.A. Peplau, and D.R. Peterson (eds) *Close Relationships*. New York: W.H. Freeman.

Mandler G, (1984). *Mind and Body*. New York: Norton.

Mandler, J.M. and Johnson, N.S. (1977) "Remembrance of things parsed: story structure and recall." *Cognitive Psychology*, 9, 111–51.

Markus, H. (1977) "Self-schemata and processing information about the self." *Journal of Personality and Social Psychology*, 35, 63–78.

Miller, G., Boster, F., Roloff, M., and Seibold, D. (1970) "Compliance-gaining message strategies: a typology and some findings concerning effects of situational differences." *Communication Monographs*, 44, 37–51.

Minsky, M. (1977) "Frame-system theory." In P.N. Johnson-Laird and P.C. Wason (eds) *Thinking: Readings in Cognitive Science*. Cambridge: Cambridge University Press.

Mischel, W. (1968) *Personality and Assessment*. New York: John Wiley.

Nisbett, R. and Ross, L. (1980) *Human Inference*. Englewood Cliffs, NJ: Prentice-Hall.

O'Keefe, B.J. and Delia, J.G. (1982) "Impression formation processes and message production." In M.E. Roloff and C.R. Berger (eds) *Social Cognition and Communication*. Beverly Hills, CA: Sage.

Ostrom, T.M. (1984) "The sovereignty of social cognition." In R.S. Wyer, Jr and T.K. Srull (eds) *Handbook of Social Cognition*, vol. 1. Hillsdale, NJ: Lawrence Erlbaum.

Patterson, M.L., Reidhead, S.M., Gooch, M.V., and Stopka, S.J. (1984) "A content-classified bibliography of research on the immediacy behaviors: 1965–82." *Journal of Nonverbal Behavior*, 8, 360–93.

Planalp, S. (1983) "Relational schemata: an interpretive approach to relationships." Unpublished PhD dissertation, University of Wisconsin-Madison.

—— (1985) "Relational schemata: a test of alternative forms of relational knowledge as guides to communication." *Human Communication Research*, 12, 3–29.

—— and Hewes, D.E. (1982) "A cognitive approach to communication theory: *cogito ergo dico*?" In M. Burgoon (ed.) *Communication Yearbook V.* New Brunswick, NJ: Transaction-International Communication Association.

—— and Honeycutt, J.M. (1985) "Events that increase uncertainty in personal relationships." *Human Communication Research*, 11, 593–604.

Rosch, E. (1978) "Principles of categorization." In E. Rosch and B. Lloyd (eds) *Cognition and Categorization*. Hillsdale, NJ: Lawrence Erlbaum.

Roseman, I.J. (1984) "Cognitive determinants of emotion: a structural theory." In P. Shaver (ed.) *Review of Personality and Social Psychology*, vol. 5. Beverly Hills: Sage.

Rothbart, M. (1981) "Memory processes and social beliefs." In D. Hamilton (ed.) *Cognitive Processes in Stereotyping and Intergroup Behavior*. Hillsdale, NJ: Lawrence Erlbaum.

Schank, R.C. and Abelson, R.P. (1977) *Scripts, Plans, Goals and Understanding*. Hillsdale, NJ: Lawrence Erlbaum.

Schneider, W. and Shiffrin, R.M. (1977) "Controlled and automatic human information processing: I. Detection, search, and attention." *Psychological Review*, 84, 1–66.

Schustack, M.W. and Anderson, J.R. (1979) "Effects of analogy to prior knowledge on memory for new information." *Journal of Verbal Learning and Verbal Behavior*, 18, 565–83.

Searle, J.R. (1969) *Speech Acts*. Cambridge: Cambridge University Press.

Sillars, A.L. (1980) "The stranger and the spouse as target persons for compliance-gaining strategies: a subjective expected utility model." *Human Communication Research*, 6, 265–79.

Snyder, M. (1984) "When belief creates reality." In L. Berkowitz (ed.) *Advances in Experimental Social Psychology*, vol. 18. New York: Academic Press, 247–305.

—— and Swann, W.B., Jr (1978) "Hypothesis-testing processes in social interaction." *Journal of Personality and Social Psychology*, 36, 1202–12.

Spiro, R. (1980) "Accommodative reconstruction in prose recall." *Journal of Verbal Learning and Verbal Behavior*, 19, 84–95.

Taylor, S.E. and Crocker, J. (1981) "Schematic bases of social information processing." In E.T. Higgins, C.P. Herman, and M.P. Zanna (eds) *Social Cognition: The Ontario Symposium*, vol. 1. Hillsdale, NJ: Lawrence Erlbaum.

——, ——, and D'Agostino, J. (1978) "Schematic bases of social problem-solving." *Personality and Social Psychology Bulletin*, 4, 447–51.

Tracy, K., Craig, R.T., Smith, M., and Spisak, F. (1984) "The discourse of requests: assessment of a compliance-gaining approach." *Human Communication Research*, 10, 513–38.

Van Dijk, T.A. and Kintsch, W. (1983) *Strategies of Discourse Comprehension*. New York: Academic Press.

Wegner, D.M. and Vallacher, R.R. (1977) *Implicit Psychology*. New York: Oxford University Press.

Zajonc, Robert B. (1980) "Feeling and thinking: preferences need no inferences." *American Psychologist*, 35, 151–75.

11 Cognition and communication in the relationship process

Leslie A. Baxter

For the past six years, I have been researching how people communicatively accomplish romantic relationship development, maintenance and repair, and disengagement (Baxter 1979, 1982, 1983, 1984, 1985, in press; Baxter and Bullis, in press; Baxter and Philpott 1980, 1982; Baxter and Wilmot 1983, 1984, 1985; Bullis and Baxter 1986; Dindia and Baxter 1986; Wilmot and Baxter 1983, 1984; Wilmot, Carbaugh, and Baxter 1985). To a large extent, personal relationships research has mirrored other social scientific work in viewing communication as a mere conduit of more causally forceful psychological and sociological factors (Pearce and Cronen 1980). By contrast, a view of relationships as communicative accomplishments presumes that communication is a central force in its own right. The significant role accorded communication in creating the social order can be traced to the later Wittgenstein's (1953) focus on language-in-use. However, a view of relationships as communicative accomplishments should not be taken as a deterministic stance toward the power of communication. Rather, communication and the social order relate dialectically with communication constructing people's conceptions of the social order just as the constructed social order frames our understanding of communication. The dialectic or reflexive relationship between communication and the social order also has its roots in the later Wittgenstein's (1953) work, in particular his metaphor of "language games." Language-in-use (i.e. communication) gains its meaning because of the context in which it is framed, and simultaneously such language use enacts the contextual frame. For example, the choice of a given chess move is made in the context of knowing the rules of the game of chess and the move gains its meaning only through that contextual frame; simultaneously, the particular chess move accomplishes and makes real a game of chess. The Wittgensteinian assumptions that frame my research program are evident in several contemporary social theories, including the Coordinated Management of Meaning (Pearce and Cronen 1980), symbolic interaction (Blumer 1969; Mead 1934), language action (Frentz and Farrell 1976), ethogeny (Harré 1980), and structuration (Giddens 1979).

Collectively, my program of research affords insights into two aspects of relationship cognitions or knowledge. First, this research suggests that relationship parties have a cognitive repository of relationship process knowledge in addition to their conceptions of various static relationship types. Such process cognitions or schemata serve to frame any given communicative action, thereby assisting actors in their communicative choice-making and in making sense of such communicative actions. Second, this research program gives insights into the functions and uses of relationship cognitions in the communicative interaction between relationship parties. Specifically, the argument will be advanced that relationship process knowledge allows relationship parties to use ambiguous communicative actions to their advantage in creating certain relational outcomes.

Extant work in social cognition and relationships focuses largely on one type of relationship knowledge: cognitive conceptions of various relationship types (Argyle and Henderson 1984, 1985; Davis and Todd 1982, 1985; La Gaipa 1979; Rands and Levinger 1979; Wish and Kaplan 1977; Wright 1985). Although researchers in this domain may differ on the form such relationship knowledge takes, i.e. whether it is in the form of prototypes, systems of behavioral rules, or underlying dimensions (cf. Planalp 1985), they collectively give us insight into people's conceptions of such relationship types as acquaintanceship, platonic friendship, and the romantic relationship. Insightful as this body of work is, however, it generally affords us a static state view of relationships, in contrast to a dynamic view of processes of relationship emergence and change. Relationship types do not materialize instantaneously but rather are constructed over time through the interactions of the relationship parties. Further, once a given relationship type has formed, it is not static but typically is ever-changing and fluid. In short, extant work in social cognitions of relationships has de-emphasized relationship processes in favor of relationship products. It is a primary thesis of this chapter that interactants are guided by relationship process cognitions in addition to their conceptions of various static relationship types. Relationship process cognitions appear to be organized into two orders of specificity: (1) cognitions relevant to various relationship trajectories, i.e. conceptions of how relationships typically develop and dissolve; and (2) cognitions relevant to relationship-ing, i.e. conceptions of strategic actions by which to accomplish various relational outcomes.

In addition, existing work in social cognitions of relationships deals largely with the psychological functions of such cognitions for the individual, rather than the social and communicative functions (Clark and Delia 1979). Although we know that relationship cognitions affect the person's information acquisition and retrieval functioning (Planalp 1985; Roloff and Berger 1982), relatively less attention has been given to how this relationship knowledge is communicatively used in interaction between relationship parties (the substantial research program by Berger and his colleagues is a notable exception [see Berger and Bradac 1982; Berger, this volume]). It is a second thesis of this chapter that relationship cognitions allow relationship parties to rely heavily on indirect cueing to accomplish much of their relationship interaction, rather than using direct communication about their relationship. Contrary to the popular stereotype encapsulated in the expression "What we need is communication" (Katriel and Philipsen 1981), the typical relationship process is not dominated by open, direct relationship communication, but rather involves the construction of a web of ambiguity by which parties signal their relationship indirectly.

With this overview in mind, the chapter first turns to a discussion of the two types of relationship process knowledge that have surfaced in the research program. Process trajectory knowledge provides a general framework of what growth and dissolution processes are like; it provides a cognitive backdrop for the more particularized knowledge relationship parties have of strategic actions that can be performed during these processes. Reciprocally, however, such strategic actions are the "stuff" of which relationship trajectories are constituted. Thus, cognitive knowledge of process trajectories and strategic actions mutually inform one another and jointly reveal what people think of relationship *processes*.

RELATIONSHIP PROCESS KNOWLEDGE: TRAJECTORIES AND STRATEGIC ACTIONS

Process trajectory cognitions

Several of the studies in this research program suggest that people have cognitive schemata, i.e. coherent conceptual frameworks (Craik 1979), for the ways relationships grow and disengage. Built on the basis of observation and experience, these relationship trajectory schemata allow the relationship parties to make sense of the sequence of episodes that occur when relationships are forming and breaking up. In the formative state of romantic relationship growth, for instance, the parties' growth trajectory schemata allow them to gauge whether the relationship's progress is "on course," to predict which sorts of events should occur next in the trajectory sequence, and to make retrospective sense of episodes that have occurred already in the relationship's interaction history. Such trajectory schemata are distinct from the parties' relationship type schemata; whereas the former address the issue of how romantic relationships form (or decline), the latter address the issue of what constitutes the romantic relationship type.

Process trajectory schemata have been derived from two types of data across several studies in the research program: respondent reactions to hypothetical relationship situations, and respondent verbal accounts of their own relationship experiences. In response to hypothetical scenarios, the assumption is that respondents "call up" their schemata of the ways in which such situations play themselves out in real life (Harré and Secord 1973). In providing accounts of their own relationship experiences, the assumption is that respondents use their schemata as a guide to sense-making, focusing on features of their experience that are salient in their own schemata (for a complementary perspective on accounts, see Weber *et al.*, this volume). Both types of data affirm the author's belief in the subjectively constructed nature of social life. Thus, no claims are made about objectifiable behaviors enacted by relationship parties in actual relationship encounters. Based on the assumption that reality is subjectively constructed, actors' perceptions and schemata are valid sources of data about relational life. Obviously, however, a useful complement to the research in this program would be observation of relationship interaction in order to determine how relationship knowledge plays itself out in actual communicative action (for a discussion of the relationship between social cognition and social action, see Berger, this volume).

In an attempt to determine whether people have growth trajectory and disengagement trajectory schemata, Wilmot and Baxter (1983) presented 263 subjects with hypothetical conversations that were attributed to one of two relationship types (cross-sex friends or cross-sex romantic partners) and to one of two relationship trajectories (growing closer or growing apart). Although the conversational stimuli were identical for all subjects and afforded substantial specificity of information, subjects interpreted the relational meaning of the conversations quite differently depending on the process trajectory in which the conversations were framed. The growth trajectory frame produced perceptions of the conversations as more disclosive, honest, and direct than the conversations framed in the dissolution trajectory. The relationship type did not affect perceptions of the conversations, suggesting that process trajectories do not differ for these two relationship types. The results of this study support the claim that people do indeed have process trajectory schemata which they use to interpret relationship interactions. Further, these schemata point to disclosive and direct communication as an important feature that differentiates growth and dissolution trajectories.

Additional work in the research program has elaborated on both the growth trajectory and dissolution trajectory schemata. In an attempt to move beyond hypothetical relationships and to expand our understanding of the growth trajectory schema, the relationship partners from forty cross-sex romantic couples were interviewed independently for all of the

significant turning points that occurred in the development of their relationships (Baxter and Bullis, in press; Bullis and Baxter 1986). Because the
extant analyses of these turning point interviews have focused on facets of
the relationship other than the growth trajectory schema, I will use this
occasion to delve into this account data in some detail.

It is apparent that two mutually exclusive pattern variations exist in
people's growth trajectory schema: the proverbial love-at-first-sight, which
we labeled the Whirlwind trajectory, and the gradual Friendship First
trajectory. Both of these thematic variations featured reported increases in
disclosure and directness over time, but both were heavily punctuated by
instances of indirectness and incomplete disclosures, as well.

Only a minority of the respondents actually reported experiencing the
Whirlwind trajectory, yet several verbal accounts made reference to this
type of commonly known growth trajectory. One female respondent indicated surprise in experiencing a Whirlwind trajectory because she didn't
think "it" happened that way: "We got together at a party, no big deal, and
then he kissed me goodnight. And then the next day I saw him and it just
happened. Those kinds of things usually never happen. I mean, if something happens at a party it's usually disastrous. It usually never works out."
By contrast, a male respondent expressed pleasant surprise that his romantic relationship did not experience a Whirlwind trajectory but instead
typified the second type of growth trajectory people made reference to, the
Friendship First trajectory:

> [The relationship] was totally different. . . . It just doesn't seem like
> what you're supposed to do. You're supposed to catch her first
> glance and fall in love, but this was more like the 6000th glance. . . .
> I think it's real important to a relationship to grow the way we did, a
> gradual year of becoming real good friends and then deciding that
> there might be something more that you want to experience.

The most frequently reported growth trajectory was the gradual progression from friendship to romantic involvement. For some respondents,
this Friendship First trajectory reflected the opinion expressed above by the
male respondent that friendship was a desirable antecedent foundation for
a romantic relationship. For other respondents, the Friendship First trajectory occurred out of necessity, as when the other party was hesitant to
commit to a romantic relationship due to a third party rival or general
caution against involvement. For yet other respondents, the Friendship
First trajectory was a safe and secure way to continue enjoying one
another's company without worrying about loss of autonomy in becoming
a couple.

In addition to the basic conceptual distinction between Whirlwind and
Friendship First trajectories, three secondary themes emerged in respondent accounts: perceived symmetry of involvement, perceived effortfulness,
and perceived degree of autonomy separate from the couple relationship.

These secondary themes were evident in the accounts of both Whirlwind and Friendship First trajectories. The theme of symmetry of involvement captures whether both relationship parties were in agreement on the progress of their relationship (the symmetrical condition), in contrast to the asymmetrical state in which one party wanted a romantic relationship more than the other party. The asymmetrical state was described by respondents in terms of distinct pursuer–pursued roles, as this verbal account excerpt from a male indicates: "I was kind of surprised to find us caught up in the whole pursuit thing. I was the definite pursuer and she was the pursuee. I thought I was in a commanding portion of the market. Then I was invaded by a competitor [a rival] and needed to reanalyze my strategies."

Although unequal involvement creates an effortful situation for the more involved party, the effortful–effortless theme surfaced in other respondent accounts, as well. In general, this dimension captures whether or not the growth trajectory is conceived of as an inherently problematic phenomenon that necessitates interactional work to overcome difficulties. One female indicated the presence of the effortfulness feature in her growth schema by expressing surprise that her relationship's history had been so problem-free:

> We got to know each other *really* quickly. And spent a lot of time together. . . . It seems like things are too perfect sometimes and they shouldn't be like that. It [the relationship] just keeps elevating itself and I don't know if there are any specific times . . . we haven't had any times when things have declined.

A male respondent repeated the effortfulness theme in his declaration that "All relationships have their ups and downs." Yet another female respondent supported the same theme in her statement that "All relationships are kind of crazy at first; everything's so idealized. Then reality catches up." In contrast, several respondents revealed that the presence of effort and interactional work signalled that the relationship "just wasn't meant to be" or that it "wasn't natural." As one male expressed the effortless theme: "In my view of relationships, you can't push and you can't hold back. You just 'be.' Some people are lucky and they have similar backgrounds and environments – they just fit real well together. For others, it just won't work out."

The third theme captures the degree of individual autonomy the relationship parties maintained during their relationship's growth. Some couples' growth trajectories were characterized by limited autonomy, or what one female respondent aptly referred to as the "glue couple syndrome." Other relationship histories were characterized by greater independence by the relationship parties, either throughout the entire relationship's history or after experiencing an intensive "glue syndrome" stage. One female respondent referred to this more independent trajectory as "knowing that you're always two separate individuals apart from the relationship that's forming."

Given that the majority of relationships described in the turning point interviews illustrated the Friendship First trajectory, it is useful to enquire whether respondents have clear conceptions of how the transformation from friendship to romantic partners occurs. The transformation issue is an important one, given that there are fuzzy boundaries between the cross-sex friendship and cross-sex romantic relationship types with many attributes in common (Davis and Todd 1982; Wilmot and Baxter 1984). Relationship parties do have clear conceptions of what events transform the relationship to one of romantic involvement. The first display of physical affection (Wilmot and Baxter 1984) and the first "date," as opposed to simply "spending time together" (Bullis and Baxter 1986), are the salient schema features that transform a relationship from platonic friendship to romantic involvement.

In sum, two basic growth trajectory schemata are suggested: the Whirlwind trajectory and the Friendship First trajectory. These two basic patterns capture how quickly the relationship parties become romantically involved. In addition, three secondary schema themes surfaced in people's talk about relationship growth: symmetry of involvement, degree of effort, and degree of autonomy the parties maintain outside the relationship. These three secondary themes emerged with both of the two basic trajectory types.

Two studies in the research program have further explored the dissolution trajectory schema. Baxter and Philpott (1980) presented respondents with a story completion task whose story start involved a couple desiring unilateral or bilateral disengagement. In completing the story the way they thought it would really happen, two break-up patterns were evident. One trajectory was characterized by themes of procrastination, equivocation, and indirect hinting by the breaker-upper, leading to several escalatory exchanges between the parties of increasing frustration, hurt, and anger to both parties. Labeled the Protracted Indirectness trajectory, this pattern matches quite closely the schema of reduced disclosure and directness found in the Wilmot and Baxter (1983) study reported above. The second trajectory, labeled the Swift Directness trajectory, featured a less protracted exchange between the parties with direct expression of wants and desires. Although negative emotional reactions were present in this trajectory as well, they were generally envisioned as less intense than in the Protracted Indirectness trajectory.

Although these two dissolution trajectories were created in response to hypothetical relationship situations, they match quite closely the accounts respondents have provided in making sense of their own relationship break-ups (Baxter 1984). In analyzing the accounts of ninety-seven romantic relationship break-ups, Baxter (1984) noted the salience of four schema themes: (1) whether the break-up was unilaterally or bilaterally desired; (2) whether the dissolution was negotiated directly or indirectly; (3)

whether the dissolution was relatively swift as opposed to protracted with several cycles or rounds of negotiation; and (4) whether the parties experienced ambivalence and sought repair actions at some point. The most common pattern was a unilateral, protracted, and indirect trajectory, a finding that bears close resemblance to the Protracted Indirectness trajectory noted above. That is, the typical disengagement was reported as one-sided in which the breaker-upper sought to signal his/her desire to end the relationship through indirect cues such as hinting; such hinting usually failed which led to additional "rounds" of signalling from the breaker-upper to the broken-up-with. Much less common was a pattern of swift and direct dissolution.

On the whole, many of the themes evident in the dissolution trajectory schema appear similar to those for the growth trajectory schema. The protracted–swift rate of dissolution accomplishment appears to parallel the gradual–immediate distinction noted in the growth trajectories for onset of romantic involvement. The symmetry of involvement theme noted for the growth trajectory schema bears close resemblance to the unilateral–bilateral desire to seek dissolution. Effortfulness appears to be pervasive in all variations of the break-up trajectory schema, perhaps with the single exception of the bilateral, direct, and swift scenario (Baxter 1984), whereas growth trajectories allowed both effortful and effortless variations. Last, the ambivalence experienced during dissolution bears on the issue of autonomy vs. interdependence that was noted for the growth trajectory schema. In short, people appear to make sense of relationship beginnings and endings by using the same basic set of relational themes.

The growth trajectory and dissolution trajectory schemata that have emerged in this research program are quite general in nature. They do not entail a detailed sequence of events but rather capture the overall themes of the two processes. Subsequent work is needed to determine whether people have detailed event-by-event sequential conceptions of these processes. Work is needed, as well, on people's conceptions of the "middle process" between the end-points of growth and dissolution. Do people have schemata of the process dynamics once relationship parties have established a mutually acceptable relationship state? The next section discusses an initial piece of research related to this stage of relational life, but much more work is needed. Research also needs to address people's schemata for relationships "at risk." What conceptions do people have of what a troubled relationship looks like? Obviously, this middle process between formation and dissolution holds enormous importance for how the parties choose to function in established relationships.

This section of the chapter has addressed people's general trajectory schemata of what relationship growth and dissolution processes are like. It has painted a broad portrait of how people regard these processes. The next section attempts to fill in some of the details of this broad portrait in discussing people's conceptions of strategic actions during the processes of relationship growth, maintenance and repair, and dissolution. Although cognitions of strategic actions are at a different level of specificity than the trajectory schemata just discussed, they obviously hold relevance to people's process knowledge of relationships.

Strategic action cognitions

Many of the studies in this research program have probed people's conceptions of the strategic actions that collectively comprise the relationship processes of developing, maintaining and repairing, and dissolving romantic relationships. "Strategic action" refers to the rational means–ends nature of communicative activity regardless of whether the parties are consciously aware of their strategic choice-making at the time of its enactment. Indeed, as Duck (1985) suggests, relationship parties probably do not invest much conscious cognitive effort in their day-to-day relationship encounters. Baxter and Philpott (1985) have found that conscious strategic choice-making occurs only in circumstances of high importance, difficulty, or unpredictability. Conceptualization based on rational means–ends rather than cognitive effort locates strategic action as a social as opposed to psychological phenomenon. That is, from a Wittgensteinian view, communicative action takes on the meaning of "strategic" based on properties of the social context in which it is embedded. Cognitive structures about strategic action have been variously referenced in the literature, e.g. scripts (Abelson 1981), memory organization packets (Schank 1980), and procedural records (Greene 1984). Greene's (1984) action assembly theory posits a hierarchical order of specificity to such cognitive structures, with four basic levels of abstraction:

1   The interactional representation, i.e. a general conception of how current interaction goals are to be achieved.
2   The ideational representation, i.e. the level at which the specific content of discourse is conceived.
3   The utterance representation, where syntactic, lexical, and phonological features are conceived.
4   The sensorimotor representation, the most specific of the levels, in which the action is actually produced.

The strategic action work discussed in this section can best be captured at the interactional representation level.

Individuals usually have multiple goals in any given encounter (for a related discussion on goals, see Berger, this volume). What are the types of goals most salient in relationship dynamics? Consistent with Berger's uncertainty reduction theory (Berger and Bradac 1982; Berger and Calabrese 1975), relationship parties seek to acquire information relevant to the current situation before them in order to reduce uncertainty. Second, as articulated in the politeness theory of Brown and Levinson (1978), relationship parties seek to maintain the face of self and the other. A useful distinction has been drawn between two types of face: (1) positive face, i.e. one's desire to be liked, respected, and valued; and (2) negative face, i.e.

one's desire to maintain a sense of control or freedom from constraint (Brown and Levinson 1978). Third, the relationship parties seek to establish their desired relational outcomes, whether formation of a mutually acceptable romantic relationship, maintenance and repair of same, or dissolution of the relationship.

In order to expedite the discussion of strategic action interactional representations, research will be organized around the three process stages of relationship formation, maintenance and repair, and dissolution.

Relationship formation

The person seeking to form a specific relationship with another faces several informational burdens. As articulated elsewhere (Baxter and Philpott 1982), this person must establish two critical attributional perceptions in the other party: (1) that one is interested in having the relationship with the other party; and (2) that one is worthy of the other party's investment in such a relationship. Clearly, these two perceptions are not entirely independent of one another, as one's interest in the relationship can constitute evidence of one's worth. The critical feature about these attributions is their conjunctive nature, i.e. both are necessary. How the person strategically establishes these two perceptions in the other party is dependent on what information has been obtained about the other party relative to: (1) his or her realization that one is interested; and (2) his or her realization that one is worthy and that the relationship is desirable.

Direct relationship communication affords the most efficient strategic action for both acquiring information on the other party's current perceptions and for altering those perceptions. Direct talk maximizes clarity, thereby reducing the likelihood of misunderstandings. However, strategic action during the growth trajectory is not typified by direct relationship communication, but rather features highly selective instances of directness embedded in a dominant pattern of indirectness. Such indirectness, if appropriately enacted, allows the relationship parties to acquire and present information "off the record," thereby reducing risk to positive and negative face (Brown and Levinson 1978). If a person indirectly indicates his or her desire for romantic involvement with the other party and is rebuffed, the person's face nonetheless can be maintained. An indirect "bid" for involvement entails sufficient "slippage" to allow the person to deny the attributed meaning. Indirect as opposed to direct self-presentation of oneself as a worthy relationship partner also maintains the person's face; excessive directness runs the risk of being disliked because of too little modesty. In addition, a rebuff from the other party would probably occur indirectly as well, further contributing to the person's face-saving. Further, indirect strategic action maintains the other party's face as well. A "bald on record" declaration of one's desire for romantic involvement or a direct enquiry about feelings puts the other party "on the spot" by demanding an answer, potentially threatening his or her negative face.

Several studies in the research program document the salience of indirect strategic action over direct relationship communication during the relationship development period. In a study of "taboo" topics in opposite-sex relationships, Baxter and Wilmot (1985) found that the status of the relationship was a pervasive topic partners avoided, especially if the relationship was in a transition between platonic friendship and a romantic relationship. The reasons given by respondents for avoiding direct relationship talk shed insight into their conceptions of the relationship growth process. The most frequent reason expressed by respondents for a taboo against relationship talk was the threat such directness would pose for the relationship. Many respondents perceived that commitment levels were not yet equal; explicit talk about the relationship would force recognition of this discrepancy, thereby jeopardizing the relationship's future. Interestingly, the concern over a discrepancy in commitment levels was equally present for both the more committed and the less committed parties; the more committed did not want the less committed to feel pressured by the discrepancy in feelings, and the less committed did not want the more committed to become angry by the imbalance. Clearly, these respondents perceived themselves embedded in the asymmetrical involvement trajectory presented above. The second most frequent reason for the relationship talk taboo was vulnerability to the individual's face posed by the possibility of something the other party would say. The third reason expressed against direct relationship talk was the perceived effectiveness of tacit strategic action, an issue addressed in further detail in the section on social cognitions in relationship interaction, (p. 208). Fourth, some respondents expressed a taboo against relationship talk because it constituted interactional work in what was ideally conceived as an effortless process, reflecting the effortful–effortless theme discussed above. Last, respondents avoided direct relationship talk because it was premature, appropriate only in already close relationships. The last reason is quite consistent with the turning-point data discussed above, in which respondents reported avoiding relationship talk about significant turning-points in the early stages of development (Baxter and Bullis, in press).

The perception that increased disclosure and directness characterize the relationship growth process, as reported above, appears to be contradicted by the avoidance of direct talk about the state of the relationship. The contradiction may be more apparent than real. Direct relationship talk may be used for symbolic purposes to confirm and validate relationship closeness once the parties have assured that closeness through tacit and indirect strategic actions, in contrast to use of direct relationship talk as a strategy of negotiating greater closeness. This analysis is consistent with the final reason expressed above for avoidance of direct relationship talk. This almost ritualistic use of relationship talk has also been noted by others (Katriel and Philipsen 1981).

In addition to the avoidance of direct talk about the state of the relationship, the taboo topics study (Baxter and Wilmot 1985) revealed other subject areas that are strategically avoided in developing relationships. Activities outside of the relationship, prior romantic relationships, relationship norms (especially sexual norms), and known issues of disagreement were also taboo because of their perceived threat to the relationship's growth potential. Collectively, people's taboo topics strongly suggest a conception of relationship growth as a fragile endeavor best handled through the perceived safety afforded by indirect strategic actions.

But what indirect actions are likely to be employed? Baxter and Wilmot (1984) found a rich repertoire of strategic actions that relationship parties reported employing to discern the other party's perceptions. Labeled "secret tests," these strategies are unknown to the partner and test his or her relational feelings concerning the worth of the relationship investment. Most commonly reported were endurance tests that reduce the other's rewards in order to determine his or her depth of commitment. For instance, the person might create a situation in which the partner must choose between the relationship and something else that is desired. Second most frequently mentioned were triangle tests, in which the person creates a situation with a real or hypothetical third party where the other party can be checked for fidelity or jealousy. For example, one might create a fictitious rival in order to see whether or not the partner displays jealousy. To test fidelity one might strategically monitor how the partner behaves with an attractive member of the opposite sex in a party situation. Respondents also reported use of separation tests in which contact with the other party is broken in order to monitor whether and when the other initiates re-uniting. Other indirect secret tests mentioned less frequently than the strategic actions just mentioned include: (1) enquiry with third parties who might have information about the partner's feelings; (2) public presentation as "a couple" in order to check the partner's reaction to the presentation; and (3) a variety of "testing the water" tests through hints, jokes, etc. Taken as a whole, these secret test strategies suggest that evidence of commitment is exceedingly important to the growth trajectory. In fact, many of the significant turning points people identified in the growth of their relationships revolved around this salient feature (Bullis and Baxter 1986).

People also have a repertoire of indirect strategies for conveying their interest in the other party and in convincing the other party to become involved in a relationship. Baxter and Philpott (1982) found that strategies for relationship initiation can be reduced to five basic types:

1   *Other Enhancement:* the giving of compliments or other signals that demonstrate that one thinks highly of the other.
2   *Similarity Display:* the demonstration of commonality with the other.
3   *Self-Presentation:* the presentation of a unique and favorable image of oneself to the other.
4   *Favor Rendering:* the doing of favors or giving of rewards.
5   *Inclusion:* activity that brings the other person into one's interaction proximity.

The strategies of Other Enhancement and Inclusion appear most directly related to the perceptual attribution that one is interested in and likes the other. Similarity Display and Self-Presentation permit one to display attributes by which to prove one's worthiness to the other party. Favor Rendering would seem to contribute simultaneously to both key attributions – that one is interested and that one is appealing. Because a display that one likes the other is nothing more than positive face work, the detailed set of positive politeness tactics presented by Brown and Levinson (1978) has direct relevance to the relationship initiation process. Recent work in affinity-seeking (Bell and Daly 1984) also holds relevance, as does the chapter in this volume by Berger.

Although the various elaborations of strategic action repertoires that have emerged in the research differ in detail and labels, they collectively affirm that relationship parties seek to establish the two critical attributes of liking the other and being likable. Further, these various strategy repertoires support the strong role that indirect cueing plays during the growth trajectory process.

Relationship maintenance and repair

As noted above, this research program has not yet examined people's maintenance and repair trajectory schemata. However, some initial work has recently been completed on people's strategic actions for maintenance and repair, and the findings of this research shed some beginning insight on the conceptions people hold of this middle process between relationship formation and dissolution. An initial study with both partners from forty-five marriages followed by a replication with fifty marital couples (Dindia and Baxter 1986) revealed a rich repertoire of over fifty strategies by which parties attempt to maintain and repair the marital relationship, which conceptually reduce to a much smaller set of basic strategy types. The respondents in this study, married an average of fourteen years, were asked to list all the things they did when attempting to accomplish preventive maintenance, i.e. to keep their relationship healthy, and to accomplish restorative repair, i.e. to restore their relationship's health in the presence of problems. Space limitations preclude an exhaustive review of all of the study's findings, but the most frequently listed strategy types merit discussion for what they reveal about people's conceptions of maintenance and repair processes. Overall, the most frequently reported strategies were increased time spent together and increased general interaction (e.g. talk about the day). The conception of relational difficulty implicit in these two strategies appears to be a drifting apart of the relationship partners. In other words, these strategies suggest relational drift as a central theme in people's cognitive schemata of the middle period of relational life.

Spending more time together and general interaction perhaps offset such relational drift. However, if the sorts of difficulties experienced by marital partners are more complex than relational drift, as the literature on marital complaints would suggest (Harvey, Wells, and Alvarez 1978; Kelley 1979; Kitson and Sussman 1982), general talk and increased contact might be quite ineffective if not counterproductive. Research is needed on the actual efficacy of strategic repertoires used by relationship parties in maintaining and repairing their own relationship.

Although maintenance and repair goals shared several strategies in common, including the two mentioned above, specialized strategies emerged for each type of goal. Specifically, direct relationship talk was likely to be used for repair purposes and strategically avoided for relationship maintenance. By contrast, relationship maintenance was significantly more likely than repair to involve the strategies of introducing novelty to offset routine and more responsible execution of one's marital role obligations (e.g. lawn work, house cleaning, etc.). This partial specialization of strategies suggests that preventive maintenance and restorative repair are related but different processes as conceived by these respondents. Additional work is needed to tease out the similarities and differences in these processes. As Duck (1984) has recently argued, coping with relational difficulty is not a monolithic phenomenon but rather a complex set of processes that vary in important ways. The findings of this study support Duck's analysis.

At a minimum, the ability of these marital partners to generate strategies of maintenance and repair is suggestive of their conception of the middle period of relationships as inherently effortful with ongoing interactional work. More particularly, the strategies suggest a perceived need to counter the problem of relational drift. Finally, the strategies suggest that preventive and restorative interactional work are perceived as partially similar but also distinct processes.

Relationship dissolution

Many studies in this research program have been devoted to strategic actions by which parties dissolve their relationships (Baxter 1979, 1982, 1983, 1984, 1985, in press; Baxter and Philpott 1982; Baxter and Bullis, in press; Wilmot, Carbaugh, and Baxter 1985). Following Duck's (1982) stage model of dissolution, Baxter (in press) suggests that strategic actions vary depending on where the parties are in the dissolution phase.

The initial stage of dissolution, the so-called private decision-making stage, involves a private assessment of the other party and of the relationship as sources of satisfaction and dissatisfaction. The party's primary goal is to decide whether or not to dissolve the relationship. This period is high in uncertainty (Duck 1982), motivating the person to strategically acquire information about the other party's likelihood of resisting a dissolution "bid," the other's motivation to make changes necessary to make the relationship more satisfying, and the possible reactions of social network members to a dissolution of the relationship. Direct relationship talk potentially affords the greatest efficiency of action, just as it does during the growth trajectory. However, relationship parties who are contemplating dissolution opt instead for indirectness, largely because its threat to face is less than the threat posed by bald-on-record directness (for a detailed discussion of this point, see Baxter [in press]). Thus, this preliminary phase of dissolution is conducive to indirect secret test strategies, as noted above for the growth trajectory. However, the purpose of such tests is obviously different than during the relationship development stage.

Assuming that a person concludes the private decision-making stage with a decision to dissolve the relationship, the information burden shifts to that of informing the other party of one's desire and persuading him or her to accept it. Baxter and Philpott (1982) argue that dissolution at this stage involves the mirror opposites of the conjunctive attributions discussed above for relationship initiation. That is, the two critical attributions to create for the other party are: (1) that one no longer is interested in the relationship; and (2) that one no longer is worthy of the other's continued investment in the relationship. However, unlike relationship initiation in which the counterparts of these attributions function conjunctively, Baxter and Philpott (1982) suggest that one of these attributions may suffice to accomplish dissolution. That is, one could employ strategic actions that signal one no longer is interested in the relationship *or* one could employ strategies so costly to the other party that he or she initiates dissolution action. In practice, these two attributions often overlap at the level of strategic action. The mere realization that one's partner doesn't wish to continue creates relational spoilage that is often sufficient evidence that the relationship is no longer worthy of continued investment (McCall 1982). Further, as discussed above under the dissolution trajectory schema, how one signals the first attribution often convinces the other party of one's lack of worth.

Although many levels of specificity could be discussed in terms of reported strategic dissolution actions (see in particular Baxter [1982, 1984, 1985]), the functional thrust of these strategic actions is their relevance to these two critical attributions. Because it is generally less stressful psychologically to view oneself as the breaker-upper rather than the broken-up-with (Hill, Rubin, and Peplau 1976), most of the strategic actions concentrate on the first attribution, i.e. conveying that one no longer is interested in a relationship with the other.

Basically two clusters of strategic action have emerged concerning this first attributional task (Baxter, in press). The first, labeled Distance Cueing, involves a variety of indirect signals to the other party that convey loss of interest, e.g. reduced breadth, depth, and valence of self-disclosure. The second cluster involves direct relationship talk with the other about one's feelings. These two clusters of strategies hold implications for both parties' face. Because of the likelihood that directness will be met with anger and hostility from the other party, the disengager's positive face is better served by the indirectness of Distance Cueing. Relationship talk is perceived as more effortful than Distance Cueing, thus evoking greater threat to the disengager's negative face in his or her desire for freedom from constraints. Unfortunately, face-saving on behalf of the disengager is often at odds with the other party's face. The other's positive face is threatened under any circumstance, but the threat is probably greatest with Distance Cueing for it doesn't even show the basic courtesy of a face-to-face accounting (Wilmot, Carbaugh, and Baxter 1985). Similarly, the other party's negative face is likely to be more threatened with Distance Cueing; at least a direct talk allows the other party some sense of control in the situation.

As noted above, indirectness is a frequent strategic choice by the disengager, who clearly opts for his or her own face instead of face-saving on the other's behalf. However, directness does become more likely under some circumstances: when the other is not culpable in the relationship's demise (Baxter 1982), when future contact with the other party is anticipated (Baxter 1982), and, most importantly, when the prior relationship was very close (Baxter, in press). The greater likelihood of directness in very close relationships may imply that parties' close relationship schemata obligate face work on the other's behalf as just compensation for the former good times once experienced in the relationship. Alternatively, directness may be employed in close relationships simply because the web of interdependence is so complex that indirectness is inadequate to the dissolution task (e.g. determining who gets which household goods).

The second attribution, which involves giving the other party sufficient cause to seek dissolution himself or herself, is accomplished by a myriad of tactics, which collectively are labeled Cost Escalation (Baxter 1985). Such actions as becoming hypercritical toward the other may drive the other party to the conclusion that the relationship is no longer worth the investment. However, Cost Escalation is probably a strategy of last resort for two reasons. First, as noted above, it is more desirable to be perceived as the breaker-upper than as the broken-up-with. Second, in light of the costly face implications for the other party that accompany the Distance Cueing strategies, these frequently employed strategies targeted at the first critical attribution simultaneously accomplish the second critical attributional task as well.

Taken collectively, the dissolution strategies research supports the dissolution trajectory schema presented above in featuring reduced disclosure and reduced directness. Although directness is evident in some selected circumstances, indirectness is a prevalent strategic action. Both Distance Cueing and Cost Escalation fall short of directly confronting the other party with one's dissolution desire.

Although direct relationship talk may afford the greatest efficiency in accomplishing one's relationship goals due to its clarity, the strategic action research consistently suggests that relationship parties opt instead for a variety of indirect actions. Such indirectness serves the face work needs of the user. The final section of this chapter addresses the functional value of relationship process cognitions in allowing such heavy reliance on indirect cueing actions.

THE FUNCTIONS OF SOCIAL COGNITIONS IN RELATIONSHIP INTERACTION

The central argument of this section is that it is people's well-developed relationship process cognitions that allow indirectness to be employed quite efficiently in relationship interaction. In turn, such indirectness reduces the face threat otherwise present in direct communication; because indirect meanings are not formally codified, the user has some "slippage" through which to deny attributed intentions if they prove damaging or ineffectual. Certainly, indirectness lacks the explicit clarity of bald-on-record direct talk and thus is not as efficient as directness; indirectness does increase the likelihood of misunderstandings because it is more ambiguous by definition. But relationship parties, heavily reliant on indirectness, *do* manage to accomplish relationship-ing. If misunderstandings were omnipresent, indirectness would be totally inefficient and relationship parties would be incapable of conducting their relational lives. Obviously something intervenes to prevent ubiquitous misunderstanding of indirect signals. That "something" is commonly understood relationship process knowledge.

As King and Sereno (1984) argue, the relational meaning derived from any action is based on Grice's (1975, 1978) principle of implicature. In Grice's view, implicated meaning is triggered when a communicative act violates what is expected for the situation at hand. Thus "the date" evokes the implicated meaning that the relationship is being transformed from platonic to romantic; the event violates the norm of platonic relationships and makes relational sense only at the implicated level. Similarly, a Distance Cueing tactic such as reduced self-disclosure violates an expectation that romantic partners disclose openly to one another; this violation triggers the implicated meaning that the relationship is being transformed to one of reduced closeness. Our ordinary language use is characterized by many instances of strategic implicature that have become conventionalized through frequent and reoccurring use. Similarly, many of the indirect signals used in relationship-ing can be regarded as conventionalized. They are commonly used and commonly understood, comprising the substance of our process cognitions about how relationship processes work. However, because such implicated relational meanings are not formally codified by the culture, the user has the "slippage insurance," which assures him or her reduced threat to face. It is difficult to deny meaning that is directly coded; implicatures, by contrast, can be denied if this is useful. In short, then, our relationship process cognitions consist of many conventionalized implicatures about relational meaning. Conventionalization produces the efficiency of indirect cueing. Thus, indirectness is interaction work designed to "have one's cake and eat it too:" sufficient efficiency with minimized threat to face.

However, it is important to challenge the assumption that all misunderstandings constitute inefficiency. As Sillars and Scott (1983) observe in their review of the perceptual agreement research in close relationships, not all perceptual disagreements harm the relationship. Baxter and Bullis (in press), for example, noted the absence of a significant correlation between current satisfaction with the relationship and whether or not the two partners agreed in the perceptions of important turning-points in their relational history. The crucial issue is whether the discrepant cognitions are compatible with one another or whether they block one another's constructions of social reality (Sillars and Scott 1983).

Indirect cueing, which involves compatible but different process schemata between the two relationship parties, may be quite functional to the relationship, especially early in the developmental process. Early on, the two parties lack a stockpile of relational investments and rewards necessary to cope effectively with difference and conflict (Altman and Taylor 1973). Direct relationship talk at that point would force premature realization of cognitive differences, whereas indirect cueing allows the parties to maintain the illusion of agreement so long as the parties' schemata do not block one another. Thus, indirect cueing may "buy time" for the relationship parties, allowing them to construct a relational foundation sufficient to cope at a later point in time with differences and conflicts surrounding how relationships can and should function.

SUMMARY

This chapter has summarized the author's research program in romantic relationship processes as it relates to the content and functions of people's relationship process cognitions. An important distinction was made between cognitions about relationship *types* and cognitions about relationship *process*. Most relationships research focuses on cognitions of relationship types, affording a static state vision of relationships. By contrast, the research summarized here concentrates on process cognitions. In particular, relationship process cognitions at two levels of specificity were examined: cognitions surrounding the process trajectories of growth and dissolution, and more specific cognitions surrounding the strategic actions by which relationship partners accomplish growth, maintenance and repair, and dissolution processes. The primary function of relationship process knowledge is to allow the relationship parties to rely on indirect cueing rather than direct relational communication. Such indirectness affords efficiency in accomplishing process goals with minimized threat to the face of the user. Further, such indirect cueing may "buy time" for the relationship parties in perpetuating the illusion of agreement until the relationship bond is on firmer ground to withstand difference and conflict.

ACKNOWLEDGMENTS

The author would like to thank Patrick McGhee for his helpful comments on this chapter.

REFERENCES

Abelson, R.P. (1981) "Psychological status of the script concept." *American Psychologist*, 36, 715–29.

Altman, I. and Taylor, D. (1973) *Social Penetration: The Development of Interpersonal Relationships*. New York: Holt, Rinehart & Winston.

Argyle, M. and Henderson, M. (1984) "The rules of friendship." *Journal of Social and Personal Relationships*, 1, 209–35.

—— and —— (1985) "The rules of friendships." In S. Duck and D. Perlman (eds) *Understanding Personal Relationships*. London: Sage, 63–84.

Baxter, L. (1979) "Self-disclosure as a relationship disengagement strategy: an exploratory investigation." *Human Communication Research*, 5, 215–22.

—— (1982) "Strategies for ending relationships: two studies." *Western Journal of Speech Communication*, 46, 223–41.

—— (1983) "Relationship disengagement: an examination of the reversal hypothesis." *Western Journal of Speech Communication*, 47, 85–98.

—— (1984) "Trajectories of relationship disengagement." *Journal of Social and Personal Relationships*, 1, 29–48.

—— (1985) "Accomplishing relationship disengagement." In S. Duck and D. Perlman (eds) *Understanding Personal Relationships*. London: Sage, 243–65.

—— (in press) "Self-disclosure and relationship disengagement." In V.J. Derlega and J. Berg (eds) *Self-disclosure: Theory, Research and Therapy*. New York: Plenum.

—— and Bullis, C. (in press) "Turning points in the development of romantic relationships." *Human Communication Research*.

—— and Philpott, J. (1980) "Relationship disengagement: a process view." Paper presented at the Speech Communication Association, November.

—— and —— (1982) "Attribution-based strategies for initiating and terminating friendships." *Communication Quarterly*, 30, 217–24.

—— and —— (1985) "Conditions conducive to awareness of communication activity." Paper presented at the Western Speech Communication Association Convention, February.

—— and Wilmot, W. (1983) "Communication characteristics of relationships with differential growth rates." *Communication Monographs*, 50, 264–72.

—— and —— (1984) "Secret tests: social strategies for acquiring information about the state of the relationship." *Human Communication Research*, 11, 171–201.

—— and —— (1985) "Taboo topics in close relationships." *Journal of Social and Personal Relationships*, 2, 253–69.

Bell, R.A. and Daly, J.A. (1984) "The affinity-seeking function of communication." *Communication Monographs*, 51, 91–115.

Berger, C.R. and Bradac, J. (1982) *Language and Social Knowledge: Uncertainty in Interpersonal Relations*. London: Edward Arnold.

—— and Calabrese, R. (1975) "Some explorations in initial interaction and beyond: toward a developmental theory of interpersonal communication." *Human Communication Research*, 1, 99–112.

Blumer, H. (1969) *Symbolic interactionism: perspective and method*. Englewood Cliffs, NJ: Prentice-Hall.

Brown, P. and Levinson, S. (1978) "Universals in language usage: politeness phenomena." In E. Goody (ed.) *Questions and politeness: strategies in social interaction*. New York: Cambridge University Press, 56–289.

Bullis, C. and Baxter, L. (1986) "A functional typology of turning point events in the development of romantic relationships." Paper presented at the Western Speech Communication Association Convention, February.

Clark, R.A. and Delia, J.G. (1979) "Topoi and rhetorical competence." *Quarterly Journal of Speech*, 65, 187–206.

Craik, F.I.M. (1979) "Human memory." *Annual Review of Psychology*, 30, 63–102.

Davis, K. and Todd, M. (1982) "Friendships and love relationships." In K.E. Davis and T.O. Mitchell (eds) *Advances in Descriptive Psychology*, vol. 2. Greenwich, CT: JAI Press, 79–122.

—— and —— (1985) "Assessing friendship: prototypes, paradigm cases and relationship description." In S. Duck and D. Perlman (eds) *Understanding Personal Relationships*. London: Sage, 17–38.

Dindia, K. and Baxter, L. (1986) "Strategies used by marital partners to maintain and to repair their relationship." Paper presented at the International Communication Association Convention, May.

Duck, S. (1982) "A topography of relationship disengagement and dissolution." In S. Duck (ed.) *Personal Relationships 4: Dissolving Personal Relationships*. New York: Academic Press, 1–30.

—— (1984) "A perspective on the repair of personal relationships." In S. Duck (ed.) *Personal Relationships 5: Repairing Personal Relationships*. New York: Academic Press, 163–84.

—— (1985) "Social and personal relationships." In G. Miller and M. Knapp (eds) *Handbook of Interpersonal Communication*. Beverly Hills: Sage, 655–86.

Frentz, T. and Farrell, T. (1976) "Language-action: a paradigm for communication." *Quarterly Journal of Speech*, 62, 333–49.

Giddens, A. (1979) *Central problems in social theory*. Berkeley, CA: University of California Press.

Greene, J.O. (1984) "A cognitive approach to human communication: an action assembly theory." *Communication Monographs*, 51, 289–306.

Grice, H.P. (1975) "Logic and conversation." In P. Cole and J.L. Morgan (eds) *Syntax and Semantics: Speech Acts*, vol. 3. New York: Academic Press, 41–58.

—— (1978) "Further notes on logic and conversation." In P. Cole (ed.) *Syntax and Pragmatics: Pragmatics*, vol. 9. New York: Academic Press, 113–28.

Harré, R. (1980) *Social Being*. Totowa, NJ: Littlefield, Adams.

—— and Secord, P. (1973) *The Explanation of Social Behavior*. Totowa, NJ: Littlefield, Adams.

Harvey, J., Wells, G., and Alvarez, M. (1978) "Attributions in the context of conflict and separation in close relationships." In J. Harvey, W. Ickes, and R. Kidd (eds) *New Directions in Attribution Theory*, vol. 2. Hillsdale, NJ: Lawrence Erlbaum, 235–60.

Hill, C.T., Rubin, Z., and Peplau, L.A. (1976) "Breakups before marriage: the end of 103 affairs." *Journal of Social Issues*, 32, 147–68.

Katriel, T. and Philipsen, G. (1981) "'What we need is communication': 'Communication' as a cultural category in some American speech." *Communication Monographs*, 48, 301–17.

Kelley, H.H. (1979) *Personal Relationships: Their Structures and Processes*. Hillsdale, NJ: Lawrence Erlbaum.

King, S.W. and Sereno, K.K. (1984) "Conversational appropriateness as a conversational imperative." *Quarterly Journal of Speech*, 70, 264–73.

Kitson, G. and Sussman, M. (1982) "Marital complaints, demographic characteristics, and symptoms of mental distress in divorce." *Journal of Marriage and the Family*, 44, 87–101.

La Gaipa, J. (1979) "A developmental study of the meaning of friendship in adolescence." *Journal of Adolescence*, 2, 201–13.

McCall, G.J. (1982) "Becoming unrelated: the management of bond dissolution." In S. Duck (ed.) *Personal Relationships 4: Dissolving Personal Relationships.* New York: Academic Press, 211–31.

Mead, G.H. (1934) *Mind, Self, and Society.* Chicago: University of Chicago Press.

Pearce, W.B. and Cronen, V.E. (1980) *Communication, Action, and Meaning: The Creation of Social Realities.* New York: Praeger.

Planalp, S. (1985) "Relational schemata." *Human Communication Research*, 12, 3–29.

Rands, M. and Levinger, G. (1979) "Implicit theories of relationship: an intergenerational study." *Journal of Personality and Social Psychology*, 37, 645–61.

Roloff, M.E. and Berger, C.R. (1982) *Social Cognition and Communication.* Beverly Hills, CA: Sage.

Schank, R.C. (1980) "Language and memory." *Cognitive Science*, 4, 243–84.

Sillars, A. and Scott, M. (1983) "Interpersonal perception between intimates: an integrative review." *Human Communication Research*, 10, 153–76.

Wilmot, W. and Baxter, L. (1983) "Reciprocal framing of relationship definitions and episodic interaction." *Western Journal of Speech Communication*, 47, 205–17.

—— and —— (1984) "Defining relationships: the interplay of cognitive schemata and communication." Paper presented at the Western Speech Communication Association Convention, February.

——, Carbaugh, D., and Baxter, L. (1985) "Communicative strategies used to terminate romantic relationships." *Western Journal of Speech Communication*, 49, 204–16.

Wish, M. and Kaplan, S.J. (1977) "Toward an implicit theory of interpersonal communication." *Sociometry*, 40, 234–46.

Wittgenstein, L. (1953) *Philosophical Investigations.* New York: Macmillan.

Wright, P.H. (1985) "The acquaintance description form." In S. Duck and D. Perlman (eds) *Understanding Personal Relationships.* London: Sage, 39–62.

Section Three

Constructing relationships: representation, reality and rhetoric

12 Adding apples and oranges: investigators' implicit theories about personal relationships

Steve Duck

"You can't add apples and oranges," they used to tell us at school. They did not go on to talk about the nonequivalence of categories, the usefulness of superordinate classes or the value of reconceptualizing incomparable items as members of such superordinate classes so that they could be added – but we eight-year-olds knew that that is what they really meant.

The same is true in scientific studies of personal relationships: you can't always learn very much from comparing studies that are looking at entirely different things unless the work of scholarship can reconceptualize them as equivalent members of a superordinate class and draw out their bearing on one another. That's obvious. What is less often regarded is the fact that it is equally difficult to compare, and so learn anything useful from, studies of the same thing if the various investigators have used radically different approaches or have chosen to study different parts of the same phenomenon from different angles, using different measures and different forms of analysis. In other words, apparently similar items can be incomparable: beneath similar labels can lurk important differences, whether these be differences of method, of conceptualization, or of implicit theories about the phenomena. The scholarly work usually entails comparisons of different explicit theories, drawing out the superordinate truths from differences of detail, and the integration of work from different parts of the totality of research.

This chapter will explore some of the *implicit* theories about relationships as they are encapsulated in the analogies contained in the investigators' work, the metaphors investigators use, and the "stories" they have for guiding their work. It will be the argument of this chapter that these representations are not merely trivial ways of conceptualizing items of no significance but that they influence the means by which investigators conduct their work. In a broad sense, the "methodological" tools we choose on a given occasion are chosen because of their coherence with the investigator's implicit "story" about the phenomena and amount to a *substantive* theoretical viewpoint (Levy 1976). The usual dichotomy of "methodological" versus "substantive" misses the point that both "theory" *and* "method" (rather than "theory" alone) contain assumptions that both reflect and direct an investigator's thinking (Duck 1977).

THE ORIGIN OF "PERSONAL RELATIONSHIPS"

The most obvious ancestor of the new field of Personal Relationships has been the old and much narrower field of Interpersonal Attraction and the influences of this forebear are strong and complex (Duck 1985, 1986; Duck and Perlman 1985). We learned a lot – some of it directly useful and some of it useful only insofar as it provides warnings for our future efforts and shows paths that need to be avoided in our future journeys.

One major problem in the old field is illustrative of the point I am making here, and we can learn much from it. A major cause of the lack of progress in the field of interpersonal attraction (i.e. attraction to strangers) was the looseness and variety with which investigators used the term. Some investigators (e.g. Byrne 1971) used the term "attraction" to refer to a specific context where a response to a (fictitious) stranger was studied. Others (e.g. Riggio and Woll 1984) use it to refer to selection of dating partners, whilst yet others use the term as an attitudinal construct roughly co-terminous with "liking" (Berscheid and Walster 1978) or attraction to a relationship, an internal force binding long-term relationships together (e.g. Levinger 1974). These phenomena do not necessarily have the same underlying truths behind them, as investigators began to realize, and different studies with the same apparent purpose were soon seen to have the same jacket on the outside but rather different contents in the books themselves, as it were (Duck 1977).

If I believe that attraction is an attitude then I measure it on an attitude scale and take no measures of its behavioral consequences or the effects of that "attitude" in the social life of the person holding it, for instance: I am interested in the factors that produce the attitude rather than in its use. In other ways the conceptualization of the phenomena affects the study of them: if attraction is merely a cognitive or attitudinal response to a set of stimuli, then it makes perfect sense to study it as a pure response in the laboratory, rather as one may study eye-blinks as a response to sudden flashes of light. If, on the other hand, I regard attraction as an important element in the long-term conduct of relationships then that sort of measurement would be inappropriate. For this reason, any ignoring of the tiny methodological or analogical differences between studies is an ignoring of theoretical or perspectival differences and invites theoretical confusion.

Nonetheless, the language of "attraction" did have one set of similar influences on investigators' beliefs and ways of approaching things. It set us all to think of the processes of attraction in a particular conceptual framework. To use the term "attraction" in the first place gets us into the language of magnetism – similar poles; opposite poles; the notion that one item causes the other to pull towards it willy-nilly. To treat attraction as a magnetic force only is implicitly to conceptualize attraction as a static and contextless occurrence with no consequences for the lives of the subjects beyond the encounter being studied. It also presupposes that two entities pull towards one another on the basis of inherent qualities, properties, or characteristics without them having to *do* anything. In short, the magnetic analogy encourages us to play down the interpersonal processes of attraction and focus on the "stimulus properties" of the two attracted entities.

CARVING THE PHENOMENA

Although the general terms can affect our ways of approaching the phenomena as a whole, the real problem comes when similar terms are used to describe different phenomena in more subtle and evasively incomparable ways. To take another example from the old field of Interpersonal Attraction, there may be some important differences between "liking" expressed after a meeting lasting two hours and "liking" expressed after a meeting lasting five hours, but both could be studied by different investigators and rightly described as "studies of extended first encounters." Some years into such research, it was shown, however, that prediction of liking on the basis of personality similarity can be made more accurate if different measures are used after brief meetings, after one week of repeated meetings, after four weeks, and after three months (Duck and Craig 1978), yet various other investigators have used each of those measurement points as their criterion for "extended interaction in real life" (see Duck 1977). Furthermore, such different studies were nevertheless often compared and scholars attempted to explain differences in findings in ways that took no account of the different time-points used as measurement criteria.

Another good example is provided by the research on similarity and liking that constituted the largest part of work on "interpersonal attraction" for many years. Most methods of studying the role of personality similarity in relationships implicitly assumed that there was only one kind of similarity possible (viz., a global or general similarity of whole personalities) and that more or less any measures of it were equivalent. Not only this but "personality" was also assumed to be a uniform concept equivalently measurable by any given set of personality tests, at the investigator's own choice or preference, irrespective of differences underlying the particular tests and personality theories that they represented.

According to this view there was nothing wrong with comparing different studies that assessed similarity in different ways or used different personality tests. If they assessed personality and they measured levels of similarity then they must really be about the same sorts of things. Not surprisingly, the resultant literature was highly confusing and studies pointed in many different directions. Yet whilst many commentators recognized that there were probably different sorts of *relationships* that could be studied, and that they should not be compared without qualification, there was little comment about the different measures of similarity.

It is necessary only to assume that personality has many sides and is hierarchically organized, or even only that it is "released" to outsiders in a staggered kind of way – as Social Penetration theory assumes in other contexts (Altman and Taylor 1973) – to unravel some of these mysteries at least.

In the interactions and acquaintances of everyday life, persons disclose their own personality and discover their partner's gradually. Accordingly the focus for similarity-seeking will change over time as the relationship develops and partners build up a more detailed picture of one another, have needs for different sorts of knowledge, and so forth (Berger and Bradac 1982; Duck 1977). If a measure successfully matches the depth of personality characteristics that the partners are engaged in exploring at the given point in relationship growth then it will expose the basis of similarity underlying the relationship but if it does not then it will fail to do so. Accordingly, Duck and Craig (1978) found that different measures of personality could be ordered according to their degree of grossness: those that measured personality in terms of gross dichotomies (e.g. introvert–extrovert) were most useful at that stage of a relationship where partners had made only such gross judgements about one another. Later and more sophisticated measures of the detail of personality (such as those categorizing personality into eighteen dimensions, like the California Psychological Inventory) were more useful later, when partners had learned enough about each other to be in a position to make equally sophisticated categorizations of one another. Those measuring personality in terms of extremely fine reactions and dimensions, such as Kelly's (1955) Reptest, could predict friendship choices made at the point where partners were knowledgeable about one another and had a good grasp of the fine detail of one another's thinking and personal styles.

A similar argument applies to the types of measures used to assess the degree of similarity existing between two partners (see Duck [1977, ch. 6] for a review). Similarity can be assessed in terms of a total score on a set of items or in terms of matched scores on individual items. Both forms of measure of similarity have been used in the attraction literature (e.g. Day 1961; Griffitt 1966). In the former case, however, the same total scores may be arrived at by different answers to individual questions and in the extreme case, two people could score exactly the same total by answering a set of questions in exactly opposite manners, each getting half "right." Their totals would be the same even though they had acted exactly oppositely in answering their scales and presumably took opposite view-points on the issues individually. They would be pronounced similar in gross personality whilst actually being opposite at the detailed level. It would not be surprising to find some researchers who used this type of measure and concluded that similar subjects were not more likely to be friends than were randomly paired subjects – even if the "similarity hypothesis" were actually true. A measure of similarity that took account of the precise ways in which each person answered each question would arrive at a conclusion about their similarity more in keeping with the answer that could be arrived at by the individuals in the course of their daily interactions with one another. It would therefore provide a better reflection of the likely impact of similarity on the actual conduct of social lives.

A more subtle version of the ways in which investigators of Interpersonal Attraction ignored the relational processes of real life by embodying static measurement assumptions into their data collection techniques is the following. If a researcher believes that acquainting partners must be aware of similarity between them before it can influence their relationship then he or she will measure it in a way that mimics real-life displays of similarity (e.g. Beier *et al.* 1961). If on the other hand the investigator thinks that the true nature of similarity exerts an influence independently of the partners' awareness of it then no such attempt will be made (e.g. Griffitt 1966).

As we develop further into the field of living personal relationships, therefore, then we need to bear in mind the lessons that can be learned from this past. Our use of a given measurement language reflects our beliefs about the phenomena and is tantamount to a tacit theoretical standpoint. It embodies our theories and makes assumptions about the data. If investigators do not either speak the same language or note the differences between them, then many different sides to relationships will be inevitably confused and pointless comparisons between incomparable items will occur. This is particularly true now that the field of Personal Relationships has begun to focus so strongly on process variables (Duck and Sants 1983) and longer term relationships between real people.

For instance, "the study of dating behavior" sounds like a good topic and it sounds as if we should be able to group the studies on that topic and learn something by sifting them through. However, we soon realize that some investigators look at the initial choices made by clients of video-dating services (e.g. Riggio and Woll 1984), whilst others explore the conflict behavior of the dating couple (e.g. Lloyd and Cate 1985), yet others the sexual negotiations of the premarital couple (Christopher and Cate 1985) and others the experience of violence in dating (Deal and Wampler 1986). Clearly these are all entirely legitimate topics for study in their own right and our general understanding of the mechanics and dynamics of dating will be increased by their pursuit. Nevertheless, the fact that they are all conducted under the same verbal umbrella does not mean that they are "about" the same things and we could not necessarily usefully compare each of them with each of the others in the hope of finding common threads. These are some relatively obvious ways in which the task of research scholarship can be made more tricky. Clearly an adequate review of such studies would take pains to note that these different topics were studied under the same rubric and some attempt may even be made to order them in a way that showed how each could cast light on the others or contribute to a general understanding of the big picture.

One lesson to learn from the past, then, is that metaphor and analogy require to be explored carefully at the general level in interpreting approaches to the phenomena. Also worth learning, however, is the point that such metaphors and analogies run deeper than this and influence conceptualization of the nature of phenomena at fundamental as well as global levels. This is particularly noticeable in the presently emerging fields of personal relationships where investigators are now beginning to think more carefully about the interpersonal processes that guide and constitute the development, maintenance, breakdown, and repair of personal relationships (Duck and Sants 1983; Huston *et al.* 1981).

McCall (1982) makes the point that the language used by couples with relational problems can give a careful and attentive therapist useful insight into the ways in which that couple views its particular problems. Someone who talks of relationship breakdown seems to be saying that something in the relationship is not working rather than that their partner has become unattractive to them. Someone who talks of being stuck on a partner is giving us a particularly vivid analogy that emphasizes the possible one-sidedness of their relationship to the partner. A person describing the relationship as a cage is telling us that his or her freedoms are perceived to be restricted rather than that they have found another partner who is more attractive. McCall is right to teach us that the language used by people in their ordinary descriptions is chosen because it is vivid and appropriate to the ways in which they construe their circumstances.

SOME LINGUISTIC VARIATIONS IN PERSONAL RELATIONSHIPS

What is sauce for the subject is sauce for the investigator also. We can expect to find that investigators who use one form of language – for instance, those who talk of relationships making progress – continue to investigate them in particular styles consistent with the original analogy – for instance in terms of their paths or trajectories. Other investigators might talk of the relationship changing form or shape as it develops and these are more likely to use methods designed to assess the importance of different dimensions at different times in the mutating relationship. Whilst both investigators may believe that the label of "relationships" means that they are truly investigating the same thing, they are not doing so in the same ways. One acts as if relationships are on a track and our task is to map out the tracks that are possible; the other acts as if relationships transform themselves during the course of their lives and our task would be to see how each form grows from each other form – perhaps being connected to its previous form only in hardly recognizable ways.

Following the above argument, however, let us look at some illuminating ways in which the apparently identical analogy (pathways, trajectories) actually contains different assumptions not only about method but also about the phenomena – which create important ways in which the underlying viewpoints do not coincide. In the case of the trajectory analogy, there are differences in assumption about routes taken: Huston *et al.* (1981) write as if they assume that the goal of the trajectory is known at the time of the beginning of the relationship (an assumption perhaps reflected in the fact that their subjects *do* know the goal: they are married subjects asked to map the trajectory of their previous courtship); Delia (1980), however, assumes that subjects do *not* know the goal of their trajectory and suggests methods that plot the actual course taken as the relationship unfolds – as much for the participants as for the observers. The same analogy is used, but different underlying assumptions are reflected in different "methodological" recommendations. What Huston *et al.* (1981) actually studied was not what their title states, namely, "Mate selection as an interpersonal process," but models of courtship progress as reflected in subjective retrospections about a relationship known to have reached its goal.

Such work leaves out an important element of the actual conduct of relationships in real life that could seriously affect the course actually taken in a given case: namely the uncertainty that comes from social relating and ties into inevitable doubts about the intentions and commitment of the partner to the relationship (Duck and Miell 1984). One can never know these things and the uncertainty is critical to the judgements that one makes in reality about the course which the relationship shall take (Duck and Miell 1986).

Trajectory analogies thus take two forms, the route-planning version (as when a driver sets out to arrive at a given end-point by following a map and a known route) and the medieval artillery version, where a given missile takes a given course aimed at a particular goal but may or may not fail to reach it and is more likely to fail than to reach – or may, indeed, be more or less random and uncertain.

There are several different analogies that researchers have used to conceptualize relationships and these are not necessarily compatible at the "deep" level (Duck 1984). *The film analogy* (e.g. Altman and Taylor 1973) treats relationships as developing their full form from the attributes that the two partners bring to the relationship to begin with. Relationships have a chemistry to them independent of the activities of the persons involved. On this analogy the development of a relationship is like a movie and the breakdown is like a film shown in reverse (Altman and Taylor 1973). The assumption of this analogy is that investigators can predict the outcome of a relationship more or less by knowing the attributes of the partners before they meet and working out the ways in which those attributes will interact "chemically." Needless to say, this is the implicit model of the dating agencies.

The horticultural analogy sees relationships developing from seeds, growing, blossoming, and, perhaps, fading. In this analogy the ideal form of the relationship is predetermined by its inherent "genetic" structure, but its achievement of the final form can be influenced by its surrounding environment (e.g. it fails to reach perfect form because it is starved of affection or is grown in inequitable soil); the partners merely affect its achievement of a final form that is inherently predetermined. Researchers with this implicit theory conduct work that explores the ways in which partners' behavior either constrains the achievement of the ideal form or promotes the relationship's growth (e.g. Equity Theory, Hatfield and Traupmann 1981).

Mechanical model analogies tell us that relationships can run into disrepair and can break down or run smoothly. For investigators in this tradition, the relationship is the sum of the behavioral interactions of the participants and the task of research is to comprehend the components of which relationships are constructed. The implication is that the necessary relational skills can be inculcated into those persons and those relationships where they are presently absent (e.g. Jones, Hansson, and Cutrona 1984). In this tradition "a smoothly functioning relationship is a natural and predictable product of well-honed and properly arranged component pieces" (Duck 1984, p. 510).

Such analogies are not disruptive of progress in given specified areas of our field where it tends to be true that workers with common interests and goals also share common analogies. The lesson for our future progress, however, is that attention to such things can help us to unravel the larger pattern that covers the whole field. There may not be only one way to look at the field of personal relationships any more than there need be only one, jointly agreed way to look at a given relationship between two persons (Duck and Sants 1983). What is needed in both cases, however, is a sense of the meaning of discrepancies between perspectives – even those embodied in the language and communications of the parties involved.

CONCLUSIONS

Researchers into relationships need to be aware of the fact that they too share the human tendency to think in terms of analogies and metaphors. In their case the result can lead them into particular styles of research that may be marginally incompatible with those of other investigators. As with many other scholarly problems, this one can be dealt with if it is kept in perspective and researchers act in awareness of the differences between them. We may then realize that, in a very special sense, the study of social and personal relationships is like a fruit salad.

REFERENCES

Altman, I. and Taylor, D. (1973) *Social Penetration*. New York: Holt, Rinehart & Winston.

Beier, E.G., Rossi, A.M., and Garfield, R.L. (1961) "Similarity plus dissimilarity of personality: basis for friendship?" *Psychological Reports*, 8, 3–8.

Berger, C. and Bradac, J. (1982) *Language and Social Knowledge: Uncertainty in Interpersonal Relations*. London: Edward Arnold.

Berscheid, E. and Walster, E.H. (1978) *Interpersonal Attraction*. Reading, MA: Addison-Wesley.

Byrne, D. (1971) *The Attraction Paradigm*. New York: Academic Press.

Christopher, F.S. and Cate, R.M. (1985) "Premarital sexual pathways and relationship development." *Journal of Social and Personal Relationships*, 2, 271–88.

Day, B.R. (1961) "A comparison of personality needs of courtship couples and same-sex friends." *Sociology and Social Research*, 45, 435–40.

Deal, J. and Wampler, K.S. (1986) "Dating violence: the primacy of previous experience." *Journal of Social and Personal Relationships*, 3, 457–71.

Delia, J.G. (1980) "Some tentative thoughts concerning the study of interpersonal relationships and their development." *Western Journal of Speech Communication*, 44, 97–103.

Duck, S.W. (1977) *The Study of Acquaintance*. Farnborough: Gower.

—— (1984) "A rose is a rose (is a tadpole is a freeway is a film) is a rose." *Journal of Social and Personal Relationships*, 1, 507–10.

—— (1985) "Social relationships." In G.R. Miller and M.L. Knapp (eds) *Handbook of Interpersonal Communication*. Beverly Hills: Sage.

—— (1986) *Human Relationships: An Introduction to Social Psychology*. London: Sage.

—— and Craig, R.G. (1978) "Personality similarity and the development of friendship." *British Journal of Social and Clinical Psychology*, 17, 237–42.

—— and Miell, D.E. (1984) "Towards an understanding of relationship development and breakdown." In H. Tajfel, C. Fraser, and J. Jaspars (eds) *The Social Dimension: European Perspectives on Social Psychology*. Cambridge: Cambridge University Press.

—— and —— (1986) "Charting the development of friendship." In R. Gilmour and S.W. Duck (eds) *The Emerging Field of Personal Relationships*. Hillsdale, NJ: Lawrence Erlbaum.

—— and Perlman, D. (1985) "The thousand islands of personal relationships: a prescriptive analysis for future exploration." In S.W. Duck and D. Perlman (eds) *Understanding Personal Relationships*. London: Sage.

—— and Sants, H.K.A. (1983) "On the origin of the specious: are personal relationships really interpersonal states?" *Journal of Social and Clinical Psychology*, 1, 27–41.

Griffitt, W. (1966) "Interpersonal attraction as a function of self-concept and personality similarity–dissimilarity." *Journal of Personality and Social Psychology*, 4, 581–4.

Hatfield, E. and Traupmann, J. (1981) "Intimate relationships: a perspective from Equity Theory." In S.W. Duck and R. Gilmour (eds) *Personal Relationships 1: Studying Personal Relationships*. London and New York: Academic Press.

Huston, T.L., Surra, C., Fitzgerald, N., and Cate, R.M. (1981) "From courtship to marriage: mate selection as an interpersonal process." In S.W. Duck and R. Gilmour (eds) *Personal Relationships 2: Developing Personal Relationships*. London and New York: Academic Press.

Jones, W.H. Hansson, R.O., and Cutrona, C.E. (1984) "Helping the lonely: issues of intervention with young and older adults." In S.W. Duck (ed.) *Personal Relationships 5: Repairing Personal Relationships*. London and New York: Academic Press.

Kelly, G.A. (1955) *The Psychology of Personal Constructs*. New York: Norton.

Levinger, G. (1974) "A three level perspective." In T.L. Huston (ed.) *Foundations of Interpersonal Attraction*. New York: Academic Press.

Levy, P.M. (1976) "Methodological and substantive issues: is there a difference?" *Bulletin of the British Psychological Society*, 333, 221.

Lloyd, S.A. and Cate, R.M. (1985) "The developmental course of conflict in dissolution of premarital relationships." *Journal of Social and Personal Relationships*, 2, 179–94.

McCall, G.M. (1982) "Becoming unrelated: the management of bond dissolution." In S.W. Duck (ed.) *Personal Relationships 4: Dissolving Personal Relationships*. London and New York: Academic Press.

Riggio, R. and Woll, S. (1984) "The role of nonverbal cues and physical attractiveness in the selection of dating partners." *Journal of Social and Personal Relationships*, 1, 347–58.

13 The social construction of an 'us': problems of accountability and narratology

John Shotter

'There was no plot', said William, 'and I discovered it by mistake.'
(Umberto Eco, *The Name of the Rose*, 1980, p. 491)

ACCOUNTING FOR AND IN THE MAKING OF PERSONAL RELATIONSHIPS

As Duck and Gilmour (1981) and Mikula (1984) point out, early inter-personal relationships research was concerned with interpersonal attraction phenomena, with first impressions, and with superficial encounters. However, it has become clear that initial attraction, as typically studied, is at best of limited value for a proper understanding of the dynamics of real-life relationships. First, it did not take into account the fact that even an initial attraction is a *developmental* phenomenon, and second, it also neglected the *social context* in which personal relationships are embedded. To attempt to make good both these deficiencies is my concern below.

Two ways to make an 'us': personal and community relations

Elsewhere (Shotter 1984, 1986b), I have discussed the origins of the developmental processes involved in the socially creative construction of social identities, i.e. the development of an 'us' and of the individual identities constituting that 'us'. There I was concerned with accounting for the growth (the social making) of infant members of a community into distinctive, morally autonomous individuals; I wanted to understand how it was possible, in a vague and uncertain world, for people to develop an ability to act deliberately, to sense themselves as knowing what they are doing, and to be able to account for at least some of their behaviour as *their own*, experiencing it (and allowing for others to experience it) as issuing from within themselves rather than as caused in them by external forces. Central to that discussion was the concept of *joint action* and its *formative* powers (see Ginsburg [1985] for a very succinct and clear outline of my position and of the central concepts I introduce).

Here I want to make a central use of the concept of joint action again in discussing the process of people's further growth together, and the ways in which, in the course of that growth, they account for their behaviour to one another. For the fact is that under certain conditions, people who can *already* be considered to be morally autonomous individuals (if not psychologically autonomous), can continue their psychological development by beginning to form, in interaction with others, a new 'us', an enclave within the larger 'us' of which they are already a part, an 'us' in which they themselves can be further psychologically and morally transformed – an 'us' *relative* to which and in terms of which they can account for themselves to each other (and to themselves).

In particular, I want to discuss problems to do with accounting for the different transformations possible in certain kinds of what have now come to be called 'close' personal relationships (Kelley *et al.* 1983), especially with accounting for what seems to be involved in 'falling in love'. But also I want to discuss very generally the accountability problems to do those kinds of social *movements* in which a new reality is created, and I say 'accountability' rather than 'attributional' problems, because the issue is not only to do with *locating* the relevant influences, but with *formulating* a characterization of them. For in many such movements a reality of an extraordinarily vital kind is created that gives rise to new powers and possibilities of being, and that seems, if not to subvert, to at least violate one's current mundane reality – for the new unity breaks with something in the old. For this, and for other reasons, accountability problems arise with social movements, which tend to create new social realities. And it is my purpose in this chapter to attempt to clarify some of these accountability problems.

The 'psychologist's fallacy' and the unaccountable outcomes of joint action

Accountability problems can arise because, from the point of view of the old, displaced reality, the active positing of a new reality is disturbing, unintelligible, unexpected; it calls the old reality into question in the most powerful way possible, i.e. not theoretically, but practically. Faced with such a threatening form of activity, the tendency has been to act as if it is invisible; it is as if its true nature must be repressed; it is either ignored or described (i.e. misdescribed) as mundane, when in fact it is quite extraordinary.

But this is not the only, nor the major reason why such behaviour is so difficult to account for. Another reason – and this is a difficulty people themselves face in accounting for their own behaviour from *within* transitional relationships – is that they are involved in a creative or developmental process *still in progress*, rather than in an outcome or product of such a process. In other words, whatever has been so far achieved, practically, in the relationships is still *incomplete*. As such, it is still open to, or able to take on, or be 'lent' further specification. And this is exactly what happens in our attempts to describe it: we describe incomplete processes by their supposed final product.

William James (1890, p. 196) describes this tendency as 'the psychologist's fallacy', saying that 'the most fictitious puzzles have been introduced into our science by this means'. The form of the fallacy is as follows: A vague event E occurs. What was it? As it could come to completion, say, as an A, there is a tendency to label it as such. In reality, however, it is still the event E, what it was originally. Wittgenstein (1980, I, no. 257) also warned against the unwarranted completion (in our descriptions) of essentially incomplete human activities still in progress; often one must just accept, he says, that 'Here *is* the whole. (If you complete it, you falsify it.)'

However, the 'psychologist's fallacy' is still not the main reason for our difficulties. That is to be found in the fact that the activity involved is *joint action*, i.e. it is activity *between* people, in which not only unintended joint outcomes are produced (rather than outcomes intended by the individuals involved), but as a part of that outcome, a 'situation' is created that the participants experience themselves as being 'in' (Shotter 1984). The realm of joint action is, in fact, quite common, almost the rule rather than the exception; for in almost all face-to-face activities involving concerted social action, individuals cannot produce an outcome according to a prearranged plan of their own. There would be no point to conversations, negotiations, to mothers playing with their children, to games, or the writing and reading academic papers, etc. unless there was a possibility of an unforeseen, creative but contingent outcome. An outcome appropriate to a joint 'situation' is required – an intelligent response to it as it changes moment by moment. And often, we clearly can respond as required. Yet such a process is difficult to account for. Why?

Joint action has two major features:

1   As all human action, whether autonomous or joint, has an *intentional* quality to it, it always seems to 'point to', or to 'indicate', or 'to be related to something other than or beyond itself'; in joint action, however, something is created that is not 'in' any of the people involved, but is apparently 'in' (or 'of') the situation constituted between them.

2   As people must co-ordinate their activity in with that of others, and are constrained to 'reply' to others in their actions, what they as individuals might desire and what actually results in their exchange are often two different things; in short, joint action produces unpredictable and unintended consequences.

Thus its results, appearing to be *independent of any particular individual's wishes or intentions*, appear to be nobody's; they cannot be attributed to an author (Heider 1958). They must, therefore, have an 'external' or 'objective' quality attributed to them; and rather than their *reasons*, one feels that one ought to seek their *causes*. For rather than being deliberate actions *done* by an individual for a purpose, in their 'objective' nature they have the quality of events that just *happen* (see e.g. Buss [1978] on the causes – reasons distinction in attribution theory). Yet this is still an unsuitable attribution, for although their nature is independent of the wishes of any individuals, they lack the *completeness* of truly objective entities. In their incomplete or open nature, they are intentional in so much as what so far is 'rationally visible' in them (to use a phrase of Garfinkel's [1967]), specifies what further developments they will permit, afford, or allow (see also Eco [1979] for an extended account of 'open' and 'closed' texts in this same respect).

In other words, although such outcomes lack an author, they none the less have the quality of 'authored' things; they cannot just be treated as caused events – that is to ignore their developmental or historical nature, and the fact that they have a significance to people. Thus, when viewed retrospectively, they seem to have the appearance of unfolding as if in accord with an as yet untold story or design, authored by an individual – but they are not! As occurrences, they are neither done by anyone in order to bring about an end, nor caused in any clear way by antecedent events; *at the time of their occurrence, their nature is truly vague* (see Gavin [1976], James [1890, p. 254] and Shotter [1983] on the central importance of the 'vague' in human affairs). This means that, while their significance may be accounted for practically, *in the context of their occurrence*, logically, it *cannot* be accounted for in any context-free way without distortion: they are 'ordering processes' still in progress, rather than already 'ordered structures'; they are still on their way towards a structure, so to speak.

Ex post facto facts

The consequences of such a state of affairs are profound: it means, as we shall see, that even the attempt to describe the making of relationships in terms of narratives, stories and plot structures runs into trouble. Witness the making of sexual approaches. 'I'm just off to the cinema', says a woman in the vicinity of a man she is attracted to, in the hope that he will respond as she desires. The significance of her utterance is not yet complete, however. If he says, 'Oh, can I come too?' then he has completed its significance as an 'invitation', and she is of course happy to accept it as having been as such. If he just says, however, 'Oh, I hope you enjoy the film', then he completes it simply as an 'informative statement'. Embarrassment has been avoided by her not having to issue a direct invitation, which might risk a direct refusal. The real indeterminacy of utterances often allows for their significance to be determined retrospectively.

But if he did turn her down, was it because to go to a film at that time was truly impossible for him, or because he truly did not want to be with her? Clearly, the significance of the situation between them is still somewhat vague, and thus requires further practical investigation between them if they are to clarify it further. Let us imagine that he did accept her invitation, and as they walk out of the cinema after the film, she then says, 'Would you like to come back for a coffee?' He says, 'Oh, yes please!' and goes to put his arm around her. But she draws back and says, 'Whatever gave you that idea?' He is taken aback. He knows what gave him the idea, it was the whole way she offered the original 'invitation': it seemed to imply an invitation to greater intimacy – but at the same time, as both she and he were aware, it did not explicitly request it. The character so far of the relationship they are in is 'open' to such reversals as these; while perhaps unexpected they are not unintelligible.

Relevant here too is Sartre's (1958, pp. 55–6) analysis of 'bad faith', in which he discusses the example of a woman who, in conversation with a man she knows cherishes certain sexual intentions regarding her, allows him to take her hand, but leaves it limp within his, 'neither consenting nor resisting – a thing' (p. 56). Her 'bad faith' as he sees it, is in not treating the event with its proper significance. For, by allowing him to take her hand, she lets him risk requesting a greater physical intimacy:

> To leave the hand there is to consent in herself to flirt, to engage herself. To withdraw it is to break the troubled and unstable harmony which gives the hour its charm. The aim is to postpone the moment of decision as long as possible.   (p. 55)

Sartre does not say how the relationship went on, but perhaps she shortly afterwards broke it off. But isn't that what she intended to do all along? Not necessarily, perhaps originally she had intended it to flourish. While that is what it later resulted in, that is not what it began as; its significance later was not the same as at the time of its origin.

Again, an accountability problem arises in such circumstances, one of a very special kind. Ossorio (1981) calls it the 'ex post facto facts' paradox. It is a much more complex version of the 'psychologist's fallacy': it is the claim that something that has already occurred *must have had* a certain significance, because of what occurred later. The fallacy has the following form: The vague event E could be seen as signifying either A or B; if X follows from it, it *must have been* A; if, however, Y results, then it *must have been* B. In fact, of course, it was and still is the vague event E. The

230 Accounting for Relationships

fallacy is in seeing the origin of a process being an event of a definite kind
because of what followed from it, of assigning a particular form to an
earlier event because of the form of a later one, even though at that earlier
time the event did not have that form. It is a very obvious fallacy but none
the less a very beguiling one: it occurs in seeing human actions, or human
history, retrospectively, as simply a progression of events through time
with each event possessing its own 'correct' interpretation. And, finding
ourselves puzzled as to why an outcome occurred (because of the real
indeterminacy of the factors involved), we feel that that 'correct' interpretation must exist somewhere. Thus the project of searching for it
appears to be quite a legitimate one. But if Ossorio is right, there are no
such 'correct' interpretations to be found. In human affairs, things do not
happen in time in a simple progression, as if according to rules, scripts,
plots, etc. – there are no plots, and if we discover them we discover them
by mistake.

There are many dangers of the *ex post facto* kind. They can occur even
in attempts to use the most innocuous, undramatic kinds of plots – in, say,
the story that people are like isolated atoms in motion according to certain
laws. For instance, in the language of Kelley *et al.* (1983),

> two people are in a relationship with one another if they have *an
> impact* on each other, if they are 'interdependent' in the sense that a
> change in one person causes a change in the other and vice versa.
>
> (p. 12, my emphasis)

And the relationship is '"close" if the amount of mutual impact two
people have on each other is great or, in other words, there is high
interdependence' (p. 13) – the image of billiard balls is not far beneath the
surface here, with changes *caused* by 'impacts'. They then go on to say
that 'a causal analysis of interaction regularities *requires* the inference of
relatively stable "causal conditions" that act on the relationship to produce
and maintain these regularities' (p. 14, my emphasis). But if what Ossorio
has to say about *ex post facto* facts is correct, such changes cannot be
predicted on the basis of such a 'causal analysis'. For, although once an
event has taken place and been seen as an instance of a 'regularity', as a
useful 'relationship descriptor', and tied 'to properties of the interconnected activity pattern that can be recorded and agreed on by impartial
investigators' (p. 13), this does not mean that along with all such other
instances it was occasioned by the same circumstances. In other words,
ignoring the *ex post facto* fallacy, they infer from outcomes what their
causes *must have been*. Upon what justification? Well, they say that the
causal analysis 'requires' it. Rather than responding to demands arising
from practical involvements in personal relationships, and justifying their
claims by appeal to those involvements, they use another framework of
interpretation altogether, with quite a different justification: 'We believe
that the basic framework itself is largely dictated by the common principles and assumptions that underlly all scientific endeavours' (p. 15). Quite!

Being true to science is more important than being true to the phenomena: but it engenders a way of seeing that leaves one blind to the genuinely interpersonal processes involved.

There are other dangers also of the *ex post facto* kind. There is the danger, for instance, in the appeal to retrospective reports, in empirical investigations of the growth of personal relationships: because of what seems to be a current outcome, what in reality could still be open to many interpretations is treated as if it had already become something clearly identifiable. This problem is discussed, for instance, by Duck and Miell (1984): they are quite aware that 'the drawback of retrospective accounts ... is that the final known outcome of a relationship will inevitably colour the retrospective accounts given by the subjects in specifiable and predictable ways' (p. 236). But they go on later to raise what they call a 'pseudo-methodological problem', i.e. whether asking people in a developing relationship to provide data upon it by keeping *diaries* will not only 'colour' the data gathered, but also disrupt in some way the developmental course of the relationship. They rule this possibility out, however, on the following grounds:

> Might it not be the case that, even at the time of the interaction, the subjects are reviewing the information available to them, and trying to place any incoming information about the partner or the relationship into the broader context of its history and expected future?
>
> (p. 238)

Indeed! This is exactly what they *might* be doing – *but not if they are engaged in genuine joint action.* Only if they are acting individualistically would they be acting in such a reflective manner. A truly joint exchange is best analysed, as we shall see, as being *passionate*, i.e. as neither simply caused, nor as reflective.

Thus, to sum up this section: the concept of joint action is important in attempts to account for the development of social and personal relationships for the following reasons: (1) within the relationship, each person's action produces a 'new organized setting or situation' *into which* the others must direct their next actions; (2) thus the formative influences on people's actions (the enabling-constraints provided by the momentary setting) are not to be found wholly within themselves, i.e. they are not completely aware of the determinants of their own conduct and thus logically, cannot give a clear account of it; (3) however, that does not mean that they lack an awareness of their immediate circumstances and are unable to act in a way inappropriate to them; (4) it simply means that people must, in every instance, respond in a moment by moment fashion to the specific, local contingencies arising, moment by moment in the settings they create between themselves, and account to one another for what they do in terms of such contingencies. This means that, in attempting to account for occurrences within still-continuing processes, not only can one fall foul of the simple mistake of describing processes by their products, but one can also mistakenly see the workings of an author's intention where none such exist – thus to seek the as yet untold story, or design, or rules, guiding the progression of the action.

PASSIONATE EXCHANGES AND ACCOUNTING

Above, it was suggested that, although the origins of joint action are vague, it unfolds progressively over time, and as it does so, it introduces a greater and greater degree of specificity into its outcome, i.e. into the 'relationship' it produces. Thus a relationship in progress, while having so far produced a certain degree of specification in itself, still leaves itself open to yet further specification, but now, *only of an already specified kind* (Shotter 1980). What occurs next must 'fit in with' the totality so far specified or determined. Thus each new action must be directed *into* a context, the situation produced by previous actions, and fitted in with what that situation invites, affords or allows, thus to develop it further. In such circumstances, we cannot be held wholly responsible for what we do: for what we do is not wholly up to us, other people's actions are just as much a formative influence in what we do as any plan, rule or script within ourselves. Thus, to an extent, our actions can be said to be of a *passionate* nature (the term 'passion' being derived from the Latin *pati* which means 'to suffer' or 'undergo change'). We simply find ourselves *happening* to act in a certain way, spontaneously; and this passive aspect of passionate activity is expressed colloquially by such phrases as 'falling' in love, being 'gripped' by anger, 'seized' by fear, 'torn' by jealousy, 'transported' by joy, etc. (Averill 1980a). We do not happen to act as we do, however, out of mere subjective impulse, for we act in a *reasonable* manner, i.e. in terms of a practical awareness of our circumstances. And the criteria we use in judging whether people have understood the nature of the exchange they are involved in do not depend upon what occurs in their heads, but upon what they actually *do* in relation to their situation, the appropriateness of their actual response to it. The traditional disassociation of reason from emotion, and emotion's placement in opposition to it, at least in the realm of practical activities, is a serious mistake.

Passionate actions, practical reason and transitory social roles

We can see this, i.e. practical reason at work in people's passionate exchanges, in, for instance, a passage taken almost at random from Marilyn French's (1978, p. 171) *The Woman's Room*. The central character Mira is speaking about Natalie's husband, Hamp:

> 'And he hates. God, he hates. All of us. All women.'
> 'Not quite all', an acid voice behind her put in.
> She turned. Natalie was glaring at her, slowly waving the rest of the packet [of letters]. 'There's one woman he likes. Just one.'

Mira frowned. She didn't understand Nat's tone. 'What do you mean?'

'Don't tell me you don't know!' Natalie accused. At Mira's look of incomprehension, she burst out. 'They're to you! Are you going to say you didn't know?'

Mira sank into a chair. 'What?'

'Love letters. Oodles of them.'

Here, Mira is at first puzzled by Natalie's tone and responds to it with a request for clarification. Natalie at first refuses to respond to the request, she treats it as false. Mira is still confused, her look of incomprehension suggests her innocence. So finally Natalie accounts for her tone by telling Mira about the love letters to her (Mira) she had found among her husband's possessions. But Mira had never received any such letters.

Three points are illustrated by this exchange: (1) mostly, the activities depicted are *not* actions, each momentary response is just that: *a response* and not an action, i.e. it is not properly accounted as an activity done deliberately, upon reflection, according to a prior plan in order to bring about a particular outcome; (2) in other words, in such exchanges people's expressions are mostly *indexical* expressions, i.e. they make the particular sense they do only in relation to the context of activity in which they occur; and (3) thus it would be odd to ask Mira why she had 'decided', for instance, to be puzzled by Natalie's tone; for she would say that it wasn't something she had *decided* to do at all, but that it was Natalie's tone that had *made* her puzzled. In other words, the exchange above is best analysed as a *passionate* one (which it clearly is), for the activities involved have the general form of passions – for, as I said above, a passion is accounted as something for which we ourselves are not wholly responsible, we didn't plan to act that way, we say that something 'made' us act as we did. Yet they are activities appropriate in some way to their circumstances. Following Averill (1980a, b), who focuses upon what practically people *do* in such situations, rather than upon what they might think or experience, I shall treat passionate activities as like the performance of, as Averill puts it, *transitory social roles*.

The metaphor of transitory social roles for passions is very appropriate. For consider the moral nature of the social world: it is simply not open to us to do what we want when we please. What we have a right to do on one occasion we have no right to do on another; conditions we have no obligation to satisfy here we must attempt to satisfy there; privileges accorded to us now may be taken away from us tomorrow; and so on. The moral setting for our activities is thus an ever-changing sea of opportunities and limitations, risks and invitations, enablements and constraints – with our 'place' or 'status' within it transformed by each of our and other people's activities within it. Now Goffman's (1959, p. 27) definition of a social role is that it is 'the enactment of the rights and duties attached to a given status', i.e. it is the way one responds to the enabling-constraints afforded one by one's momentary situation. Given Goffman's definition, we can see the point of Averill's description. He takes passions as neither opposed to reason, nor to social convention; he treats them as intelligent activities whose sense is grounded in their immediate social context.

Barthes (1983) also expresses a similar view to Averill: 'I take a role', he says (p. 161), 'I am *the one who is going to cry*; and I play this role for myself, and *it makes me cry*: I am my own theatre.' As Averill points out, people who say to others 'That makes me angry' or 'I love you' are not simply labelling an internal state; they are entering into a complex relationship with another person, as if playing a role which makes them act as they do (1980b, p. 314). So, from a practical point of view, acting emotionally is not just a matter of 'labelling an internal state' (Schachter 1971), it is *behaving* in a certain kind of, as Averill puts it, 'socially constituted way'. Passions, then, are much more common in social life than we care to admit; furthermore, many of them are positive, i.e. they are the major currency, so to speak, in terms of which, as I mentioned above, most of our face-to-face exchanges are conducted. Why is it so difficult for us to admit this?

Averill has discussed the paucity of terms in our language for the description of positive emotions (Averill 1980a). He concludes that, compared with actions, passions are thought to be uncharacteristic of the individual in question, irrational, intuitive, impulsive, intense and persistent, and that most of these connotations have a slight negative quality. Such terms are thus less applicable to positive behaviours. But this is not the only reason for the paucity of positive emotions:

> Unlike crimes of passion, which are legion, good deeds of passion are rare, not necessarily because evil is more prevalent than goodness. Rather, it is because responses with positive outcomes are not typically described as emotional, for that would imply a diminished responsibility on the part of the individual for his [or her] behaviour.
>
> (Averill 1980a, pp. 24–5)

While the typical act of courage has many of the characteristics of a passion, the individual is praised and honoured for it; thus only if it is not treated as passion, not treated as beyond the person's control, but as an action, can the praise be justified. This, Averill suspects (and I agree), is why there is a reluctance to describe emotional responses that lead to a positive outcome as passions – they undermine our hard-won modern conception of our individuality and moral autonomy. However, if Averill is right, only if we reinstitute passionate activity between people as activity on a par with the supposed rational actions of individuals, have we a chance of properly understanding joint action as a non-instrumental, creative activity, and thus the making of personal relationships (Unger 1984). How might such passionate interpersonal processes – processes which, if they could ever come to completion in their own terms, would disturb established social realities – how might the nature of such processes be properly described?

Narratives

Gergen and Gergen (1983), noting that they involve *historical* processes, entailing changes through time, suggest that a *narrative* structure is required for a proper explanatory account of such real-life developments. And here one must agree: it is only within a narrative order – which allows for the description of different conflicting forces and different points of view, and their attempted resolution – that the human *drama* can be properly characterized; a theoretical order, which demands a single, supposedly universal, context-free standpoint for the description of an orderly, sequential progress towards an outcome, is quite inadequate to the task. Gergen and Gergen go on, however, to claim that the narratives required must be *coherent* narratives; that unless we can see systematic connections between life events, we are prone to see our lives as a rather meaningless sequence, as just 'one damned thing after another'.

Gergen and Gergen's (1983) requirement of coherency, however, suggests that we treat a person's life as if it contained an *untold* story, one which requires discovering as 'the' story of that person's life – as if they possessed an already determinate history that guided them in the living out of their life, and the project of accurately discovering it was a possibility. Another objection I have to it is that, rather than each action in a sequence of action being in response to local and contingent conditions, a matter of practical reasoning about one's social circumstances, it again makes people's actions a matter of individual reflection, a matter of planning, plotting and deciding, as if the intelligent adaptation to contingencies as they occurred played no part in them living their lives.

I would, therefore, like to put forward a third view, one that accepts to an extent that life just 'is' one damned thing after another, but which also recognizes the importance of the human story-telling capacity. In my view it works *retrospectively*, to make some sense of what has happened so far, to gain hints as to what one might do next. While the raw material of a biography, the facts (in which any narrative we may produce must be grounded), may at first appear as an 'and then ... and then ... and so on' chronicle of events, this does not preclude their retrospective embedding in a narrative, to give or lend them *structure*, a structure they do not in themselves possess but which none the less they will afford or allow. Indeed, we may embed them in any one of an indefinite number. However, to repeat what I have already said above, this is not to say that we can embed them in any narrative we please; stories not grounded in facts are fictions.

To repeat: while a fictional narrative creates its own free-floating but none the less ordered mental space, the ordered mental space created by a historical narrative must be grounded or rooted in actual facts, whose nature is not wholly predetermined, i.e. they are vague facts which are thus given or lent a determinate nature and ordering by the story in which they are embedded. As White (1978) and Mink (1978) persuasively argue, this is the case in historiography; the bare chronicle of the historical record can be 'emplotted' in different ways – as comedy, romance, tragedy, or as satire – where the *ways* chosen (but not the content) depend, not upon evidence, but upon irreducible imaginative preferences or choices, i.e. upon the existential projects or the projected forms of life envisaged in the accounts constructed. The same is clearly the case in accounting for the making of relationships; no plot is 'the' plot. All grounded plots can be explanatory in some way; though none of them tell us 'the' way it was, only 'a' way (Goodman 1972).

But is this good enough? In the light of what I said above about the distortions introduced by 'plot structures' about their suppression of local and momentary contingencies, and their valorizing of individual reflection, should we refer to plots at all? Doesn't this leave us in the position of Eco's hero William: 'I behaved stubbornly, pursuing a semblance of order, when I should have known well that there is no order in the universe' (Eco 1980, p. 492). By imagining an erroneous order, we may still discover something, Adso, William's assistant, says to him in trying to console him. But William is not convinced; we are not prepared to accept its erroneous nature and to throw it away after use: 'The only truths that are useful', he says (p. 492), 'are instruments to be thrown away' – but the trouble is people are prepared to die for them, and live by them. People warrant their actions by reference to them, rather than to the facts, to their beliefs rather than their circumstances. A story is treated as the Truth. Is there an alternative to plots and the distortions they introduce?

Lexicons and 'image repertoires'

Is there an alternative way of presenting what it is one knows – when one knows about something such as love, say – that makes the knowledge available to others as a *practical resource* without distorting its nature? Barthes (1983, pp. 7–8), in discussing this problem, says:

> Every amorous episode can be, of course, endowed with a meaning: it is generated, develops, and dies; it follows a path which it is always possible to interpret according to a causality or a finality – even if need be, which can be moralized ... this is the love story, subjugated to the great narrative Other, to that general opinion which disparages any excessive force and wants the subject himself to reduce the great imaginary current, the orderless, endless stream which is passing through him, to a painful, morbid crisis of which he must be cured, which he must 'get over' ... the love story ... is the tribute the lover must pay to the world in order to be reconciled with it.

What then is an alternative to it, to the 'love story'? Barthes (1983) says:

> Very different is the discourse, the soliloquy, the *aside* which accompanies this story (this history), *without ever knowing it*. It is the very principle of this discourse (and of the text which represents it) that its

figures cannot be *classified*: organized, hierarchized, arranged with a view to an end (a settlement): there are no first figures, no last figures.

What it is one knows is known in an unformulated way. There can be, in other words, no story, no order, no rules, or principles, no completeness to the lover's life in actual fact. This does not mean to say that none can be *constructed*. But if one is, then it cannot be *the* story.

Hence, to avoid falling into the traps discussed above, Barthes refuses to provide a narrative account of love, yet he wants to write about love only in a way that the facts will allow. How, if not as a narrative? Well, as indicated above, he thinks the knowledge possessed by the lover of the loved one, of the other (indeed, of any kind of 'otherness') is, he claims, 'atopos', i.e. unclassifiable, of a ceaselessly unforeseen originality. It can be given or lent whatever form its nature will allow by the use of tropes, figures of speech, metaphors and suchlike. And the figures available to the lover for the ordering of the lover's experience, constitute what Barthes calls the lover's 'image-repertoire', a body of knowledge *without* any pre-imposed order. Thus, 'to let it be understood', he says (p. 8), 'that there was no question here of a love story (or of a history of a love), to discourage the temptation of meaning, it was necessary to choose an *absolutely insignificant order*'. Indeed, such knowledge has the same character as that claimed by many writers for the nature of all everyday, practical common-sense knowledge. Common-sense knowledge in general is, says Heider (1958, p. 2), 'unformulated and only vaguely conceived'; 'it embraces the most heterogeneous kinds of knowledge in a very incoherent and confused state' (Schutz 1964, p. 72); it is 'immethodical' (Geertz 1983, p. 90), i.e. it caters both to the inconsistencies and diversity of life, it is 'shamelessly and unapologetically *ad hoc*. It comes in epigrams, proverbs, *obiter dicta*, jokes, anecdotes *contes morals* – a clatter of gnomic utterances – not in formalized doctrines, axiomatized theories, or architectonic dogmas' (ibid.). Yet strangely, as Geertz goes on to say, for all its disorder, such knowledge has 'accessibleness' as another of its major qualities, or, as Barthes (1983, p. 214) says, 'the power of the Image-repertoire is immediate: I do not look for the image, it comes to me, all of a sudden', on occasion after occasion, called out by (internal or external) accidents of one's situation, at 'the whim of trivial, aleatory circumstances' (Barthes 1983, p. 3).

Rather than as a particular story, what it is one knows when one knows about such a topic as love should be presented, Barthes feels, not as a representation, a 'picture' of love, but in such a way as to communicate 'the very substance I employ in order to speak [the lover's discourse]' (Barthes 1983, p. 59). The figures he provides function as a set of instructions or devices for constructing, so to speak – from different moments and situations dispersed in space and time – the different affects felt by lovers. The active principle of a figure is not, he says, what it says but what it articulates: by and large, it is only a 'syntactical aria', a 'mode of construction'. For instance, if the lover awaits the loved object at a rendezvous, a sentence-aria keeps running through his head: '*All the same, it's not fair* ...'; '*he/she could have* ...'; '*he/she knows perfectly well* ...'; knows what? It doesn't matter, the figure 'Waiting' is already formed. Such sentences are matrices of 'figures precisely because they remain suspended: they utter the affect, then break off, their role fulfilled.   (p. 6)

Hence, instead of an account of love, what Barthes provides is a kind of lexicon or dictionary of love's figures – the forms of order it will allow – with entries in an *alphabetical* order, figures that merely indicate in a metonymical manner the 'topics' or 'sites' where, as he says (p. 5), 'each of us can fill in th[e] code according to his own history; rich or poor, the figure must be there, the site (the compartment) must be reserved for it'. It is as if there is an imaginary space whose 'places' or (topos) topics 'lend' it an existence. It is as if the nature of love – what the transitory roles played by those in love are – can only be grasped by locating them somewhere. While in fact, of course, in reality, it cannot be so located; it is essentially non-locatable – 'An emotion has duration; it has no place; it has characteristic "undergoings"' (Wittgenstein 1980, vol. 1, no. 836).

Here Barthes's concerns parallel those discussed by Mink (1978), who points out that in historiography generally today, while one would not want to deny that there was 'something' for historiography to be about, most would want to deny that its task was the telling of *the* as yet untold, single story of what actually happened. History no longer has a unified subject-matter; there are histories but no History. As there is no universal history, argues Mink, there is no universal historiography either, i.e. no one single kind of story about human cultural development.

> One simply cannot generalize over cultural histories as easily as one can over political history. The history of mankind thus becomes dispersed into an encyclopedia of biographies, customs, ideas, local institutions, languages, peoples, and nations. The dispersal was summed up in Carlyle's dictum that history is 'the essence of innumerable biographies'.   (p. 139)

In other words, there is a past, but it is we who determine its significance, and we do it by locating it in an order of relationships represented only in the *construction* of one or another kind of narrative form; it is we who make the past determinate according to our concerns of the moment.

Summary

I have set out what seems to me to be the main problem in accounting for interpersonal relationships: that many such relationships are creative ones, continually involving passionate exchanges, with people as if in transitory social roles. In other words, they involve still incomplete social movements or processes. And what has to be accounted for are the moment by moment changes, this way and that, as the process develops. In such developments, however, the momentary state of affairs so far achieved is incomplete; it is open to, invites or affords further specification. Within a medium of communication, when a still incomplete state of affairs must be described, it *is* specified further. For the purposes of communication, it is treated *as if* complete, and described either in terms of its supposed final product or in terms of the plan or plot an individual would have to follow to produce such a product. Thus, for example, as 'being in love' is the end result of 'falling in love' (if all goes well, although very often it doesn't), the transitory, passionate process is described in terms either of the much cooler, more stable, reasoned state, or in terms of 'the love story' – the process is described in terms of the product of the process, or the process as a sequence of products. In short, the circumstances are given or lent a structure *they do not in fact have*; a reality is described in terms of a fiction, a fiction that preserves our other individualistic fictions about ourselves. But couldn't we write other kinds of stories, ones that emphasize more our interdependencies with other people? How might we best account for 'falling in love', relationships in motion, so to speak? If we are still to have recourse to stories, why should some stories be judged as better than others; what are the criteria for 'good' stories? What should such stories be about; what should be their substance; what their point?

'FALLING IN LOVE' AND 'BEING IN LOVE'

In Kurt Vonnegut's novel *Mother Night* (1973) – of which, incidentally, the moral is, he says, that 'we are what we pretend to be, so we must be careful about what we pretend to be' i.e. be careful about the stories we tell ourselves – he writes (p. 23) of a young playwright thinking of his next play:

> I was sitting alone on a park bench in the sunshine that day, thinking of a fourth play that was beginning to write itself in my mind. It gave itself a title . . . 'Nation of Two'.
>   It was going to be about the love my wife and I had for each other. It was going to show how a pair of lovers in a world gone mad could survive by being loyal only to a nation composed of themselves – a nation of two.

The intuition Vonnegut expresses is apposite here, that lovers, who are in one sense already complete individuals, can begin to constitute between themselves something they experience as a third entity with its own nature, a 'nation', or something very like a nation, which then becomes part of their identity, a part of what they are to themselves. For etymologically a nation is a unity with a sensible continuity and a common origin (or birth), a unified region of social activity whose unity is so strong that, no matter what might disturb it, it is continually reborn as that same unity. In other words, falling in love is not *sui generis*; it is, as I have already said, a special kind of joint action, and an extreme case of a social *movement*.

Accounting relative to being in a two-person 'us'

What makes falling in love to an extent special, however, is that it is only a two-person relationship, and two-person relationships are special because the thirdness created between the two of them is not a thirdness on behalf of which a third party can speak. So, although it is a thirdness that provides the terms in which the couple must discuss and account for the details of their relationship together, it is not a thirdness that can in itself create a discord – by authorizing one person's version of 'the facts' over the other's. In other words, *all* expressions in two-person exchanges are, and must remain, 'indexical' expressions, i.e. they can work only by indicating something in the context of their usage. They cannot be reconstructed as 'objective' expressions, i.e. as intelligible to anyone, to third-person observers. For that would require of an expression: (1) that it be not only about something that 'forces' itself upon one, i.e. it 'makes' or 'compels' one to feel this or that way; but also (2) it is about something all *others* can experience in the same way also, i.e. it is independent of people's (emotional) involvements with one another, independent of any situation existing only between two people. It is this second criterion that cannot be met in two-person relationships. Hence, occurrences in two-person relationships cannot be made sense of 'objectively'; they are accounted for in terms solely *relative* to the implicit 'situation' the two persons constitute between themselves; third-person, uninvolved observers, who are not party to that situation, must make sense of events between the two by embedding them in another framework.

Consider the episode below, extracted from Tom Stoppard's (1982, p. 19) play *The Real Thing*, in which Stoppard exploits this fact:

HENRY:　No, no – buck's fizz all round. I feel reckless, extravagant, in love, and I'm next week's castaway on *Desert Island Discs*.
MAX:　Are you really?
HENRY:　Head over heels. How was last night, by the way?
CHARLOTTE:　Hopeless. I had to fake it again.
HENRY:　Very witty woman, my present wife. Actually, I was talking about my play.
CHARLOTTE:　Actually, so was I. I've decided it's a mistake appearing in Henry's play.
MAX:　Not for me it isn't.
CHARLOTTE:　Well, of course not for you, you idiot, you're not his wife.
MAX:　Oh, I see what you mean.
CHARLOTTE:　Max sees what I mean. All those people out front thinking, that's why she got the job. You're right, Max.
MAX:　I never said anything!

Three people are involved in this somewhat opaque episode; it will perhaps become somewhat less opaque if you know that Max and Charlotte, who is married to Henry, are actors in a successful play by Henry. The episode mostly consists in a succession of two-person exchanges. Their nature is such, however, that the most obvious 'topic' constituted by the audience to the play (from the actors' utterances on stage) is *not* the one constituted by the characters in the play. They (the characters) seem to suffer from continual misunderstandings (and so do we, although ours are different from theirs).

For them (and for us), their continual misunderstandings are (a) understood as such, and (b) successfully repaired without impairing the flow of conversation between them. At every point, a topic, or topics, is constituted *between* a speaker and a listener that has (emotional) currency *only* in the situation between them. For instance: (1) when Max says, 'Are you really?' we as third-person outsiders can see that, implicated in this response, is a reference to Henry's appearance on *Desert Island Discs*. Henry, however, misunderstands, and takes it that the implication is a reference to him (Henry) saying he feels 'in love'. And this is the point: it is because people within the flow of a two-person exchange make sense to one another *only* in terms of what goes on *within* the exchange that such misunderstandings can arise. But what about the next exchange? (2) Here, Stoppard surely plays an *ex post facto* trick on us. Henry says to Charlotte, 'How was it last night?' We, still with love in mind, interpret her utterance – 'Hopeless, I had to fake it again' – as to do with their love life as husband and wife. But Henry had switched in his previous utterance (had he?) from the topic of him being in love to his play. (3) Consider next Charlotte saying, 'You're right, Max', and Max's reply, 'I never said anything!' Again a possible topic, that of an audience thinking about Charlotte being Henry's wife, appears to be implicated in their exchange. Max appreciates the implication but declines to allow it.

These rather brief remarks are inadequate to unpack the complexity implicated in the episode above, but limitations on space will not allow further analysis here. I cannot go further here, either, into the special qualities of two-person exchanges compared with three-person ones, and what it is that makes for the kind of 'objectivity' we seek in science, and why that is impossible to achieve in relation to two-person relationships without distortion. Suffice it to say that there are some relationships whose understanding depends upon local and momentary contingencies. And 'procedures of enquiry', in which a class of speakers (scientists) are privileged, by being allowed to speak with an authority way beyond the range of their merely personal situation and power, i.e. to speak as if their utterances were context-free, are quite unsuited to their proper (undistorted) understanding. If we continue to act simply as if in all close relationships there just 'are' (to be found somewhere) sets of events that (a) are in themselves objective, and (b) will explain the conduct of the relationship, but which (c) we have not yet discovered, then we shall trap ourselves in paradoxes and illusions of our own making. *And* we shall prevent ourselves from ever discovering this fact. To see how such illusions can come about, I would like finally to turn to an analysis of why 'falling in love' is even more special than just being a two-person relationship.

Falling in love: illusions of passion

Love is blind; the wisdom of the fool and folly of the wise; like a ghost everybody talks about and few have seen; the encounter of two weaknesses; the child of illusion and the parent of disillusion: thus is love disparaged and derided. But falling in love with someone is much more than being fascinated by, or infatuated with a person's features. Such perceptions are no more than a starting-point. If we love another person, we certainly love him or her for what he or she 'is'; but at the same time we love them for what they *might be* – as Plato points out in *The Symposium*. Indeed, he goes further and suggests that it is love that works to produce the *movement* from what is to what might be. Although from a mundane point of view lovers may be 'blind' to one another's imperfections, in another sense they are far from blind: they see new *possibilities* in each other's activities and being. Their love for one another allows them to detect within the vague, incomplete responses they give one another, satisfying and gratifying ways of completing those responses; in their intense involvement with one another they see details in each other missed by those less concerned. With our eyes fixed upon an *image* we construct we are indifferent as to how far it is reflected and realized in the actual state of our loved ones, for we see through, in and behind what our loved one 'is', what he or she can become, as when mothers see their child's facial movements *as if* their child is 'smiling at them' and respond appropriately (Shotter 1974), and so on. We measure our loved one against our own ideal image of them, and continually present it to them as *their* ideal, as *their* project: to become fully what so far they are only partially – as if, *ex post facto*, they must become what in fact they have been all along. This creates the illusion that, as researchers, we can study retrospectively, in mundane terms, what it was that made for happiness between them (Argyle and Henderson 1985) – when the characteristics studied are the outcome of such processes of concern and attention, not their cause. The practical result of such research is information about how to describe the *criteria* met by happy couples (in case one needed a written account to help one recognize happiness), but no practical help at all in recognizing the *circumstances* that might *allow or afford* the occurrence of happiness.

And what of our lover's effect upon us? Again, here is a puzzling *ex post facto* outcome. When we fall in love, we fall in love with a particular person; but it was not that particular person we needed before falling in love with them. They *became* the needed person in the process of our 'falling for them'. And as our 'falling' progresses, and we 'discover' our relationship with the other to be both satisfying and gratifying, our vague need for a relationship becomes specific – as a need for that particular person. But what is the nature of this discovery about ourselves, for we neither simply discovered it, for it occurred in a process of 'falling', nor was it constructed, made or arbitrarily chosen by us. Indeed, 'we' as such change in the process, we come to need the other person in our very being. None the less, we often treat this discovery as if we had simply made a discovery about *ourselves*: *ex post facto*, we view ourselves as having lacked and needed this relationship all along, as if it was something only to do with us. This illusion is what might be called an 'illusion of discourse' for it arises out of a need to talk in a particular way, to talk in the currently acceptable language of self-explanation. And that way of talking *requires* that we make sense of all our activities in terms of events and actions, happenings and doings, *located* either 'in' us or 'outside' of us, not floating somewhere mysteriously 'between' us. In the idiom I am employing here, however, in my attempt to speak *practically*, as if from a position of involvement in two-person relationships, the matter looks different. Our relation to our circumstances becomes of crucial importance, and we must characterize the 'discovery' as a *creative discovery*, for in our relationship to the other person we *find* that the *making* of a new order of significance not ever before encountered is allowed us.

Those who treat close relationships as consisting merely of a succession of states, of causal events, have failed to recognize its nature as a *formative* movement, of which Plato (in *Phaedrus*) was already shrewdly aware – 'a cause whereby anything proceeds from that which is not, into that which is'. It is a creative process involving *novelties*. As Scheler (1954, p. 153) puts it:

> Love does not simply gape approval, so to speak, at a value lying ready to hand for inspection. It does not reach out towards given objects (or real persons) merely on account of positive values inherent in them, and already 'given' *prior* to the coming of love. For this idea still betrays that gaping at mere empirical fact, which is so utterly uncongenial to love. Love only occurs when, upon the values already acknowledged as 'real' there supervenes a movement, an intention towards potential values still higher than those already given and presented. In so doing, love invariably sets up an '*idealized*' *paradigm of value* for the person actually present.

It is the imaginative order, and its function in producing 'images', 'paradigms' and 'figures' in terms of which to give form to one's feelings, and the use of such forms in guiding the *developmental movements* involved in personal (and social) transformations, that are ignored, derided, distorted and ultimately repressed by current empirical approaches aimed at understanding (for the purposes of their management) interpersonal relations. For, in fact, in a practical reality, their extraordinary features are not amenable to an orderly, coherent account of a mundane kind.

CONCLUDING REMARKS

My concerns in this chapter have been of both a positive and of a negative kind. On the positive side, I have tried to describe what a social world, and especially a two-person, interpersonal one, might look (or feel?) like from the practical (rather than theoretical) point of view of first- and second-person participants in it, and especially to describe its *formative* nature, i.e. the circumstances it affords for personal development. On the negative side, I have been concerned to point out some of the distortions introduced into the attempt to understand interpersonal relationships within the current scientific framework, which views such relationships as manifesting a merely causal sequence of events, requiring description from a third-person, external observer point of view. I have been especially concerned to emphasize the way in which it suppresses concern for both the developmental and social context of such relations. I have argued that currently the 'image repertoire' from which we draw what we call our experiences of ourselves is that provided to us in the common-sense language of psychological explanation – the language we use when we are called upon to reflect upon our actions to justify them to others. In place of it I have been attempting to talk in the same idiom as that we use in conducting our activities, our language in practice.

Why is this not done in the rest of psychology? Why do we, as professional psychologists, persist in basing ourselves only in the language of justification? We do it in the service of retaining unchanged a whole set of established procedures in terms of which many other aspects of our everyday social activities are regulated and co-ordinated (Foucault 1979). And our accounts are thus concerned with (a) fitting what otherwise seems a marginal activity into an already existing framework, and (most importantly) (b) rendering it *as if* it is marginal, because of its formative creative nature, because of its potential disturbing effect upon established social orders. We are, I think, wrong in taking this approach. And above I have given my reasons for saying this. Here I want to add that I think we are wrong in a way that is *dangerous* to us all. For at least, at the moment, love functions in the gaps, so to speak, of the current 'disciplinary matrix', as Foucault (1979) calls it; we are thus still able to experience in our personal relationships what has, as MacIntyre (1981) claims, been obliterated from our social life at large: i.e. a continually renewed sense of surprise at other people's ceaselessly unforeseen originality and at the novel situations in which they involve us. And this can be compared with the desperate experience of turning continuously the wheel of routine, and function as a hint of better things.

This can be expressed more explicitly: the current project of making interpersonal relations an object for science can be seen as the continuation of a project concerned with the reconstitution of all human relationships as power relations, with, as MacIntyre puts it, the obliteration of the distinction between manipulative and non-manipulative social relations, and with eradicating joint action and its passionate, creative tendencies. Those such as Kelley *et al.* (1983), who are determined, as a result of their *observation* of close relationships, to describe them as if *caused* by certain *conditions*, possess (quite possibly unconsciously) an implicit aim in their method. It is to make the prediction and control, the disciplining and regulation of other people's activity possible, i.e. to make it possible for people *deliberately* to act as if in a 'close' way according to rational principles, to *simulate* a close relationship, but without the subversive threat to the dominant social order presented by the creative nature of genuine relationships. To make close relationships mundanely accountable is to make them – i.e. if they are to be *proper* close relationships – as if they *ought* to be conducted with certain rules in mind:

> He who is subjected to a field of visibility, and knows it, assumes responsibility for the constraints of power; he makes them play spontaneously upon himself; he inscribes in himself the power relation in which he simultaneously plays both roles; he becomes the principle of his own subjection.   (Foucault 1979, pp. 202–3)

If we did, however, allow ourselves to recognize the real formative nature of such relationships, we would be recognizing the character of our loss, which is the loss of the creativity of passion. But we don't, even though it is because of the practices *already existing* between us that we call certain of our relationships 'relationships' and treat others as not worthy of the name. What we need is a 'better' story, a better way of formulating the nature of personal relationships than the current 'causal story', a story that makes 'rationally visible', so to speak, the processual, formative nature of such relationships, and that reveals what certain 'illusions of discourse' at the moment repress. We need a story that 'fits in with' the *practice* of personal relationships, rather than in with the established practices of science – for in personal relationships, too, we can check, evaluate and elaborate the truths we make, as we make them. Practically, even love is not blind.

REFERENCES

Argyle, M. and Henderson, M. (1985) *The Anatomy of Relationships and the Rules and Skills Needed to Manage Them Successfully.* Harmondsworth: Penguin Books.

Averill, J. (1980a) 'A constructivist view of emotion'. In R. Plutick and H. Kellerman (eds) *Theories of Emotion.* New York: Academic Press.

—— (1980b) 'On the paucity of positive emotions'. In K. Blankstein, P. Pliner and J. Polivy (eds) *Advances in the Study of Communication and Affect*: vol. 6 *Assessment and Modification of Emotional Behaviour.* New York: Plenum Press.

Barthes, R. (1983) *A Lover's Discourse.* New York: Hill & Wang.

Buss, A.R. (1978) 'Causes and reasons in attribution theory: a conceptual critique'. *Journal of Personal and Social Psychology*, 36, 1311–21.

Duck, S. and Gilmour, R. (1981) *Personal Relationships*: *1: Studying Personal Relationships.* London: Academic Press.

—— and Miell, D. (1984) 'Towards a comprehension of friendship development and breakdown'. In H. Tajfel, C. Fraser and J. Jaspers (eds) *The Social Dimension: European Perspectives on Social Psychology*, vol. 1. Cambridge: Cambridge University Press.

Eco, U. (1979) *The Role of the Reader: Explorations in the Semiotics of Texts*. London: Hutchinson.

—— (1980) *The Name of the Rose*. New York: Harcourt Brace Jovanovich.

Foucault, M. (1979) *Discipline and Punish: The Birth of the Prison*, trans. Alan Sheridan. Harmondsworth: Penguin Books.

French, M. (1978) *The Women's Room*. London: Sphere Books.

Garfinkel, H. (1967) *Studies in Ethnomethodology*. Englewood Cliffs, NJ: Prentice-Hall.

Gavin, W.J. (1976) 'William James and the importance of "the vague"'. *Cultural Hermeneutics*, 3, 245–65.

Geertz, C. (1983) *Local Knowledge: Further Essays in Interpretative Anthropology*. New York: Basic Books.

Gergen, K.J. (in press) 'The language of psychological understanding'. In H. Stam, K. Gergen and T. Rogers (eds) *Metapsychology: The Analysis of Psychological Theory*. New York: Hemisphere.

—— and Gergen, M. (1983) 'Narratives of the self'. In K. Scheibe and T. Sarbin (eds) *Studies in Social Identity*. New York: Praeger.

Ginsburg, G.P. (1985) 'Taking talk seriously: a revision of the field'. *Contemporary Psychology*, 30, 872–4.

Goffman, E. (1959) *The Presentation of Self in Everyday Life*. New York: Doubleday; Harmondsworth: Penguin Books, 1971.

Goodman, N. (1972) 'The way the world is'. *Problems and Projects*. New York: Bobbs-Merrill.

Heider, F. (1958) *The Psychology of Interpersonal Relations*. New York: John Wiley.

James, W. (1890) *Principles of Psychology*, vol. 1. London: Macmillan.

Kelley, H.H., Berscheid, E., Christensen, A., Harvey, J.H., Huston, T.L., Levinger, G., McClintock, E., Peplau, L.A. and Peterson, D.R. (eds) (1983) *Interpersonal Relations: A Theory of Interdependence*. New York: John Wiley.

McIntyre, A. (1981) *After Virtue: A Study in Moral Theory*. London: Duckworth.

Mikula, G. (1984) 'Personal relationships: remarks on the current state of research'. *European Journal of Social Psychology*, 14, 339–52.

Mink, L.O. (1978) 'Narrative form as a cognitive instrument'. In R.H. Canary and H. Kozicki (eds) *The Writing of History: Literary Form and Historical Understanding*. Wisconsin: University of Wisconsin Press.

Ossorio, P.G. (1981) '*Ex post facto*: the source of intractable origin problems and their resolution'. Boulder, Colorado: Linguistic Research Institute report No. 28.

Sartre, J-P. (1958) *Being and Nothingness: An Essay on Phenomenological Ontology*, trans. Hazel Barnes. London: Methuen.

Schachter, S. (1971) *Emotion, Obesity, and Crime*. New York: Academic Press.

Scheler, M. (1954) *The Nature of Sympathy*, trans. Peter Heath. London: Routledge & Kegan Paul.

Schutz, A. (1964) *Collected Papers II: Studies in Socal Theory*. The Hague: Martinus Nijhoff.

Scott, M.B. and Lyman, S. (1968) 'Accounts'. *American Sociological Review*, 33, 46–62.

Shotter, J. (1974) 'The development of personal powers'. In M.P.M. Richards (ed.) *The Integration of a Child into a Social World*. Cambridge: Cambridge University Press.

—— (1980) 'Action, joint action, and intentionality'. In M. Brenner (ed.) *The Structure of Action*. Oxford: Blackwell.

—— (1981) 'Telling and reporting: prospective and retrospective uses of self-ascriptions'. In C. Antaki (ed.) *The Psychology of Ordinary Explanations of Social Behaviour*. London: Academic Press.

—— (1983) '"Duality of structure" and "intentionality" in an ecological psychology'. *Journal for the Theory of Social Behaviour*, 13, 19–43.

—— (1984) *Social Accountability and Selfhood*. Oxford: Blackwell.

—— (1986) 'A sense of place: Vico and the social production of social identities'. *British Journal of Social Psychology*, 25, 119–211.

Stoppard, T. (1982) *The Real Thing*. London: Faber & Faber.

Unger, R.M. (1984) *Passion: An Essay on Personality*. New York: Free Press.

Vonnegut Jr, K. (1973) *Mother Night*. London: Panther.

White, H. (1976) 'The tropics of history: the deep structure of the *New Science*'. In G. Tagliacozzo and D.P. Verene (eds) *Giambattista Vico's Science of Humanity*. Baltimore: Johns Hopkins Press.

—— (1978) 'The historical text as a literary artifact'. In R.H. Canary and H. Kosicki (eds) *The Writing of History: Literary Form and Historical Understanding*. Wisconsin: University of Wisconsin Press.

Wittgenstein, L. (1953) *Philosophical Investigations*. Oxford: Blackwell.

—— (1980) *Remarks on the Philosophy of Psychology*, vol. 1. Blackwell: Oxford.

14 The representation of personal relationships in television drama: realism, convention and morality

Sonia M. Livingstone

THEORETICAL AND EMPIRICAL APPROACHES

Introduction

> In trying to understand the meanings persons place on experience, then, it is necessary to work through a theory of fictions: a theory explaining how these forms operate, the semantic devices they employ, the meanings they sustain, the particular glow they cast over experience. This is a process of making large claims from small matters.
>
> (Carey 1975, p. 190)

The representation of personal relationships on television constitutes a substantial part of television content. The formation, maintenance and dissolution of personal relationships, with their associated emotions, problems and social ramifications, are the mainstay of each dramatic genre on television (e.g. situation comedy, crime series, soap opera and the single play). It is frequently assumed, although not often demonstrated, that the representation of relationships provides a source of information, contrast and analytic frameworks for viewers' own representations of their own and other people's relationships (Alexander 1985; Fallis, FitzPatrick and Friestad 1985). This chapter is concerned with the approaches taken towards these representations, as a prerequisite to understanding the roles that they play in the lives of their viewers.

For a social psychologist attempting to understand people's everyday social reality, the cultural representations, with their conventions and constraints, which mould people's interpretative processes, are of central concern. For a media researcher attempting to understand the contribution of the media to people's everyday social reality, the conventions and constraints that mould the construction of a programme are also of concern. As Carey (1975) suggests above, both concerns require an appreciation of semantic devices, dramatic genres, communicative aims, and so forth. It may turn out that media research, which draws upon literary and anthropological analyses of cultural texts, will contribute to social psychological research by providing a theoretical resource for thinking about the way people place meanings on their experience (Murray 1985). More important, however, is the proposal that the two research enterprises are mutually dependent: the construction of representations, of which the media form a subset, and the interpretation of representations cannot be independently conceived, for each occurs in the context of the other (Eco 1979).

Psychological approaches to television programmes often ignore the social and communicative nature of viewing, and regard viewing simply as a matter of individual response to an individual stimulus. In contrast to this position, I wish to emphasize that the production of television programmes and their interpretation by viewers occur within and are dependent upon broadly the same, usually implicit, cultural background. Second, both processes occur in the context of specific, and more explicit, sets of ideas about the other. Thus the production team uses its knowledge and opinions of the viewers' interests, capabilities and prejudices, and viewers have some awareness of the context of production, of temporal and financial constraints, of when they are being patronized, and so forth.

This chapter considers the ways in which television drama may contribute to viewers' understandings and images of personal relationships. Specifically, the discussion will focus on the realism of representations, and on how conceptions of the text implicate conceptions of the audience, and vice versa. While the discussion will be fairly general to television drama, much of the current research and theorizing concerns soap opera. As my own research has also focused on soap opera, this chapter will centre upon this popular genre. Soap opera is the prime locus for television's treatment of personal relationships. As Cantor and Pingree (1983) note, 'love, duty, family, and intimate relations are at the core of the soap opera world' (p. 13).

The main theoretical and empirical approaches adopted towards representations in the media, particularly of personal relationships, will first be outlined. I make no claims to offer a comprehensive review, and given limits on space, I shall inevitably raise more issues than can be resolved here. However, I shall first highlight some problem areas in current research, particularly in terms of the interface between media and social psychological research. In view of these problem areas, I shall then discuss some broad theoretical distinctions by which current research strategies should be reappraised if we are to achieve an integration between the more promising theoretical approaches to the media and the social psychological approaches to interpreting social representations.

Either of two incompatible approaches are typically adopted to study the representation of a given phenomenon by the media. Each makes a particular set of assumptions about the semantics of texts and the process of textual interpretation, to be described later. It is important to note that both approaches are distinct from, and to some extent theoretically prior to, psychological questions about the effects (cognitive, affective, behavioural or interpersonal) of the media. The present paper will focus on representational rather than 'effects' research on relationships and the media. The two main approaches towards media representations will now be outlined, together with research conducted on the representation of personal relationships. These will then be contrasted with Moscovici's (1984) theory of social representations, a social psychological approach to similar issues.

Cultural studies

This draws upon a variety of sources, particularly literary criticism, semiotics, social anthropology and theories of ideology, in order to analyse the latent meaning structures beneath the surface content of the programme (Davis and Walton 1983; Hall *et al.* 1980; Masterman 1984). These are placed in relation to their mechanisms of production and their socio-structural context. Behind this research lies the assumption that television makes an important contribution to the symbolic reality of its viewers, and it is argued that in order to appreciate the nature of this contribution, one must focus upon television's ideological, mythic and institutional determinants, its implicit or latent meanings, its cultural precursors, and, as has been emphasized more recently, its semiotic openness to the interpretative contribution of viewers.

Relationship portrayals provide a useful forum for the dramatic treatment of morality, social problems and contemporary myth (Allen 1985; Hobson 1982; Mander 1983; Silverstone 1981). In this respect, they implicate ideological or mythic levels of meaning beyond those of the referential or manifest meaning of the particular relationship portrayed. For example, Mander (1983) argues that the interpersonal conflicts in *Dallas* mediate treatment of contemporary moral dilemmas concerning family life and social/institutional responsibility. Hobson (1982) shows how current social problems such as teenage pregnancy and abortion are carefully discussed through the interactions of soap opera characters. Skidmore and Skidmore (1983) trace a metaphoric parallel between current affairs (Watergate in their example), and the hero/villain conflicts of comic books.

Booth (1980) discusses how television deliberately attempted to alter people's conceptions of relationships in order to halt the substantial increase in broken marriages after the war. In 1953, a four-part drama-documentary entitled *The Pattern of Marriage* was broadcast by the BBC with the explicit aim of re-establishing the 'happy family' life of viewers. In this case, television embraced its responsibility to viewers and would have accepted that: 'The media's function is the provision of social realities where they did not exist before, or the giving of new directions to tendencies already present' (Halloran 1970, p. 31).

The programme portrayed an ordinary couple surmounting, successfully, their marital problems, so as to guide viewers through their own problems and thus maintain the family as the basic structural unit of society. Booth argues that the programmes were essentially evasive and conventional, avoiding treatment of the social causes of marital breakdown, and advocating traditional morality as a sole curative.

While television explicitly focuses upon the intra- and inter-personal levels of experience, it thus appears to omit or, more accurately, disguise, the socio-political, with either benevolent or manipulative aims. Television drama has developed a set of generic conventions, and viewers a set of interpretative expectations, which dictate that macro-level concerns are treated (for they cannot be excluded) through the medium of the intimate or personal. Buckman (1984) comments on soap opera thus: 'All problems on the soaps have to be personalised, and the personalities involved must conform to stereotypes whose views reflect majority thinking' (p. 146). 'Unless politics are personalised, the soaps can't handle them' (p. 31). Similarly, another researcher concludes:

> It is important to realise, however, that like pastoral devoid of irony, soap opera reflects and communicates a form of social seeing that legitimates a preoccupation with solely private lives. As such, it continues to make a major contribution to the domestication of American woman.   (Porter 1982, p. 131)

As a consequence, it is often through the representation of personal relationships and the exploitation of the conventional opposition of the personal and political, that historical and political meanings are encoded. An emphasis upon latent and ideological analysis, not merely upon the manifest content, is required to detect this. The judicious focus upon the personalities rather than social roles of those in the news (Lerman 1983), the use of soap opera to convey socio-structural messages (Allen 1985; Hobson 1982), the choice of the single play by many socially critical authors (e.g. *Cathy Come Home*) to argue a political case and provoke social action in response to personal indignity, are all instances of the use of relationships by television to carry more significance than relationship information *per se*.

Occasionally, the media adopt a more explicitly educative role, although little attention has been paid to this. One analysis of women's magazines reveals the development in 'rhetorical visions' offered in advice on managing relationships. In the 1950s, magazines contained the rhetoric of un-selfish togetherness, with an endorsement of traditional sex roles, an emphasis on security, and a strong sense of the right and wrong way to manage a relationship – the 'ten easy steps to a happy marriage' genre. This has changed since the 1960s to views of challenging, developing, creative relationships, with negotiated meaning and no set standards – the 'we can talk it out' genre (Kidd 1979).

Content analysis

This is a largely sociological and social-psychological enterprise (Berelson 1952; Cassata and Skill 1983; Gerbner and Gross 1976) which attempts to follow Berelson's original prescriptions for an avowedly 'scientific' approach to content by developing a 'research technique for the objective, systematic, and quantitative description of the manifest content of com-munication' (Berelson 1952, p. 18). Conceiving of television's contribution to symbolic reality through the explicit contrast between television repre-sentations and the parallel phenomena in everyday life, content analysis aims to describe the biases and selections in the television representations presented to viewers.

The bulk of relationship research has been conducted by content analysts, and I briefly summarize the results below. Each study is based upon a quantitative and 'objective' analysis of several months or years of (usually prime-time) American television entertainment programmes (see Cassata and Skill [1983] and Wober and Gunter [1987] for more detailed reviews). In the domain of relationships there is almost no research to date conducted on British television. One exception is a content analysis of British 'family theme' programmes (Jones 1984) based on one week of British television. There is some British research concerning the representa-tion of individuals, particularly in relation to gender, from which infer-ences about relationships may be drawn (Durkin 1985; Livingstone and Green 1986). In general, television drama contains more men than women, few children or elderly people, few employed women or working-class people of either sex, and almost no ethnic minorities. Family relationships provide a central theme of much drama, and this is integrated with issues of morality, power and romance (Jones 1984).

Relationship 'life events'   Serials such as *Dallas* and *Dynasty* emerge as 'anti-family' dramas, with a high rate of divorce, cohabitation, miscarriage and abortion, and remarkably few images of married bliss (Goldsen 1975).

Family structure   Only about one-third of television families are nuclear families, there are many single-parent families, and many comprise miscel-laneous family groupings with members of the extended family although central relationships do concentrate on the immediate family (Hines, Greenberg and Buerkel 1979; Jones 1984). However, the vast majority of television characters are not portrayed as part of a family at all, as few characters have any children (Phelps 1976, cited in Wober and Gunter 1987).

Marriage Family and relationships are portrayed as more important to women than to men (McNeill 1975). Mothers are less likely than other women to have any life outside their family (Phelps 1976, cited in Wober and Gunter 1987). In the home, women defer to their husbands for support and authority, while women who have successful careers tend to have problems in their relationships with men (Roberts 1982, cited in Wober and Gunter 1987). Problems arise when the wife and not the husband is the sole breadwinner (Jones 1984). The marital status of women is more salient than that of men (Silverman *et al.* 1978, cited in Wober and Gunter 1987), so that women are primarily represented in relational roles, which to them are seen as all-important, while men are shown independent of relationships. The majority of marital relationships are conflictual, and this is due to interpersonal rather than socio-structural problems (Jones 1984). Marriage appears less satisfying to women and responses to conflict are often fatalistic (Jones 1984).

Interaction patterns within relationships Familial roles in general are portrayed as largely conflict-free relationships, with an emphasis on affection and altruism (Fisher 1974) and a minimum of negative or rejecting interactions (Greenberg *et al.* 1980). Where conflict does occur, it is concentrated between spouses and between siblings, with children rarely involved in parental disputes. Across generations, interactions are more common between same-sex parent/child pairs (Greenberg *et al.* 1980) or between parents and teenage children (Jones 1984). The solutions to conflict tend to reinforce the normative values of our culture (Barcus 1983). Difficulties faced by families in real life (money, aging relatives, educational problems) are rare on television (Barcus 1983), although British programmes, especially soap operas, often aim to reflect the lives of their viewers. Interestingly, the problems caused by unemployment in the family are receiving increasing attention (Jones 1984).

Sex Sexual relations, usually heterosexual, have long been portrayed on the cinema screen, but television has avoided the issue, partly due to children in the audience, but more because of beliefs concerning the conservativeness of the adult audience (Cassata and Skill 1983). LaGuardia (1983) has documented the gradual inclusion of sex in American daytime soap operas. Greenberg, Abelman and Neuendorf (1981) compared incidence of sexual behaviours on daytime and prime time television, and found that daytime television (i.e. soap opera) includes sexual intimacies short of intercourse, with the exception of some rapes, and prime time television includes fewer such intimacies, but more intercourse, prostitution and homosexuality. By and large, sexual interaction is more verbal than physical (Jones 1984).

In sum, there have been two major concerns for content analysts: first, how far do television representations mirror the real-life distribution of relationship phenomena; and second, in so far as television representations are a 'distortion' of real life, is this in the direction of increased or decreased normativity or morality? From the above evidence, one can conclude that television provides a highly distorted representation of personal relationships and that, further, these distortions or biasing of reality are fuelled by two, sometimes contradictory, concerns: to increase viewer interest by sacrificing realism for dramatic incident; or to improve the viewers' moral understanding by sacrificing realism for a moral ideal.

The theory of social representations

Moscovici's (1984) theory of social representations is not explicitly concerned with the media at all, but it constitutes the most complex and provocative theory recently offered by social psychology concerning the nature and status of culturally given representations of everyday phenomena. As the above two domains of research show, television constitutes a major source of representations and frameworks for understanding everyday social phenomena. We must ask how straightforwardly social representation theory can be applied to television representations. The concept of 'social representation' may be relevant to television in any or none of the forms proposed specifically by Moscovici, or by social psychologists more generally as a catch-all for such representational concepts as stereotypes, scripts, attributions or schemata. However conceived, the peculiarities of television representations and of their manner of interpretation should be, although rarely are, taken into account.

Consider the following definitions:

> pictures of the world, the definitions of the situation and problems, the explanations, alternative remedies and solutions which are made available to us (Halloran 1970, p. 53)

> concepts, images, statements, explanations, perceptions, theories, branches of knowledge, words, mixtures of all these and: cognitive matrices which coordinate the above (Potter and Litton 1985, p. 87)

The first definition refers to television representations, the second to Moscovici's social representations. Clearly they are very similar in terms of content. But as communicative acts, the roles of these two types of representation are rather different, and before one makes the convenient assumption that television is 'just another source' of representations, let us briefly consider the differences. Moscovici, indeed social psychology generally, is often vague about the origins of the social representations whose psychological or group identity consequences are studied. Yet television representations have a relatively clear source, although the sources upon which they themselves draw are the very social representations whose origins remain unspecified or hidden. Programmes are constructed according to a unique set of criteria, and the meanings they make available to viewers must in part reflect those constraints. These criteria variously concern institutional constraints (time, finance, facilities), medium constraints (technology, scheduling), professional constraints (legality, decency, artistic merit), viewer constraints (ratings, conservatism, presumed intelligence), ideological constraints (morality, consumerism) and literary constraints (genre, cohesion, narrative structure).

Alternatively, one could regard the media as prime examples of social representations which usefully and clearly illustrate in a relatively concrete form many of the features attributed to social representations. One can analyse the institutions and communicative intent that produce media representations, the programme structure and, with more difficulty, the cultural environment and the viewer's interpretation. Drawing on the vast body of media research may facilitate development of a comprehensive theory of social representations and clarify present shortcomings of the theory. Unfortunately, we do not at present have either a representation-based or an interpretation-based categorization of types of social representation, leaving the typicality of television representations uncertain.

A further dilemma in the integration of social representation theory and the study of television representations is where one locates the social representation in the complex communicative process that Hall (1980) has termed the 'production cycle'. Consider that we must integrate what the production team wanted to communicate, the television programme made as a consequence, and what viewers perceived. Which of these is the social representation, and what are the consequences of selecting any one of these? While a psychologist might identify a consensus in viewers' interpretations as the social representation, it seems more usual to identify the initial presentation of the phenomenon (the book, the programme, the rules our parents teach us) as the social representation. The ways in which people make salient or interpret these phenomena is then a matter of the use of rather than the construction of social representations. This use constitutes a further problem for it draws upon social knowledge which may too be regarded as social representations. The argument concerns the status of social representations in the various processes by which meaning is constructed. The many ways in which our symbolic world is endlessly created and recreated in all its variety are such that there is no one role for representations. Consequently, if the term social representation is not to be over-extended, merely a fashionable gloss for any work concerning the construction or power of meaning, then it is this entire communication process that must be examined. A theory of social representations will inevitably involve this implicitly, so we should attempt to be explicit, otherwise we may fail to distinguish between social representations created by a powerful few for the general public and those which are, instead, emergent from people's ordinary activities. On issues of the locus of social representations Moscovici's work is weak. Social representations appear from a nebulous social source, in a coherent and intrinsically meaningful form, and 'irresistibly thrust' themselves into the consciousness of the defenceless masses. But for the deletion of the source, Moscovici often reads like the hypodermic model of critical mass communication theory, which held that the process of media influence is analogous to the wholesale injection of pre-produced images (Curran, Gurevitch and Woollacott 1982). Indeed, many of the arguments concerning social representations have already been rehearsed and developed in the field of mass communications.

TELEVISION AND REALITY

The problem

Each of the above three approaches to media representations is problematic in various ways. Cultural studies is often seen as subjective, or non-scientific, imposing its own theoretical and political stance upon the phenomena, offering insight but no definitive answers. The theory of social representations has already been discussed, but essentially the theory is still insufficiently developed. Content analysis, developed to circumvent the problems of subjectivity, has generated most research on television representations. It is important, therefore, that we are aware of its considerable limitations and the extent to which these qualify or undermine the results obtained.

There are three reasons to be dissatisfied with content analytic research. First, there is a limit to how much can be counted; the requirements of 'manifest', 'reliable' and 'objective' built into the enterprise preclude much of the more subtle, ambiguous and interpretative aspects of the representations. For example, one can count the denotative far more easily than the connotative, and the included more easily than the excluded.

Second, there is little facility for integrating findings beyond merely listing results as was done above. For example, the significance of the recent inclusion of sex in soap operas transcends the mere facts of its existence, and is revealed through its relation to narratives and characterization (Kreizenbeck 1983). Thus, good women find sex 'icky', and put their careers second, while bad ones use sex as a weapon in their relationships, are openly seductive, promiscuous, committed to their careers, and unhappy: 'The soap opera, by presenting characters who flaunt the values and morals of the audience, strengthens that audience's resolve to hold on to those abused ideals ... the family is the soap source of spiritual and emotional strength' (Kreizenbeck 1983, p. 176). Such conclusions depend on the integration of findings in the context of relevant generic and narrative conventions which frame the meaning of any units quantified. Comedy, melodrama and soap opera place quite different frames on the 'same' events.

Third, and most important, is the fact that content analysis brings with it a particular and problematic view of the relationship between the psychology of the viewer and the semantics of the text. This problem encompasses the two previous points, and itself hinges upon the wider issue of the relationship between television representations (or social representations more generally) and the everyday reality of the viewer. If we are to go beyond the mere accumulation of questionable data, the relationship between media representations and the viewers' reality must be explored more fully. As argued earlier, these two domains are interdependent. Cultural studies (and, more recently, social representation theory) depend on and may founder on their unexamined assumption that the levels of meaning, narrative conventions and textual constraints proposed by their analyses of programmes (representations) have psychological reality for the viewer, whether consciously or not. Conversely, psychological approaches to the media, which favour content analysis for its scientific approach, founder upon their limited conception of the programme, a conception that severely restricts the range of programme 'effects' that can be sought.

Media research is ultimately concerned with the relation of television representations to the everyday reality of the viewer. Research variously examines the opposition, correspondence, causal interrelatedness or mutual indivisibility of these two. Beneath any research one can identify a commitment for or against the independence of television representations and everyday reality. Content analysis takes the position most aligned with common-sense assumptions. Indeed, it is its intuitive plausibility that has enabled this research to proceed on such an atheoretical 'I wonder if . . .' path. Such research follows what Grant (1970) has termed 'Conscientious Realism', a critical approach to literature, and by extension to the media, which itself draws upon a correspondence theory of truth in its conception of the representation/reality relation. This he opposes to 'Conscious Realism', based upon coherence theories of truth.

This distinction is pertinent both in relation to the above issues, and also because different television genres make different implicit claims about the degree to which they mimic reality. Chesebro (1982), in an analysis of popular American television series shown over several years, has revealed that 'mimetic' programmes, those which purport to portray life as the viewer knows it, with characters 'just like us', are increasingly becoming the dominant form, while leader-based, romantic, and other genres are on the decrease. This suggests that the media itself endorses conscientious realism and sees its role as mimicking the world of the viewer. Barthes (1973) has argued forcefully for the critical analysis of that which appears 'natural'. It is the common-sense, 'just like us', appeal of such programming that is disturbing because an essential prerequisite of this genre is that it denies or 'mystifies' its own production processes. It is therefore least likely to be labelled as 'fantasy' and most likely to become confused with viewers' understandings of everyday life.

Conscientious realism

This is assumed by content analysis and adopted by most psychologists who study the media. It conceives of two sources of social information for the viewer: the real or direct knowledge obtained from daily experience, and the unreal or indirect knowledge obtained from representations (literally) of daily experience as presented by the media. This latter is held to be a powerful alternative to direct knowledge, especially when there is little direct access to the phenomenon represented. Where there are any discrepancies between the two sources of knowledge, the television representation is assumed to bias or distort the viewers' understanding. It is thus the duty of the media to faithfully parallel the reality outside, and the duty of social research to act as the conscience of the media, pointing out any deviations, compelling an ever-closer correspondence. Correlational research, which shows the connection between television representations and viewers' attitudes answers the obvious question 'why should the media attempt this parallelism?' by revealing the adverse consequences of 'reality distortion'. When contrasted with an alternative theory of realism, many of the semantic assumptions of this position appear limiting if not highly misleading.

Conscious realism

This is premised upon the coherence theory of truth. For this, knowledge is not dependent upon the degree of correspondence with an external reality. Instead knowledge is held to be created in the processes of perception and language, and similarly the media are not seen as an image or reflection of reality but as an instrument that realizes reality. Consequently, for conscious realism, literature/media do not simply imitate but actively create reality. They are not merely a commentary upon but an indivisible part of reality. The representation/reality distinction is false, especially with respect to the symbolic reality of people's everyday social understanding.

A comparison

The semantics of these two positions are very different. The essence of the contrast can be represented on a number of basic oppositions. On each of these, conscious realism appears superior (see also Shotter, this volume, for a related distinction between referential and rhetorical theories of meaning).

First, the emphasis upon reference is different: for conscientious realism meaning is reference, it lies in the correspondence between the unreal text and the real world outside; for conscious realism, reference is a relatively unimportant aspect of meaning. Conscious realism places more emphasis upon, for example, Halliday's (1973) interpersonal function of language, which concerns meanings created by placing the hearer/viewer in a particular relation to the speaker/text. This is of particular interest in relation to the media because television programmes are constructed, via various institutional and professional codes, so as to appear in an informal and egalitarian relation with the viewer while in fact retaining a superior and powerful position in relation to the meanings constructed for and by the viewer: 'Content analysts assume that *what* a soap opera means can be separated from *how* a soap opera means, that the production of meaning in soap operas is simple and unproblematic' (Allen 1983, p. 97).

In the second opposition, conscientious realism treats the meaning of representations as transparently available rather than as multiply layered. This is the major focus of attack by semiotics (closer to conscious realism), which is concerned with relations between the superficial and more latent or 'deep' levels of meaning. A common distinction is between the denotational, or referential, and the connotational. It is at this latter level that interpretation centres, this being the level that connects not with the external physical world of chairs and tables but with the symbolic world of which it is a part, the world of myth and ideology (Barthes 1973). Hence the content analysts' finding that wives defer to their husbands on television is not itself of particular interest. The interest lies in the connotative level of meaning, the level that adds evaluation (i.e. approval), moral prescription (this is how it should be in real life), normativity (this is how it is in real life), connection with ideology (this is how it always has been, bringing social stability and all things good), and myth (what happens when the rule is broken). For this, one must go beyond content analysis.

Third, conscientious realism holds that there is a reality independent of the media 'out there', which is simply being described by the media. For conscious realism, the media are as much contributors to the psychological reality of the viewer as are the viewers' interactions with the people among whom they live and work. This is because interactions with people or television are significant primarily in their connotative or symbolic meanings rather than because of their physical nature.

> This [viewing soap opera] is not escapism, or confusing fact and fantasy: it is enlarging your own experience by borrowing from someone else's, something one does all the time with one's friends, and even more with one's mentors. To the soap addict, the characters *are* friends and mentors, invented though they may be. Of course they exert a behavioural influence.   (Buckman 1984, p. 170)

Fourth, conscientious realism focuses solely upon what is present, instead of conceiving of meaning as inherent in the relation between the present and the absent: 'The premise of [conscientious] realism is a Trojan horse which carries within it a highly selective, synthetic, and purposeful image of the facts of life' (Gerbner and Gross 1976, p. 178).

This point has been made by many other media researchers concerned to oppose the view that television merely reflects and does not create symbolic reality (Dyer 1982; Tuchman 1981). The point is not that television representations, say, indicate, correctly or not, that most women want to get married, or that they incorrectly reflect the proportion of parents to non-parents in our society, but that these representations 'set the agenda' for viewers' thinking on these issues. Such representations thus suggest, for example, that there is no viable alternative to marriage and that having children is an uninteresting and unimportant activity. Omission is not meaningless: 'Representation in the fictional world signifies social existence; absence means symbolic annihilation' (Gerbner and Gross 1976, p. 182).

OPEN AND CLOSED TEXTS: THE ROLE OF THE READER

These two approaches to the realism of a representation embody either implicitly or explicitly a theory of the psychological role of the viewer. To pursue this point, I shall draw upon Eco's (1979) semiotic theory of the 'role of the reader'. This is the most psychologically oriented of a variety of theories concerned with Reception Theory or reader-response criticism, which itself is an attempt to integrate the semiotics of texts with the interpretation of readers (Sulieman and Crossman 1980). Conscientious realism, in combination with the positivism of content analysts seems to assume that the meanings encoded are identical to the meanings decoded, that the coders' 'reading' of the text is the only reasonable reading and that deviations of viewers are uninteresting. Reception theorists, on the other hand, see the text as contexted within and therefore as only one of several contributions to the symbolic reality of the reader. The existence of other sources of representations, rhetoric or organizing frameworks then operates so as to place interpretative distance between text and reader. The task of reception theorists is then to account for the relation between the two. Eco postulates what can be seen as a continuum between textual closure, with unitary legitimate readings, and textual openness or interpretative flexibility.

This corresponds to a parallel theory of the role of the reader which, depending on the degree of textual closure, involves a passive acceptance or an active construction of the text. All texts are seen as embodying a 'model reader', which is anticipated during text construction, but the model reader varies with the normativity or closure and moral prescriptiveness of the text. Different television genres, or different communicative or production aims, can thus be encompassed by this open/closed continuum, and different levels of textual cohesion and viewer activity can be envisaged as a consequence. Conversely, different levels of viewer knowledge and motivation correspond to different levels of divergent or creative meaning construction. Relationships are a theme about which all viewers have considerable personal and social knowledge (although see Burnett, this volume) and this is, presumably, brought to bear when interpreting a television drama. In the domain of relationships, then, inference from media representation to effect will be complicated, because interpretative distance is placed between what Eco terms the virtual and the realized text, the text or social representation that is offered as sensible and the text or social representation sense-making creates. Any textual openness will be fully exploited by viewers.

The distinction between open and closed texts, which imply creative or normative model readers respectively, and the distinction between conscientious and conscious realism together allow us to understand the theoretical stances taken by the three basic media research strategies outlined earlier. Content analysis is firmly within conscientious realism, approaching a programme with the question 'does this representation distort or give a fair view of the phenomenon?' As psychologists, such researchers are concerned when distortion occurs, and unconcerned when the representation accords with 'reality'. Implicitly, the psychological process of viewing is therefore seen as one of comparing the passively received representation with what is known of 'reality' and then, if there is a mismatch, distorting 'reality' to fit. Further, content analysis presumes both closed texts and closed readers, regarding the television programme as a transparent stimulus of unitary and unambiguous meaning and the viewer as one who takes up these meanings offered with no interpretative effort and no integration with social knowledge.

Cultural studies researchers, on the other hand, take the opposite viewpoint. They argue for conscious realism, where television representations contribute to the never-ending psychological process of constructing one's 'reality'. Whether it is the accepted and normative or the unconventional and alternative that is presented by television, both are of interest. In fact, it is possibly the former rather than the latter which is of more concern, because viewers have less defence against the more invisible, normative readings. Usually, as a consequence of their focus on the more detailed and complex levels of meaning, rather than the more gross categories of content analysis, they also argue for the openness of texts, even in popular culture, where many reception theorists would perceive closure. Eco argues that not only are apparently straightforward and natural texts in fact the product of many complex and constructed textual devices, but also that the superficial naturalness requires completion through the constructive role of the reader, whether viewer or theorist. This role necessarily draws upon often invisible, conventional and normative knowledge. Allen (1985), Dyer et al. (1981) and Mander (1983) regard soap opera as a form of contemporary myth, not in the closed sense of providing clear solutions to everyday problems, but in the open sense of grappling with and airing practical alternatives to those moral dilemmas that naturally occur in viewers' own relationships. This coincides with the dramatic purpose perceived by viewers. For example, Hobson (1982) discusses the treatment of abortion by the soap opera *Crossroads*. While abortion, the more controversial option was rejected by the programme for a more morally acceptable alternative, in her interviews with viewers Hobson found it was the discussion of possibilities rather than the final normative conclusion that viewers focused upon. If we can rely upon self-report, this suggests that media influence in this case is mediated by viewers treating the text as more open than closed.

Interestingly, Moscovici's (1984) attempt to place social representations on the psychologists' agenda takes an intermediate theoretical stance. His concern with the role of representations in creating rather than simply mirroring symbolic reality places him firmly within conscious realism, and yet he gives a far greater power to representations than do theorists in cultural studies. Thus he too makes no distinction between the virtual and realized text, and seems to assume that all representations are closed and all determining. Moscovici has claimed of social representations that 'they impose themselves upon us with irresistible force' (1984, p. 7). Yet, particularly in respect to personal relationships, viewers' considerable personal experience, plus access to a wealth of cultural myth and rhetoric concerning the nature of relationships, allows them to distance themselves from the television representation. Further, the totality of media or other social representations do not constitute a coherent and harmonious whole, and consequently their omissions, ambiguities and contradictions allow considerable leeway for individual interpretation and selection. Together, these facts must make us question the power of television to impose its new social realities so forcefully upon the viewers. The degree to which television delimits or stimulates ways of thinking remains an open question.

AN EXAMPLE: THE DRAMATIC REPRESENTATION OF ADULTERY

To focus the above discussion, I shall briefly present a section of a more extensive semiotic analysis of a *Coronation Street* narrative (Livingstone 1985) shown in November 1984. The narrative centred on the classic 'eternal triangle' theme, in which the marriage of two central and popular characters was threatened when the husband became attracted to his secretary. Although no affair in fact took place, the story aired a variety of opinions about contemporary sexual morality and explored the reasons for which people commit adultery. The programme thereby fulfilled its mythic role of tackling and grounding in practical experience a distressing and morally perplexing social problem. See Weber, Harvey and Stanley (this volume) for a more detailed discussion of the functions served by explanations or accounts of relationships. The ten quotations below represent the categories of explanation (one might almost call them 'rules of relationships') offered for adultery or sexual behaviour. The participants are Ken Barlow, the husband, Deidre Barlow, the wife, and Sally Waterman, the secretary.

1 The old values, which prohibited adultery, are no longer respected: e.g. 'Very little shocks me these days. You've only got to read the paper to see that the ten commandments are just a joke now ... it's just that you treat it so casual. Oh, you know what I'm talking about. I just can't get used to that' (an observer).

2 Sexual relationships are part of living life to the full: e.g. 'I've missed out all down the rotten line. Nothing's ever touched me. Not your affluent society or your permissive society ... I might as well have been dead these fifteen years ... at least she [the secretary] knows what a forbidden fruit is' (an observer).

3 Extramarital attraction is irrational and out of control: e.g. 'My private life is becoming an obsession with you' (secretary to husband).

4 Adultery arises out of marital difficulties: e.g. 'Look, Ken, if there's just something going wrong with your marriage ...' (secretary to husband).

5 Adultery is the husband's attempt to regain his virility, a specific case of the middle-aged man's need to attract younger women: e.g. 'I suppose I'm a classic case really ... the onset of middle age, the male menopause. Y'know, you must have heard all the jargon' (husband); and 'I can see how a bloke of your age would be a bit chuffed to pull a young bird like her [secretary]' (said to husband's rival).

6 Adultery is an immature failure to cope with adult commitment: e.g. 'This is all turning into some kind of daft adolescent fantasy' (husband).

7 Prolonged contact with an attractive woman inevitably arouses male lust: e.g. 'She [secretary] works for him [husband]. They spend all day together in a tiny little room' (an observer); and 'She [secretary] is there, in the office, and she's not exactly ugly' (husband).

8 Some women prefer the challenge of catching a married man: e.g. 'We might as well be in the paper, with me cast as a slaggy bit of crumpet trying to get her hooks into somebody's husband' (secretary to husband).

9 Adultery by one partner legitimates retaliation by the other: e.g. 'I lied to you, didn't I? When I had that affair with Mike Baldwin, I lied to you. So now –' (wife), 'So now it's my turn, is it?' (husband).

10 Jealousy revives a dull marriage: e.g. 'I bet you told Deidre you went to bed with me ... some men like to boast, don't they? Even to their wives. Especially to their wives' (secretary to husband).

Naturally, for a complete picture one must consider these explanations in their narrative context, for they were made as everyday asides, comments and gossip by a variety of different characters whose personalities context the explanations. Content analysis, so comprehensively applied to more gross features of programmes has difficulties with connotative aspects of meaning. Allen (1983) argues that infrequent viewers of soap opera perceive only the syntagmatic aspects and miss the paradigmatic aspects. One requires only fairly basic social knowledge to perceive the plot structure, and the sequence of events. To appreciate the significance of any one event or utterance, one must relate it to its paradigm of alternative possibilities, of what could have been said or what might have happened, and to the implicit contrasts and similarities that frame the understanding of events. Knowledge of the paradigms requires experience with the programme and with the genre of soap opera. To lack this is to make an aberrant reading of the text. If what happened, who was attracted to whom, and who found out, constituted the syntagmatic aspect of the narrative, then the explanations above must be understood paradigmatically, in relation to and contrast with each other, and this requires a semantics that goes beyond the manifest and present. That one explanation places responsibility on the husband (10) must be contrasted with those which assign cause but not blame to him (3), those which involve current moral rhetoric (1) contrast with those concerned with individual circumstances (9), and so forth.

A further problem for conscientious realism becomes apparent when we look beyond the representation of simple events to the treatment of more complex themes of relationships, as in the present example. If we hold that television has a duty to portray reality fairly, at least when the genre is one that professes representativeness, what then is the reality with which television should be compared? Should the above explanations for adultery match the true causes of adultery in everyday life if we are not to be concerned about the distorting effects of such explanations on viewers? This seems an impossible requirement. Or should they merely match the viewers' own explanations of adultery? In this case, we would be requiring television to reinforce the normative and not to challenge or propose alternatives. Instead of suggesting that culture should stimulate and undermine absolute or easy conclusions, this is to require television drama to reinforce old prejudices and assumptions. It seems preferable to regard the above explanations as a contribution to the symbolic reality of the viewer, more particularly as a social representation that contributes to the viewers' awareness of the range and character of social understandings of adultery.

Although conscientious realism typically assumes textual closure, and conscious realism open texts, the theory of social representations reminds us that other positions are possible. My arguments throughout this chapter have been in favour of conscious realism, in contrast to the standard psychological position. This is a theoretical preference. The issue of textual openness versus closure, upon which hangs the issue of the role of and influence upon the reader, can only be considered within conscious realism. However, the extent to which particular programmes or programme genres are open or closed is an empirical question. The above example highlights some considerations for research. The narrative does not offer a single view of adultery, as is clear from the multiplicity of explanations. To this extent, it offers a role for the viewer in discriminating between, selecting from, and contrasting these different viewpoints on adultery, its cause, and the appropriate locus for blame or sympathy. But despite the variety of explanations, each is none the less well within conventional, moral rhetoric, which is easily available, requires no rethinking and is well grounded in normative assumptions concerning related issues such as gender and sexuality. Furthermore, an agenda has been invisibly set. There are no explanations concerning marriage as a social institution, religious views, the tension between moral prescriptions and human practice, or the socio-structural position of the characters involved. In both of these respects, the narrative closes off possibilities for the viewer, and directs him/her down well-worn and familiar pathways with minimal discomfort. Both aspects of the text, the open and the closed, must be considered before a role for the reader can be uncovered. Whichever aspect predominates in any particular text should, then, indicate likely psychological implications for the viewer.

I should like to end with an example of the activity of viewers in constructing and reconstructing narratives presented to them in soap opera. When a sample of regular viewers were asked to recall the above narrative over one year after transmission, one subject answered thus:

> We had weeks of Ken being worried about his feelings for Sally changing from those of a boss to those of a potential lover, and it eventually culminated in him kissing her and embracing her in the office.... Deidre began to suspect Sally and Ken long before anything was actually going on. ... She began listening to rumours and gossip and instead of confronting Ken and asking straight out what was happening bottled up all her feelings inside her. ... Mike started paying Deidre a lot of attention ... Deidre being very upset about what she heard about Sally and Ken.... A few nights later Mike turned up on Deidre's doorstep asking her to go away with him. ... It was all an anti-climax; she and Ken did not split up. There was a showdown with Mike in the Barlow's house. Ken and Deidre ended up going away for a holiday to patch things up.   (Woman, 25)

This story is a plausible but quite inaccurate account of two cases of adultery, for they are recalled in the wrong order. In other words, the affair between Deidre Barlow and Mike Baldwin took place several years before the Ken Barlow and Sally Waterman story, but the Ken and Sally story did indeed end with the married couple, Ken and Deidre, going on holiday. So, to produce a more satisfactory situation, in which the wife 'gets her own back', this viewer has inventively but unconsciously reorganized remembered events so as to introduce a moral twist to her representation. Neither psychologists nor media researchers have so far got to grips with such phenomena. Yet it is the study of such small matters as they relate to the complexity and partial openness of television representations that will eventually substantiate the large claims often made for television's contribution to the social reality of the viewer.

ACKNOWLEDGEMENTS

I should like to thank Peter Lunt, Michael Argyle, Roz Burnett and Patrick McGhee for their help and criticism during the writing of this chapter.

REFERENCES

Alexander, A. (1985) 'Adolescents' soap opera viewing and relational perceptions'. *Journal of Broadcasting and Electronic Media*, 29 (3), 295–308.

Allen, R.C. (1983) 'On reading soaps: a semiotic primer'. In E.A. Kaplan (ed.) *Regarding Television: Critical Approaches – An Anthology*. Los Angeles, CA: University Publications of America.

—— (1985) *Speaking of Soap Operas*. Chapel Hill: University of North Carolina Press.

Barcus, F.E. (1983) *Images of Life on Children's Television: Sex Roles, Minorities and Families*. New York: Praeger.

Barthes, R. (1973) *Mythologies*. London: Paladin.

Berelson, B. (1952) *Content Analysis in Communication Research*. Glencoe, IL.: Free Press.

Booth, J. (1980) 'Watching the family'. In H. Baehr (ed.) *Women and Media*. Oxford: Pergamon Press.

Buckman, P. (1984) *All for Love: A Study in Soap Opera*. London: Secker & Warburg.

Cantor, M. and Pingree, S. (1983) *The Soap Opera*. Beverly Hills, CA: Sage.

Carey, J.W. (1975) 'Communication and culture'. *Communication Research*, 2, 173–91.

Cassata, M. and Skill, T. (1983) *Life on Daytime Television: Tuning-in American Serial Drama*. Norwood, NJ: Ablex.

Chesebro, J.W. (1982) 'Communication, values, and popular television series – a four-year assessment'. In H. Newcomb (ed.) *Television: The Critical View*. Oxford: Oxford University Press.

Curran, J., Gurevitch, M. and Woollacott, J. (1982) 'The study of the media: theoretical approaches'. In M. Gurevitch, T. Bennett, J. Curran and J. Woollacott (eds) *Culture, Society and the Media*. London: Methuen.

Davis, H. and Walton, P. (1983) *Language, Image, Media*. Oxford: Blackwell.

Durkin, K. (1985) 'Television and sex-role acquisition: 1. Content'. *British Journal of Social Psychology*, 24, 101–13.

Dyer, G. (1982) *Advertising as Communication*. London: Methuen.

Dyer, R., Geraghty, C., Jordan, M., Lovell, T., Paterson, R. and Stewart, J. (1981) *Coronation Street*. British Film Institute Television Monograph No. 13.

Eco, U. (1979) *The Role of the Reader: Explorations in the Semiotics of Texts*. Indianapolis: Indiana University Press.

Fallis, S.F., Fitzpatrick, M.A. and Friestad, M.S. (1985). 'Spouse's discussions of television portrayals of close relationships'. *Communication Research*, 12 (1), 59–81.

Fisher, C.D. (1974) 'A typological approach to communication in relationships'. In B. Rubin (ed.) *Communication Yearbook 1*. New Brunswick, NJ: Transaction Press.

Gerbner, G. and Gross, L. (1976) 'Living with television: the violence profile'. *Journal of Communication*, 26 (2), 173–99.

Goldsen, R.K. (1975) 'Throwaway husbands, wives, lovers (soap opera relationships)'. *Human Behaviour*, 4, 64–9.

Grant, D. (1970) *Realism*. London: Methuen.

Greenberg, B.S., Abelman, R. and Neuendorf, K. (1981) 'Sex on the soap operas: afternoon delight'. *Journal of Communication*, 31 (summer), 83–9.

——, Buerkel-Rothfuss, N., Neuendorf, K. and Atkin, C. (1980) 'Three seasons of television family role interactions'. In B.S. Greenberg (ed.) *Life on Television*. Norwood, NJ: Ablex Press.

Hall, S. (1980) 'Encoding/decoding'. In Hall, S., Hobson, D., Lowe, A. and Willis, P. (eds) *Culture, Media, Language*. London: Hutchinson.

——, Hobson D., Lowe A. and Willis, P (eds) (1980) *Culture, Media, Language*. London: Hutchinson.

Halliday, M.A.K. (1973) *Explorations in the Functions of Language*. London: Edward Arnold.

Halloran, J.D. (1970) 'The social effects of television'. In J.D. Halloran (ed.) *The Effects of Television*. London: Panther Books.

Hines, M., Greenberg, B. and Buerkel, N. (1979) *An Analysis of Family Structures and Interactions in Commercial Television: Project CASTLE* (Report No. 6). Department of Communication, Michigan State University, East Lansing.

Hobson, D. (1982) *Crossroads: The Drama of a Soap Opera*. London: Methuen.

Jones, M. (1984) 'The family on television: the portrayal of the family on British television'. In *The Family on Television: A Comparative Study by Content Analysis of the Way Television Portrays the Family in Denmark, Great Britain, Hungary and Australia*. München: Stiftung Prix Jeunesse International.

Kidd, K. (1979) 'Happily ever after and other relationship styles: advice on interpersonal relations in popular magazines, 1951–1973'. In G. Gumpert and R.'Cathcart (eds) *Inter/Media: Interpersonal Communication in a Media World*. Oxford: Oxford University Press.

Kreizenbeck, A. (1983) 'Soaps: promiscuity, adultery and new improved cheer'. *Journal of Popular Culture*, 17 (2), 175–81.

LaGuardia, R. (1983) *Soap World*. New York: Arbor House.

Lerman, C. (1983) 'Dominant discourse: the institutional voice and control of topiç'. In H. Davis and P. Walton (eds) *Language, Image, Media*. Oxford: Blackwell.

Livingstone, S.M. (1985) 'A semiotic analysis of a *Coronation Street* narrative'. Unpublished paper, February.

—— and Green, G. (1986) 'Television advertisements and the portrayal of gender'. *British Journal of Social Psychology*, 25, 149–54.

McNeil, J. (1975) 'Feminism, femininity and the television shows: a content analysis'. *Journal of Broadcasting*, 19, 259–69.

Mander, M.S. (1983) '*Dallas*: the mythology of crime and the moral occult'. *Journal of Popular Culture*, 17 (2), 44–50.

Masterman, L. (ed.) (1984) *Television Mythologies: Stars, Shows, and Signs*. London: Comedia/MK Media Press.

Morley, D. (1980) *The Nationwide Audience: Structure and Decoding*. British Film Institute Television Monograph No. 11.

Moscovici, S. (1984) 'The phenomenon of social representations'. In R.M. Farr and S. Moscovici (eds) *Social Representations*. Cambridge: Cambridge University Press.

Murray, K. (1985) 'Life as fiction'. *Journal for the Theory of Social Behaviour*, 15 (2), 173–88.

Porter, D. (1982) 'Soap time: thoughts on a commodity art form'. In H. Newcomb (ed.) *Television: The Critical View*. Oxford: Oxford University Press.

Potter, J. and Litton, I. (1985) 'Some problems underlying the theory of social representations'. *British Journal of Social Psychology*, 24, 81–90.

Silverstone, R. (1981) *The Message of Television: Myth and Narrative in Contemporary Culture*. London: Heinemann.

Skidmore, M.J. and Skidmore, J. (1983) 'More than mere fantasy: political themes in contemporary comic books'. *Journal of Popular Culture*, 17 (1), 83–92.

Sulieman, S. and Crossman, I. (eds) (1980) *The Reader in the Text*. Princeton: Princeton University Press.

Tuchman, G. (1981) 'Myth and the consciousness industry: a new look at the effects of the mass media'. In Katz, E. and Szecsko, T. (eds) *Mass Media and Social Change*. London: Sage.

Wober, J.M. and Gunter, B. (1987) *Television and Social Control*. Aldershot: Gower.

15 Narratives of relationship

Kenneth J. Gergen and Mary M. Gergen

SOCIAL ACCOUNTS AND THE VANISHING MIRROR

Social scientists have traditionally occupied themselves with the task of furnishing accurate descriptions and explanations of human conduct. The presumption is that scientific discourse about human conduct is (or ideally should be) a reflection of what people actually do. Yet, within recent enquiry into social accounting and accountability we discern a shift in sensibility that is both subtle and profound. The newly emerging questions concern the function of social description and explanation within social life: how do people justify or excuse their actions, create positive impressions, establish and maintain their 'moral careers' or gain others' agreement that X is the case and not Y. (See e.g. Antaki 1981; Harré 1983; Sabini and Silver 1982; Schlenker 1980; Semin and Manstead 1983; Shotter 1984). This work is invaluable in sensitizing us to the pragmatic purposes to which person talk is put within social relationships. Yet, just as our sensitivity to the social function of person description is increased by such undertakings, so our confidence in objective accuracy is undermined. If persons are successful in shifting the definition of their motives, emotions, intentions, beliefs, and the like, as they move through time and social context, then what is to be said of objective constraints? How and by what are such accounts to be corrected – either in science or everyday life? As descriptions and explanations come to be viewed as 'tellings,' as opposed to 'reports,' then the semantic link between word and action is eroded. Person description ceases to operate as a mirror of reality. Rather, it becomes a linguistic device for carrying out relationships. This is not the context for a discussion of principled impediments to a picture theory of language. The major point is that enquiry into a social accounting liberates the investigator to consider the form and function of person description in its own right – independent of its truth value.

One of our chief concerns in this regard has been with the process of story-telling in human relations. Stories furnish some of the first organized accounts of human action to which we are exposed in our lives. They absorb us as we read novels, biography, and history; they occupy us at the movies, the theater, and before the television set. And, possibly because of this intimate and long-standing acquaintanceship, they also serve as a critical means by which we make ourselves intelligible within the social world. We tell extended stories about our childhoods, our relations with family members, our years at school, our first love affair, the development of our thinking on a given subject, and so on. We also tell stories about last night's party, this morning's class, or lunch with a companion. We may even create a story to relate how we cut ourselves while shaving or scorched the breakfast muffins.

Given the prevalence of story-telling as a means of rendering accounts, we are confronted with a series of challenging and absorbing questions. Among them, for example, what rules or constraints govern the process of story-telling; can we identify major story forms within the culture; what are the historical antecedents of these forms, what functions do such stories serve within·social life; what is the relationship between such stories and patterns of action; and to what extent are scientific accounts also governed by the story form? Enquiry into a number of these issues is underway – both within psychology and adjoining disciplines of literary theory, philosophy of history, and anthropology. However, it is the chief aim of this paper to illuminate narratives of relationship – stories about and within social relationships. The enquiry is divided into three parts. First, we clarify certain aspects of narrative accounting – specifically, its rules, forms, and functions. We then turn to the issue of relational (as opposed to individualized) discourse, and enquire into its historical emergence. Finally we bring together these two concerns to treat forms and functions of relational narratives in social life. Here we shall be centrally concerned with narrative change across time.

THE WELL-FORMED NARRATIVE

If our concern is with the process of telling stories, we must have available a working definition of a story; how is a story to be differentiated from other forms of accounting? This issue is more than terminological, as in articulating the criteria for a proper story we are also beginning to elucidate fundamental rules of account-giving. That is, when we understand the restrictions on how we may tell stories about ourselves, we confront the limits of our ability to make ourselves understood. We cannot, without danger of becoming unintelligible, tell stories that break the rules of story-telling. To go beyond the rules is to engage in tales told by idiots. An outline of these rules can be derived from literary theory (Genette 1980), historiography (Mink 1969), and certain social scientific work (Bertaux and Kohli 1984; Labov 1984; Sutton-Smith 1979). This literature, in combination with some analytic work of our own, suggests that the well-formed narrative possesses at least the following components:

(1) *The establishment of a goal state.* In order to count as an acceptable story one must first establish a goal state, an end-point, or an event to be explained. For example, the end-point may be the protagonist's well-being ("how I narrowly escaped death"), the discovery of something precious ("how we fell in love"), or locating the meaning of events ("how we solved the mystery"). To tell a story without a goal state is essentially "to have no point." The rudimentary tale told by a child about his/her day at school is often lacking in just this component; the child seems to wander aimlessly from one detail to another (often to a parent's frustration). As adults we scarcely tolerate stories without established end-points, and these end-points are typically suffused with value.

(2) *Selection of events relevant to the goal state.* Once a goal is established it serves to dictate the kinds of events that can subsequently figure in the account. The myriad candidates for "eventhood" are reduced to but a small fraction by the establishment of the goal. An intelligible story is one in which events are selected that serve to make the goal state more or less probable. Thus, if one's story is about the winning of a football match ("how we won the game"), the kinds of events that are relevant are those that bring the goal closer or make it more distant (e.g. "Tom's first kick bounced off the goal, but with a thrust of his head he was able to deflect the ball into the net"). Only at great risk would one introduce into the story of a football match a note on fifteenth-century monastery life or a hope for future space travel.

(3) *Arrangement of events in chronological order.* At least on the level of informal story-telling, one is generally required to arrange the relevant events in a linear, temporal sequence. For example, certain events are said to occur at the beginning of the football match and these precede events that are said to take place toward the middle and the end. It is tempting to say that the sequence of related events should match the sequence in which the events actually occurred. However, this would be to confuse the rules of intelligible rendering with what is the case. Temporal ordering is, after all, a convention that employs an internally coherent system of signs; its features are not required by what is the case. Rather, the system may be applied or not to what is the case depending on one's purposes. Clock time may not be effective, for example, if one wishes to speak of one's "experience of time passing in the dentist's chair;" nor is it adequate if one wishes to describe relativity theory in physics. That yesterday preceded today is a conclusion demanded by rules of rhetoric and not events as they occur.

(4) *Establishing causal linkages.* By contemporary standards the ideal narrative is one in which the events preceding the goal state are causally linked. ("Because the rain came we fled indoors;" "As a result of his operation he couldn't meet his class.") This is not to subscribe to a

narrow, Humean view of causality. Rather, causal accounts are discursive forms in which the specific articulation of one event or series of events is said to require the occurrence of a subsequent event. What may be included within the acceptable range of causal forms is historically and culturally dependent. Thus, many scientists wish to limit discussions of causality to the Humean variety; social philosophers often prefer to view human action as caused by reason; botanists often find it more convenient to employ teleological forms of causality. However, when events within a narrative are related in a causal sense the outcome is a more coherent form of story.

(5) *Demarcation signs.* Most properly formed stories employ signals to indicate a beginning and ending. As Young (1982) has proposed, the narrative is "framed" by various rule-governed devices that indicate when one is entering the "tale world," or the world of the story. "Once upon a time ...," "Did you hear this one ...," "You can't imagine what happened to me on the way over here ...," or "Let me tell you why I'm so happy ..." would all be signals to the audience that a narrative is to follow. Endings may also be signaled by phrases (e.g. "So now you know what happened ...") but need not be. Laughter at the end of a joke may indicate the ending of the tale world; often the description of the story's point is sufficient to indicate that the tale world is terminated.

These five components appear to be critical to the well-formed narrative in contemporary western culture. This is not to say that all components are employed on all occasions. Just as in the case of grammar or dance forms, performances may vary considerably in the degree to which they approximate the ideal form. And, too, the concept of the narrative may and does evolve over time. Contemporary novelists, for example, often violate the existing forms and thereby invite the reader to consider alternative forms of intelligibility.

FORM AND PROCESS IN NARRATIVE CONSTRUCTION

Given these rudimentary constraints over the construction of contemporary narratives we may turn to related issues. We have elsewhere attempted to delineate common narrative forms – or story plots – and to enquire into their various social functions. Although literary and dramatic theorists have frequently tried to establish the "fundamental plots" available to the writers (cf. Frye 1957), such accounts have generally proved unsystematic or narrowly constraining. We believe that the present approach allows us to escape some of the traditional problems. Specifically, the present analysis makes it possible to derive available forms of plot from the components of narrative outlined above. As we have first seen, a story's end-point is weighted with value. Thus, the victory, the consummated affair, the discovered fortune, or the prize-winning paper, all might serve as valued goal states or story-endings. On the opposite end of the evaluative continuum would fall the defeat, the lover lost, the fortune squandered, or the profes-

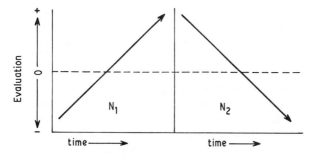

Figure 15.1 Progressive (N_1) and regressive (N_2) narratives

sional failure. Further, we can then view the various events that lead up to the story's end (components 2 and 3 above) as moving one through two-dimensional, evaluative space. As one approaches the valued goal over time, the story-line becomes more positive, and as one approaches failure, disillusionment and so on, one moves in the negative direction. All plots, then, may be converted to a linear form with respect to their evaluative shifts over time.

To clarify, let us consider two primitive plots. The first may be termed the *progressive narrative*. In this case there is a valued end-point, and the related events simply move steadily toward the accomplishment of this point. Voltaire's Pangloss, for example, professes that each year the world becomes better and better until the best is reached; this story would approximate a progressive narrative (see Figure 15.1). In contrast, to tell of the death of a friend in which each successive incident was increasingly dire, would constitute a *regressive narrative*. The goal state is negative, and each event brings the protagonist ever closer to the end-point (see Figure 15.1). Given these rudimentary narrative forms one can expand the scope to consider other commonly encountered prototypes. In previous work, for example, we have documented the trajectory of the tragedy, the Aristotelian comedy, the epic saga, the happily-ever-after-tale, and the dialectic progression (Gergen and Gergen 1983; in press). Further, by taking into account the direction and acceleration in the slope line we have been able to offer several insights into the creation of dramatic engagement – or the sense of dramatic excitement.

For present purposes, however, we wish to terminate this discussion with a consideration of the pragmatic functions of stories. Stories are often told for purposes of entertainment, and in such cases the creation of dramatic engagement is central. However, in most instances of everyday accounting, entertainment would appear to be of secondary significance. As it is commonly said, narrative accounts are used for purposes of conveying information. Yet, it would be a mistake to assume that what is meant by "conveying information" is the furnishing of an accurate portrayal. There is nothing about the nature of experience that demands any particular rendering of it. As we saw at the outset, in the focus on accounts, reality recedes from view. In this light it seems more appropriate to view the "conveying of information" in terms of illocutionary effects (Austin 1962). That is, we should be less concerned with the validity of narrative accounts than with the implications of such accounts for subsequent action – both on the part of the source and the audience. In this sense, narrative accounts are more like invitations to a dance than mirrors of reality; they suggest to the audience a range of actions that appropriately follow. They suggest to the audience how the source is to be treated or regarded and what they may anticipate from him or her.

Consider, for example, the use of the simple progressive and regressive narratives within a relationship. When a person portrays him/herself as demonstrating ever-increasing success, improvement, status, skill, and the like, there are important illocutionary effects. For a prospective employer such a narrative is a promise of future accomplishment, for a potential competitor it may be used to intimidate, and for a potential lover it is to demonstrate the advantages of union. Similarly, the regressive narrative may be employed for a variety of purposes within relationships. On certain occasions it may be used to elicit sympathy ("See what a miserable state I have fallen into"), and at others to obtain support ("Without your help I don't have a chance"). At still other times the regressive narrative may be used to dissociate one from a seeming position of inferiority (e.g. "You should realize that at one time I was the most deeply honored visitor here"). In all these instances, we find the narrative possesses important pragmatic functions within social encounters.

FROM THE INDIVIDUAL TO THE RELATIONAL NARRATIVE

Most of our work to date has been concerned with individuals' accounts of themselves, from brief self-portrayals to full biographical renderings. Although this analytic dissection is useful for certain purposes, it is also clear that the demarcation between self and others cannot be fully warranted. At the outset, as our earlier analysis demonstrated, individualized accounts typically include other persons – a supporting cast as it were. One's identity in such stories vitally depends on how members of the supporting cast are constructed, and vice versa. One cannot portray oneself as a leader unless others are constructed as followers; to regard oneself as altruistic requires others who agree they have been helped; to be a favorite daughter requires others who were less favored and so on. As one expands the focus to include the stories of others (often various audience members) it is rapidly realized that we exist in a state of ontological interdependence, where each participant's biographical constructions are dependent on the construals of others.

A second analytic departure is thus invited, one that distinguishes between a language of relatedness and a language of individuals. We must shift from a consideration of "I," "he," "she," or "it" to the narrative of

"we" and "they" – from individual narratives to stories of the superordinate form. In the remainder of the chapter we wish to open discussion on
narratives of relationship. We shall first consider the historical emergence
of relational accounting more generally, and then turn to their position
and deployment in narrative constructions.

ANTECEDENTS OF RELATION ACCOUNTS

Within the empiricist tradition it is held to hold that concepts about the
world are (to the extent that they are not mere fictions) derived from or
dependent on observations of the world. In effect, the scientist's vocabulary of understanding should ideally spring from the process of careful and
systematic scrutiny. Yet it has become increasingly clear within recent
decades that this view of the origins of concepts is deeply flawed. There is
little about observation (and this concept itself suffers from ambiguity)
that requires any particular array of categories. We are essentially free to
construe and reconstrue the world in any way that the culturally embedded rules of intelligibility will permit. Yet, if concepts do not spring from
the soil of observation, how are we to understand their genesis? At least
one important answer to this question emerges if we abandon the prevailing assumption that concepts are mental entities lying somewhere in the
skull. If one is willing to entertain this possibility it is no longer necessary
to grapple with the 2,000-year-old philosophic problem of determining
how ideas (concepts) spring from incoming sense data, and the equally
intractable problem of how concepts (as psychological elements) can ever
be converted into physical action. Rather than viewing concepts as mental
events or entities, it is more congenial within the present framework to
consider them as units within social discourse. For, after all, it would
appear that we use publicly shared words to name and to classify; whether
words have anything to do with a "mental world" of concepts remains
moot. If we make this shift from mind to discourse, we are positioned to
take a fresh look at the origin of concepts.

At least one important function served by discourse practices is that of
directing or influencing social action. If a mother can convince her children
that "sharing" is a virtue, she may enjoy hours of tranquility. If a suitor
can demonstrate that he is replete with fine qualities, he may win the love
he so desires. If a lawyer can persuade the jury that his/her client intended
to slay a bear rather than a business colleague, the client may go free. In
effect, if one's linguistic framing of the world prevails, the outcomes may
be substantial. Failing to achieve intelligibility in construction is to have
little role in the co-ordinated set of activities from which life satisfactions
are typically derived. From this perspective we may anticipate that fresh
concepts will be developed as they are required to move social proceedings
in various directions. Terms will be borrowed from other contexts (as in
the case of metaphors), they will be used in new composites (e.g. "air-
craft," "Fernsehen" – television, lit. "far-see"), or they will be developed

afresh by weaving various words and phrases into new definitions (e.g. "psychological burnout"). In each case the terms are employed for purposes of furthering a given project of action. The "domino" metaphor was used by American government administrators to garner public support for involvement in the war in Vietnam; the concept of "family therapy" enables therapists to justify a new set of therapeutic practices; and "star wars defense" enables President Reagan to pursue an increased defense budget.

To turn more directly to the issues at hand, it may fairly be said that within western culture the single individual has served as the chief subject of narrative explication. That is, people generally furnish accounts of themselves – "my past," "what I did," "what happened to me," and other singular entities. The individualized form of narrative accounting is favored by a wide variety of cultural constructions in western culture. Within the Judaeo-Christian tradition it is the individual who is held accountable for his/her actions. For Christians it is the individual who must repent, seek salvation, and who will face the final judgment. Similarly, within courts of law it is traditionally the individual who stands trial, whose intentions are judged, whose insanity is in question, and so on. Even when corporations are involved in crime, the responsibility is traced to single individuals. Similarly, democratic political institutions are built around the assumption of individual decision-making; each individual has a right to a vote, to an opinion, to free speech, and so on. The western concept of knowledge also lends itself to practice of individual accounting. As we saw, the traditional western belief is that concepts – or the adaptive representations of the world – are stored within the brains of single individuals. Thus, educational and assessment practices are typically focused on the mental processes of single individuals. Western economic practices, with their emphasis on the economic rationality of the single individual, and the associated practices of individual ownership, consumership, and employment are consistent with the individualized orientation of the culture more generally. The pragmatic benefits of individualized accounting are thus considerable.

The particular emphasis given to the individual has hardly escaped the notice of analysts and critics. In his analysis of Balinese culture, Geertz (1975) contrasts the role-centered emphasis – which tends to view persons as occupying niches within the more general system – with the more western view which holds that actors are fundamentally independent of systems (unless they voluntarily choose membership). In a similar vein Dworkin (1977) has differentiated between rights-based and duty-based ethical codes. The former, which place a strong emphasis on the rights of individuals (and which are largely western), are contrasted with the latter in which it is the society that is prior to the individual and to which the individual owes allegiance. While western culture tends to emphasize the former, cultures such as the Hindu (see Shweder and Miller 1985) tend to understand individuals primarily as they are situated with respect to the group. In his analysis of Marquesan culture, Kirkpatrick (1985) also makes note of the distinct lack of interest in individuality. In most instances in which individual characteristics are denoted, it is for purposes of bringing about relationships of mutual acceptance within a community. And, within cross-cultural social psychology, investigators have distinguished between cultures emphasizing individualized as opposed to collective values (Marin 1985). South American cultures are often contrasted with North American in their preferences for group as opposed to individual centered values.

Such distinctions have been paralleled by an energetic array of criticism of the western, individualized mode of accounting. Bellah and his colleagues (1985) argue that the priority given to the individual militates against the possibility for intimacy or commitment in the marital context. Lasch (1979) sees the emphasis placed on the individual as approximating a form of cultural narcissism. Sampson (1977, 1986) has attacked the idealization of the "self-contained individual" in psychology for its obscuring the potential of co-operative relationships and its ultimate threat to world peace.

Such critiques seem particularly appropriate, and worthy of the most serious consideration. However, it would be a mistake to conclude that western culture is peculiarly lacking in relational accounts. Albeit more obscured, less differentiated, and often implicit, relational discourse is available to cultural participants. In crudest form the shift from an individualistic language to the collective requires only a simple alteration in personal pronouns – from "I" to "we," from "he" and "she" to "they." However, there are more extended languages of description and explanation reserved for collectivities as opposed to individuals. In this light it is interesting to consider the emergence of one major form of relational language – that employing micro-social or face-to-face encounters.

RELATIONS, PASSIONS, AND THE FEMININE VOICE

One of the most fundamental units of relationship in western culture is that said to exist between man and woman. Some argue that this relational unit, typically built around the bearing and sustenance of children, is primeval in origin (Westermarck 1921). Others propose that the more discrete sub-unit of the family was preceded by a tribal phase (Morgan 1877; Muller-Lyer 1931). That is, a language of verbal identity may have been available before one that singled out family and particularly couples as the significant units. Employing such materials Frederick Engels (1942) advanced the thesis that the tribe or class as the fundamental unit gave way to the family as variations began to emerge in patterns of material possession. As certain individuals acquired land, cattle, food, and so on, the language of community was eroded. Further because of such differences in economic power, and the fact that women were generally among the have-nots, women came to be rightful possessions of men. "Family" was thus a term employed by males to single out a range of persons (wife, children, and others) under their ownership. Yet, one must also suppose that "the family" as the major unit was also a valuable construct for those who were protected by their membership. By virtue of "family membership" their sustenance and security were preserved. To the extent that this concept could be buttressed by artefact (by adding family names, crests, trades, and so on), fleshed out with a language of role differentiation (e.g. father, mother, son, brother, sister, etc.), furnished with a sense of history (as in the "family tree"), and endowed with some form of sanctity (as enjoyed, for example, within the Judaeo-Christian tradition), both ownership and protection could be ensured.

Yet there was an additional and more variegated language that was necessitated in the familial arrangement. From earliest times to the present century women have typically (but not always) occupied a position of lesser power than men within the family system. Saint Paul, in his epistle to the Ephesians, counsels women to obey the master of the house. Early Greek wedding ceremonies treated the woman much as property. In medieval times, for example, a marriage ceremony typically required the woman to kneel before her new master (her husband) and swear her allegiance. However, this position of diminished power was typically coupled with a high degree of insecurity. The woman could be abandoned at the will of her master. To again use the medieval illustration, new wives were often viewed as "intruders" into their master's household, objects of powerful and long-lasting distrust. Their primary task was to bring into the world a male heir. To control the blood-line their dedication to the master was under closest scrutiny. In contrast, the master was virtually unconstrained in his activities. Thus, the wife could be repudiated by the husband for any extra-marital attachment, for failure to produce an heir, or because she proved less desirable than a new favorite (Duby 1978). Further problems confronted the wife in the age of industrialization (and to the present). As Dizard and Gadlin (1985) propose, the increased availability of employment outside the home (the family-run farm or cottage industry), decreased the male's dependency on the family unit. Rather, the male became increasingly committed to a dependent outside the factory or market for sustenance (and often companionship). As a result the position of the female was again jeopardized. The male was economically and socially supported; the female was left with the task of securing his continued commitment.

This perennially precarious position of the female, it may be proposed, invited the development of a more elaborate language of relations. In particular, for the female there was a need for a specialized language that could enhance the power of the female in the domain of informal interchange, bond the male more securely, and thereby enhance the sense of security. In part the establishment of "unithood" could be accomplished through the apotheosis of sexual congress. Heterosexual intercourse could be conceptualized as a fundamental form of relatedness and endowed with deep and sometimes mysterious value. The rudiments for such a construction were long available within the history of western culture. In particular the imagery of sexual intercourse lent itself uniquely to a language of unity. Further, there was reason for others (especially males) to agree with such a conception. It was in the male's interest to sanctify the relationship as a means of threatening those (including his wife) who might otherwise corrupt the blood-line. Both the Christian and Jewish faiths had also placed a value on the relationship, largely, it would appear, to ensure that there were social units that could be entrusted with imparting the faith to succeeding generations. And finally, the courtly tradition had also idealized the heterosexual relationship, largely it appears because of a male/female ratio in which the female was a scarce commodity (Secord and Guttentag 1985).

However, the establishment of the male and female as a bonded and valued unit was but a crude implement for influencing the course of events. More variegated in its potential for altering the course of interaction, from initial encounter onward, was the discourse of emotion. Emotional terms serve as major tools for distinguishing among states of relationship and their value. As DeRivera (1984) has pointed out, most emotion terms are inherently relational. One feels love *toward* another; hatred, envy, admiration, pity, scorn, and the like all have an object. In effect, emotion terms cannot easily be made properties of single individuals. Each term implies a state of relationship between one person and another. Such terms can be contrasted to the mental predicates of the Enlightenment, such as "reasoning," "thinking," and "planning." Such terms do not presuppose a necessary connection between the individual and others. Further, emotion terms are inherently valuational. The manner in which they are used places a high value on the state of love, while devaluing states of anger or hatred. Each term within the emotional vocabulary thus acquires particular, pragmatic implications. To say "You don't love me any more" furnishes a request or demand for one kind of reaction, while "I detest you" has dramatically different implications for subsequent activity. Likewise, declaring the presence or absence of "passion," "fear," "jealousy," "anger," and so on are each useful as means of guiding the course of human interchange.

In this sense we can appreciate why women have generally exceeded men in their capacity to employ the arts of emotional language (cf. Komarowsky 1967, 1976; Levinger, Rands, and Talaber 1977). Further we can understand why men have traditionally been guarded in emotional expression, and wary of women for their seeming preoccupation with emotion. As we see, women employ emotion discourse (and associated performances) for purposes of securing and retaining the commitment of the male. They will become adept at emotional performances as a means of challenging the male's inclinations toward independence. They will seek to justify the significance of emotion in human life (as in poetry, music, art, religion), as a means of increasing its impact within the pragmatic process of negotiating their degree of "bondedness." In contrast, males will typically find emotion talk (and associated performances) alien if not bizarre (the woman as inscrutable), and so develop a linguistic arsenal that will combat its effects (typically the language of the individual, with its emphasis on rationality and objectivity). They may mount various critical attacks both on the emotions and on those who display them.

Already within the classical Greek period Logos, or reason, was associated (by males) with light, the higher regions of the divine, and with the man. In contrast, Pathos (or the passions; also the root for passive) was equated with darkness, the nether regions, and with woman. The male antipathy toward female emotion continues into the eighteenth-century European society and the rise of rationalism among the ruling élite. To cite only one vignette, as it was said of the latter period, that "when you have written a genuine bit of love poetry, the last place ... in which you think of seeking the applause of a congenial audience, would be the smoking room of your [men's] club" (Stephen 1904, p. 81). The prominent Lord Chesterfield was said to be in admiration of deRochenfocould, whose writing on women "always speaks of them with true aristocratic contempt." Chesterfield believed that "a man of sense will humor [women] and flatter them; he will never consult them seriously, nor really trust them, but he will make them believe that he does both. They are invaluable as tools, though contemptible in themselves" (Stephen 1904, p. 113).

Of course, much the same antinomy continues to shape contemporary life. Social psychological research indicates, for example, that males in western culture are typically characterized (by both men and women) as unemotional, independent, objective, not excitable, logical, and able to separate ideas from feelings (Rosenkrantz, Vogel, and Bee 1968). In contrast, females are said to be aware of feelings of others and expressive of tender feelings. So long as the romance novel, the soap opera, and religious organizations continue to cater predominantly to a female audience, the female's edge in matters of "emotional knowledge" – and thus their roles as keepers of the relationship – is likely to remain.

Vestiges of these differential discourse capacities are also evident in the academic sphere. When scholars such as Carol Gilligan (1982) and Norma Haan (1985) attack Kohlberg's theory of moral reasoning on grounds that it ignores the relational quality of mature, moral decision-making, and for its emphasis on reasoning capacities (cool, empty, and arrogant), they are doing far more than engaging in a topical scholarly debate. In their attempt to embed moral decision-making in ongoing relationships, they are engaging in an enduring cultural ritual. They are bringing the rhetoric of relationship into the domain of male-dominated scholarship and they are adding further lustre to the rhetoric of relationship by demonstrating its advantages over the rhetoric of individuality to which male scholarship has so long been committed. Similarly, when feminist scholars attack the traditional scientific methods of experimentation for both their inhumanity and their implicit value biases, they are again bringing the language of the hearth into the male-dominated sphere of the scientific laboratory. In recognizing the inherent relationship between subject and object and the values (emotional investments) underlying scientific propositions, they are undermining an epistemological position that has long been essential to the individualized argot of the masculine world.

THE PRAGMATICS OF THE RELATIONAL NARRATIVE

With a preliminary understanding of narrative accounts, and the emergence of relational language, we now turn to a wedding of these two domains. We do this by focusing on the way in which narrative accounts are deployed within social settings. As we have seen, narratives are important as practical implements in carrying out social interchange; and we have further discussed how relational language has also served to increase protection, support, commitment, and the like. In linking the narrative format with the language of relations we open a new set of vistas related to the pragmatics of relational narratives. Let us explore some of the more prominent features of this union. Specifically, we explore the pragmatic implications of three broadly shared relational narratives and the manner in which they unfold within an ongoing interchange.

Unification myths

At the outset, means are required for replacing individualistic language in favor of a relational discourse. One of the major means of achieving this end is through what may be termed *unification myths*, i.e. stories that depict the transition from the individualized status to that of relational member and endow the latter with value. Most married couples, for example, possess a shared story of "how we got together" or moved from a state of singlehood to being "joined in matrimony." Religious sects often help their members develop stories of their "becoming one with Christ." A similar function may be played by initiation processes (e.g. army boot camp, fraternity hazing); such initiation rights furnish the raw materials out of which unification myths can be developed. The difficult training regimen that many athletic teams demand of their players before the season often serves the same end. Through these various means one "sees the light," "becomes close," "develops brotherhood," "joins the gang," and so on. By use of the story form, the reality of relationship is achieved.

It is hardly accidental that most unification myths take on the form of a progressive narrative. That is, they are stories in which unification serves as the goal state, while the condition of individualization is treated as a devalued starting-point. As the story unfolds the individual moves from the devalued status of being an individual to the goal of unification. The loneliness, directionless, and incompleteness of singlehood is at last relieved by the merging with the other. For fundamentalists, one moves from a state of being a lost soul, damned to hell, to a state of grace in God. For military units, clubs, teams, and the like one is typically viewed as naive, undeveloped, weak, and the like before becoming one of the group.

By adopting the form of the progressive narrative, and anchoring it with the negative state of individualization on the one side and the positive goal of relational unity on the other, the latter state is imbued with value. The state of unity is vindicated, and a subsequent return by either member to a more individualized form of accounting (or to practices said to be individual-centered) are subject to criticism and correction. Thus, in the telling and retelling of the story of "our romance," "finding Jesus," "becoming a team member," and so on, the power of the relational rhetoric is continuously reinvigorated. With the mythologizing of the road to unification, patterns of commitment are further buttressed.

After unification: the plight of regression

Perhaps the chief problem with unification myths is indeed their progressive character. As we have seen, such myths indirectly treat the act of unification as a goal or a positive end-point. As a result, the collaborators in the construction are left at the beginning of their fully recognized relationship in an ascendant position. They have at last achieved transcendent status. How is the subsequent narrative then to proceed? From the theoretical standpoint outlined earlier there are three possibilities, and two of them prove to be problematic. The first is to continue the trajectory – "our story" – in the positive direction. However, this option is inhibited because the putative goal of the story has already been achieved. The goal of unification is secured; bliss is at hand. This is not to say that fresh progressive narratives cannot be achieved. When a couple plan a baby, a team vows to work toward a winning season, and a business group sets out to achieve a new sales high, they are setting the stage for a fresh, progressive narrative. However, in each case the participants must face the task of hammering out the new goal state and organizing events around it.

The second possibility for the participants is the establishment of a stability narrative, i.e. a story of "our continuing success." In this case the participants continue to boast of their achievement of unification, their membership, their interdependence, and the like (see the Gergen and Gergen [1983] discussion of the "happily ever after" narrative). However, this option also possesses difficulties. For a start it furnishes to others, and to the participants as well, a picture of stagnation. It violates the common value placed on growth, development, or positive change (the progressive narrative). Further, the stability narrative is essentially without dramatic force. As explained in earlier treatments (cf. Gergen and Gergen 1983), the dramatic impact of a narrative construction is primarily dependent upon (a) rapid ascent or descent along the narrative slope, or (b) a change in the direction of the slope line itself. Drama occurs when one is rapidly reaching a positive goal state, rapidly approaching a negative goal state, or undergoing a change in fortune (from success to failure, or vice versa). The stability narrative precludes such possibilities, and thus burdens the participants with the sense of ennui. "Nothing ever happens to us," "we are in a rut," "we are going nowhere," "the organization has lost its vitality," etc.

The result of these difficulties is that participants in a relational construction are left with the temptation of engaging in a regressive narrative. If new goals are not established and the drama of relationship is not to be lost, the participants must begin to entertain the possibilities of failure. "I fear we are falling out of love," "our relationship is going to the dogs," "our friendship is not as close as it used to be," "the sense of fraternity is being lost," "I don't think we really trust and depend on each other like we did last year," "this organization is really coming apart at the seams." All such phrasings are common constituents of the regressive narrative. They are readily available and invited by those who have made themselves out to have achieved the goal of communion, and who wish to retain a sense of drama within the relationship.

Yet, with each movement into the abyss, the possibilities for positive development are reinstated. Further, as the goal of re-established communion presents itself, the possibility for dramatic engagement is furthered. For, as we have seen, the sense of drama is intensified when the direction of the narrative slope is altered – in this case from negative (failure) to positive (growth). In the prospects of a change for the better, drama is rekindled. Thus, the confrontation of loss furnishes the participants with the possibility of new progressive potential. "Let's try to find each other again," "a holiday is just the thing we need to recover our romance," "some new programs would help us to recreate our sense of mission." In each case a new and potentially exciting story is about to begin.

The romantic saga and the emergence of "deep communion"

As we see, unification myths serve a vital function in creating the reality of relationship, and such myths lend themselves to subsequent narratives of regressive form. The latter, in turn, give rise to the renegotiation of goals and the subsequent unfolding of a progressive narrative. Yet, as rapidly discerned, as the new summit is approached the context is again set for stabilization and the attendant sense of lethargy. In effect, the problem created by the initial myth of unification is reinstituted. With the summit once again attained, there is virtually nowhere to go but down. Over time, this alteration of pro- and regressive narratives should give rise to a new form of story – what we have termed the *romantic saga* (see Figure 15.2). In the romantic saga the protagonist(s) confront(s) life as a series of battles won and lost. Each victory leads to a subsequent loss – the hero defeats an enemy, only to find that he/she has played into the hands of a new foe. The couple finds that their precious goal of unification confronts them with defeat at the hands of stultification; they respond by seeking new interests they may share together, only to find that their new hobby is leading them into painful competition with each other.

It is our experience that there is one highly significant outcome of the

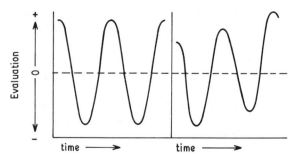

Figure 15.2   Romantic saga and deep communion narratives

romantic saga for the definition of the relationship. Preliminary explanation is required. Social definition is essentially contextual in character.
That is, when words are employed to etch out the existence of an event,
one moves from the accepted realm of existants, forming the context of
understanding, into the vacuum of the unformed. We must employ an
existing context of understandings to forge a new event. The more extended the existing context, the more clearly and powerfully the newly
formed event can be inscribed. To illustrate and make relevant, persons
who have experienced only scant interchange will have considerable difficulty in declaring that they have a "relationship." There is simply not
enough raw contextual material upon which they can draw to make out a
case for a "tangible" sense of unification. To create a sense of relatedness
requires a context of events ("Do you remember when we did ...," "what
happened when ...," "our day at ...") from which definition of relatedness can be derived. The greater the number of these events, the stronger
or more palpable the construction of "our relationship."

   In the case of the romantic saga, the participants are creating as by-
products of an extended context of events. They are creating memorable
high-points, troughs, and dramas of change. As a result they are positioned
to establish a new and more palpable definition of relatedness. This definition, which can be termed *deep communion*, will be of a specific kind: at
its core it will define relatedness as a movement through highs and lows.
The earlier unification myth will be replaced. No longer will relatedness be
the result of a constant progression toward a positive goal state. It will be
the result of goods and bads, thicks and thins, sickness and health, wins
and losses. However, this emerging definition of deep communion should
engender a greater sense of reality than that resulting from the initial
unification myth.

   In the case of communion myths the progressive form was employed to
give an enhanced sense of value to the goal of relatedness. With minor
alteration in historical reconstruction this same tactic may be used to
intensify the value of deep communion. In particular one may view the
array of peaks and valleys as positively accelerated: over time the peaks
become higher and the valleys shallower (Figure 15.2). In effect the highs

and lows are leading to a "new and more profound" condition. As it is professed, the hostility, depression, boredom, and anxiety were all essential as entry fees to the state of mature connection.

CONCLUDING CAVEATS

We have now unfolded a story of narratives in developing relationships. It is a story with a beginning (independence) and an end ("the reality of relatedness"); the chapters in the story are causally linked – each follows ineluctably from the preceding account; and as we have told it, the narrative slope is positively inclined (the final goal of deep communion is achieved). Our account has thus approximated the demands of narrative accounting, and generated what we thereby hope to be a sense of intelligibility. However, intelligibility in this instance is bought at a dear price. There are opposing understandings of persons and relations that stand in the wings, and whose appearance has been painfully prevented by the demands of our analysis to this point. Our account must be qualified in several important ways.

As we have seen, narrative accounts can serve a wide variety of pragmatic functions. They may be used to create various kinds of expectations, to challenge, to gain sympathy, to create a sense of union, and so on. Pragmatic requisites may also shift rapidly with time and circumstance. A relational narrative that was serviceable in one condition may not be in another. As a result, we should not anticipate a high degree of consistency among narrative constructions across time. People may well reverse or abandon any given story on another time or occasion. The emerging love story may be abandoned when a worthy competitor arrives to make his/her bid for intimacy; the progressive story of the business organization may be obscured if a threat of failure is required for enhancing enthusiasm to a new sales enterprise; the departure of a group member may lead to a self-protective retelling of the group history, and so on. Thus, the route from the unification myth to deep communion may be subject to frequent disruption.

As we have also proposed, once a goal state is established it helps to determine how the preceding reality is to be constructed – what is to be counted as an event and how it is to be related to other such realities. To tell the story of a bitter failure requires that the preceding reality be divided into events that bear on this conclusion. What might have been an "interesting exchange of opinions," "a clearing of the air," or even a non-event in one story, may be counted as a "bitter attack" if figuring in a tale of why one quit one's job. As narrative constructions are developed for various purposes over time, one accumulates an array of events without necessary connection or coherence. One has at one's disposal a range of symbolic artefacts from an assortment of often conflicting realities. And, in spite of their potential disarray, each of these events may seem fully compelling – constituting the "really real." Such an accumulation may frequently stand in the way of constructing a smooth and coherent narrative in any future occasion, and may inhibit the kind of narrative unfolding we have outlined above. Past "realities" can creep into consciousness at any time, and prevent an easy reconstruing. Such difficulties may be especially great when the realities are shared – a product of interdependent negotiation. One may greatly resent it when a "deeply touching moment" of a past unification myth is reduced to trivia in a subsequent regressive challenge. Sedimented realities stand as impediments to historical reconstruction.

SUMMARY

The present chapter has centered on the way in which people construct realities. We have first been concerned with the rules that govern the way we make ourselves intelligible through stories. If we are furnishing biographical accounts to others, how must we proceed? We then opened consideration on relational accounts. In western culture we traditionally accept the reality of individuals. However, relational constructions also play an important role in social life, and their emergence in western culture is of interest. Finally we joined these two strands to consider relational narratives. As we found, such narratives often progress in a characteristic way as persons tell of their lives together across time. This is not to say that such a trajectory is inescapable, only that it is invited by contemporary convention. Surely the tale of regression that many men and women make of their lives together stands in contradiction to the present analysis. The question raised for the future is why a sense of deep communion fails to be achieved in such cases. A new story is required.

REFERENCES

Antaki, C. (ed.) (1981) *The Psychology of Ordinary Explanations of Social Behaviour*. London: Academic Press.

Austin, J. (1962) *How to Do Things with Words*. Cambridge, MA: Harvard University Press.

Bellah, R.N., Madsen, R., Sullivan, W.M., Swidler, A., and Tipton, S.M. (1985) *Habits of the Heart*. Berkeley, CA: University of California Press.

Bertaux, D. and Kohli, M. (1984) "The life story approach: a continental view." *American Sociological Review*, 10, 215–37.

DeRivera, J. (1984) "The structure of emotional relationships." In P. Shaver (ed.) *Review of Personality and Social Psychology*. Beverly Hills, CA: Sage.

Dizard, J.E. and Gadlin, H. (1984) "Family life and the marketplace: diversity and change in the American family." In K. Gergen and M. Gergen (eds) *Historical Social Psychology*. Hillsdale, NJ: Lawrence Erlbaum.

Duby, G. (1978) *Medieval Marriage*. Baltimore: Johns Hopkins University Press.

Dworkin, R. (1977) *Taking Rights Seriously*. Cambridge, MA: Harvard University Press.

Engels, F. (1942) *The Origin of the Family, Private Property and the State*. New York: International Publishers.

Frye, N. (1957) *Anatomy of Criticism*. Princeton, NJ: Princeton, University Press.

Geertz, C. (1973) *Interpretation of Cultures*. New York: Basic Books.

Genette, G. (1980) *Narrative Discourse*. Ithaca, NY: Cornell University Press.

Gergen, K.J. and Gergen, M.M. (1983) "The social construction of helping relationships." In J.D. Fisher, A. Nadler, and B. DePaulo (eds) *New Directions in Helping*, vol. 1. New York: Academic Press.

—— (in press) "Narrative form and the construction of psychological theory." In T. Sarbin (ed.) *The Narrative Perspective in Psychology*. New York: Praeger.

Gergen, M.M. and Gergen, K.J. (1984) "The social construction of narrative accounts." In K. Gergen and M. Gergen (eds) *Historical Social Psychology*. Hillsdale, NJ: Lawrence Erlbaum.

Gilligan, C. (1982) *In a Different Voice*. Cambridge, MA: Harvard University Press.

Haan, N., Aerts, E., and Cooper, B. (1985) *On Moral Grounds*. New York: New York University Press.

Harré, R. (1983) *Personal Being*. Cambridge, MA: Harvard University Press.

Kirkpatrick, J. (1985) "How personal differences can make a difference." In K.J. Gergen and K.E. Davis (eds) *The Social Construction of the Person*. New York: Springer-Verlag.

Komarowsky, M. (1967) *Blue Collar Marriage*. New York: Vintage.

——, Burke, R.J., Weir, T., and Harrison, D. (1976) "Disclosure of problems and tensions experienced by marital partners." *Psychological Reports*, 38, 531-42.

Labov, W. (1981) "Speech actions and reactions in personal narrative." In D. Tanner (ed.) *Analyzing Discourse: Text and Talk*. Washington, DC: Georgetown University Press.

Lasch, C. (1978) *The Culture of Narcissism*. New York: Norton.

Levinger, G., Rands, M., and Talaber, R. (1977) "The assessment and rewardingness of close pair relationships." Unpublished manuscript.

Marin, G. (1985) "Validez trans-cultural del principio de equidad." Paper presented at the Interamerican Congress of Psychology, Caracas, Venezuela.

Miller-Lyer, F. (1931) *The Family*, trans. F.W. Stella Browne. London: George Allen & Unwin.

Mink, L.A. (1969) "History and fiction as modes of comprehension." *New Literary History*, 1, 556–69.

Morgan, L.H. (1877) *Ancient Society*. New York: World Publishing Co.

Rosenkrantz, P.S., Vogel, S.R., and Bee, M. (1968) "Sex-role stereotypes and self-concepts in college students." *Journal of Consulting and Clinical Psychology*, 32, 287–95.

Sabini, J. and Silver, M. (1982) *The Moralities of Everyday Life*. London: Oxford University Press.

Sampson, E. (1977) "Psychology and the American ideal." *Journal of Personality and Social Psychology*, 35, 767–82.

—— (1986) "Deconstructing psychology's subject." *Journal of Mind and Behavior*, 4, 135–63.

Schlenker, B.R. (1980) *Impression Management: The Self Concept, Social Identity and Interpersonal Relations*. Monterey, CA: Brooks Cole.

Secord, P.F. (1984) "Love, misogyny and feminism in selected historical periods: a socio-psychological explanation." In K. Gergen and M. Gergen (eds) *Historical Social Psychology*. Hillsdale, NJ: Lawrence Erlbaum.

Semin, G. and Manstead, A.S.R. (1983) *The Accountability of Conduct*. London: Academic Press.

Shotter, J. (1984) *Social Accountability and Selfhood*. Oxford: Blackwell.

—— (1985) "Social accountability and self specification." In K.J. Gergen and K.E. Davis (eds) *The Social Construction of the Person*. New York: Springer-Verlag.

Shweder, R.A. and Miller, T.G. (1985) "The social construction of the person: how is it possible?" In K.J. Gergen and K.E. Davis (eds) *The Social Construction of the Person*. New York: Springer-Verlag.

Stephen, L. (1904) *English Literature and Society in the XVIIIth Century*. London: Duckworth.

Sutton-Smith, B. (1980) *The Folkstories of Children*. Philadelphia, PA: University of Pennsylvania Press.

Westermarck, E. (1921) *The History of Human Marriage*, vol. 1. London: Macmillan.

Young, K. (1982) "Edgework: frame and boundary in the phenomenology of narrative communication." *Semiotica*, 41, 277–315.

16 From self-reports to narrative discourse: reconstructing the voice of experience in personal relationship research

Patrick McGhee

> What is truth? A moving army of metaphors, metonymies and anthropomorphisms, in short a summary of human relationships that are being poetically and rhetorically sublimated, transposed, and beautified until, after long and repeated use, a people considers them as solid, canonical, and unavoidable. Truths are illusions whose illusionary nature has been used up and have lost their imprint and that now operate as mere metal, no longer as coins.
>
> (Nietzsche, in Culler [1983, pp. 203–4])

In this chapter I want to suggest that much of the research being carried out under the 'personal relationship' (PR) banner is radically misconceived. Central to this misconception are (1) the lack of any explicit theory of the main methodological tool, the self-report and (2) a pre-theoretical and implicit commitment to a representational 'cinematic' epistemology. Since PR research seems to need more than anything else a conception of what people are doing when they speak of their personal experience, recent attempts by linguists to analyse 'experience talk' will be reviewed. At an elementary level the motivation of this piece is the notion that coherent conceptual analyses are a pre-condition for intelligible empirical studies and to examine experience talk in its natural habitat – the conversational account – as a positive response to contemporary misgivings about self-report methodologies.

A SCIENCE OF PERSONAL RELATIONSHIPS?

The current 'scientific' approach to personal relationships (representational epistemology, non-reflexive, objective, neopositivist) seems only able to address phenomena by characterizing relationships as the internal emotional and cognitive residue of external interpersonal occurrences rather than as interpretative activity and this has had particular consequences for the study of people's relationship 'experience'. Goffman (1974) reminded us how attempts to make 'cinematic' (representational) copies of reality are fundamentally misconceived because 'what the cinematic version would be a copy of, that is, an unreal instance of, would itself be something that was not homogeneous with respect to reality, itself shot through with various framings and their various realms' (Goffman 1974, p. 561). It is my argument here that PR research attempts to make copies of reality but behind this official activity is the necessary business of dealing with the shared interpretative frameworks in which personal relationships are lodged; such dealings being required to accomplish the social episode(s) of the research situation. In a sense PR research presents itself as an intellectual voyage of discovery – but can be reconsidered as a process of rediscovery through our own backyards. The reality-modelling aspect of empirical PR work as executed and reported occludes the interpretative practices that necessarily attend the elicitation of self-reports. These practices are so routine and regularized as to be invisible and as routinized structures of interpretation operate to make empirical studies feasible and research reports intelligible.

THE SELF-REPORT QUESTIONNAIRE

Recognized problems of the self-report in psychological research

Over 65 per cent of empirical papers published in the *Journal of Social and Personal Relationships* (first seven numbers, n = 35) used a simple form of questionnaire self-report. More striking, less than 10 per cent comment on the validity of their methodology (McGhee 1985). Just what is involved in giving a self-report seems to be of no interest to PR researchers. Certainly, the self-report attitude scale has been the subject of numerous criticisms over many years and has been specifically criticized in the field of PR by McCarthy (1981). For example, it has been stated countless times that report scales are fakeable, that they assume both an attitude–behaviour correlation that is in fact notoriously low and that it is meaningful for subjects to attend to the component parts of their beliefs or attitudes. Additionally Harré (1979) has highlighted the process of the social construction of data in the laboratory and argued that there is not necessarily any research data prior to the posing of the research question. In general it is taken for granted that the marks on scales are transparent for both subject and researcher. It is doubtful whether researchers and subjects achieve any great level of mutual comprehensibility and highly unlikely that, to the extent that it is achieved, it is in the way desired by the researcher. Overall there is the faith in the capacity of the subject to map the scale onto the dimensions of his experience and to reflect the latter in the former. McCarthy's observation has been universally ignored:

> Since many of the questions researchers ask in the area of personal relationships concern participants' motivational and other cognitive/ affective responses on occasions in the past, the implications of the Nisbett and Wilson thesis for the ways in which we go about our research activities are profound.   (McCarthy 1981, p. 28)

The way this disattention appears in the PR research report will be covered in detail later.

The theory of PR that underlies the use of self-reports

Linguistic communication in the form of a truncated paper and pencil questionnaire conversation is seen as an unproblematic technical resource for the PR researcher – a way of getting information from one place to another, with, hopefully, minimal transmission distortion – yet the tele-mentational theory of language that tacitly underwrites such a practice is a myth (Harris 1981). As pointed out by De Carlo (1981) psychologists have no real explicit model about what people are doing when they fill in a self-report. In the absence of an official theory of method the question arises: why do PR researchers feel that asking people about their relationships is a way of examining those relationships? As regards the ideology of the person that underlies this pre-theoretical decision a number of factors are probably at work that might be termed the doctrines of co-extension, participant status, homeostasis and internality, all of which are required to legitimize the use of the subject as an access to the relationship.

First, there would seem to be the assumption that overall there is a general co-extension of subject and object – a person's relationship cannot be where the person is not. Yet, if we pay any heed to sociologists at all then this is not a necessary decision; gossip, medical records, artefacts and property about and of the couple are in a sense partly constitutive of 'the' relationship within a society. Similarly, since a relationship cannot be accomplished in isolation from social structures and beliefs the distribution of knowledge necessary for the bringing off of a relationship is not limited entirely to the couple.

Second, there is the notion of the subject's 'participant status' with respect to the relationship – s/he is presumed to be privy to certain information about the relationship, has certain rights of agency over and within it, and certain obligations of effect (a 'duty to attend'); in other words psychologists ascribe a sort of chronic 'mutual presence' between partners – they are assumed to be monitoring the actions and decisions of the other (see Goffman 1955).

Third, there would seem to be a separate but equally general notion that as individuals people do not just experience PRs, but that they experience them increasingly clearly and unequivocally. In other words, that people monitor their experience and will actually do something about it, ultimately achieving some kind of perceptual and experiential homeostasis in their relationships.

Fourth, the decision by PR researchers to use self-report scales in the way they do betrays a belief on their part that relationships are primarily *internal experiences* (rather than, say, particular kinds of social organizations), and as such fundamentally non-linguistic – yet also that those (reactive) experiences can be given linguistic form.

As regards what might traditionally be called the *cognitive* assumptions typically made in these studies, it is clear that (in contrast to their colleagues in mainstream cognitive psychology) PR researchers have an operational model of their subjects for the purposes of research that treats them as having a spectacular amount of cognitive insight, as being in possession of an impressive long-term memory – though possessing distinctly limited *computational* abilities – but, above all else, as pathologically high self-monitors. In general, the idea is that subject self-reports are readouts rather than deployments of knowledge. There would thus appear to be a major contradiction characteristic of social psychology in general and PR research in particular: subjects are assumed to be reasonable people to get information from about the social world because they are assumed to be active, monitoring agents intimately involved with understanding and interpreting their interpersonal experiences, yet it is that very reflexive interpretative, computational ability that has to be put into suspended animation in order that questionnaires can be used as technical instruments that find rather than construct a particular interpretation.

It is worthwhile to sensitize ourselves to the rhetoric of the psychological research report. It can be observed for example that statistics, as well as providing an opportunity for occasional mathematical pyrotechnics, serve to facilitate the subtle shifts from discourse on that which is, to discourse on that which is said to be.

Latour and Woolgar (1979) have pointed out how scientific discourse is sustained by all parties to it subscribing to conventions of rationality and consequently authors are required to *introduce* logic into their papers – as opposed to reason being an intrinsic property of the scientific enterprise itself. The major task for the researcher reporting his or her study is to establish that their engagement with reality is such that it actually touches upon that which they claim to be building a theory about. In PR research this is inordinately difficult to do. And since theories are rooted in profoundly equivocal concepts researchers are able to collapse the grammars of reality and of self-reports into one and present their work as a metaphysical excursion beyond both.

A grammar of PR research reports

As an analytic framework with which to approach official glosses of PR research (i.e. the journal research report) I propose the following simple schema, which can be applied to any standard research report to highlight where we are likely to find ontology shifts. What I want to suggest is that one of the ways PR researchers finesse the problems of self-report validity is to write up their research reports as a Drama of Nouns (as does to a large extent a great deal of social psychology which uses questionnaires). Characters in this drama pass through various episodes in various worlds, each with its own grammar. Popular heroes in this genre include 'Satisfaction', 'Age', 'Commitment' and 'Attraction'. The drama usually has four acts: in the Introduction section of the paper the nature of relationships and the scientific puzzle is described in R-mode (reality mode); then the method and statistical analyses are described in D-mode (document mode) ('subjects' ratings were subjected to cluster analysis'). Following on directly from this Results are summarized in S-mode (statistical mode) ('there was a main effect for satisfaction'), 'Conclusions' are summarized in P-mode (Platonic mode) ('Satisfaction seems to lead to less Communication – i.e. despoiled of all human, scientific or mathematical embodiment'), and then the Conclusions are discussed in R-mode. The S → P move is the major transition point in this little narrative. The argument here is that the nouns are all that hold the action together – without them there is no plot – yet different actors seem to be playing the same role.

Let us now consider each of these dramatic episodes in detail:

(1) *R-Mode* (reality mode). Here the 'actual' nature of personal relationships is speculated upon in various ways using common sense, other papers, author's observations, etc. All these fragments attempt to construct an image of what it's like out there, beyond the paper, beyond what we know this study is going to be like. The author wanders down the by-passes and cul-de-sacs of being in love or whatever. R-mode is characterized by particular kinds of grammatical forms. Relationships and people 'are', or 'are likely to be' X, Y and Z. A few points here: it is critical to note that even in studies that eschew the paradigmatical form of the self-report (the Likert scale) or one of its close approximations, the mode of discourse is still R-mode. 'That' paper did not capture reality because 'that' paper used such and such a research methodology, however, 'this' paper because it uses (new, improved) 'this' methodology, *will* capture reality – and we will find out whether people 'are' X, Y or Z. The issue of 'reality-catching' is never itself held to account. In the Introduction section of the scientific report such a reflexivity would be *un*grammatical. It is reality we are trying to capture and reality hunting we shall go. It is the *raison d'être* for the paper as scientific report – for that is the convention

of comprehension that sustains our reading of the report – a convention of Truth. And in this case it is, specifically, a correspondence notion of truth, a form of conscientious realism (see Livingstone, this volume).

(2) *D-mode* (document mode). Here the terms under consideration are cast in the form of document elements/document activity (as in 'Subjects filled in a 26-item scale of satisfaction'). A curious set of contradictions are discernible here – all statistical studies in an academic community stuck with the heritage of logical positivism depend classically upon a notion of 'operational definition' – yet the PR researcher cannot bring him/herself to use such 'precise' terminology, so instead talk as if the document activity was an exemplar of *both* the theory/theoretical model/theoretical term identified in their Introduction *and* of the category in the *real world*. Here the R-mode and the D-mode are in potential conflict since the latter is clearly not the former. Given that we are using terms like 'love' and 'fairness' or 'friendship' this will be manifestly seen to be so. The tension is too great if common-sense terms are used so, by warrant of the conventions of scientific discourse, they are simply avoided and the drama of nouns pursued.

(3) *S-mode* is the statistical mode where the nouns of the study are embodied as variables and are connected by correlations or 'significant' differences.

(4) *P-mode* is the platonic mode. Here the nouns seem to exist independently of any actual, mathematical or linguistic embodiment but just *are* (as in 'Satisfaction has a definite effect on Attraction'). This is a necessary preliminary for the return to reality mode, a transitional state between scientific and everyday/theoretical reality. P-mode characterizes the way of talking that occurs at the end of the Results section and at the beginning of the Discussion section.

D-mode and S-mode are, of course, necessary preliminaries for P-mode, the reader's attention has to be turned away from what is actually happening in the study, i.e. subjects are being asked questions and giving answers about their private lives as opposed to doing it, as it were. The reports are severed from their source and become first 'subjects' ratings' and then simply 'scores on scales'; finally as numbers they achieve transcendental status prepared for Platonic status. This disembodiment procedure is necessary if scientific readings of the paper are to be achieved because it is the only way to get back to reality-talk in R-mode; yet it betrays the underlying tension for the 'scientific psychologist': s/he is trying to connect two things that have the same grammar of description in logical positivism, a third party description of the world (the theory) on the one hand, and the way the world actually is, on the other, by way of something which is neither: people's statements about the world. The R-D-S-P-R grammar is required because as researchers they cannot follow their nouns down the road towards reality (i.e. in questionnaires on Likert scales) because they are in fact 'gobbled up' by it (into subjects' heads) – and indeed spat out by it in fairly unrecognizable form (i.e. self-reports). PR researchers have to cover up the tracks of their nouns as they trot off into their subjects and talk of something else – namely how subjects' reactions/responses make sense in the researchers' documentary and statistical grammars. There is a sense in which PR researchers and psychologists cannot *afford* to have a theory of language use while they subscribe to the logical positivist myth of the disjunctions between theory, reality and enquiry. It is only by regenerating their nouns in an alternative form of embodiment (main-effects and significant correlations between document numbers) that concepts can achieve the status of non-embodiment (P-mode), which constitutes the metaphysical inference about our empirical episode. It could be said that contemporary PR research reports share many of the properties of medieval morality plays in the way they sustain their own intelligibility by the use of assumptions of the active roles of essentially fictional agencies of sub-componential psychological traits and abilities (see also Harré 1983, ch. 1). From this we should see how researchers cannot in fact afford to raise the issue of the origins of self-reports since they are committed *pre-theoretically* to identifying the documents as analogically isomorphic to the activities they are *really* interested in.

Unquestioning use of self-reports has been criticized because such studies are typically retrospective, restrictively structured or because it is not actual behaviour. Various empirical responses embody each of those 'doubts' about the prototypical form of self-report. I will not consider each of these (but see Miell, this volume; Weber, Harvey and Stanley, this volume) but will concentrate on the Rochester diary and some recent suggestions regarding open-ended accounts (Duck and Miell 1986).

THE ROCHESTER DIARY STUDIES

Perhaps the most vaunted method of getting away from the standard form of self-reports is to get the subject to describe his PR *as he is doing it*. The idea here presumably is that if you are going to have reports of relationships then you may as well *stand up close to them* when you are doing it – or in the words of Wheeler and Nezleck (1977) get subjects who 'both emit the behaviour and record it'. And you can't stand much closer than that.

The studies under consideration here are Wheeler and Nezleck (1977), Reis, Wheeler and Nezleck (1980) and Wheeler, Reis and Nezleck (1983). This work is intensive, exhaustive and technically excellent, and demonstrates some unavoidable problems within the current PR paradigm. The technique used by these workers, the 'Rochester Interaction Record' (RIR), argue Duck and Perlman (1985), has 'led to quite a revolution in the relationship field. It is now possible to study not only the characteristic ways in which people spend their day, but also such mediating variables as physical attractiveness ... loneliness ... and gender' (p. 16). This is a large billing to live up to but if Duck and Perlman are right then major advances for the study of personal relationships might be very close.

Leaving aside the language games involved in casting 'loneliness' as an 'intermediate variable' let us look at what is actually involved in the RIR. (N.B. Interestingly the word 'diary' never actually appears in the original paper – or indeed in any of the subsequent ones.) Subjects are asked to record on experimenter-designed forms (documents again) the time, place and duration of all social interactions that occurred that day, along with the number and sex of any present. These scales are taken away by subjects into their everyday lives and out of the laboratory – certainly a refreshing, and critical, use of self-reports. This would seem to be the state-of-the-art experience ethnography and psychological enquiry at the very limits of the self-report methodology.

In the original study subjects were told prior to data collection that their forms were to be filled in at least once per day. In a subsequent paper (Wheeler, Reis and Nezleck 1983) it is reported that 'It was suggested to subjects that they fill out the records at a uniform time, such as before going to sleep' (p. 945). So the RIR is a Likert scale filled in by subjects at the end of their interaction-packed day. Many of the points made above regarding self-report scales are applicable here since these diaries are simply bed-time rating scales of social episodes and not on-line recording of relationship experience (whatever that might be). Obviously there are many elementary limitations that could be pointed to here such as recall, effect of anticipation of ratings, knowledge of likelihood of cross-checking of their reports, etc. However, the Rochester studies are interesting because of the intriguing tension between the attempt by Wheeler and his colleagues to get at 'reality' and the practices they have to engage in to establish a coherent interpretation of their data that superficially sustains but ultimately vitiates their scientifically sanctioned intellectual enterprise.

We are exploring here in detail the ways in which investigators' theories operate to pre-define the dimensions and 'meaning' of the social episodes the subjects are asked to report on and the negotiation of legitimacy to make such reports. Notionally, the sheer cognitive load of saying everything about one's day clearly rules out asking subjects to 'write down everything that happened to you today', and common-sense theories rule out the using of items in the RIR such as 'how many times did you look the other person(s) straight in the eye?' or 'how many verbs did you use?' etc. because people are not taken to be able to say anything about these things – they are not held and cannot be held accountable for them. The RIR is pitched at a level that is taken as being 'acceptable' to the subjects themselves and to the scientific community at large.

The kind of actual scales used is itself revealing. The number and specific structure of the scales changes somewhat across the studies but certain assumptions are clear. Taking Wheeler, Reis and Nezleck (1983), for example, it is assumed that intimacy, disclosure, pleasantness, satisfaction, initiation and influence are the key elements in social interaction and relations. Further, it is assumed that 'superficial' and 'meaningful' are diametrically opposed, that 'quality' of interaction is a question of more or less pleasant interaction, that 'satisfaction' is experienced relative to that level of satisfaction expected and that initiation and influence are each one-party actions, excluding joint initiation or equal and strong influence over the course of the interaction. Finally, the scale assumes a distinction between work, tasks, pastimes, conversations and dates: so it already contains a theory of the size of the experiential aperture and of whether people can report on the middle level of events that constitute their social relationship experience.

In a sense the RIR is *already* a theory of what constitutes 'the way people lead their everyday lives' and what the results tell us is how competent people are in using that theory to make rational sense of their experiences. Given the implicit theory and the inevitable orientating of subjects towards the practical matters of when, where, how and why they are to fill the RIR in, and given the linguistic presuppositions of questionnaires themselves, it is clear that the question of 'accuracy' of correspondence is not relevant here, since the RIR, like any questionnaire, like any scale, indeed like any everyday conversational question, by exploitation of presuppositions constructs the very model of the world in which responses or answers to it will be intelligible. The scales trade on a linguistic competence that is taken as external and prior to the experiences being reported upon and as such is considered an unproblematic methodological resource, but is rendered invisible by the research endeavour.

Wheeler and his colleagues are anxious to document the interactions they have with their subjects, presumably in the belief that if we are to 'look at' people's 'real' lives then this delicate process must be described in detail. Reading through their account of what occurred we can see that subjects were given a detailed and debatable definition of what was to count as a social episode and what was not. 'A social interaction was defined as any ... interaction lasting longer than ten minutes in which the participants attended to one another and adjusted their behavior in response to one another', e.g. sitting next to someone in a lecture was not appropriate, whereas talking to someone for ten minutes was (see Wheeler and Nezleck 1977, p. 745). We might wish to complain that this 'leaves something out' (out of what?) or that 'radically' we should 'let the subjects decide' what should count. But that would be to miss the point somewhat. We can ask if it is *possible*, let alone desirable, to provide well-understood definitions of a social episode?

What is the status of Wheeler's concern to effect some kind of consensus for the notion of 'social interaction'? Does he think that his subjects do not *know* what the words 'social interaction' mean? No, he is teaching them, ostensively, the semantics of the RIR. The subjects are told the range of the semantic terms, various conceptual wanderings and doubts that are anticipated by the researchers. They then endeavour to draw out for them the territorial geography of significance in which the subjects' narrative RIR identity will be located; a necessary prerequisite if the scale items are to be *answered* (a mutually comprehended symbolic act), as opposed to 'written on' (a physical behaviour of indeterminate significance). Such ante-research conversations are only possible if Wheeler and his colleagues are already familiar with the way the students spend their lives around campus and the moral identity implicatures of various social episodes.

It is necessarily the case that researchers have to weave a fabric of significance around the scales so that there will be a set of constructed communicative assumptions in which to ground subsequent research inter-pretations of subjects' reports. This idea of the apprentice–theoretician subject is strengthened when we pursue the text of Wheeler and Rezleck further. On the one hand we have the interesting (and rare, and so inevitably intriguing) comment that subjects were afforded the title of co-investigators. But as we shall see, this 'status' is provisional upon the subjects learning the logic of the RIR. Thus the subjects earn the right of avowal on the matter of their own private personal lives if they show the capacity to use the scales properly. To move away from the Rochester studies briefly and consider the general issues here it would seem clear that subjects and researchers can only attempt to use report scales if the former *already* knows what it means to describe his personal life. And using that knowledge as a shared communicative resource the researcher attempts to draw his new boundaries of meaning and application. Further, scores of self-report inventories have been used in the usual way by PR researchers without pre-negotiating the meaning of the items, because it is claimed such scales are 'self-explanatory'. But if they are self-explanatory, they must be mutually comprehensible, and if they are mutually comprehensible then subject and researcher must *already* share the capacity to engage in a dialogue about relationships. And *that* means they already share a theory about what the constituents and grammar of PRs are. Either subjects understand what we say to them or they don't; if they don't then the whole exercise is absurd in any sense, but if they *do* understand us then *what* is it they understand? What makes PR research possible *at all*?

PR researchers attempt to see whether there are common representations of relationship trajectories, episodes, communicative strategies, rules and understandings generally by utilizing research methodologies that depend entirely upon such representations being reciprocally and routinely avail-able. Of course, Wheeler *et al.*'s results are non-random and certainly not arbitrary, so don't they mean *something*? But in the absence of a theory of the task it is difficult to see what that something might be, and of course to make such a defence is to presume that the products but not the processes of communication about social relations will display a patterned structure. As is so often the case, a study does not tell us something new but arbitrates by institutional warrant on the relative 'legitimacy' among the members of a set of *already* understood patterns of common-sense interpretation.

The use of questions in surveys seems to be parasitic upon the principles of natural conversation yet abuses them (see Adler 1984). In a self-report questionnaire of any kind it is true to say that while questions can be ignored, misunderstood or queried at a semantic distance, *answering* them requires submission to their *interrogative logic*. In order to get people to do the scales, write the account, we have to frame the interrogation so that they understand what to do. That 'interrogative frame' draws upon, and sometimes takes the form of, natural conversation. Yet it is abused – the research questionnaire is a truncated conversation as no further negotiation is allowed. We cannot frame the responding by conversation and then take the responses as though they were unframed by conversation. No matter how we attempt to construct a valid questionnaire all we do is construct a new speech act – a linguistically realized social action in itself, not an image of one.

In their paper Reis, Wheeler and Nezleck state that 'throughout the study a collaborative, non-deceptive atmosphere was maintained, which we believe aided the gathering of valid data' (Reis, Wheeler and Nezleck 1980, p. 606). Similarly Wheeler, Reis and Nezleck (1983) report that 'the students' role as collaborators in this naturalist research was stressed' (p. 945). In the next paragraph it is reported that

> At the conclusion of the record keeping period, a brief interview with one of the researchers was held. During that session, the interviewer probed for difficulties, ambiguities and potential sources of inaccurate data.... Based on their responses, the data of five of the participants were discarded.

What is the moral order (Harré 1979; 1983, pp. 244–6) that permits someone to be a collaborator one minute and discarded the next? The use of the word 'probe' in this context is interesting. The idea of probing 'beyond' a text to see what lies behind it (reality or not-reality) is an illusion noted, amongst others, by Barthes (1975). He points out how, by holding back crucial information until the end, texts, by an illusion of the 'hermeneutic code', give the appearance of presenting a 'hidden truth' through a veil of confusion and uncertainty. What counts as inconsistent will vary and there are numerous *ex post facto* rhetorical and interpretative possibilities at the speaker/writer's disposal. To say on Tuesday that you like someone, and then on Saturday that you don't will be consistent in some contexts and inconsistent in others. Further, the justifications and excuses, or more generally the 'accounts' made in response to suggestions of ambiguity or allegations of inconsistency will affect whether actors are taken to be ambiguous or inconsistent. It would be interesting to speculate on the rules of consistency used by Wheeler, Reis and Nezleck (1983). Note that Wheeler, Reis and Nezleck do not have to subject *themselves* to scrutiny when they claim *they* were 'non-deceptive' towards their subjects. Wheeler, Reis and Nezleck, by virtue of the conventions of scientific reporting, achieve 'truthfulness' in their reported dealings *performatively* from within the scientific paper, while the subjects are put to achieving the status of accuracy and coherence for their part in the study *conversationally*, i.e. their truth is negotiable, that of Wheeler, Reis and Nezleck is not.

What are we to take from all this? First, we should see the practical difficulties involved in studying relationships that preclude subjects from even attempting to constantly record their experience 'as it happens' (the Rochester team avoid this by having records filled in at the end of the day). In order to get subjects to understand what they are *supposed* to be doing, researchers are forced to enter into a discussion with subjects as to what is to count as a part of a relationship and further how to use the scales in that context. To create the research episode we have to draw upon the very reservoir of knowledge that we presume to discover. To make such research possible at all we already have to share with our subjects a model of the worlds in which relationships routinely and unproblematically occur. What kind of *discoveries* are possible here? Yet PR researchers have no explicit model or theory about how this process of orientating subjects towards the empirical episode, of drawing a structure upon the world we presume they will understand, affects or matches, or even how it is already a part of that which we are trying to study – the nature of relationships in society.

EXPLOITING 'BIAS': INCONSISTENT CONSISTENCY

Duck and his colleagues (Duck 1985; Duck and Miell 1986; Duck and Perlman 1985; Duck and Sants 1983) have regularly suggested that any suspected biases in subject reports are potentially open to direct investigation, even though there is, they say, little empirical evidence to believe that they are biased in any critical way. It is worth examining these claims more closely since they hit at the heart of the confusion concerning the relations between perspectives, accounts and texts and readings thereof in PR research. Duck and Miell (1986), like many researchers in the field, see the problem of understanding subjects' reports as being primarily one of identifying and separating out subjects' *cognitive* biases and limitations. They see retrospective reports as being liable to being distorted by 'rationalisation, selective forgetting, reconceptualisation and idealisation' (Duck and Miell 1986). Elsewhere Duck (1985) has suggested specifically that such retrospective distortions might, at least in part, have their origins in the periods of out-of-relationship reflection. Further, Duck and Sants (1983) have suggested that the examination of discrepancies between accounts might be informative for researchers regarding the nature of stability in relationships. The conceptual advance entailed by Duck's suggestions is crucial because it represents a shift away from the study of realities of relationships to the explicit study of (textual) accounts of relationships. Fascinatingly, however, the elevation of bias to theoretical object, accredited with a formative influence on partners' conceptions of relationships, has, interestingly, led to it being utilized by others as a justification of several studies that use self-report methodology as a tool for examining actual relationships. The justificatory account here runs as follows: 'My study uses self-reports, but self-reports could be biased;

therefore my model of reality could be biased. However, Duck says bias is an intrinsic aspect of relationship construction, so therefore my research strategy is warranted. I can make conclusions about reality.' Of course the reasoning is entirely spurious. If I tell you about how I sell used cars then your fear that I might be lying should not be allayed by your *separate* suspicion that I use lies to sell my cars by saying 'lies are an integral part of selling used cars so it doesn't matter if he is lying now'.

The first point to make with respect to Duck's claim that the study of account 'bias' (and that means for Duck an inconsistency between accounts) is to remind ourselves that the identification of 'inconsistency' is not a theory-free activity: it is not objective, it is a category of interpretation that may or may not be appropriate or useful. The identification of inconsistency within or between texts is a judgement as to whether *both* the candidate elements can exist simultaneously within the conceptual logic of a theory in which those elements have meaning. Supposing I wrote in a Duck diary that 'Today I must say I love my wife . . .' and then seven days later wrote 'I haven't liked anyone for over a year . . .'. In what sense and in what way would a judgement of inconsistency be warranted here? Would such a judgement be debatable? These articles suggest that we should not dismiss relationship accounts (here, essays) as useless or invalid just because they are inconsistent or in conflict with other accounts. Instead they say such properties are worth studying because they tell us something about the way people bias their perceptions of relationships.

The problem, of course, is *how* do you decide whether two essays are in conflict or internally inconsistent? We could ask the authors (subjects) of such essays whether they thought the essays were inconsistent or contradictory or whatever (see Wheeler and Nezleck 1977, p. 745, footnote 1), but then we would be examining their practices in interpreting texts to another person, which is a separate matter and not what Duck has in mind at all (he wants to examine the nature of the cognitive biases that create a gap between reality and representation). What would a set of rules about how to identify two accounts (essays) as discrepant look like? What would a set of rules attempting to identify two accounts as *consistent* look like? What would be the substance of such rules? And how would we be sure that, when classifying two essays as discrepant, *we* were acting consistently under those rules? Lalljee, Abelson and Brown (1984), for example, have argued that the nature of consistency between attitudinal statements and behaviour is essentially a conversational achievement accomplished by means of culturally intelligible accounting practices. A further point is that it is generally assumed that accounts will only be inconsistent with respect to *other* accounts and that the accounts themselves will not be *internally* contradictory. This is largely because accounts here are seen as essentially the 'printout' of perspectives and not linguistically realized constructions in their own right. Yet when we accept the idea that accounts have internal contradictions we are again faced with the problem of establishing a firm footing for our interpretations of those textual accounts as contradictory, interpretations that depend upon culturally ratified assumptions of the taken-for-granted aspects of relationships.

More crucial perhaps is the problem that Duck and his colleagues consider themselves, when confronted by an 'inconsistency', to be dealing with a distinctively and exclusively *psychological* bias. It is as if one could get a transparent account by securing a text free from memory distortions and 'reconceptualizations'. But to talk of written account as 'distorted' begs the question 'distorted from what?'. In fact what we have here is yet again a form of Harris's (1981) psycho-centric myth of language use – i.e. taking psychological talk as being (approximately) representative of a non-linguistic psychological substrate (see Shotter, this volume). Duck (1985), in his synthesizing overview of relational communication, has no difficulty in accepting the constructivist model of communication when thinking of people as partners in a relationship talking to *each other*, but when it is a question of considering the talk of subjects *in an experiment*, he regresses to a pre-constructivist Representational Augustinian 'cinematic' model of discourse. Duck and Miell (1986) expect us to accept their discursive claims to rational coherence even if part of that claim includes a judgement of inconsistency, of rhetorical error, upon claims made by others, which were nevertheless statements about the speakers' own relationship.

The third-person account of Duck and Miell is privileged over the first-person accounts of their subjects. The identification of consistency, inconsistency or any other kind of 'bias' is *logically* as much a consequence of Duck and Miell's implicit theory of relationship 'integrity' as it is of that of their subjects. One way of progressing here is to realize that there is no reason why Duck and Miell might not offer *more than one* reading of their subjects' accounts, and there is no reason, in principle, why *those* separate readings cannot be of a form that they would label 'mutually incompatible'. We must be aware of the fact that the identification of an account as inconsistent, accurate, revealing or informative is itself an interpretative activity of essentially comparable status, and further, that no single particular interpretation of an experience description is necessary any more than any particular description of experience is demanded by 'experience' itself.

ACCOUNTS AND THE DISCOURSE OF EXPERIENCE

Accounts as tellings

Given the fundamental difficulties and contradictions that seem to lie at the heart of PR researchers' use of the self-report it is appropriate to consider whether there are more suitable ways of approaching relationship talk. In the following sections I wish to explore whether contemporary linguistics, in particular pragmatics, in relation to discourse analysis and conversation analysis, are in a position to offer PR researchers a framework for engaging people's communications about their relationship experiences. It would appear that these approaches to 'experience talk' offer much that is interesting, challenging and potentially useful, but nevertheless have several puzzles and questions to which PR researchers, in their study of accounts, may be able to make a positive contribution. Let us begin by considering what occurs when we read an account of an extended personal relationship of the kind presented in this volume by Weber, Harvey and Stanley. Weber's accounts are intelligible precisely because as readers bringing cultural expectations to the texts about 'angst', 'despair', 'exhilaration' of Love and Passion, or whatever, we are privy to the metaphorical and narrative conventions with which the writer constructs this particular written story of her experiences. The significance of 'my palms were sweaty' is appreciated without any further specification because it is conventionally understood as a sign of anxiety and nervousness. Further, we understand the connectivity or syntagmatic coherence of 'I was confused and didn't understand my reaction' and 'since he had not even touched me or held my hand' because we have, and are anticipated by the writer to have, the appropriate background knowledge and the requisite conversational competence to make the appropriate inferences for her to make her point. It is precisely these discursive properties of experience accounts, which are obviously central to many problems of PR research, that I wish to explore in this section. In particular I wish, along with Shotter (1985; this volume) to develop a rhetorical account of the rhetorical practices that constitute personal relationship accounts based on the notion that accounts are primarily perceptual/instructive, intrinsically bound with local and general moral orders (Harré 1983) and exploit the formative power of language.

What I want to develop here (in my own way) is the *situated conversational* dimension of Shotter's 'knowing-from' – 'a contextual form of knowing which takes into account, in what is known, the situation within which it is known' (Shotter 1985, p. 447) as the basis for a rhetorical approach to the study of PR talk. Accounting for relationships is in this sense situated, contextualized and narrativizing (White 1980) – in other words exclusively and exhaustively designed to enable 'going on'. There are a number of ways of approaching conversation as a rhetorical accomplishment. Following Leach (1983), I take the study of linguistic phenomena as rhetorical in the sense of affording an analytic primacy to the regulative, principled, goal-directed, problem-solving, functional and interpersonal nature of communication over the (constitutive-) rule-governed, conventional, formal and ideational aspects. To this perspective, however, I wish to add the face-work mechanics of accounting identified initially by Goffman and recently reviewed and synthesized by Semin and Manstead (1983).

What is happening when a social actor provides an account of his personal relationship? Shotter (1985) has suggested following Garfinkel in suggesting that accounts, understood in a number of senses, are primarily instructional in that they typically operate to tell the requester of the account how to see the conduct of the actor as intelligible and rational.

> *Accounts* can be distinguished from theories in the sense that an account of an action or activity is concerned with talking about the action or activity as the activity *is*. It is an aid to *perception*, functioning to instruct one as to how to constitute an otherwise indeterminate flow of activity as a sequence of recognisable events, events of a kind already known about within a society's way of making sense of things. Rather than being a *report* about a state of affairs which can be evaluated as to its falsity, an account works in a quite different way: it *tells* us something, it informs or instructs us as to how practically to go about seeing what the 'is' is, that is, what we ought to see as the 'is'.   (Shotter 1985, p. 451)

The structure of communication

It seems useful to think of the agency behind these tellings identified by Shotter as a Goffmanian *principal*. In some of his later work on the structure of talk, Goffman (1974, 1981) made useful distinctions between the *animator* ('the thing the sound comes out of'), the *author* ('who formulated and scripted the remark being made') and the *principal* ('who believes personally in what is being said and takes the position that is implied in the remarks' [Goffman 1981, p. 167]). Further, Goffman (1974, p. 517) describes the principal as 'the party who is held responsible for having willfully taken up the position to which the meaning of the utterance attests'. Although these three functions can be associated with different human beings for a single utterance they are characteristically all realized by the mouth, mind and public image (as it were) of the same individual. Interestingly, there are striking parallels between Goffman's principal and the Gricean notion of 'speaker' in the terms of his definition of meaning-nn (Grice 1957). Meaning-nn can be defined as follows: *S meant-nn Z by uttering U if and only if (a) S intended U to cause some effect Z in recipient H; and (b) S intended (a) to be achieved simply by H recognizing that intention (a)*, where S is speaker, Z some belief or cognition, U is some utterance and H is the hearer (from Levinson 1983, p. 16).

As Levinson points out, this definition provides a useful conceptual starting-point for the domain of pragmatics within linguistics. One gloss of meaning-nn is: We cannot separate the words used from the speaker's reciprocally apprehended decision to use precisely those words. We hear the words from within the frame of 'This is what I have to say at this point; know that this is what I intend to have you understand.' In a sense this also provides the basis of the formative and rhetorical power of communications and emerges to support the structure of advocacy, and indeed the logic of speech acts in general.

A recent attempt to develop a way of approaching talk about personal experience (and also narrative discourse of personal experience) is the work of discourse analysts Labov and Fanshel (1977). This will provide the ground for developing the notion of a rhetorical approach to relationship talk.

LABOV AND FANSHEL'S A AND B EVENTS

The myth of privileged access

Labov and Fanshel (1977, p. 100), in developing a general framework for the analysis of natural dialogue, offer the following classification scheme for events, which, they suggest, provides the basis for predicting how utterances mentioning such events are routinely heard by co-conversationalists: 'A-events' (events known only to the speaker); 'B-events' (events known only to the listener); 'AB-events' (events known to both speaker and hearer); 'O-events' (events known to others present); 'D-events' (events the truth of which are disputed). 'Known' in this context does not however mean known in the epistemological sense of 'true factual belief', but events to which one has 'privileged access' and about which one cannot be reasonably contradicted, 'such as A's own emotions, experience, biography and so on' (Stubbs 1983, p. 118). This would seem to be a useful classification in that we can apparently unequivocally assign relationship accounts as consisting of entirely 'A-event' statements, but there are several difficulties here.

This formulation seems to assume that statements about experiences are reports of those experiences but morally vacuous – a position avoided if we take statements about experiences as commentaries upon them. It is a misconception to say that statements about internal states are reports on internal states to which the speaker has privileged access. The doctrine of privileged access is an early casualty of Wittgensteinian and Rylian philosophy. First-person statements are essentially avowals not reports and as such more or less felicitous or warranted rather than true or false. The idea that experience when mentioned linguistically is a matter of reporting on privileged access has been scotched recently by Coulter (1979) with respect to recollections, thoughts, perceptions, motives, intentions and sensations; by Averill (1980) with respect to emotions and by Harré (1979) and Schafer (1980) with respect to biography. The notion of privileged access underpinning the everyday language of experience is simply no longer tenable.

The depth of the confusion underlying Labov and Fanshel's system is further revealed when they argue that statements about A-events, because the speaker has privileged access, characteristically evoke 'minimal acknowledgement'. Just what we are to make of this with respect to statements such as 'I love you', 'I'm pregnant', 'I am not happy in this relationship', 'Deep down inside my soul I really detest you' is not clear (see Toolan [1985] for similar criticisms of other discourse analytic schemes). Statements about B-events, argue Labov and Fanshel, are essentially 'requests for confirmation'. This does not deal with utterances such as 'you really are screwed up inside' and so on and so on.

It seems that what determines what a statement about oneself or another is taken as expecting depends quite simply not upon the location of the referent but upon the rights of advocacy associated with the referent and concomitantly, the moral evaluation of the listener entailed by the statement in a way that clearly overrides Labov and Fanshel's rules. Further, even when B-events *have* been mentioned in prior discourse (and thus stop being B-events and become AB-events), a summary statement about those events still seems often to be heard as a request for confirmation. However, the request is not about confirmation that the events occurred but that A's interpretation of them is legitimate (N.B. not correct or necessarily the speaker's 'intended' meaning). In other words, Labov and Fanshel's rule for confirmation requests is neither necessary or sufficient to cover the effect of statements about A and B events.

This all seems to suggest that what is at issue here is not 'privileged access' and requests for information about the truth or falsity of propositions about such events or states, but rather a matter of *rights of advocacy* over avowals and ascriptions made regarding the position or line taken by co-conversationalists·with respect to various *evaluative and moral stances*. What is required is a classification of referents into those over which particular speakers have rights of advocacy and those over which they have not, a classification that is in no way co-extensive with that produced by the 'privileged access' criterion. If we take Goffman's 'principal' as the element of speakers that have rights of advocacy, then we can define a rhetorical position as the asserted moral status of the principal with respect to the ongoing discourse; this enables us to propose as an alternative to Labov and Fanshel's rule the following 'interpretative' rule: If other makes a statement over which you have rights of advocacy, then hear it as a rhetorical position being given to you. The sense of 'request for confirmation' that these statements yield comes from the more general rhetorical principle: Avoid ambiguity in your rhetorical position. The sense of need for confirmation is actually a sense of 'What do you have to say for yourself now?' In short, irrespective of whichever principal actually makes the remark, ascriptive statements are spoken on behalf of the principal who has the rights of advocacy over that of which the ascription is made – it is up to the principal to cancel if he so wishes and if he can.

Over-arching all statements such as 'I am a very sick man', 'I am the right man for you/I love you/We could do wonderful things together', 'I am jealous' and 'I am innocent!' are the institutionally and morally conferred rights of advocacy. Subjective experiences are negotiable and self-ascriptions are necessarily provisional since they have to be ratified as appropriate, understood, intelligible and accepted from *within* the conversation. The achieved orderliness of talk of each other's experience comes from a conventional system that regulates claims, avowals, ascriptions and defeasibility in discourse (see Coulter [1979] for a thorough account). It is not the case, as Labov and Fanshel would seem to be arguing, that 'privileged access' underwrites the right to speak about experiences, but rather that rights of advocacy are constitutive of the privilege to speak of experiences as a person in a way that has particular rhetorical consequences (see Harré 1983). In that sense the matter of establishing what is to be, and what can be, taken to be the case for the purposes of the conversation, for the possibility for 'going on', is established intra-linguistically and not by reference to some separate reality frame. It is in this sense that relationship communication can be seen to be accomplished rhetorically (see Shotter, this volume).

NARRATIVE DISCOURSE

The story-telling aspects of accounts are clearly crucial ones, yet consideration of the narrative dimensions cannot be considered in isolation from the overall conversational and face-work context in which the account occurs. A characteristic of many accounts and a potential characteristic of them all is that embedded within them are other accounts, and that they themselves are embedded within the rhetorical structures of the conversation that provides both the antecedent conditions and consequent 'up-take' of their contribution to the discourse. Simplistically, for present purposes, we can say that social episodes contain conversations that contain speaker turns that contain accounts that contain narratives that speak of the actions of characters. The narrative account speaks from within the speaker turn and has significant consequences for the illocutionary force that empowers or compromises the turn in much the same way that the rhetorical force of turn will empower or compromise the face of the speaker. But by what authority does a narrative speak into a conversational turn? This is a key issue because traditionally the narrative has been studied as a self-contained unit within the conversation and as such its relation to the discourse of the Goffmanian principal has been largely neglected (even Goffman [1974, ch. 13] limits discussion to the matter of what is essentially 'narrative voices' and leaves the perlocutionary consequences for face of principal narration largely untouched). This state of affairs has been buttressed by the fact that the huge body of work in literary theory on narratology considered the integral but isolated literary text as its point of departure – analysis of the consequences or occasioning grounds for the literary story-telling being explicitly detached from the study of the conventions of narrative form as such (see Rimmon-Kenan 1983).

THE RELATION OF NARRATIVE ACCOUNTS TO ONGOING DISCOURSE: INTERNAL OR EXTERNAL WARRANTS?

Labov (1972), Labov and Waletsky (1966) and Labov and Fanshel (1977) have argued for a universal structure of narratives – Abstract, Orientation, Events, Evaluation, Coda. The Abstract, they suggest, will be along the

lines of 'Let me tell you something funny/amazing/fascinating/fantastic/
peculiar/that happened', i.e. they announce the 'reportability' of the tale
(Labov and Fanshel 1977, p. 107). Somewhat in contradiction to this
characterization of narrative discourse as being exclusively of the 'anec-
dote' genre they point out that narratives are, however, tightly integrated
into the conversation and function as equivalent to *individual speech acts*
the evaluative point of the narrative is the contribution to the conversation. Whatever the force of that idea few literary theorists would accept
their definition of a narrative as 'one means of representing past experience
by a sequence of ordered sentences that present the temporal sequence of
those events by that order' (Labov and Fanshel [1977, p. 105]; see also
Romaine [1985] for a critique of their universality thesis). This is clearly a
position that requires and so accepts unquestioningly the representational
thesis and the difficulties with their view that follow from this. Specifically,
they see the evaluative component of a narrative as being external to its
structure, as 'inserted devices' such as intensifying modifiers, complex
syntactic devices, the use of negatives, and so on.

White (1980) makes it clear that the structural devices of narrative itself
provide more than sufficient resources for effecting an evaluative move. If
we search for evaluative appendages alone we will be blind to the moralizing power of structure itself. We can construe the social actor's task as
analogous to that of the historian, and just as there are histories there are
accounts of varying degrees of intelligibility and cogency. In discriminating
between three kinds of history, White (1980) suggests that the power of
the chronicler's account of historical events over that of the annalist is that
the former utilizes a 'notion of a social center by which to locate them with
respect to one another and to charge them with ethical or moral significance' (White 1980, p. 15). However, as White himself goes on to point
out, a moral/logical centre is still insufficient for an account to be a
narrative one – the events must be presented in such a way that they are
'revealed as possessing a structure, an order of meaning, which they do not
possess as a mere sequence'. This structuring process, considered as an
active operation in communication, is probably the key area for developing the study of natural accounts of experience.

Particularly interesting here is the work of such narratologists as Bremond (1966) and Prince (1973). Intrinsic to both their attempts to establish the basic structure of narrative is the idea of character transition from
one moral state to another. For Bremond this emerges from a pattern of
potential for action → action realized → success/failure. For Prince, the
basic pattern is *temporally sequential events, causal effect, inversion*.
Further, Labov and Fanshel elevate a possible discursive pattern into an
obligatory rule, namely that if a request for information is met with a
narrative then assume that the evaluative point of the narrative provides
the information requested. However, this ignores the fact that a narrative
account will be provided if the information is face-threatening, i.e. a
dispreferred (see Levinson 1983; ch. 5), and that the evaluative insertion

(or evaluative move inherent in the narrative structure) provides *not* the information requested but demonstrates that presuppositions of the question are inadequate while trying to save the face of the requester. As Wolfson has pointed out, however, most stories examined by these theories have been collected as part of the standard socio-linguistic research interview. In those episodes the narrative is requested by the researcher within what is essentially a moral vacuum. The abstract seems to announce the general tellability of the story – an announcement required precisely because beyond the request of the researcher there is no reason for its being told there and then. By contrast, in 'normal circumstances' faces will be on the line and speakers are being held to account. When giving an explanation as an account for conduct narratives need no abstract, their place within the conversation being legitimized by the threat hanging over the the face of the speaker. In that sense abstracts are consequences of moral vacuums.

The problem here is that it depends what counts as a story. If we accept only the self-contained narratives we get in response to questions like 'Tell me about a time when you fought a guy bigger than you ...' then abstracts will proliferate because the speaker has to write a promissory note that the story is worth the floor time. But if we are interested in the forms and deployments of narratives as realized in accounts of conduct then abstracts are going to be largely unnecessary because the grounds for rendering intelligible, for telling others how to see your actions is *already* a summary of the story.

From within the moral structure of the discourse the *tacit abstract* of accounts is 'My moral status is secure thus ...' and similarly their *tacit coda* is 'See? I am a rational, acceptable and intelligible social agent after all ...'. In natural discourse the speaker's turn will be taken as completed whenever sufficient information has been provided by the speaker to make the point of his turn and knows that the point of his turn is heard as having been made. The point of the conversational turn is defined here as sufficient information being provided by the speaker for the listener to be able to go on. That such a juncture has been reached will be characteristically marked by 'interruptions' such as 'I see' or 'Right', or whatever. In other words when the move 'So what?' is no longer rhetorically intelligible and will not be from within that turn, 'So what?' as presented by Labov (1972) seems to confound the idea of listeners' monitoring of relevance to the narrative account with general moral disinterest. But, of course, one could, in a narrative account of why person X did action Y in the context of being a bystander, offer a story where the relevance of a remark from within the story is not immediately apparent to a listener and be interrogated in a similar but amoral fashion: 'So what?/ How do you mean?/Eh?' etc.

When some offence or enigmatic behaviour has occurred, ratified participants in a conversation can sanction, ignore or challenge (Goffman 1955). Clearly a challenge constitutes an audience preference over disattention or a poke in the ribs and to that extent constitutes, paradoxically, a *licence* to instruct, an invitation to do the 'cognitive' work of the audience – to 'author' in the Goffmanian sense mentioned earlier, an interpretation of the world. That is, when an actor has been called upon to give an account, it is not just a 'fractured social reality' that is presupposed but that those calling on the actor to account have preferred challenge to immediate sanction. Punishing transgressors is often a very effective way of sustaining realities. In everyday life the moral difference between a challenge and a sanction within the episode that occasions a choice between them is the basis of the instructional force of the account. The instructional force of the account trades on the invitation to render intelligible, which is itself significant within the conversation with reference to the possibilities of immediate sanction or moral stricture.

The distinction is often made within literary theory between the events, the story and the telling thereof within a narrative (or *histoire, reçit* and *narration*). It is the third category that is most often neglected and it is that category that corresponds most closely to the activity of the Goffmanian principal and Shotter's 'knowing-from'. In a sense this is what Duck and Miell (1986) and Weber, Harvey and Stanley underestimate; the actual situated activity of telling the listener (or psychologist) the story, with all its qualificatory, deictic, conversationally co-operative and discursive techniques – the actual practical linguistic (and not cognitive) construction of the relationship account. Given that accounts are perceptual-instructive, i.e. occasioned by invitations to render comprehensible within and for the sake of the social encounter, their point within conversation is just the moral force of their narratives and should felicitously speak directly to the invitation. When we account of our own behaviour a well-formed narrative is one in which the moral transition is not just intelligible, rational and compelling, but, on the part of the speaker with respect to that particular speech act, *wittingly* so, i.e. not just incidentally or potentially so but understood to be intended as such.

White (1980), Schafer (1980), Shotter (1985) and Gergen and Gergen (this volume) do not explicitly exploit this 'non-natural meaning' aspect (Grice 1957) of stories. The felicitous use of the metaphors of experience requires not just an ability to privilege alternatives agencies (Culler 1983, p. 188) but an intimate familiarity of the moral implications for those who use them as well as of the implications for those of whom they are used. When we listen to someone's account of their experience we hear not just the story but the eternal Gricean sub-text of, 'I am happy to have you understand that this is where I stand on this issue ...'.

NARRATION, TEXTUAL RHETORIC AND THE GOFFMANIAN PRINCIPAL

All accounts are given in the shadow of their own illocutionary force. The overpowering logic of conversational structure ensures that previous conversational moves specify the range of possible hearings open to any given subsequent utterance. Most compellingly, analysis of the significance of *silence* shows how powerful the rational system that organizes turns is (see Levinson 1983, p. 299; Manning, in press). However, to the extent that the speech act possibilities and their associated identities of a turn or move are *under*-specified by the antecedent discourse then internal specification of illocutionary force becomes a correlatively more powerful rhetorical resource. This 'illocutionary latitude' is a resource for all but is perhaps most easily used in three-party conversations where speakers can, as it were, move in and out of conversational sequences.

Let us pursue this aspect further. If the principal does attempt to subvert the conversational logic (which is of course precisely what provides the speaker with the floor in the first place), then early specification of his or her 'preference' over the default force/hearing is possible and efficient in terms of rational discourse, but not necessarily appropriate given rhetorical–moral considerations. Again, the difference between the default and the ultimately accomplished act is part of the rhetorical significance of the utterance. In that sense Conversation Analysis, in providing us with aspects of descriptions of conditional relevances, preferred patterns and so on, provides us only with the 'unmarked expectations' or raw material the competent social speaker is assumed to be able to do something *with* (see Levinson [1983, p. 367] and also in this context de Lajarte [1984] and his analysis of the crucial distinction between *discursive formations* or pre-conditions for talk and *concrete discourses*). Possibly, also a factor here is the degree of perceived communicational/cognitive work seen to be done in disabusing listeners of their Labovian prejudices, work such as spelling out who has understood and misunderstood who on what and why etc. If this is so then it suggests that a Gricean-nn reading of Goffman's 'authorial' function is possible.

To see illocutionary force as an achievement of statements that felicitous utterances accomplish by virtue of fulfilling the prerequisite requirements is to court a particular kind of *ex post facto* fallacy (see Shotter, this volume). In other words, to describe what makes a request a request and then infer that the start of statements so classified are the start of requests is to underestimate the 'groundwork' done *within* utterances. Labovian pre-conditions for requests, questions, and so on (Labov and Fanshel 1977) share many common features and at the beginning of an utterance a number of speech acts could in principle be realized. In some situations it is precisely this initial ambiguity of whether the speaker is on his/her way to making a justification or an excuse that enables him/her to retain the floor and amass as much evidence or accounting resources as s/he has available and more time to monitor the back-channels. Challenges, assessments, disclaimers, apologies, justifications and excuses are almost always much longer than their minimal conditions would require. The textual rhetoric of ongoing face work is under-researched and Leach (1983) considers only the principles of clarity, processibility, economy and expressivity. However, in extended utterances such as narrative discourse illocutionary force is indeterminate, non-discrete and above all provisional; the general force is built up, piece by piece, subsequent parts trading on the frames established by earlier ones. The final, overall effect of an utterance might indeed be a request or condemnation or whatever but we must be careful not to ignore that it started as an assertion or eulogy and in that situation *could* only have started thus. Similarly, accounts of and in relationships can, by virtue of the conventions of description and narration, exploit expectations established by remarks and comments made at some earlier point.

Overall, psychologists and sociologists seem, when analysing accounts or theorizing about attitude statements, consistently to place the emphasis on the *conscientious realism* of the pre-utterance circumstances (i.e. between the speaker's alleged knowledge state and the world) at the expense of the *conscious realism* between the utterance and the post-utterance circumstances (see Livingstone, this volume, for a explanation and discussion of these terms). By doing this these analyses underestimate the *forward and enabling* aspects of claims about experience and the way subsequent talk 'backs up' prior discourse, not by appealing to some extra-linguistic arbitration but through intra-linguistic rhetorical operations such as analyses, comparisons, re-namings, rule-invocation, and so on. In that sense, in the analysis of *both* conversational and written accounts, we must be careful not to underestimate the syneidectic (retrospective moralizing) resources of speakers. Statements can be made on the basis of the speaker's faith in his or her own ability to construct retrospectively from within the discourse the cogent grounds for the claims s/he commits him/herself to, i.e. statements can be *made* to make sense (see Antaki [1985] for an empirical approach to the study of the backing up of claims).

CONCLUSION

This is what narrativizing discourse achieves: the presentation at the same time as a way of perceiving, the results of that perception such that a transition from one moral 'state' to another is accomplished by the speaker as a character in his/her own story. This transition is primarily internal to the story, not an appendage. But as pointed out earlier, it is crucial that this transition is appropriate for realizing the point of the story. From within the frame of a demand/request for an explanation of some morally ambiguous occurrence, a narrative is spoken under the shadow of being a story that will provide a point such that a hearing of justification can be taken as heard (a state of affairs that narratives themselves can exploit or subvert). But further, the means of presenting the material for the case of the point will be *wittingly* organized around the trajectory of moral transittion.

While the shift away from attempts to construct scientific theories that more or less portray what people 'actually' do, and towards providing accounts of how people go about using various linguistic devices to effect social action is long overdue in psychology, we must not forget that there is no 'representational security' in the 'higher order' discourses either. To say that someone has 'justified their actions' is hardly less problematic than saying 'he is attracted to her' since socially constructed (rhetorical) interaction no more yields a single necessary interpretation than actions yield a single necessary description. Nevertheless, in the same way that from the dialogue of competing accounts of action new interpretative resources emerge (e.g. moral ascendency) so too do divergent interpretations of accounts of action yield greater understanding of the practice of interpretation itself. In such a case the essential provisionality of accounts and interpretations should be seen less as an acknowledgement of the concessions required in the face of the limitations of discursive analysis and more as a *primary resource* for an intellectual community addressing the power and contradictions of meaning. Further, of course, there is the completion of the practical hermeneutic circle – interpretation of accounts feeds back into accounting practices just as they, in turn, feed back into the construction of intelligible conduct and empower new configurations and realizations of order in action. PR researchers have to apply their models of communication reflexively to their own empirical enquiries and explore more vigorously the forms of talk that sustain relationships, both internally and externally to the relationship. The collection of written and spoken accounts, for their own sake and for an understanding of what. they are, is fundamental to the analysis of social relations in a number of senses.

It should be no surprise that PR research does not, despite a period of intense activity, seem to be about to solve the technical difficulties of measurement identified by McCarthy in his review of the methodologies of the 1970s. PRs are not tangible objects, they are social constructions sustained by networks of accounts, and as such their examination will always require us to have more knowledge than we can articulate or formalize about them – and so discoveries seem inevitably to be in terms of reorganizations and re-analyses of what we already know. *That* does not mean we do not need to add to what we have to organize, but simply that there are no algorithms for collecting precisely the bit of knowledge we might think we want. We feel we need and want to know about the way relationships actually are – but this *is* how relationships actually are, practical activities with no general rules. Traditional experimental studies in PR research (and arguably social psychology generally) should be afforded the same status as the computer in cognitive psychology – a crucible for competing descriptions of self-consciously 'artificial' problems; a way of stumbling across possible configurations of behaviour or thought, to be evaluated as much in terms of what new ideas it provides on the nature of configurations as anything else.

This overview of the current and possible uses and conceptions of self-reports has been neither exhaustive nor even-handed. It has attempted to articulate discontent at a self-confident period in the the study of PRs.

Although it has favoured broad coverage rather than deep defence, polarization rather than synthesis, it is hoped that it also defended a largely eclectic way in which the basic sympathies of PR research might move.

ACKNOWLEDGEMENTS

I would like to thank David Clarke, Bob Hoyle, Peter Manning and Rom Harré for many helpful criticisms and suggestions made on earlier drafts of this paper.

REFERENCES

Adler, J.E. (1984) 'Abstraction is uncooperative'. *Journal for the Theory of Social Behaviour*, 14, 165–81.

Antaki, C. (1985) 'Ordinary explanations in conversation: causal structures and their defence'. *European Journal of Social Psychology*, 15, 213–36.

Averill, J. (1980) 'A constructivist theory of emotion'. In R. Plutnik and H. Kellerman (eds) *Emotions: Theory, Research and Experience*. New York: Academic Press.

Barthes, R. (1975) *S/Z*, trans. R. Miller. New York: Hill & Wang.

Bremond, C. (1966) 'La logique des possibles narratifs'. *Communications*, 8, 60–76.

Coulter, J. (1979) *The Social Construction of Mind*. London: Macmillan.

Culler, J. (1983) *The Pursuit of Signs: Semiotics, Literature, Deconstruction*. London: Routledge & Kegan Paul.

De Carlo, N. (1981) 'La quantificazione ovverro il numero come segnale'. *Psicologia Contemporanea*, 40.

de Lajarte, P. (1984) 'On literary practice'. *Diogenes*, 127, 123–41.

Duck, S.W. (1985) 'Social and personal relationships'. In G. Miller and M. Knapp (eds) *Handbook of Interpersonal Communication*. Beverly Hills: Sage.

—— and Miell, D. (1986) 'Charting the development of friendship'. In R. Gilmour and S.W. Duck (eds) *The Emerging Field of Personal Relationships*. Hillsdale, NJ: Lawrence Erlbaum.

—— and Perlman, D. (1985) 'The thousand islands of personal relationships: a prescriptive analysis for future explorations'. In S.W. Duck and D. Perlman (eds) *Understanding Personal Relationships: An Interdisciplinary Approach*. London: Sage.

—— and Sants, H. (1983) 'On the origins of the specious: are interpersonal relationships really interpersonal states?' *Journal of Social and Clinical Psychology*, 1, 27–41.

Goffman, E. (1955) 'On face-work'. *Psychiatry*, 18, 213–31.

—— (1974) *Frame Analysis*. New York: Harper & Row.

—— (1981) *Forms of Talk*. Oxford: Blackwell.

Grice, H.P. (1957) 'Meaning'. *Philosophical Review*, 64. (Reprinted in D. Steinberg and L. Jakobovits (1971) *Semantics: An Interdisciplinary Reader in Philosophy, Linguistics and Psychology*. Cambridge: Cambridge University Press.)

Harré, R. (1979) *Social Being*. Oxford: Blackwell.

—— (1983) *Personal Being*. Oxford: Blackwell.

Harris, R. (1981) *The Language Myth*. London: Duckworth.

Labov, W. (1972) *Language in the Inner City*. Philadelphia: University of Pennsylvania Press.

—— and Fanshel, D. (1977) *Therapeutic Discourse: Psychotherapy as Conversation*. London: Academic Press.

—— and Waletzky J. (1966) 'Narrative analysis: oral versions of personal experience'. In J. Helm (ed.) *Essays on the Verbal and Visual Arts*. Seattle: University of Washington Press.

Lalljee, M., Brown L.B. and Ginsburg, G.P. (1984) 'Attitudes: dispositions, behaviours or evaluations?' *British Journal of Social Psychology*, 23, 233–45.

Latour, B. and Woolgar, S. (1979) *Laboratory Life*. Los Angeles: Sage.

Levinson, S. (1983) *Pragmatics*. Cambridge: Cambridge University Press.

McCarthy, B. (1981) 'Studying personal relationships'. In S.W. Duck and R. Gilmour (eds) *Personal Relationships 1: Studying Personal Relationships*. London and New York: Academic Press.

McGhee, P. (1985) 'Public and private accounts of friendship and the family: impression management in young adolescents'. Paper presented at the British Psychological Society Social Section Annual Conference, Cambridge, September.

Manning, P.K. (in press) 'Structuralism and social psychology'. In N. Denzin (ed.) *Studies in Symbolic Interactionism*, vol. 8. Greenwich, Connecticut: JAI Press.

Prince, G. (1973) *A Grammar of Stories*. The Hague: Mouton.

Reis, H.T., Wheeler, L. and Nezleck, J. (1980) 'Physical attractiveness in social interaction'. *Journal of Personality and Social Psychology*, 38, 604–17.

Rimmon-Kenan, S. (1983) *Narrative Fiction: Contemporary Poetics*. London: Methuen.

Romaine, S. (1985) 'Grammar and style in children's narratives'. *Linguistics*, 23, 83–105.

Schafer, R. (1980) 'Narration in the psychoanalytic dialogue'. *Critical Enquiry*, 7, 29–53.

Semin, G.R. and Manstead, A.S.R. (1983) *The Accountability of Conduct: A Social Psychological Analysis*. London: Academic Press.

Shotter, J. (1985) 'Accounting for place and space'. *Environment and Planning D: Society and Space*, 3, 447–60.

Stubbs, M. (1983) *Discourse analysis: the sociolinguistic analysis of natural language*. Oxford: Blackwell.

Toolan, M. (1985) 'Analysing fictional dialogue'. *Language and Communication*, 5, 193–206.

Wheeler, L. and Nezleck, J. (1977) 'Sex differences in social participation'. *Journal of Personality and Social Psychology*, 35, 742–54.

——, Reis, H. and Nezleck, J. (1983) 'Loneliness, social interaction, and sex roles'. *Journal of Personality and Social Psychology*, 43, 943–53.

White, H. (1980) 'The value of narrativity in the representation of reality'. *Critical Enquiry*, 7, 5–27.

Endpiece

Rosalie Burnett

The over-arching subject is sufficiently broad and the chapters diverse enough to indicate a final summary overview of the various facets and their connections, supplementary to that which was set out in the Introduction. That is, there are several complementary sub-themes which may not be immediately apparent under the 'account–accounting' mantle which forms the integrative framework for this volume. (It may be useful also to refer back at this point to the typology of 'accounts' provided by Charles Antaki in his chapter.) In addition, a note to underscore the importance of this framework could be helpful, preliminary to my colleague's Postword about developments for the future.

The 'accounting' concept has served to link together research reports and theoretical discussion of such diverse topics as, for instance: formulation of perspectives in new relationships; the connections between relevant knowledge and achievement of objectives; conceptual biases in academic accounts of relationships; types and functions of laypersons' relationship accounts; and problems in their use as a research tool; the emotional bases of interpersonal knowledge and decision; communication about relationships, and reflections about them; the cultural context of relationship expectations, and of relational language; the origins and implications of relationship representations and narratives.

The collective underlying theme which connects the contributions is the creation of our relationship experiences and realities by our 'accounts' of them. Such accounts are formed and activated on several interrelated levels. Thus 'accounting for relationships', in some part, involves our emotional grasp and conscious reasoning, our implicit knowledge and acquired beliefs, conversations and silences, reported explanation and joint interpretation, academic theories and cultural representations. Each is variously included in the negotiation and realization of meaning in our personal lives. Alternative conceptualizations of the 'accounting' perspective have been bracketed together by their common concern with representational aspects as distinct from relationship action and events as objective realities.

Each chapter provides a metaperspective of complementary but varying pertinence to personal relationship understanding. As indicated, 'accounting for relationships' has multiple meanings wherein there are distinctions and overlap. In applying this rubric, we mean accounting as a *capacity* and *achievement*, whereby sense is attained and some level of understanding is reached, whether the process is beyond conscious awareness or involves reasoning and deliberate processing of knowledge. We mean also accounting as an *activity*, done in a social setting and used to achieve social goals, such as theories shared, excuses made, personal dramas re-enacted and relationship stories told. We use the concept, therefore, to denote both accounting as a *process* and accounts as a *device*.

Perhaps the major differentiation to be drawn, crudely corresponding to microstructural and macrostructural perspectives, is between *private* accounting, done intrapersonally or between the dyad, frequently without words and often unconsciously, and *public* accounting, a long-term collective process, reliant on language and social systems. These mirror divisions within the research literature and the same polarization is to some extent reflected in the structure of the book, in the contrast between Section One and Section Three, with Section Two containing bridging chapters. Collectively, they occupy what is, arguably, the 'true space of psychology' (Harré, Clarke and De Carlo 1985).

Not all our contributors would necessarily agree with this amalgamation and might regard opposing extremes as in conflict with their own position. In his chapter, Antaki suggested that: 'There is what looks like an unbridgeable gap between those who see an account as a social interaction ... and those who see it as a private unconscious cognition.' By connecting these together, we are consciously aiming to avoid such a gap and to enable a more coherent view by juxtaposing different levels of analysis, following early advocations for integration and unity of different subdisciplines and levels of analysis (Hinde 1979, 1981; Duck and Gilmour 1981). In this, we are cognizant of the interdisciplinary character of personal relationship research and the need for the present endeavour to be thus extended.

Contained in the different contributions are implications for us all as *participants in relationships* – such as arise from the possibilities that emotional dominance and joint agency leave us with less rational control and less individual control over our relationships than previously believed; and knowledge about the various sources of our received relationship truth and the functions and goals of our internalized versions of it. Additionally, there are implications for *academics* in accounting for relationships – for instance: how they obtain their data; what should be their point of concern; theoretical and methodological biases; fallacies and assumptions.

We are attaching importance to the accounting framework for good reason. A view of their interrelations is facilitated by presenting intrapersonal and dyadic accounting patterns and processes as framed and influenced by social structures and practices. A depth and breadth of perspective is enabled, necessary for advancement in the study of personal relationships if the fruits of investigation are to be widely received and swallowed, and in keeping with developments in social science in general.

Personal relationships are very much about individuals: by definition, *who* the relationship is with is especially significant. Yet, paradoxically, the book represents a move away from individualism – though this is without neglecting the key role of individual construal (Section One), set in the wider context of collectivism. Thus, it is a paradox that a phenomenon of great intimacy, personal relationships, requires investigation of public and collective practices and processes: although by definition private and micro-scale, investigation at other levels and from a wider context are of relevance to full understanding. Even a phenomenon as intimate as a relationship has social derivatives, and so personal relationship research needs a social context. But equally, we must be wary of over-socializing the prevailing conceptions of relationships. The part of individuals (self-concept; interpretation; effort after meaning; individual goals, etc.) must not be neglected. Hence the range here, from implicit schemata and tacit knowledge embedded in perception, to declared opinion, publicized views and official dogma embedded in social context.

Having once emerged as an official research area, 'Personal Relationships' has served to provide a focus for diverse research projects and problems, and has very rapidly established itself as a lively and thriving research domain. Even greater activity in the form of a 'boom' period is forecasted (Duck, in press). Relatively little concerted attention has previously been given to work under the 'accounting for relationships' mantle, and we are confident that this volume constitutes an important early contribution to the maturing approaches and concerns of the future. The desirability of broadening-out to correct imbalances inherited from the restrictive experimental antecedents of the field has been identified by Duck and Sants (1983), and the accounting paradigm will be a decided move in that direction.

Another paradox with respect to relationships is their critical importance to the persons concerned whilst at the same time they are likely to be experienced as trivial and mundane much of the time, and regarded as a refuge from the serious occupations of life (Burnett 1986). This same uncertain status – commonplace but crucial – is indicated in changing scientific evaluations of the subject. Prior to the 1980s, social psychologists' enthusiasms were caught up with more esoteric if less immediately relevant matters, and a contempt for their familiarity may have contributed to the neglect of relationships. Indeed, an assumed sufficiency of knowledge was identified by Hinde (1979) as one of the 'obstacles to a science of personal relationships'. Approximately a decade ago, Brain, an anthropologist, summarizing prevailing attitudes, cynically decried the lack of importance attached to relationships: 'for many ... it may be impossible to accept that a person's identity as an individual, society's character as truly "human", and our survival as members of that society, may depend on anything so vague, so unstimulating, so humanistic as love and friendship' (1977, p. 207). Less damningly, Hinde (1981) pointed out that 'The study of interpersonal relationships forms the meeting point of a number of different scientific disciplines, but the central focus of none' (p. 1).

It is perhaps surprising therefore when relationships, the home of predictable and trivial exchanges and not traditionally regarded as requiring explanation, are described as critical to our understanding of social meaning, and when claims are made that advancement in human psychology must depend on a relational perspective. But, following belated appearance as a worthy research topic, 'we now see the emergence of the relationship conception as the focal point for psychological theorizing and empirical investigation' (Rychlak 1984, p. 364). Further, there are '"currents in the wind" that point to the study of relationships as not just another branch of the study of people, but as perhaps the central endeavour of the social sciences' (Lock 1986, p. 98). Fulfilment of such a role requires allowance for dialectical interaction between society and relationships (Hinde 1979; Duck and Gilmour 1981), and attention to individual processing, joint interpretation and social construction of meaning, such as are evident in the present volume.

The slant of this collection towards an ethogenic approach and constructivism, and away from mainstream experimental psychology, is less radical than it may appear in contrast to more specific, experimental work being conducted in the field. Indeed, some of the underlying positions are far from new: antecedents include symbolic interactionism and ethnomethodology, which in turn contain early ideas hailing from Mead and from Wundt, and through them traceable back to Darwin (Farr 1980). Further, the broadening of perspective, and changes in assumptions and purpose are fast becoming orthodox. Contributions here flow with the tide of change, conceptually, methodologically and in objectives. Contained assumptions regarding the social origins of meaning, ambiguity and temporality, the pluralism of mental processing, and a more emotional and less self-contained concept of the individual, are reflections of trends in psychology as a whole, and accord with contemporary models of humanity and paradigm shifts in social psychology. This is not the place to re-explicate such changes, but the new student of social psychology is now likely to be brought up on a more eclectic and interdisciplinary approach, less distinct from and more at one with other disciplines, the links between social psychology and sociology, linguistics, communication science and philosophy in particular being stressed.

Taken as a whole, this volume is in keeping with the present spirit of social psychology, and the shape it is now in following the crisis-of-confidence years and subsequent adjustments. Stretching in coverage from the private-individual sphere to the public-social sphere, the work reported here reflects theoretical and methodological diversity to cater for social life being momentary and set in history, and demonstrates that new paradigm positions and more conventional approaches need not be in conflict. The study of personal relationships, still relatively fresh research territory, always threatened to be a challenge to the academic investigator, characterized by conceptual density and empiricism-defying breadth and depth, some questions thus evading easy answers (McCarthy 1981). The volume is not replete with answers and leaves gaps, especially for a developmental perspective and the contributions of other disciplines. But there is sufficient within the preceding pages to support belated scholarly acknowledgement that, far from being simply about intimate affairs and of subsidiary interest, when investigated from the broad representational perspective of this volume, personal relationships are at the heart of all the issues of perennial importance to social scientists.

REFERENCES

Brain, R. (1977) *Friends and Lovers*. St Albans: Paladin.
Burnett, R. (1986) 'Conceptualisation of personal relationships'. Unpublished DPhil thesis, Oxford University.
Duck, S.W. (in press) *Relating to Others*. Milton Keynes: Open University Press.
—— and Gilmour, R. (1981) Preface. *Personal Relationships 1: Studying Personal Relationships*. London: Academic Press.
—— and Sants, H.K.A. (1983) 'On the origin of the specious: are personal relationships really interpersonal states?' *Journal of Social and Clinical Psychology*, 1, 27–41.
Farr, R.M. (1980) 'Sunk with hardly a trace: on reading Darwin and discovering social psychology'. In R. Gilmour and S.W. Duck (eds) *The Development of Social Psychology*. London: Academic Press.
Harré, R., Clarke, D.D. and De Carlo, N. (1985) *Motives and Mechanisms: An Introduction to the Psychology of Action*. London: Methuen.
Hinde, R.A. (1979) *Towards Understanding Relationships*. London: Academic Press.
—— (1981) 'The bases of a science of interpersonal relationships'. In S.W. Duck and R. Gilmour (eds) *Personal Relationships 1: Studying Personal Relationships*. London: Academic Press.
Lock, A.J. (1986) 'The role of relationships in development: an introduction to a series of occasional articles'. *Journal of Social and Personal Relationships*, 3, 89–99.
McCarthy, B. (1981) 'Studying personal relationships'. In S.W. Duck and R. Gilmour (eds) *Personal Relationships 1: Studying Personal Relationships*. London: Academic Press.
Rychlak, J.F. (1984) 'Relationship theory: an historical development in psychology leading to a teleological image of humanity'. *Journal of Social and Personal Relationships*, 1, 363–86.

Postword: the idea of the account and future research

Patrick McGhee

The study of personal relationships is a huge undertaking, simple gener-alizations are seductive and misleading. It is not wrong, however, for a society to expect its behavioural and social scientists to make comprehensi-ble and practical interpretations about the everyday experiences, emotions, passions, thoughts and activities that constitute social and personal rela-tionships. As Duck has pointed out in his chapter the way we conceive of and articulate the nature of relationships in our questions anticipates particular kinds of answers. Our belief is that the study of relationships must recognize the structured, practical, symbolic nature of human affairs if it is to make either sense or headway. The shorthand term for the raw material of such a perspective we, and our contributors, have used is that of an 'account'. That we *do* need such a sensitivity to fundamental issues of 'representations in use' is a claim we make in the current context of the emergence of strains and tensions in identifying a basic subject-matter for a science of relationships. It is probably too early to look *back* at the history of the new upsurge in interest in relationship research but it is never too early to look forward and ask ourselves where we are meant to be going. In this concluding chapter I wish to attempt to identify some of the possible future directions potentially offered by following the work reported in the preceding chapters.

PERSONAL RELATIONSHIPS AND THE HISTORY OF THE PRESENT

Personal relationship (PR) research has come into its own in the past decade, and the history of that process has been documented elsewhere, and will, no doubt, be documented again, so it need not be pursued here.

Yet, as Shotter (following Foucault) points out in his contribution to this volume there are histories of the past and there are histories of the present. The former is the traditional retrospective, assertive and documentary-based kind familiar to all of us; the latter, however, is something quite different. The history of the present is not concerned with drawing a picture of the past but rather attempts to clarify the future as it is produced by our history and is present in our circumstances *now*. Its aim is not one of representation but of empowerment, with instructing us in the possible opportunities and barriers to the actions that now confront us, as a result of our past action. Consistent with its enabling aims it tells us how to act by the telling of stories – of context-breaking. This story-telling history, which speaks directly to us, and of us, begins not with the assumption that we have completed a journey to the present but with the assumption that we are, unavoidably, in the process of moving on – it is instructional, empowering and opens up new ways of seeing and acting; in short, it is an account.

ACCOUNTS

The common thematic trunk of the articles in this volume is a *commitment to some kind of concept of structured representations of experience designed for practical purposes* as being useful in the study of PRs. As a consequence there is the primary concern to explore the properties of such structures, model their use, and identify the consequences and functions of different kinds of descriptions by examining the systems in which such representations operate. The ways in which having or making one kind of representation rather than some other have been identified and explored in a number of ways.

And yet certainly no single property is common to all the branches of the trunk. Overall, we have attempted merely to privilege the symbolic over the material, the relational over the absolute, the cognitive over the behavioural and the qualitative over the quantitative. By entailment, the model of communication that emerges is functional and formative rather than one of information transmission, and, in general, language is seen largely as a tool for social action. Cognitive processes have been taken to be systemic, intimately related to emotional states, temporally extensive, strongly inter-psychic and, above all, as guiding and directing action rather than accumulated registrations of experience. Further there is a general emphasis on the role of practical utility in social action rather than computational efficiency. Behaviours are seen as structured, directed, co-ordinated and symbolic; not constitutive of episodes but symbolically significant acts within them. Emotions are cast as social and cognitive rather than exclusively biological, integral to action and knowledge, not detached from them. Further, they are identified as active and organizing rather than as passive consequences. Overall, a picture emerges of relationships surviving on a repertoire of interpretations, understandings and knowledge that have grown out of, and are continually pitted against, a reality that is unfixed and uncertain, yielding no single correct or necessary account of itself.

Many of the properties of the account are characteristic of the cognitive structures that guide and direct action in the social domain. Just as linguistic commitments afford some lines of action and erase others, so too do emotional and cognitive representations prefigure future possibilities of action; this is not just because they are the 'source template' for action but because, like linguistic commitments, such representations are only possible because they are *already* embedded within matrices of interpersonal understanding and as such are collectively accomplished. A combination of efficient and formal causation, action plans orientate the actor to the immediate interactional episode, self-regulating yet sensitive to changes in critical circumstances. Thus shared cognitive representations of action plans become a primary communicative and accounting resource, operating as pre-existing structurings of experience. These action scripts and shared representations of the possible realizations of those scripts serve to *formulate*, in a clearly practical sense, the interactional and communicative possibilities that sustain social relations.

Another sense of the account as structured practical social knowledge that has been dealt with in detail is that of the *scientific* account of personal relationships as presently understood and as it might be developed. This kind of account too is, despite itself, fundamentally metaphorical and linguistic in origin, and struggles to remain theoretical in the sense of being a self-contained and autonomously intelligible generalized representation and yet nevertheless it continually requires 'wrap-around' accounts to guide our use of it (Shotter 1985). Contemporary philosophers of science see metaphors as key elements in the building of scientific knowledge but the metaphors have to be explicit and their limitations recognized (Harré 1983). When explicitly held as models from another domain they enable new perceptions of phenomena to be made. The issue of the appropriate form of the scientific account, or, less prejudicially, the formal account, has been a recurrent theme in the chapters of this book. Different treatments have been proffered, but what is clear is that the simplistic representational cinematic image approach is no longer tenable, with its persistent inductivism and truth-conditionalities. A hauling of social psychological scientific practice into the twentieth century is long overdue and there are signs that it may be PR research where the need for change may be most quickly recognized and acted upon.

EMPIRICAL EXPLOITATIONS OF THE 'ACCOUNT' THEME

In this section I wish to explore some of the connections that exist between different formulations of the notion of structured practical social actions as it has been described in the preceding chapters in order to underline the utility of the idea of accounts. The themes I have selected are: reflection,

324 Accounting for Relationships

communication and gender; the long-term control and organization of relationships and emotion; linguistic accounts and interpretation; and the recall of past experience. This selection is not meant to be exhaustive or evaluative but broad, diverse and, hopefully, stimulating.

Reflection, communication and gender

As Burnett points out in her chapter we do not *routinely* reflect upon relationships in the sense of formulating an explicit appraisal from what we already know (through reorganization, inference, analysis and evaluation). This process of appraising is often, though not always, occasioned by some problematic or threatening occurrence that threatens some component of the individual's interpretative system. An interesting connection can be made here with Baxter's research programme by considering how Burnett's analysis of reflection can be mapped onto Shotter's distinction between knowing-that and knowing-from (see McGhee, this volume). Reflection is, in this sense, an attempt to actively create the former out of the latter, to construct the theoretical from the practical. A similar distinction with strikingly resonant themes is that between implicit and explicit task knowledge (Broadbent, Fitzgerald and Broadbent 1986). Men are discouraged from and refuse to 'theorize' to others (discursively in disclosure) or to themselves (cognitively in reflection), and are encouraged instead to rely upon their practical capacities to conduct relationships, a practical ability underwritten by social power and conventions of gender. Women, on the other hand, do attempt, and are encouraged to attempt, to construe explicitly their experience and conduct both cognitively and discursively. In short, the lay epistemology of men is exclusively practical, while that of women is both hermeneutical *and* theoretical – a distinction that cross-cuts the traditional rational/irrational dimension and contradicts the myth of the 'intuitive female'.

This practical knowing seems to underlie not only Burnett's unreflective males but also Baxter's indirect cueing and general indirectness in relational communication. Certainly the latter would seem at some level and in some sense to be buttressing the former. Communicative expectations entail that any given utterance need not explicitly carry its full semantic content since it is the pragmatic interaction of the linguistic and contextual that yields the full situated, performative meaning. The pragmatics of interaction would seem thus to permit males to avoid articulating a symbolically accountable statement of their plans, intent or evaluations – in short their assessment of the relationship. Baxter's trajectories as cognitive scripts not only provide an over-arching context to comprehend speaker-meaning, they also render viable a mode or strategy of communication that can be both protective of, and corrupting for, the health of relationships. Even if the epistemic distinction drawn by Shotter does not appear inevitable, an analysis of the connection between reflective concerns and communicative styles of individuals and dyads would seem to promise a number of integrating possibilities for the study of relational understanding and development.

Long-term organization and control of relationships and emotion

Clarke and Baxter both point to the function of higher order affective processes informing and directing lower level cognitive and communicative exchanges between partners. While Clarke explores the procedural aspects of these meta-episodic influences, Baxter emphasizes the representational aspect of these structures. We can ask whether the Clarke and Baxter models are (a) two perspectives of the same level of long-term structuring, (b) two perspectives of complementary features of a complex high-order system, or (c) two perspectives on two processes operating at two different metalevels. While various formulations are possible the most immediately appealing is perhaps that Clarke's superordinate 'dialogue of the emotions' is guided and directed by the specified structures of Baxter's trajectories, with the latter being construed as script-like socio-cognitive templates of rules and sequences.

Somewhat in opposition to this perhaps is the work reported by La Gaipa in his chapter that adolescent conceptions of friendship predict the affective but not the cognitive aspects of adult friendships. However, an alternative formulation is that Baxter's templates and Clarke's emotional exchanges stand in *heterarchical* relation, sharing and reciprocally engaging in control of each other and the lower cognitive and behavioural levels. For example, the current emotional state of a partner in a romantic relationship, say, *excited* (as opposed to, say, merely *happy*) will influence the likelihood that, say, a *Whirlwind* (rather than a *Friendship First*) trajectory schema will be primed for the relationship, a priming that will influence perceptions of future events and circumstances and so constrain and direct the possible emotions that are possible, these in turn affecting the priming of subsequent early- to middle-relationship schema and so on. The logic behind such heterarchical control schemes in social life has been worked out in some detail by the Palo Alto research group (Cronen and Pearce 1980). Such a formulation may offer a reconciliation of the grammatical perspective on emotion advanced by constructivists: 'what you feel is constrained by what you have learned it is possible/rational to feel in this kind of set of social circumstances' (see Averill 1980) with the contemporary social psychological perspective that levels of arousal and general emotional disposition are prior to, and are a key influence upon, cognitive categorization and decision-making (Zajonc 1984).

Obviously, specification of the dynamics and contingencies of the passing of control between these two systems is a necessary prerequisite of any exclusively empirical attack here, but a primary speculation is that long periods of reflection on relationships in depression reflect a constant flip-flop processing between the two systems, the emotional and the interpretational, each of which requires particular information from the other that the other cannot give. Part of this untangling of the control of action must inevitably involve following the lead given by Berger in modelling the planning of action, not just for the crucial initial stages but over the wider timespan. To take one example, Baxter refers to her work with Philpott, which observed that in the early stages of a relationship the major goal of an 'interested party' was to effect in the potential partner the conjunctively necessary attributions that (a) self is attractive and worthwhile, and (b) self is available and interested. We can look at this in terms of what cognitive scientists call 'anticipation of protection violations'. To the extent that these two goals have to be achieved sequentially it would appear that they constitute a classic example of the conjunction problem (Charniak and McDermott 1985, pp. 500–1). That is, attempts to establish the second of the two goals tend to involve the undermining of the already-achieved goal. In this particular case it would presumably be more efficient to establish that one is attractive and that one is available rather than that one is available and then attractive. This has resonances of the heterarchical control of emotions and trajectory processing, in that some previously brought-about state operates as the processing context for the bringing about of some other and the states are, in principle, interchangeable. To the extent that the two classic attributions of relationship initiation are mutually inhibiting, there may be discernible linguistic strategies that serve simultaneously to preserve a previously achieved goal state and contribute to the accomplishment of the other necessary conditions required for the attainment of the other social episodic goals. This may be a locus for integrating work on the connection between particular social interactions and their contribution to overall relational development with the detailed work on self/identity presentation strategies (Semin and Manstead 1983).

Finally, there is the matter of negative plans (see Berger, this volume). Most work on plan co-ordination begins with the assumption that actions serve to transform the external world from one state to another. However, for practical systems the issue is very often one of *preventing* state changes, searching for possible ways things can go wrong and stopping them from happening. While the number of such possibilities in social life is indeterminate if not infinite it is likely that representations of social interaction possibilities contain a specific set of theories of failure, i.e. theories of what is likely to go wrong. This could be a specification of the vulnerability of particular components of action plans or it could be a list of external influences that are liable to undermine various parts at an unspecified time. Different representations of failure possibilities anticipate different repertoires of countermeasures but all would presumably have some set of relatively high-level specifications along the lines of 'avoid X', 'disable Y', 'for time z do not do p', and so on. The above and other considerations lead to the interesting conclusion that a system's negative plans reveal more about its operating environment and its representation of its *own* procedures than do its 'positive' plans and instructions. Basically, it would seem to be the case that effective systems have a large repertoire of low-level positive actions (which are *marshalled* as a function of the context but are in terms of their internal structure context-invariant) and a small number of higher level context-primed (but in execution open-looped [see Berger, this volume]) negative plans. This might appear a somewhat counter-intuitive notion since typically low-level and not high-level processes are assumed to be the more context-specific but here we are referring to the particular operations the plans specify and not to the ways the values of the parameters of those operations change as a function of their interaction with the task environment.

Linguistic accounts and interpretation

In many respects the heterarchical metaphor is the information-processing analogue of the other metaphors of dual structure, such as dialectic opposition and hermeneutic analysis, that find their way into more linguistic and interpretative accounts of social life; each serves to highlight the mutual dependence between oppositions at the expense of the ideas of unilinear determination. The verbal accounts of Wilkinson and Weber's subjects are both products of, and theorizing about, the process of relationship development, and of course where such theorizing occurs within a relationship it becomes an action performed *on* that relationship. It is worth bearing these structural distinctions in mind when we approach accounts of relationships and attempt to build general principles regarding their form and function. As is often the case when we identify parallel symbolic functions, the meta-representational aspects tend to become foregrounded. As a consequence we can identify how concepts reflecting *problems of representation itself* enter into cognitive and discursive accounts; concepts such as ambivalence, uncertainty, ambiguity, change, expectation, consensus and recall become themselves represented entities (and indeed explanatory agencies) in the belief systems and narratives that support personal and social relationship images. It is perhaps here, on the question of the person perception consequences and narrative functions of different images of cognitive activity given in accounts, that the most useful and intriguing work uniting cognitive and socio-linguistic research on relationships waits to be done. Given the ambiguity and complexity of relationship experience and the semantic openness of behaviour itself, it might be expected that one of the crucial aspects of actual, ascribed or imputed partner status is that concerning the significance for identity of states and processes of representation itself. Further, it would seem a worthwhile project to survey and identify the evaluations and moralities associated with particular representational states and cognitive activity generally. Weber, Harvey and Stanley suggest that the degree of account discrepancy might be a useful index of the quality of the relationship, and this might indeed be the case, but accounts that incorporate metaphors of discrepancy and misrepresentation in their comments on other accounts are also probably particularly revealing of the state of the relationship, even if the accounts are in fact similar.

It has been often observed that several social forces conspire to dissuade men from self-disclosing, and Burnett has pointed out that similar un-codified constraints operate to divert men away from reflecting upon their relationships. It is worth pursuing social grammars of such cognitive activities in the domain of relationships in general and in that of romance and passion in particular. A preliminary observation here is that several of the assumptions that are routinely made regarding the *rationality* of others when interpreting what they do and say in order to perceive their actions and accounts as meaningful are often suspended when we attempt to understand their *passionate* romantic actions (see also Shotter, this volume). Allwood (1976) has argued, for example, that we usually assume that the actions of others are normal, intended, purposeful, wilful, moti-vated, hedonistic, efficient and feasible, yet it would seem that Allwood's assumptions are inverted when we attempt to make sense of *passionate* romantic behaviour of others, or at least the licence of passion warrants usually irrational behaviour without compromising the general long-term rational identity of the actor. It is also interesting to ask what assumptions of social rationality are made by lovers about one another. An initial project might be to explore the rhetorics of different kinds of love: *eros*, *ludus*, *storge*, *pragma*, *mania* and *agape*, i.e. not as cognitive or behaviou-ral categories but as *idioms* of love – as spoken within and about rela-tionships. Crucial here, perhaps, are the ways in which accounts of roman-tic agency present '*irrational* passion' as a legitimate and warranted gloss on the action of *rational* individuals.

The over-arching structures of specific episodes and communications do not typically reveal themselves unequivocally in accounts of the develop-ment of relationships but rather reveal the products of their operations, and it requires a sensitively rigorous and comprehensively detailed analysis to reveal the ways in which impressions guide and are guided by the developing relationship. The accounts of Wilkinson and Weber's subjects repay several rereadings – their richness and indeed their opacity makes us turn to them again and again and gives us a sense of perceiving more than one possible interpretation. There are two general points to be made here.

First, there is a negligible probability (and an even smaller utility in assuming) that there is in such accounts a single specifiable meaning to be drawn out. The vacillation of meaning reflects intrinsic equivocations and not incidental ambiguities or complexities in the texts. While from within conversations as listeners we routinely comprehend a single point or inten-tion being indicated by a speaker on that day at that place under those circumstances, from without and at several removes from the actual accounting we are perhaps paradoxically better placed to appreciate the richness of the account. Both types of understanding of descriptions of experience are legitimate tools *and* objects of research in and on rela-tionships but we must make strong distinctions between them.

Second, our sense of various possibilities of interpretation directs us as readers through our *own* repertoire of interpretational heuristics and categories – even if they are each separately more or less useful, correct or appropriate. To approach a written account of a relationship with a pre-constrained set of hypotheses is to be not only inadequate to that account as a social object, but to miss an opportunity to explore our own repertoire of interpretational categories. Of particular interest is the way accounts, internally, invite, implicitly and explicitly, their own interpretations. One segment of an account may, more or less directly, comment on the meaning of some other part – or the style of the account itself may operate to encourage, more or less disingenuously, a particular perspective on what is said.

The use of irony, humour, sarcasm and register generally has not been studied in the examination of private and public sense-making of relationships. A related enterprise is the examination of the ways in which accounts contain a history of their own development as stories. There would seem to be two aspects here. First is the way accounts present further accounts of how the speaker came to see things that way, which would involve statements about reflection, evaluation, 'insight' and so on ('Although I used to think X, I suddenly came to realize that Z ...'). A second aspect is the way accounts contain stories of their own previous tellings – possibly serving the function of providing justification for the current form of the account ('Having talked this all over with her I now think ...'). The question is whether such reflexive accounts are separate to the main account and simply presented as validational of it, or whether they are so woven into the fabric of the account that they are inseparable from it. An intriguing project here is to examine the rhetorical function of such histories of tellings and reflection as they contribute to the pragmatic aims of the current telling. This is one aspect of the 'intertextuality' of accounts, another being that indicated by the Gergens, namely how accounts of partners are concurrently cross-validating. Examination of these diachronic and synchronic interdependencies of accounts would be a major and arguably refreshing development of the rather static notion of accounts of experience perpetuated by current self-disclosure paradigms.

Recall of past relationship experience

Miell's work impressively demonstrates how explicit characterizations of past relationship growth are biased in the direction of the current state of affairs. This finding reinforces several points made elsewhere and raises several fundamental problems for current conceptions of lay epistemology and research practice. In what sense is the past a part of the present? Clearly, Miell's work indicates that any model based on a notion of a simple accumulation of traces of experience is manifestly insufficient and thus raises basic questions about the status and reliability of the retrospective interview and questionnaire as a means of gathering data about relationship development or dissolution. No matter how *influential* 'biased' memories or accounts are they are still not *accurate* memories or *reliable* accounts and researchers must be clear about whether they are (or think they are) examining talk, beliefs, perceptions about relationships or relationships 'in their own right' since methodological exigencies can only warrant such profound equivocations so far, and in PR research that boundary has long since been passed. Miell's results have much more than methodological implications, of course. A model of memory for relationship experience is still a fundamental requirement for many areas of PR research.

Sally Planalp has made a material beginning to such an undertaking by examining the long-term pro-typical and schematic knowledge structures that guide and organize perceptions and recollections of our own and others' social relations. Again this is an area where linguistically and cognitively orientated researchers can co-operate. Perhaps the most useful and interesting development here is an emphasis on the *retrieval* processes involved in the use of these and other relational representations. Much of Elizabeth Loftus's work on the retrieval of autobiographical memories seems particularly relevant here from the cognitive point of view (Loftus and Fathi 1985), while the highly interesting work of Boden and Bielby (1986) on the linguistic aspects of the articulation of distant memories provides a number of leads for the PR researcher. Also, the work of John Harvey and his colleagues (Harvey, Flanary and Morgan, in press) on the role of emotion in encoding relationship memories deserves serious attention. A grand synthesis of Miell's effects and Loftus's retrieval strategies, Boden and Bielby's linguistic formulations and Harvey's flash-bulb phenomena with mood congruency memory effects would be a profound and enduring contribution to the theory and methodology of several areas of PR research.

Finally, in this vein, might be mentioned the social constructivist claim that 'to remember' is not just (or even) to have a certain kind of cognitive experience but to be ratified as talking correctly about a previous event – as much a *discursive* achievement as an information-processing one (Coulter 1979). Considering Burnett's observations on reflection it can similarly be asked under what conditions are people satisfied that they have indeed remembered correctly and are not mistaken? This is not a simple issue of confidence ratings but of examination of self-regulating processes of evaluation and self-ratification. Again the heterarchical metaphor appeals: what is remembered will reflect the motivations, mood and context generally of the attempt to recall – is that fact taken into account in the process of *self*-ratification as it is in *other*-ratification? Are linguistic qualifiers and hedges discernible in discursive accounts that appear to reflect the processes of ratification? Clarification of the conceptual links between these various strands may ultimately prove in the long run to be at least as illuminating as empirically grounded discoveries.

Overall, then, it would appear that there are several strands of definite

empirical projects that can be pursued by fruitfully exploiting the integrating power of the notion of the account – the structured and socially
functional description – within the area of PRs. What might be noted
particularly here are the analogous properties of accounts in the intrapersonal, interpersonal and socio-cultural domains enabling interesting
conceptual translations.

EMPOWERMENT

These papers point to an epistemology of empowerment, of praxis. These
researchers have explored the subtle questions of not just which emotions?
which cognitions? which interpretations? but the questions of *in what
sense* 'emotions', 'cognitions', 'interpretation'? Studies and speculation on
what is 'in fact' the case encourage ethno-centricism, intellectual introversion, ahistoricism; the contributions to the present volume have pointed
towards the future through an uncodified but principled *epistemology of
the possible*, of personal and social construction of experience. Not that to
appreciate the powers for action is to act, or to act wisely, but without
such a reflexive appreciation of the ways 'worlds of experience' *come to be
the way they are* we are prisoners, personally and scientifically, of an
external and apparently inevitable present. Practical social knowledge
means just that: knowledge of, for and from within, social praxis. Yet with
empowerment comes responsibilities and liabilities at the level of both the·
individual and dyad, for in the same way as your experience is not just
constructed by you but *by* others, so too does your construction of your
experience compromise and ensnare the experience *of* others. From the
simple case of Berger's subjects, who in their approaches to others make of
others 'approachees', through to Shotter's consideration of the infiltration
of new moralities into a culture, the structures of experience are constructive as well as constructed, overpowering as well as empowering.

EPILOGUE

Accounts finish in many ways – with the triumphant satisfaction of a point
well-made, the carefully measured summary statement, the sudden revela-
tion, the tongued-tied silence of the story that has exceeded its own logic
or the discursive annihilation of the story that has overstayed its conversational welcome – the possibilities are as countless as those of human
experience and social interaction themselves. Janus-like, each account in its
accomplishment simultaneously betrays both its identity as the regulated
culmination of previous stories and encounters and as the foundation for
future ones – a braiding of understandings that is both the context and
realization of intimate social experience piercing equally the direction of
action and the authenticity of feeling. We hope, in conclusion here, that
this collection of accounts of the study of PRs has been sufficiently rooted
in common experiences and comprehension, on the one hand, as to iden-

tify this volume as retrospectively sense-*making* and sufficiently stimulating in suggesting possible future knowledge and understandings on the other, as to identify it as prospectively sense-*building* in the development of the scientific narrative of the study and practice of 'accounting for relationships'.

REFERENCES

Allwood, J. (1976) 'Linguistic communication as action and cooperation: a study of pragmatics'. *Gothenburg Monographs in Linguistics 2*. Gothenburg: University of Gothenburg.

Averill, J. (1980) 'A constructivist theory of emotion'. In R. Plutnik and H. Kellerman (eds) *Emotions: Theory, Research and Experience*. New York: Academic Press.

Boden, D. and Bielby, D.D. (1986) 'The way it was: topical organization in elderly conversation'. *Language and Communciation*, 6, 73–92.

Broadbent, D.E., Fitzgerald, P. and Broadbent, M.H.P. (1986) 'Implicit and explicit knowledge in the control of complex systems'. *British Journal of Psychology*, 77, 33–50.

Charniak E. and McDermott, D. (1985) *Introduction to Artificial Intelligence*. New York: Addison-Wesley.

Coulter, J. (1979) *The Social Construction of Mind*. London: Macmillan.

Cronen, W.B. and Pearce, V.E. (1980) *Communication, Action and Meaning: The Creation of Social Realities*. New York: Praeger.

Harré, R. (1983) *Personal Being*. Oxford: Blackwell.

Harvey, J.H., Flanary, R. and Morgan, M. (1986) 'Vivid memories of vivid loves gone by'. *Journal of Social and Personal Relationships*, 3, 359–73.

Loftus, E.F. and Fathi, D.C. (1985) 'Retrieving multiple autobiographical memories'. *Social Cognition*, 3, 280–95.

Semin, G. and Manstead, A.S.R. (1983) *The Accountability of Conduct: A Social Psychological Analysis*. London: Academic Press.

Shotter, J. (1985) 'Accounting for place and space'. *Environment and Planning D: Society and Space*, 3, 447–60.

Zajonc, R.B. (1984) 'On the primacy of affect'. *American Psychologist*, 39, 117–23.

Name index

Subject index